Clinical Handbook of Pastoral Counseling, Volume 3

Integration Books

Studies in Pastoral Psychology, Theology, and Spirituality
Robert J. Wicks, General Editor

also in this series

Clinical Handbook of Pastoral Counseling, Volume 3

Edited by
Robert J. Wicks
Richard D. Parsons
Donald Capps

Integration Books

paulist press / new york and mahwah, n.j.

Book design by Theresa M. Sparacio

Cover design by Tim McKeen

Library of Congress Cataloging-in-Publication Data

Clinical handbook of pastoral counseling vol. 3 / edited by
Robert J. Wicks, Richard D. Parsons, Donald Capps.
    p. cm.
    Includes bibliographical references and index.
    ISBN 0-8091-4061-6
    1. Pastoral counseling. I. Wicks, Robert J. II. Parsons, Richard D. III. Capps, Donald.
BV4012.2 .C58 2002
253.5—dc21

2002003644

Published by Paulist Press
997 Macarthur Boulevard
Mahwah, New Jersey 07430

www.paulistpress.com

Printed and bound in the
United States of America

Contents

II. Special Challenges and Opportunities for Pastoral Counselors in the Third Millennium 209

III. Special Challenges and Responsibilities of the Pastoral Counselor 319

Robert J. Wicks

Introduction

The *Clinical Handbook of Pastoral Counseling,* Volume 3 is designed to offer a broad range of practical information on helping others.

Yet, to accomplish this required not only that we select certain chapters from the previous two-volume edition of the *Clinical Handbook of Pastoral Counseling* but add new ones as well. Although naturally there were many topics that could have been chosen for inclusion here, those selected include a chapter on sexual exploitation and other boundary violations and chapters on pastoral counseling with the following populations:

- Military personnel
- The aged
- Asian Americans
- Latino Americans
- Individuals with disabilities
- Persons with sexual addictions
- Hospice patients

Once we gathered these papers and included some relevant chapters from the previous two *Handbooks,* a new breakdown was needed. Therefore, three sections were established, each with its own introduction, to provide a clear logic to the broad and varied contents of the book.

The sections are

    I. Pastoral Counseling with Special Populations
   II. Special Challenges and Opportunities for Pastoral Counselors in the Third Millennium
  III. Special Challenges and Responsibilities of the Pastoral Counselor

With the publication of the *Clinical Handbook of Pastoral Counseling,* Volume 3, the hope is to make available important contributions by some of the finest professionals in the field today. No book is ever truly "comprehensive," but this effort to bring together in one place so many essential topics and gifted authors in the field of pastoral counseling was considered both worthwhile and timely. The inclusion of some relevant chapters from the previous two *Handbooks* in this volume presented the problem of dealing with outdated statistics. While there has been an editorial effort to update these statistics in places, the reader should be aware that some earlier statistics remain in order to respect the theses of the original articles. In each case, it was determined that the pastoral content of the article is still valuable and relevant for contemporary pastoral counseling.

Although there is great interest today by social workers, psychiatrists, and psychologists in the area of spirituality and religion, the perspective of people involved in *pastoral* counseling and ministry is still unique and offers a real contribution to the field of behavioral science in general.

Pastoral counseling and care professionals are interested in sound clinical practice; they don't want to be guilty of the mistake of "spiritual romanticism." However, their purpose is not just good mental health practice—as important as this is for their work. They are also deeply concerned with connecting "the immediate" to "the ultimate" (what theologian Paul Tillich referred to as the process of "ecstatic reasoning"). And so, their interest is not only in returning persons to their faith communities in a more healthy emotional state; their interest also involves enabling those they help to resume roles in their communities that are more prophetic, compassionate, and prayerful, as dynamic persons of faith involved with a living, challenging, welcoming God. Without such ultimate religious goals as these, pastoral counseling does not exist. So, in providing clinical expertise, the following work seeks also to foster the desire to achieve a more mature and healthier faith as well as emotional equilibrium. And it is in this dual purpose that both the field and this book on pastoral counseling should finally be judged.

SECTION I
PASTORAL COUNSELING
WITH SPECIAL POPULATIONS

The articles included within section I serve as reminders to pastoral counselors of the unique nature and special relationship issues that exist when counseling people of different life perspectives and orientations.°

This section opens with a look at the role and function of the pastoral counselor within the military. Sheila Barry not only highlights the unique role and challenges confronting the pastoral counselor working as chaplain within the military but also identifies the special need for training, credentialing, and support in dealing with issues of confidentiality in light of the specific demands of the military context.

The next article, "A Feminist Perspective on Pastoral Counseling with Women," by Christie Cozad Neuger (chapter 2) highlights the sad reality that at times the practice of pastoral counseling is far from a liberating experience for female clients. Neuger suggests that often the context of pastoral counseling has "natural proclivities and natural antipathies to a feminist perspective on its work." She calls all pastoral counselors to recognize this and to use a feminist liberation approach to the counseling of women. As noted in the chapter, the author feels that such an approach is the "*only* way in which a counselor may bring real and lasting healing to women in distress."

Another population that has often been disenfranchised and that can similarly benefit from a unique perspective and special sensitivity is the aged. In chapter 3, "Pastoral Counseling with the Aged," Harold G. Koenig reviews the major problems that aging persons confront and provides suggestions for helping aging persons to overcome these difficulties.

The criticism implied in the first two essays, that counseling and therapy have been too white, male, and middle class in orientation is amplified in

---

° The reader should be aware that, while an editorial effort has been made to update statistics in places, some outdated statistics have been kept in order to respect the theses of the original articles. In each case, it was determined that the pastoral content of the article is still valuable and relevant for contemporary pastoral counseling.

the essay by Edward Wimberly (chapter 4). Wimberly challenges pastoral counselors to become cross-culturally conscious of the divergent minority groups and subcultures that exist in America. In his chapter, Wimberly provides a cultural variant model of conceptualizing cultural uniqueness of minority groups and the growth-wholeness practical model of pastoral counseling. He illustrates the utility of the model with an extensive discussion of pastoral counseling with African Americans.

The unique cultural needs and perspectives of Asian Americans is the focus of Steve Sangkwon Shim's chapter, "Pastoral Counseling with Asian Americans" (chapter 5). The author provides an extensive discussion of the unique characteristics and values of Asian Americans and the clinical issues often encountered when working with Chinese, Japanese, and Korean Americans. The author offers specific direction in terms of clinical procedures, strategies, methods, and the use of referral for the pastoral counselor working with Asian Americans.

The need and opportunity for pastoral counselors to expand their knowledge of their own cultural values, widen their theoretical framework, and increase their flexibility when working with members of diverse cultures is the theme that runs through Rebeca M. Radillo's essay on "Pastoral Counseling with Latino Americans" (chapter 6). In this chapter Radillo presents an in-depth look at sociopolitical, economic, family, and spiritual realities of the Latin American client. Through case illustration, Radillo highlights the need for every pastoral counselor to deconstruct the rigid Euro-American model of helping and begin to reconstruct a model that reflects a sensitivity and valuing of divergent cultures.

Another group for whom disenfranchisement and dis-empowerment have often been a common experience are the disabled. In his article "Pastoral Counseling with Individuals with Disabilities and Their Families" (chapter 7), William C. Gaventa, Jr., provides an insightful look into the special challenges confronting the pastoral counselor working with the disabled. Starting with the limited training typically received, through highlighting the impact of the "chronic" nature of disability and the complexity of the interaction between person and environment, Gaventa invites the reader to see challenge as opportunity. In this light, he identifies a number of suggestions for those in pastoral roles that will enable them to be both more sensitive and more supportive of those with disabilities. As he notes, "Your capacity to see strengths as well as needs, the accessibility and hospitality of your attitude and relationship, and your commitment to do what it takes to include and assist them in your ministry and service are all foundation for a pastoral relationship that may do little about the impairment, but may do wonders for the person."

Finally, the themes of insensitivity, oppression, and the need for empowerment and liberation that have been identified by the previous authors in this section is echoed in the last two chapters. In chapter 8, "Counseling Lesbians: A Feminist Perspective," Gail Lynn Unterberger offers a feminist liberation theology as a model for working with lesbian clients. In her model, the need to understand the experience of lesbian women is essential to the formulation of theological and ethical viewpoints from which to affirm the client. Unterberger urges the consideration of a gay-affirming, feminist pastoral counseling stance that determines that lesbianism per se is not a disease; rather it is a minority sexual orientation. Further, she suggests that competent pastoral counseling requires that we be aware of the systemic effects of discrimination and oppression and overall health and well-being of the lesbian parishioner or client.

The final chapter of this section, "Pastoral Counseling of the Gay Male" by Richard Byrne, provides an additional call for pastoral counselors to serve as agents of liberation. Byrne invites the pastoral counselor to take a stance of "full acceptance" of homosexual love as a way of imaging God and embodying the gospel imperative to love. Employing Adrian van Kaam's model of "intraspheric formation power," Byrne presents the twofold purpose of pastoral counseling with gay men to be (1) to assist the client in the movement toward a radical self-affirmation as a gay man, and (2) to foster an integration of the affirmed identity in the total context of the client's life field, including his relationship with the mystery that permeates this field.

Sheila Barry

1. Pastoral Counseling in the Military

Introduction

This chapter will examine the development of pastoral counseling within the context of the military community. The unique challenges and opportunities of this specialized ministry will be discussed, in the hope of affording the reader a comprehensive overview of the life of the military chaplain as a pastoral counselor. The areas of training, credentialing, and confidentiality will be explored in light of the specific demands placed on the military chaplain.

The Chaplain as Counselor

Since the creation of an organized chaplaincy in the military by an act of the Continental Congress on July 29, 1775, the opportunity for pastoral counseling has been present in the military community of the United States. Although the military chaplain has many functions and duties, including religious worship services and moral guidance, he or she is perhaps most often thought of and described in the role of pastoral counselor. Long before the establishment of the more formalized specialization of counseling, the tradition of "tell it to the chaplain" was an integral part of military history. Hutcheson (1998) quotes a paper submitted to the Secretary of the Navy in 1871 in which Chaplain G. W. Smith wrote, "The work done by a Chaplain is not simply the holding of services on Sunday as required by Regulations. That which tells most is the intercourse with individuals one by one" (p. 62).

During World War II, counseling gained an important role in response to the many and varied needs of those drafted into military service for combat. During that time of extreme stress and fear, counseling became a necessary and accepted duty of the chaplain. For the millions of Americans who fought during World War II, the clergy in uniform became well known as reliable resources of professional concern and care. In his excellent work on the chaplaincy, Hutcheson states that "this experience on the part of both

7

the clergy and lay people undoubtedly contributed significantly to the development of pastoral counseling as a specialized discipline within the ministerial profession" (p. 62).

Post World War II, the proportion of time that chaplains spent on their counseling activities continued to increase. At this point the need to develop educational programs to equip the chaplains for this counseling ministry became apparent. Some specialized programs in counselor training were developed at institutions such as the Menninger Clinic in Kansas and Catholic University in Washington, D.C., to which individual chaplains were sent. The demand was high for continuing education programs that focused on counseling skills from a large percentage of military chaplains. In the late 1960s and early 1970s, Clinical Pastoral Education training, standardization, and certification was established for chaplains in all three branches of the service. This training continues to be offered in addition to other specialized programs in counseling.

Parallel to the worldwide pastoral counseling movement, the development of pastoral counseling as a specialized ministry in the military has seen an emphasis on structure, credentialing, professionalism, and accountability. It appears that each branch of the service offers a slightly different approach to training in the area of counseling for their chaplains. The Army has developed an advanced program for family life chaplains. The venue for this training has changed over the years and is currently housed at Ft. Benning, Georgia, in conjunction with Columbus State University, and at Ft. Hood, Texas, in connection with the University of Central Texas. Twelve chaplains per year are selected for the Master's of Science program. The director and supervisor of these programs are both Clinical Members and Approved Supervisors of the American Association for Marriage and Family Therapists (AAMFT) as well as Fellows of the American Association of Pastoral Counselors (AAPC). Forty-eight hours of graduate course work are completed in the fourteen-month program in addition to a 500-hour supervised internship. The studies focus on the area of individual development, marital and family studies, research methodology, and family therapy supervision. After graduation the chaplains become directors at various Army Family Life Centers around the world, where they provide marital and family counseling, enrichment opportunities, and training for other chaplains in their ministry. It is the expressed mission of the Family Life Center to improve the quality of life for military families by providing marital and family therapy from a pastoral perspective.

The Navy offers a variety of programs that are open to chaplains from all three services. The topics range from basic suicide prevention, pastoral care of patients, and the spirituality of trauma, grief, and mourning to addressing sexual misconduct in the ministry. At the Naval Chaplains School, NETC, in Newport, Rhode Island, there is an emphasis on the importance of the role of the chaplain and its privileged communications. Through the use of articles such as those written by Michael Clay Smith (1984), the critical nature of the confidentiality issue is brought to the awareness of the chaplains in training. Selected legal cases are presented and discussed in order for the chaplains to be prepared for possible problematic situations involving confidentiality.

The Air Force stresses training in suicide prevention, trauma ministry, stress management, PTSD, grief, loss, and crisis intervention. Faced with a shift to more mobility and deployments, the Air Force is training its chaplains to deal with separation and adjustment issues for both the military members and the chaplains themselves. Clinical Pastoral Education (CPE) continues to be offered by all the services, although many chaplains now enter the military with previous training and experience in this area.

Interviews with chaplains from the three branches of the military indicate that approximately 75 percent to 80 percent of their time is spent in the area of counseling. It appears that in almost all their capacities the possibility for counseling is present, whether it be a church service, a hospital visit, an educational program, or even a social function. The chaplain is usually very visible and very available to minister to the needs of the military members and their dependents. The fact is that there are more chaplains than social workers, psychologists, or psychiatrists, and it is expected that the chaplains will be available for counseling. Thus, it becomes of primary importance that the chaplain is prepared for this major part of his ministry.

Not all chaplains come into the military service with similar or equal backgrounds. The military chaplaincy requires a chaplain to hold a bachelor's or master's degree, usually in theology, as well as ordination or ecclesiastical endorsement from a recognized religious denomination. Today's clergy are more likely to have had CPE and counseling courses in seminary than did their counterparts in the '60s and '70s. However, with chaplains coming from the four major faith groups (Protestant, Catholic, Jewish, and Orthodox), as well as the recent additions of Islam and Buddhist chaplains and the promise of Hindu and Wiccan chaplains in the near future, the training and experience that they bring can be widely varied. It therefore becomes necessary to provide training to enhance the pastoral assessment and diagnostic skills of chaplains who come on active duty with limited or no pastoral counseling courses in the seminary and perhaps very little experience in this field.

Ongoing supervision and credentialing also become very important, and all three branches continue to explore the most satisfactory means for implementing this process. This parallels the issues being dealt with by

AAPC, AAMFT, and similar groups. Given that the age of retirement from the military is fairly young (only about 1,300 military are ages fifty-five and over), many of these chaplains have the potential to continue their pastoral counseling ministry in the civilian sphere. Clearly it makes sense to continue to investigate cooperative efforts with university programs, AAMFT, and AAPC in the ongoing search for excellence.

Confidentiality

Although in today's military there are a variety of counselors provided to the military members and their families, the guarantee of confidentiality is unique to the chaplains. On the larger military installations there are apt to be alcohol and drug abuse counselors, family service counselors, educational and career counselors, and benefit counselors. These counselors are all available for the chaplain to use as referral sources, but it is most common that the individual seeks out the chaplain as the first safe contact point. It is assumed that the chaplain will have the time and expertise to give help to the troubled, and that this help will be given to all regardless of rank or religious preference. Very often the service member is reluctant to seek help from Mental Health or Family Services or Family Support on base, fearing that job, security, clearance, reputation, or promotion will be compromised. Current policy states that confidentiality with the military chaplain is total. Many chaplains will begin sessions with a disclaimer statement, saying that everything that is about to be said is confidential unless it deals with a specific area such as child or spouse abuse. Unfortunately, there have been cases where confidentiality has not been kept, and when this happens the credibility of chaplains as a whole is called into question. Overall, however, both chaplain and counselee treat the privilege of confidentiality with respect, and this contributes to the integrity of the pastoral counseling.

The privilege of communicating with a chaplain in the military is assured against the interference of third parties by the religious practices of various faith groups and by Rule 503 of the Military Rule of Evidence. Under this mandate, chaplains will not divulge communications without the express consent of the persons enjoying the privilege. This absolute privilege is accorded only to communications that take place between persons and clergymen or chaplains. The situation becomes more complicated in cases where it becomes an issue of federal law versus state law. Federal law has precedent on a military installation, and state law has precedent off the installation. Sometimes they are at odds, and it becomes crucial for the chaplain to have judicial counsel to advise the proper course of action. Military chaplains are advised to consult with the local Judge Advocate General

(JAG) representative to determine if the local jurisdiction extends the privilege in certain situations, such as marital counseling. The potential for lawsuits is a reality for the military chaplain. Smith cautions, "Standing upon the privilege may carry the risk of a contempt citation. On the other hand, a cleric might face a damage suit by a party injured if a cleric unprofessionally violates a confidence" (p. 10).

Unique Characteristics

The military chaplaincy is composed of clergy who retain their faith group but who serve people of all denominations. The military prides itself on maintaining its pluralistic setting, which presents some challenges for chaplains who have to provide for the free exercise of rights of the military members as guaranteed by the First Amendment. In turn, this means that service members may receive counsel in some form from a chaplain of another faith group. While this is certainly a common situation in the civilian sector, there is often not much choice involved if the counseling arena is on a ship, battlefield, or a remote installation. The ideal is that both the chaplain and the service member are aware of the pitfalls and challenges involved in a pluralistic setting, and in most cases this works well.

The military chaplain is also in the unique situation of being a full member of two disparate social institutions, and thus the possibility for experiencing role conflict is present even in the pastoral counseling situation. Hutcheson reports evidence that chaplains generally consider their role as clergy to be more important than the role of officer (p. 22), but also states that "the institutional duality of chaplains, as both clergy and military officers, and their two-way responsibility within the total institution to both commanders and counselees, are sources of tension" (p. 64). With some exceptions it seems that these duality issues are successfully resolved, with confidentiality being of prime importance.

Unlike many more traditional situations, pastoral counseling in the military environment often begins with a casual remark from the military person or family member: "Chaplain, do you have a minute to talk?" This could occur in the chaplain's office, on the deckplates of an engine room, in the corner of an aircraft hangar, on the deck of a ship, at the entrance to the chapel, around the edges of a bivouac area, or during a long flight. This question or a similar one could be posed just about anywhere and at any time. Thus it becomes essential to establish boundaries and safety to facilitate the counseling process. Often this presents a challenge to the chaplain, who must be both flexible and containing.

By its nature pastoral counseling in the military is often brief and crisis-centered. Chaplains often do not have the luxury of committing to long-term therapy even if they have the skills and training to do longer-term work. A chaplain is still a military officer with several roles to fill, which often means that he does not have the time available to do long-term, in-depth counseling. In addition, the military member often is not available for anything more than two or three sessions because of schedules, deployments, and transfers. Consequently, more training is being conducted in areas such as brief pastoral counseling, solution-focused therapy, or single-session therapy.

According to *Defenselink,* in 1999 there were nearly 1.37 million active duty personnel in all the services. Approximately 33 percent represent minority groups; 7 percent are women. Military men and women tend to be young. The largest group, 481,000, was between the ages of 20 and 25. 102,000 were 19 and younger; almost 307,000 were between the ages of 26 and 31. In summary, nearly 65 percent of all enlisted personnel were between 17 and 31 years of age. In addition to working with the military member, either officer or enlisted, chaplains may be brought in to work with problems involving dependents such as spouses, children, or parents. Currently the number of dependents of all active duty members totals nearly 2 million. Considering that the number of chaplains on active duty is 2,500, the ratio of chaplain to potential counselee is a staggering one. Most certainly the issue of burnout needs to be addressed on an ongoing basis.

Opportunities for Counseling

All chaplains in the military provide pastoral counseling in a variety of situations. Unless chaplains are in a hospital setting, they are usually not dealing with physical or medical problems. However, they certainly see the problems reflected in the society from which the military personnel are coming into the service. As society deals with the influences of drugs, alcoholism, lack of nuclear family support, and advanced technology, so does the military, in both its personnel and their dependents. Individual issues, marriage, family, depression, grief, death, and suicide are among the problems brought to the military chaplain. In addition, chaplains are apt to come face to face with young marriages, extramarital affairs, cybersex encounters, child abuse, spouse abuse, communication difficulties, career dissatisfaction, and drug and alcohol abuse.

However, the military life does have some unique stressors that influence the nature and intensity of the problems. Since the Gulf War and the high number of humanitarian efforts throughout the world that have required military intervention or support, the tempo of operations in all the branches of the military has increased. It is possible that most military members can expect a period of deployment for several months every two or three years. Some occupations, such as pilots, mechanics, and even chaplains, deploy their personnel as often as every year. This places a tremendous burden on all those involved—the military member, the family, and the service providers. One chaplain reported that during a one-week period when he was deployed in Saudi Arabia toward the very end of the Gulf War, he had twenty-three people come to him for counseling because they had received a "Dear John" letter or had spoken to their spouse and been told the spouse wanted a divorce.

The record number of deployments and separations from family and familiar support systems sets up countless situations where chaplains will be sought out for counsel. Many deployments are scheduled in advance, giving individuals and their families time to prepare. However, in international emergencies they can develop rapidly and with little warning. This puts added stress onto a situation that is already difficult for military personnel and their families to handle. The anxieties surrounding separation may cause existing problems to become intensified and critical. Often there will be a chaplain on one base counseling the deployed family member while another is called in to help with a situation with the family member who's left behind.

Times of return of military men and women are also occasions when the chaplain will be sought out for crises in marriages, disappointments in relationships, and issues of readjustment and re-entry. These can range from relatively simple situations where the chaplain facilitates and encourages communication and active listening to more serious issues of anger, abuse, affairs, depression, and even suicide. Mobility in our society and in the military appears to be on the rise, and it is anticipated that the problems surrounding separation, loneliness, isolation, and re-entry will need to be dealt with on a continuing basis.

Another situation somewhat unique to the military is the period of orientation, whether it is called "boot camp," "plebe summer," "basic training," or one of a number of other phrases. Every military person experiences an orientation phase during which physical and psychological limits are pushed to the maximum. For most men and women it is a limited time of considerable stress and sudden changes in their sense of identity. Individuals are expected to adapt to highly structured routines that have not been previously experienced with such intensity. Homesickness is common during the orientation period, in response to the different food, clothing, people, space, and allocation of time. Often the recruit experiences feelings of loneliness and isolation coupled with the double lack of sleep and a familiar routine.

It would perhaps be an understatement to say that the chaplain is very busy during these periods of indoctrination. Stress and anxiety often accompany change, and both physical and psychological symptoms may be present. The military chaplain needs to be sensitive to the frequency and severity of the symptoms in order to monitor for disturbances out of the realm of the normal reactions to stress.

Another critical time involves the experience of death and loss by the military member. For many individuals away from home, the experience of loss and grief is even more painful and lonely without close family support. In a youthful population such as the military, death, grief, and loss are often experienced for the first time, and the accompanying feelings of helplessness, isolation, and fear can be intensified. This can be particularly true if the death is of a friend in one's own unit. At these times the chaplain may be called upon to work both with individuals and the unit as a whole as they work through their grief.

In many situations the chaplain as pastoral counselor will be the first to break the news of the death of a military member to the immediate family. It is more frequently the chaplain than any other professional or military commander who will assume this responsibility. The chaplain is often the spokesperson for the military community's grief, and his manner and style will convey the quality of both his pastoral care and his training. At such times the chaplain must be alert for danger signals in the early, shocking grief and may also be called on to provide longer-term care for widows, children, and other significant persons in the life of the military member.

In his comprehensive history of the chaplaincy from 1975 to 1995, Brinsfield (1997) describes several recent military operations and the role of the chaplains. In his description of Joint Task Force Guantanamo involving the Haitian exodus to Cuba, he cites a period of seven-and-one-half months during which "chaplains conducted 11,606 counseling sessions with military personnel (including each other) and 13,429 with the Haitians" (p. 212). Fifty chaplains from all branches of the service and forty-one chaplain assistants handled this. Because of the large number of migrants and the humanitarian nature of the operation, the chaplains were critical assets in this operation.

With the downsizing of the military and the increase of such humanitarian missions involving military support, the demands on the chaplain corps will most probably increase. Stress and burnout among chaplains must be monitored and addressed along with increased training and support in the areas of crisis counseling. The corps itself is downsizing and the shortage of Catholic chaplains is becoming critical. What this will mean for the future of the military chaplaincy is not clear at this time.

Conclusions

The words of Isaiah 6—"And I heard the voice of the Lord saying, 'Whom shall I send, and who will go for us?' Then I said, 'Here am I! Send me'"—seem most appropriate when trying to capture the essence of pastoral counseling in the military. It is a ministry of presence, readiness, and flexibility. It is a ministry of mobility. As pastoral counselor the military chaplain has the opportunity to touch the lives of countless young, active, eager men and women and their families during periods of great stress and need. The chaplain is in the unique position of forming relationships that can encourage faith, hope, and love among persons who are struggling with their weaknesses and strengths.

Even though the majority of pastoral counseling in the military is done in the brief model, the impact can be most significant. Crisis means opportunity, and the encounter of a military member with a chaplain who is truly pastoral in his presence and skills can have long-term effects that would be almost impossible to measure. A successful experience with pastoral counseling can open the door to continued growth, which may occur with another pastoral counselor, in another time and another place, perhaps when the military member's tour of duty is completed. There is tremendous opportunity for military chaplains to touch the lives of millions of bright, healthy young men and women through a connection that may open the way for lifelong transformations.

Note

I am most appreciative of the cooperation and information I received from the Office of the Chaplains for the Army, Air Force, and Navy as well as the time and expertise shared by several chaplains through personal interviews. Chaplain Ross Trower, who authored the original chapter in a previous edition, was most generous in his permission to use his material. My former experience with the military chaplaincy was limited to my experiences as the wife of a naval officer and a staff member of the Office of the Chaplains at the United States Naval Academy. I am grateful for the opportunity to interact further with such a fine group of men and women and have the utmost respect for the very demanding ministry of the military chaplain.

References

Brinsfield, J. *Encouraging Faith, Supporting Soldiers: The United States Army Chaplaincy, 1975–1995.* Washington, D.C.: Office of the Chaplains, Department of the Army, 1997.

Defenselink. Web site prepared by Washington Headquarters Services Directorate for Information Operations and Reports, 1999.

Hutcheson, R. G., Jr. *The Churches and the Chaplaincy* (rev. ed.) Washington, D.C.: U.S. Government Printing Office, 1998.

The New Jerusalem Bible. New York: Doubleday, 1985.

Smith, M. C. "The Pastor on the Witness Stand: Toward a Religious Privilege in the Courts." *Catholic Lawyer* 29 (1984): 1–10.

Trower, Ross H. "Military." In R. J. Wicks , R. D. Parsons, and D. Capps, eds. *Clinical Handbook of Pastoral Counseling*, Vol. I (rev. ed.). Mahwah, N.J.: Paulist Press, 1993.

Christie Cozad Neuger

2. A Feminist Perspective on Pastoral Counseling with Women

A Case Study

Joan walked into the office of a pastoral counselor. She was anxious, depressed, and hopeless. She felt that her world was overwhelming her and no matter how hard she worked to make things better, she constantly failed. Her marriage was a disaster. Her husband had married her because she was pregnant and felt that, by that act, he had done all that was necessary on behalf of the marriage. She constantly tried to get him to care more for her but without success. Her job was frightening to her. She had moved into a management position and felt that all the women hated her and all the men scorned her. She wondered whether she was competent enough to handle her new work responsibilities. Her life was busy but empty. She felt guilty about her erratic mothering of two small children whom she both loved and resented. She felt spiritually dead. She experienced no connection to a God who, in her eyes, had abandoned her. She had no image of a meaningful future. She felt powerless to make things different for her and her family. And, she felt to blame for all the chaos and despair of her life.

This is the story of one woman and yet nearly every woman who reads this will feel some cords of identification and response. Much of what this woman experienced was intimately linked to living in a world in which she is devalued and limited because she is a woman. A feminist approach to pastoral counseling takes the reality of systematic sexism or patriarchy as central in the formulation of theory, theology, and clinical practice. The purpose of this chapter is to explore some of the dimensions of one feminist approach to pastoral counseling. We will return to this case later in the chapter.

A Framework for Pastoral Counseling

It is important to note from the beginning that there is a careful balance to draw in developing a theory/theology of a feminist pastoral counseling. On

17

the one hand, women share a world in which they are threatened by normative violence against them, in which they are devalued by the limited roles approved for them, and in which they are deprived of the social, economic, and psychospiritual resources necessary to a full life. On the other hand, each woman's experience in this world is different, deeply influenced by race, class, sexual preference, family of origin background, age, and life experiences. The particularities of women must be kept in mind as the broad strokes of "women's world" are painted. My own social location as a white, middle-class, well-educated, married, mother of two profoundly influences my insights and priorities in writing a feminist approach to pastoral work. For most of us, the areas of the culture from which we benefit (in my instance, class, race, sexual preference, and so on) are the areas in which we are most blind. Consequently, this chapter represents *one* perspective on a feminist approach; it needs to be complemented and challenged by other feminist/womanist perspectives.

Pastoral counseling is both deeply suited for and antithetical to a feminist perspective. Counseling of any sort is always deeply informed by a philosophical perspective. The practice of caregiving is an activity grounded in questions about human nature, the role of community, the values that guide human behavior, and the meanings of living. These philosophical/theological questions are central to our counseling work. Pastoral counseling has always overtly claimed these questions as it has developed approaches to people in need. The questions of value and meaning have been at the center of the discipline, and there has never been a claim to value neutrality.

Of these value and meaning concerns, the tendency to take up the part of the oppressed and to offer advocacy to those systematically deprived of power has been present. In addition, there has been a strong link or correlation between people's ongoing lives and the fabric of the community or culture. The phrase "the personal is political," which has been a watchword for the feminist movement, could equally apply to the dominant themes of our theological heritage. Throughout our faith histories the needs of the self could not be separated from the needs of the community. One's own sense of salvation was made manifest in a commitment to God's creation. In addition, the form of the culture affected the shape that faith positions took. Prophetic voices responded out of their own faith to the injustices of the time, which touched both the spiritual health of the prophets and that of their community. These values central to our religious traditions are congruent with a feminist liberation approach to pastoral counseling.

On the other hand, our religious traditions have consistently contributed to the oppression of women on a variety of fronts. For the most part women's stories have not been recorded in the scriptural history of the people of faith. Where women are remembered in the Bible, they have often served either as symbols of evil and seduction or as impossible ideals of self-sacrifice and perfect love. Theologians in the early church and in more recent times have used those limited symbols as ways to characterize women. Women have traditionally not been seen as worthy of public church leadership but have been expected to work behind the scenes, instrumental in the more "earthy" functions of the congregation. Many women have found considerable benefit in having a place in the church even if it was in the domestic sphere. However, there was still a message communicated to the women that they were not valuable enough to take their place in the meaning-making sphere of the church.

It becomes clear, then, that the context of pastoral counseling has natural proclivities and natural antipathies to a feminist perspective on its work. It is the responsibility of every pastoral counselor and of the discipline as a whole to take seriously this ambivalence in the ongoing theory building of its healing ministry.

It is not just the theological issues that need to be evaluated and reformulated in a feminist approach to pastoral counseling. Over the past twenty-five years pastoral counseling has borrowed from and relied heavily upon the social science disciplines of psychology, sociology, and psychotherapy. These disciplines also have been formed in the context of patriarchy and rely heavily on normative male assumptions, experience, and research. As is evident in much of the literature reporting on research done on women's lives, theory built around women's experience is very different and leads to very different therapeutic implications than that done on men's lives. Every traditional theory of psychology and psychotherapy must be held suspect of sexism and be subject to extensive critique. Some theories may not be reclaimable in any form. Others must be enlarged and reconstructed around women's experience. New theories must be born directly out of an understanding of women's lives in patriarchy. This work is underway, and the material in this chapter reflects the important work being done by feminist theorists, psychotherapists, and theologians as they seek to offer healing and empowerment to women in distress.

General Principles of Feminist Counseling

Although one must be careful not to paint in too broad a stroke, it is possible to identify some principles which are central to a feminist perspective on pastoral counseling. Some of these reflect broad agreement in various dimensions of feminist research and others are more personally compelling to my perspective. However, they reflect a general consensus in feminist work.

1. An Awareness of Patriarchy and Depression

The first and most primary principle of feminist counseling is an awareness of patriarchy as a fundamental dynamic in the formation of women's distress. As Mary Ellen Donovan and Linda Sanford conclude in their extensive study on women and self-esteem: 1) Low self-esteem is primarily the result of being female in a male-dominated culture; and 2) low self-esteem is at the root of many of the psychological problems that women experience, and attempts to cure these problems without addressing the causes of low self-esteem lead to other problems (Donovan and Sanford, 1984, p. xiv). In addition, a recent panel of the American Psychological Association, formed to study the epidemic of women's depression, decided that neither biology nor psychology could adequately explain the epidemic. The panel members stated that the depression that women of all ages, races, and classes experience is clearly linked to societal attitudes and behaviors that are detrimental to women ("Women and Depression" 1990). The reality that "the personal is political" is fundamental to looking at women's "pathology" and in developing an approach to the counseling.

The phrase "the personal is political" means that one does not treat women's emotional and psycho-spiritual distress as primarily internal and idiosyncratic in nature. Women's *dis*-ease is understood as fundamentally related to various dimensions of oppression in a world which operates to "keep women in their place." Sexism is still a real and dominant experience for women in the society. As Nicole Benokraitis and Joe Feagin state in their work on modern sexism:

> Sex discrimination is not an illusion. It is at least as robust as it was in the 1950's, 1960's, and 1970's. Why, then, are many men and women today so accepting of sex inequality and so complacent about the future? A majority of people are convinced that sex inequality is no longer a high priority problem. This conviction is based, first and foremost, on a lack of information. Most Americans rarely see or pay attention to statistics that show that sex discrimination abounds. Even when such statistics are provided, the initial reaction is denial (Benokraitis and Feagin 1986, p. 2).

The fact that all women experience sex discrimination and damage due to that discrimination is complicated by its renewed hiddenness. Women are taken by surprise when they are hurt. I have received letters from women graduates asking why we didn't tell them that sexism was alive and well out in the world. They were seduced by the greater visibility of women in positions of authority into believing that sexism was no longer a problem. It is true that women have made some visible gains, particularly in terms of economic and employment opportunities. These gains, as we shall see, are not all we would hope them to be but, nonetheless, they confuse us in our analysis of ongoing sexism. The reality is that the more subtle dimensions of patriarchy still operate powerfully upon the women in this culture. Women still live in a world which does them considerable harm because of their sex, and the hiddenness of this world makes it doubly destructive.

Women's World

I hold the basic assumption that men and women are embedded in very different worlds even as they share the same institutions and families. Women and men both have been denied systematic access to this knowledge, although women know about both worlds, at least at some level. It is crucial for women and men to be exposed to the statistics which outline these two different worlds so that the source of much of women's distress can be clearly identified. It is in knowing the world of patriarchy and its effects on the lives and faiths of women and men that we will be able to engage in effective pastoral counseling and even have a chance at working toward a more just and healthy environment for all. This is at the heart of the first principle of a feminist approach.

The purpose of the following statistics is to paint a beginning portrait of the women's world. The knowing and naming of this world is a central part of pastoral counseling with women and is the starting place for knowing women's lives and pain. The statistics about seemingly disparate dimensions of life, when seen together, begin to show the systemic oppression that women experience. These statistics become like snapshots of a system of oppression which has become a morally normative justification for the dominance of one group over another. It is again important to note here that, despite the commonality women have of experiencing a world of patriarchal oppression, each woman's class, race, family history, and life experience deeply affect the way that this oppression is experienced and understood. The particularities belong to each counseling client, and it is the larger context within which those particularities are found that these statistics reveal.

ECONOMICS

In 1987 over 26 percent of families who were singly headed by white women were below the poverty line in comparison to 8 percent of families singly headed by white males. Over 50 percent of all black families singly headed by women were below the poverty line compared to 29 percent of those singly headed by black men (Hoffman 1990, p. 561). The 2000 Census shows the same distribution of more women than men below the poverty line, and more black women than white.

In 1955 full-time women workers earned about 64 percent of the full-time wages of men. In 2000 they earned about 74 percent of men's wages. Black women earned about 61 percent of the average full-time working man, and Hispanic only about 51 percent. The biggest change is that there are many more women in the work force, but the reality of work segregation by sex has not changed much. In the mid 1980s 60 percent of all women were in either clerical, retail sales, or service jobs (Benokraitis and Feagin 1986, p. 52). Currently most women work in jobs that are still heavily female. People interpret these numbers differently, but Sara Rix writes: "Research has concluded that characteristics such as education and experience cannot account for more than one-half of the current gender gap in earnings. Moreover, on the whole, women who make comparable investments in time, preparation, and experience still advance less far and less quickly than men" (Rix 1990, p. 171).

The work hours of women are significant, too. One author suggests that what has changed in the past twenty years is that more women work at what she calls "double days" (one shift at home and one at work) (Benokraitis and Feagin 1986, p. 7). A University of Florida study found that wives average about thirty hours per week on household tasks and husbands average about six hours. Full-time employed wives do about 70 percent of the housework compared to full-time housewives, who do about 83 percent (Rix 1990, p. 33). The issue of double days is a significant factor in the lives of women who are depressed and/or discouraged about their lives.

ABUSE

Almost six million women are beaten by male friends or spouses each year. This translates into somewhere between 50 percent and 75 percent of all women being beaten sometime in their lives by a boyfriend or husband. Attacks by husbands on wives result in more injuries requiring medical treatment than rapes, muggings, and automobile accidents combined. A recent Bureau of Justice report suggests that, "based on evidence collected in the National Crime Survey, as many as half of the domestic 'simple assaults' actually involved bodily injury as serious as or more serious than 90% of all rapes, robberies, and aggravated assaults" (Langan and Innes 1986, p. 1). One-third of all women homicide victims are killed by their husbands. (Benokraitis and Feagin 1987, p. 49). And 48 percent of all domestic violence against women discovered in the National Crime Survey had not been reported to the police for reasons of fear of reprisal, desire for privacy, or fear that it wasn't important enough to be taken seriously (Langan and Innes 1986, p. 1).

Rape is another common form of abuse against women. While the U.S. Bureau of Justice reports declining rates over the past decade, there is considerable consensus that only 20 to 50 percent of rapes are ever reported. It is estimated by many that between 20 and 30 percent of women over twelve years old will be victims of attempted or completed rape sometime in their lifetime (Bourque 1989, p. 12). It is no wonder that women, though often deeply traumatized by the experience of rape, are rarely surprised by it. Several studies indicate that nearly all women live in pervasive fear of violence against them.

In addition, approximately 40 percent of all girls are sexually molested or abused by the age of eighteen—either inside of or outside of their families (MacKinnon 1987). Estimates about the occurrence of incest vary from 5 percent to 20 percent of all girl children. Women learn very early that the world is not a safe place for them.

MEDIA

It is also important to note that the media carry many of these messages of the threat of violence and the lack of worth to women. For example, a majority of children's stories still show men who achieve and women who get rescued. Male biographies outnumber female biographies, and the stories and accomplishments of women, especially women of color, are still in large part left out of our history books. These realities are changing, but very slowly. In addition, the quantity of pornography is on the rise, and it is becoming increasingly violent. There are close to two hundred pornographic magazines in the United States with about fourteen million readers. In comparison there are fewer than one million readers of feminist magazines.

There have been a variety of studies that report on the consequences of violence against women in the media, even when it is not sexual violence. A recent study by Linz, Donnerstein, and Penrod concluded: "When subjects are continually exposed to graphically depicted film violence against women, individual feelings of anxiety and depression begin to dissipate. Material that was anxiety provoking became less so with prolonged exposure....Material once found somewhat degrading to women was judged to be less so after prolonged exposure" (Linz, Donnerstein, and Penrod 1987, p. 114). In this same study the subjects also became less sympathetic to a rape trial victim and in fact judged her more harshly after watching films depicting violence against women. In other studies it was demonstrated that even after watching R-rated levels of *non-sexual* violence against women, subjects were more judgmental against rape victims then they had been before watching the movies (Linz, Donnerstein, and Penrod 1987, p. 114). Subjects also became less supportive of sexual equality, espoused more traditional views about the roles of women, and became more lenient in assessing punishment to a convicted rapist (Zillman and Bryant 1982, pp. 10–21). This kind of aggression and violence against women is pervasive in media, not only in movies and television but even in the music industry. According to some studies, more than one-half of the music videos on MTV present hostile sexual situations or show males abusing women for fun (Benokraitis and Feagin 1986, p. 10). These media presentations, in books, television, movies, music videos, newspapers, and so on seem not only to communicate the threat of violence to women, encouraging them to live in fear, but in fact increase the likelihood of violence and ongoing sexism.

IMPLICATIONS

The overall picture of these statistics portrays a part of the world in which women live. For the most part this world is minimized, trivialized, and hidden. When women are abused or devalued or made to feel crazy, they tend to believe that they are alone and to blame for this experience. It is important to communicate the world which makes these experiences normative for women so that they can begin to trust themselves and their experiences and come out from hiding to take their appropriate place in society. The pastoral counselor must first look through the lens of patriarchy rather than through the lens of personal pathology when attempting to assess the distress that a woman client is experiencing.

This lens is at the core of the principle incorporated in the phrase "the personal is political." It also reorients the goal of counseling from one of adjustment to one of empowerment. It would be destructive to help a woman adjust to a culture which is destructive to her even if it appears that it would be more comfortable. We can assume that it was adjustment to that culture that probably gave birth, at least in part, to her symptoms of distress. The counselor's goal is to empower a woman through an increased awareness of her environment and through an ability to connect with other women so that she can more readily withstand and even attempt to change the patriarchy which has been so damaging. The personal and political link means that part of women's empowerment in counseling is to begin to join other women in some form of transformation of this destructive patriarchy. Unless she does, she will continue to be vulnerable to patriarchy's power. If she joins other women in working to change the society, to work against the oppressions of sexism, racism, classism and other isms, then she will be able to move in an active way toward her own and others' empowerment. This will become more clear as we move on.

2. The Counselor/Client Relationship

A second fundamental principle of feminist thought is the nontraditional relationship between counselor and counselee. Traditionally counselors have been seen as experts who have the answers and who will tell the counselee what she needs to do in order to get "well." Usually this prescription was adjustment oriented. A feminist approach to pastoral counseling suggests that the role between counselor and counselee be egalitarian. This does not imply that there is a complete mutuality between counselor and counselee. The relationship is still a contract in which the counselor is to provide informed care and guidance for the counselee and not vice versa. However, the difference that exists is one of function not of essence, and the counselor's role is to help the counselee learn to know her own story, to believe in herself, and to claim herself in the company of other women and in the face of patriarchy. It is a role of empowerment, not one of repair or cure.

Involved in this relationship are a number of characteristics that do not fit with traditional counseling work. For example, it is often the case in a feminist perspective that the counselor is an advocate for the counselee. In other words, the counselor assumes on behalf of the counselee. Instead of looking for the "illness" she or he looks for and facilitates the client's strengths. The counselor believes in the counselee's story and her interpretation of that story, and by trusting the counselee the counselor conveys permission for the counselee to trust herself. The counselor, in this advocacy role, may also join the client in her anger or blame rather than encouraging the counselee to look rationally at all sides. This relational advocacy cheerfully breaks the myth of therapeutic neutrality and operates on behalf of the woman counselee.

Another trait of the egalitarian relationship may be that of mentor. The counselor, having gone through her own awareness and consequent struggles regarding her life in patriarchy, uses appropriate self-disclosure over the process of counseling and thereby gives hope and a sense of possibility to the counselee. It is important, of course, not to assume that the counselee's journey should or will replicate that of the counselor, but appropriate self-disclosure on the part of the counselor can be an important dimension of the counseling process. Counselor distance and withholding are not the norm in this approach.

The egalitarian nature of the therapeutic relationship should not get in the way of the counselor recognizing how much influence she or he has in the counseling process. It is not wise to ignore one's own therapeutic power or pretend that the relationship is mutual. The counselor is highly influential, and it is important to remember that the goal is that of empowerment of the counselee rather than of "fixing" her. The counselee's story and her particularities and needs and goals are the primary values in the counseling process.

3. The Group Component

A third principle in this feminist approach to pastoral counseling is the need for a group component to the counseling work. Helping a woman to experience a community of women who will hear her story and validate it through the sharing of their own stories is a fundamental dimension of this healing work. Women live in a world where they experience constant, pervasive messages about who they are and who they are not; about what is possible for them and what is denied to them; and about what they are valued for and in what ways they lack value. Women's experience, for the most part, is defined for them by the dominant culture. Most women doubt their own realities. It is a common experience for a battered woman or a rape victim to agonize over how she brought this abuse on herself. Most women who are depressed define their experience as due to their own failure. Many women who are overwhelmed by their double days of work and the unending nature of their responsibilities are puzzled and self-blaming about why they can't do what every other woman is able to do.

A counselor can only introduce the possibility that there are other ways to understand the experiences that the woman counselee has had. The counselor cannot convince or validate the systemic and widespread nature of the counselee's context. Most women do not feel entitled to see injustice toward themselves (Major 1987, pp. 124–148). They are much more able to identify abuse against other women. It is only when they join with others and hear their own stories from other women and have their own realities affirmed over and over that a new way of viewing their lives becomes possible. Reality testing, believing in one's self, building a base of trust in self and in other women, learning options for surviving and thriving—these are the activities of the counseling group for women that operates in conjunction with the individual counseling. It is in the community that one finds one's self. This is not unfamiliar to the history of the Christian church. When one lives in a world that denies that which is life giving, it is crucial to find a community in which life can be found. Women's support/counseling groups can provide the healing context in which hope and life can be found. And, almost any group in the church where women gather regularly can become this kind of support community if women are encouraged to be honest and authentic and if they are able, through their dialogue, to open their eyes to the cultural sexism and patriarchy around them.

If a profeminist man is doing this counseling work, it becomes even more crucial for a women's group to be included in the counseling plan. Churches should have ongoing women's support groups available to women at any point needed. Men cannot provide the reality testing and story sharing that a woman counselor can (and even her input alone isn't enough). Consequently, the group becomes the major part of the counseling work when a profeminist male is doing the counseling.

It is in a group that damaging behavior, ingrained in many women from an early age, gets challenged. For example, it is a lot more natural and acceptable to "good Christian women" to experience guilt and self-deprecation rather than anger in response to situations which don't live up to their own or others' expectations. It is much easier for a woman to be a giver (she is protected from accusations of selfishness and she is in control) than to be a receiver (vulnerable and able to be rejected). Women tend to give up themselves and their own "gifts and graces" for others out of a deep fear of being left alone. These attitudes and behaviors run deep in women's fragile self-esteem and are hard to challenge and even harder to give up. A women's group where these behaviors are shared and seen more clearly in one another gives both the motivation and the support to move toward more authentic and healthy ways of being.

4. A Woman-Centered Approach

The fourth general principle of this feminist approach is two pronged. It has to do with the need to take women's particularities as central in formulating a counseling approach with each woman. The first dimension to this suggests that it is important to apply consistently the counselee's values and experience, along with knowledge about women's world, as critical in exploring any issue brought into the counseling office. For example, a counselor who wishes to be an advocate for a battered woman who has come for help might feel inclined to encourage her to stand up to her spouse or to leave the home without considering the specifics of her experience and the realities for women in general. Frequently we hear counselors express frustration and confusion about why battered women don't just leave their batterers. Yet, such a woman probably has a deep fear of reprisal if she should stand up to her spouse. Since one-third of all homicides of women come from battering, it is natural for her to have fear. In addition, she might have limited financial resources or economic opportunities so that if she leaves the home, she may find herself to be part of the fastest growing homeless population—women and their young children. She may also worry about reprisals to her children or to other people dependent upon her if she looks after herself. She may very well worry about what people will think of her if she leaves her husband—she may be blamed for breaking up a perfectly viable family. She may have been told to try to be more understanding of her husband as he goes through this stressful time, a very common pastoral response to battered women. And, very likely, she has a self-esteem which is congruent with being battered and which saps her motivation and her hope of having a different, abuse-free life. If these factors aren't explored and taken seriously, if women's criteria aren't used in evaluating the circumstances a woman finds herself in, more damage may be done right in the counseling office.

The second aspect of this principle has to do with the need to consider the particularities of race, class, sexual preference, age, and so on. If the counselor belongs to a culturally dominant race or class, for example, she or he will not fully understand the race or class world of the counselee who is of color or from the working class. These particularities are not peripheral to the counseling work. They are central and the counselor must be willing to be taught the implications of these particularities. Values, responsibilities, goals—all these are profoundly affected by the particularities of race, class, sexual preference, and other dimensions of the society. The counselor must also take responsibility to learn as much as possible about the worlds to which she or he does not belong. For a white, middle-class, feminist counselor it is very important to read widely in womanist and working-class literature as well as that written by women of color.

5. The Patriarchal Context

The fifth principle of this feminist approach to pastoral counseling is hopefully self-evident. This principle has to do with the reality that both psychological and theological formulation has been done in the context of patriarchy, without much or any awareness of that context. Consequently, these sex-biased formulations have served to reinforce and reify a status quo which is destructive to women.

PSYCHOLOGY

As stated above, the psychological theories in all of the major schools of thought (psychodynamic, behavioral, humanistic, and family systems) are products of a world which has, at best, ignored women's experience and has, at worst, sought to damage women. These theories require considerable critique and cannot be utilized in working with women counselees without that critique. There has been considerable work in feminist psychotherapeutic theory and some in womanist theory, which is available to the pastoral counselor.

Much of it is eclectic and most does not address the spiritual needs of women. Nonetheless, it does give guidance to the pastoral counselor in terms of critique and construction within the context of traditional psychotherapeutic theory.

One place where the feminist/profeminist counselor of women must pay particular attention is in the dominant diagnostic categories used in the mental health system. When one explores the diagnostic categories most commonly applied to women, it is easy to see that many of the criteria for diagnosis are merely extensions of expected but exaggerated stereotypical feminine behavior. For example, borderline personality has many descriptive criteria which mirror expected feminine behavior—dependency, indecisiveness, emotionality, and so on. Depression, as we have suggested earlier, is a more acceptable affect for women (passivity, sadness, withdrawn behavior, etc.) than anger or other less passive responses. Co-dependency, as it has been extended in recent years, is an "illness" much more common in women than men and focuses on the need to take care of others and hold oneself responsible for the needs and behaviors of others. These are expected feminine behaviors. As Carol Plummer writes:

> Co-dependency is, in fact, a smorgasbord of behaviors used by all types of oppressed people when with their oppressors. It is a set of survival skills when one is in a subservient position economically, emotionally, politically, or spiritually. The list of co-dependent characteristics is true not only of women, but of workers with their bosses, or the poor with those in power. Telling women to "heal themselves" in a culture which trains them in co-dependency cannot work without transforming the context of their behaviors" (Plummer 1990, p. 10).

Plummer concludes:

> If women don't have the "disease" [of co-dependencyl, it is only because they have worked very hard against their gender socialization (Plummer 1990, p. 11).

As pastoral counselors we must be careful in our assessment work in general as we often operate with different diagnostic criteria than the field of psychiatry, which doesn't take the spiritual dimension of people seriously. In working with women we must be especially careful with these categories at the risk of perpetuating injustice and oppression.

THEOLOGY

In a like manner we must be very careful with our traditional theological categories as we work with the faith lives and concerns of our women counselees. Again, there is considerable work by feminist theologians working with deconstruction and reconstruction of theological positions available to pastoral counselors. However, the pastoral counselor must do some integrative work to make these revisions and constructions applicable to the counseling situation.

Let's look at two areas of theological concern to pastoral counselors for illustrative purposes. The first has to do with traditional theological categories, which are proclaimed from the pulpit, consistently presented in the liturgies, and reinforced by pastoral care. For example, we persistently confess in our liturgies on Sunday morning the sin of pride and for our putting ourselves first. For most women this is not a central element to her alienation from God, self, and neighbor. It is more likely that she does not think highly enough of herself or regard herself as worthy of God's care. She probably does not think of herself as able to engage publicly in the work of God's realm. She probably tends to put herself last. For her to confess consistently to pride misses the opportunity for authentic self-searching and transformation.

The same may be true when we primarily identify Christian mission with that of the suffering servant, It is not greater willingness to suffer that women usually need but a willingness to not suffer. Many pastors have told battered women who have come for advice that this is their cross to bear and that their suffering has earned them a place in heaven without ever considering that their suffering is not chosen—not redemptive—but meaningless suffering for the most part. This requires a reevaluation of some central theological tenets. Atonement and its primary metaphors need rethinking in order for them to be meaningful to women. Sin, especially sin as pride, needs deconstructive work in order to be applicable to women. In addition, women have been traditionally held to be more responsible for bringing sin into the world than men. The story of Eve's presentation of the apple to Adam is certainly better known then the stories of the women who were the last at the cross and the first at the tomb. Negative images of women in our faith traditions are intimately linked to the negative spiritual health and spiritual depression of women and to the integrative potential of the women who come to us for pastoral help. These are not dry, abstract theological luxuries for our eventual perusal. They are, rather, at the core of our pastoral counseling formulations. If, as we said at the beginning of this chapter, pastoral counseling, indeed all counseling, is at its heart a philosophical/theological enterprise, then these instances of theological destructiveness to women deeply affect our potential helpfulness in our healing ministries. We need to be about the work for which we have been particularly trained—the work of reflective theology for the sake of ministering to the spiritual needs of those in our care.

A second illustration of needed theological work has to do with imagery for God. It is clear that the predominant image for God has been, and is, that of God as father. According to a number of feminist theologians this image is not only destructive for many women, but the image itself has become an idol. We do not think of God as a father; rather God *is* a father. We have limited God in such a way that the image of father is no longer as useful in connecting with the richness of God's presence and power.

Again, this is not just an abstract concept. In research that I conducted with women in spiritual growth groups, it became clear that expanding imagery for God—especially when images included the potential for the reflection of self in the divine image—allowed women to be more active in their faith search and in their integration of their faith into the rest of their lives. A side advantage, which was not predicted, was the improvement in women's self-esteem as they found God through this new set of metaphors and images. When they were able to expand their images beyond that of a father who takes care of his daughter (replicating much of the hierarchical, paternalistic world of patriarchy) they presumably found more value in themselves. If, as we discussed earlier, much of women's problems are a result of a culture which pervasively squelches women's self-esteem, then working with imagery for God and for themselves which expands possibilities for life and faith becomes an important dimension of pastoral counseling. (For more on the use of imagination in pastoral counseling, see Neuger 1991.)

These, then, are the general principles within the feminist approach to pastoral counseling described here. They do not encompass all the dimensions to a pastoral counseling approach to women, nor do they address the specifies of counseling work with a variety of problems. They are, however, the primary elements of the lens through which a pastoral counselor should look as she or he works to formulate a counseling plan with each particular counselee. They are fundamental and foundational in approaching the psycho-spiritual distresses that women bring to pastoral counseling.

Applications

Let's take these principles and see how they apply in two commonly experienced problems women bring to pastoral counseling—situational depression, and marriage and family distress.

DEPRESSION

Depression is at an epidemic level among women. There are a variety of studies and estimates about women's depression, but at the very minimum twice as many women are depressed as men. Some studies estimate that as many as six times more women than men are depressed. There are several theories suggested for this difference in numbers of depressed men and women, but feminist research agrees that the major reason for it is "an abiding, unconscious rage at our own oppression which has found no legitimate outlet" (Greenspan 1983, p. 300). A feminist approach to counselees with depression focuses on the need for women to understand their own lives in the context of cultural sexism. Power dynamics in relationships, in families, and in institutions are taken as seriously as the psycho-spiritual symptoms that are the result of the depression. Consequently it is essential for the pastoral counselor to understand the psychological, social, and theological dynamics of patriarchy in working with women who are depressed.

There are a number of types of depressions. The type addressed here is the most common form, what would be called in diagnostic manuals "depressive neurosis." I am not talking about either major depression or bipolar depression, which seem to have biochemical roots and respond best to medication. However, depressive neurosis responds best to a counseling approach that takes seriously the sociocultural reality of the woman's depression. These sociocultural factors express themselves in various dimensions of the counselee's life—her family, her work, her faith, her social life.

This kind of depression can cause tremendous pain in a woman's life. She generally feels hopeless and powerless; she sees no possibility of change. She has generally spent a lot of her energy caring for other people and still feels unnecessary and impotent. She is frequently resentful but afraid to admit or acknowledge her anger, even to herself. She doesn't know much about self-care and even if she does, she is afraid of her own potential selfishness. She has been accused of and seen as over-involved in the family. Because she is depressed and because she has become desperate in her attempt to maintain relationships, she now seems to be the problem in the family. She is the "sick" one, and she has begun to believe this myth. Sometimes she turns to religion as a justification for her suffering and her hope is in God to help her see life as hopeful again.

By the time this woman comes to counseling her agenda is for the counselor to help her be "normal" again and stop being a drain on the family. Too many counselors buy into this agenda and work to help her adjust better to an oppressive environment. However, the role of the pastor is to empower this woman to hear and believe her own experience, to understand her life in a world that frequently is not interested in her wholeness, and to help her network with other women for the sake of ongoing support and reality testing. Finally, the hope is that she will continue to work toward her own wholeness by ongoing recognition of her role in working to change patriarchy.

This means that the counselor begins by offering hope to the woman by normalizing her depression and by listening deeply to her story. Nelle Morton, a feminist theologian, has offered us the phrase of "hearing a woman into speech," which means that we listen deeply to the pain, the hopes, the anger, the doubt, and the various life experiences of a woman until she comes to trust and know her own story. In the midst of this process she is encouraged to begin to use some of her energy to care for herself so that she loses some of her fear of helplessness in the face of abandonment. She is supported in her rage and in her ambivalence about change. After all, depression is the most familiar and acceptable way for her to be. And she is helped to develop a support community of women where she will begin to trust that her experience of hurt and deprivation is, in some form, the experience of all women. In that solidarity there is great hope and possibility.

A pastoral counselor can draw from various techniques, especially from the cognitive approaches which seem so effective in working with depression, as long as they are always used in the context of the world in which women live. All theories have been limited, even family systems theory, in that they have ignored the cultural system which is primary in the development of women's distress. As long as they are appropriately critiqued and used in the cultural context, a variety of theoretical approaches may be useful.

MARITAL DISTRESS

In many cases of women's depression, marital and/or family issues also emerge. It is very common for the dynamics of the culture to be mirrored within the family. Generally there is a considerable power difference between the spouses even though it looks as though the wife has more family power. She generally focuses her power toward the family because she does not have the broader power base that her spouse does. Further, women tend to feel powerless in the family because the major decisions are still made by the husband.

Family systems theory has not taken seriously the differences in cultural power brought into the family. The theory has tended to say that men and women have equal access to power and, in fact, choose each other in order to live out their preferred roles and rules. However, feminist family therapy suggests that the rigid rules and roles in a family are greatly influenced by the rules of the culture and both systems (the family and the culture) must be considered as changes are attempted in the counseling setting.

Case Study

When a woman comes in to counseling and talks about marital problems such as we saw in the case study that introduced this chapter, it is important to assess a number of factors. First, what are the power dynamics in the family? It is easiest to assess this if both members of the couple come to the session. Joan did not feel that her husband would come, but she did invite him. He came for the first session but was clear that he felt that the problems in the family belonged to Joan both in terms of perception and in terms of cause. He said that he was basically happy in the marriage as long as Joan did not expect anything from him. He liked his children and occasionally spent time with them on Saturdays, but for the most part he felt that his job, his social life, and his relaxation time in front of the TV comprised a fully satisfying life. When Joan shared her discontent, he said that he didn't know what he could do to change and she would just have to deal with it. He was also not willing to continue with the counseling. This meant that Joan would have to make the choice to continue alone or terminate the counseling work. She decided to continue.

Sometimes, when the family power dynamics are such that the woman feels powerless, it can be important to do some work to build self-esteem, develop self-care, and encourage an awareness of various realities of the counselee's world. Joan began to explore the world in which she lived, which included her family, her work, and her lack of a social life. She was feeling overwhelmed at work, without a support network. By advancing in her career she became afraid that she would lose any possibility of community. We worked to test this by having her take some initiative with other women in the department. She was able to develop a reasonably satisfying support community. However, this led to another problem. The group of women with whom she began to associate decided that it would be fun to go out to supper together one night a week. Unfortunately, Jim was not willing to help out at home by picking up the children from day care and making them dinner. Joan decided that it was important enough to her to hire a babysitter to pick up the children and make them dinner. After a while Jim decided that he would rather not have someone in the house, and he began to pick up the kids and make them dinner this one time a week. His willingness to do this helped Joan feel closer to him, and she did not behave with such hostility at home.

Joan also began to develop a list of self-care behaviors that she would act on during the week. They were as simple as taking a walk, reading a novel, taking a bubble bath, and so on. This self-care made her feel less needy in her marriage, and she worried less about Jim's unavailability. She became less depressed and enjoyed her life more. We worked on these issues and on her learning to trust herself and her needs more fully. We explored the images she had of herself and she did some re-imaging of her own potential. We also paid attention to the areas in which Joan was most likely to compromise herself out of her cultural and family learning. She got involved in a noontime support group of women and heard much of her story in the stories of the other women. This program of counseling helped her a great deal. However, it also made her more aware that her needs were not being met in her marriage relationship.

About this time Jim came with Joan to a counseling session. He said that he saw that Joan had made a lot of changes, and he wasn't sure that he liked them. He acknowledged that she seemed happier, but he felt that she had withdrawn from the family. The three of us agreed to work together for several sessions. During that time Joan told Jim what she had learned about herself, about the ways she had not claimed herself, and the ways in which she felt the marriage was unsatisfactory. Jim found that he did want the marriage to continue and was willing to negotiate more so that the needs of both of them could be met. This included attending church together, as they felt they had completely ignored that aspect of their lives. They felt this would be one area where they would enter at the same place and grow together. It also included going out together periodically (they had never really dated), doing without television for the hour after supper so that they could talk with each other, sharing child-care responsibilities, and developing more intimacy in various dimensions of their life together. The power bad been balanced in the relationship to a certain extent by helping Joan to know the ways in which power had been denied to her and by helping her to learn how to claim the power that was available to her. Her empowerment through counseling allowed her to have a position from which to negotiate within the marriage.

This is a very superficial description of a complex process. However, it does illustrate, at least in part, the need for the counselor to be aware of women's experience and tuned into the needs of the counselee in the face of a normatively unjust environment. Without an awareness of the systematic sexism that is mirrored in all aspects of women's lives, the counselor cannot effectively work with women individually or in families.

Conclusion

The use of a feminist liberation approach to pastoral counseling is not one option of many. It is the *only* way in which a counselor may bring real and lasting healing to women in distress. The cultural factors are central to the lives of women and cannot be seen as a side issue in pastoral counseling. They form the lens through which a counselor must look at the woman counselee, and they form the material which, when made appropriately available to the counselee, can make seemingly disparate and crazy pieces of her reality fall into place. This does not mean that the counselor lectures about patriarchy, but rather that she or he works out of the knowledge of patriarchy and shares elements of that knowledge as it becomes appropriate.

It is in keeping with the traditions of our faith to serve as advocates for people who have experienced systematic oppression. It is important to integrate that perspective into our counseling work in order to help women find the strength and empowerment authentically to know themselves, their community, and their God. In that, they will be better able to understand and respond to God's call to be full and dynamic participants in the ongoing activity of creation.

References

Ballou, M., and Gabalac, N. 1985. *A Feminist Position on Mental Health.* Springfield, Ill.: Charles C. Thomas.

Benokraitis, N., and Feagin, J. 1986. *Modem Sexism: Blatant, Subtle, and Covert Discrimination.* Englewood Cliffs, N.J.: PrenticeHall.

Bourque, L. B. 1989. *Defining Rape.* Durham, N.C.: Duke University Press.

Donovan, Mary Ellen, and Sanford, Linda. 1984. *Women and Self-Esteem: Understanding and Improving the Way We Think and Feel About Ourselves.* New York: Penguin Books.

Greenspan, M. 1983. *A New Approach to Women And Therapy.* New York: McGraw Hill.

Hoffman, M., ed. 1990. *World Almanac and Book of Facts 1990.* New York: Pharos Books.

Langan, P., and Innes, C. 1986. "Preventing Domestic Violence Against Women." *Bureau of Justice Statistics Special Report.* Washington, D.C.: Bureau of Justice (August) pp. 1–5.

Linz, D., Donnerstein, E., and Penrod, S. 1987. "Sexual Violence in the Mass Media: Social Psychological Implications." In *Sex and Gender,* edited by P. Shaver and C. Hendrick, pp. 95–123. Newbury Park, Calif.: Sage Publications.

MacKinnon, C. 1987. *Feminism Unmodified: Discourses on Life and Law.* Cambridge, Mass.: Harvard University Press.

Major, B. "Gender Justice and the Psychology of Entitlement." In *Sex and Gender,* edited by P. Shaver and C. Hendrick, pp. 124–148. Newbury Park, Calif.: Sage Publications.

Neuger, C. 1991a. "Imagination and Pastoral Care." In *Clinical Handbook to Basic Types of Pastoral Care and Counseling,* edited by Clements and Stone. Nashville: Abingdon.

———. 1991b. "Women and Depression: Lives at Risk." in *Women in Travail and Transition,* edited by Moessner and Glaz. Minneapolis: Fortress Press.

Plummer, C. 1990. "Refusing Co-dependency." *MCC Women's Concerns Report* (July–August): 9–11.

Rix, S., ed. 1990. *The American Woman 1990–91: A Status Report.* New York: W. W. Norton.

Statistical Abstract of the United States, 1987, 109th ed. 1989. Washington, D.C.: U.S. Bureau of the Census.

Swenson, N., Siegal, D., and Doress, P. 1985. "Health: Women and Aging." *The Women's Annual Number Five,* 1984–85, edited by Mary Drake McFeely, pp. 22–42. Boston: G. K. Hall and Company.

Timrots, A., and Rand, M. 1987. "Violent Crime by Strangers and Non-strangers." In *Bureau of Justice Statistics Special Report,* pp. 1–7. Washington, D.C.: U.S. Department of Justice.

Wilkinson, C. 1985. "Work: Challengers to Occupational Segregation." In *The Women's Annual Number Five,* 1984–85, edited by Mary Drake McFeely, pp. 149–165. Boston: G. K. Hall and Company.

"Women and Depression." 1990. *Chronicle of Higher Education.* 19 December 1990, p. A7.

Zillman, D., and Bryant, J. 1982. "Pornography, Sexual Callousness, and the Trivialization of Rape." *Journal of Communication.* 32:10–21.

Harold G. Koenig

3. Pastoral Counseling with the Aged

In the decades ahead, we will see more and more older adults who are in need of counseling. One reason for this will be the sheer number of elderly people in the population. While in 1998 there were 35 million persons age sixty-five or over in the United States (13 percent of the population), there will be more than 70 million by the year 2035, making up well over 20 percent of the population. Government funding of mental health services for the elderly is already coming under substantial strain. By the year 2007, the Medicare budget will increase from its current $200 billion per year to more than $400 billion per year, as national health expenditures increase from $1.1 trillion to $2.1 trillion (Smith et al. 1998).

Rates of depression and other emotional disorders requiring counseling are expected to dramatically increase among the elderly (Koenig et al. 1994). Baby boomers (those born between 1945 and 1967) have high rates of depression even now, when their health and economic status are better than those of any other generation in history. As physical health problems increase and economic well-being decreases, rates of depression are expected to soar even higher. While medical care is keeping people alive longer, many people experience chronic physical disability as they move into their later years. The estimated number of severely disabled people in the United States age sixty-five or over is expected to increase from the current number of 2–4 million to upward of 12 million in the next 30–40 years (Kunkel & Applebaum 1992). Part of the reason for this is the increase in the number of persons with Alzheimer's disease, who currently make up only 4 million of the population but who in the decades ahead will rise to nearly 14 million. Physical and mental disability are often accompanied by depression and substance abuse—as the disabled desperately attempt to cope with dependency and loss of meaning, purpose, and value. In this chapter, I will review the major problems that aging persons must deal with and suggest ways of helping aging persons overcome them.

Common Problems in Later Life

As people age, changes occur that for many create stress and emotional turmoil. In 1995, I administered a questionnaire to forty pastors or assistant pastors from Protestant (Episcopalian, Presbyterian, Lutheran, Methodist, Baptist) and Catholic traditions. These clergy were located in widely different areas of the United States, from the South and Southeast (Texas, Florida, and North Carolina) to the Midwest (Iowa and Minnesota) to the West Coast (California and Hawaii). Their ages ranged from twenty-one to seventy-two years; both men and women were included. The proportion of their congregations that were over age sixty ranged from less than 5 percent to 99 percent (average 44 percent). Over 95 percent of participants in the sample were full-time, active pastors leading congregations in small to mid-sized towns (35,000 up to 285,000). We administered the full questionnaire to twenty-seven clergy. For the remaining thirteen, we administered a briefer version that focused on the types of information clergy wanted to help them better meet the health needs of older adults and their families.

We also administered the briefer version of the questionnaire to fifty religious caregivers who attended a workshop on religion and health care of the elderly held in Tampa, Florida, in September 1995. These religious caregivers were actively involved in their local churches. Between one-third and one-half of participants were "Stephens" ministers, and one-quarter were elders or deacons. Their ages ranged from forty-six to eighty-four (average age sixty-eight); more than one-half were women; and all were Protestant. Questions in both questionnaires focused on identifying the most common reasons that older adults or their families came in for counseling.

The ten areas about which *clergy* most frequently mentioned they wanted information were the following:

1. Understanding and helping persons with Alzheimer's disease
2. Depression, grieving over loss, suicide
3. Normal physical and mental changes of aging
4. Caring for the elderly and supporting their caregivers
5. Coping with loneliness and isolation
6. Spiritual growth and development in later life
7. Help elders feel useful, needed, and able to cope with change
8. Information about nursing homes
9. End-of-life issues
10. Identifying needs of elders and community resources to meet them.

The ten areas most frequently mentioned by *religious* caregivers were the following:

1. Alzheimer's disease and memory changes with aging
2. Combating depression and maintaining hope
3. How to maintain and optimize mental and emotional growth
4. Overcoming loneliness and isolation
5. Coping with disability and dependency
6. Questions about nursing homes
7. Helping persons use their faith to cope with chronic illness
8. How to help caregivers of persons with Alzheimer's or chronic illness
9. How to maintain physical health in later life
10. Comforting persons who are terminally ill or dying.

Among the highest priority areas were understanding the normal changes of aging, coping with chronic physical illness, dealing with issues related to disability and dependency, depression and grieving, anxiety, Alzheimer's disease, caregiver stress, and loss of meaning and purpose in life. Although I review these topics briefly, a more in-depth analysis of each of these areas can be found in *Counseling Older Adults* (1997) and *Pastoral Care of Older Adults* (1998).

Changes of Normal Aging

How does one determine what is normal and what is abnormal in older persons? Many normal changes of aging are similar to and blend in with symptoms of common diseases in later life. I will focus here primarily on changes experienced in cognitive, psychological, and social functioning with increasing age.

Changes in the brain with normal aging result in mild loss of memory, which has been given the name "Aged-Associated Memory Impairment." This level of memory loss is completely normal and expected, and does not progressively worsen into dementia. Persons may have difficulty remembering names, go into the kitchen and forget why they went there, or need to carry a grocery list with them when shopping. These people, however, don't become confused or lose their orientation in familiar settings, get lost while driving (except in clearly unfamiliar environments), or become unable to balance their checkbook or pay their bills. Usually, memory changes associated with normal aging become more noticeable after a person reaches seventy-five or eighty years of age. They do not worsen rapidly, however, and never interfere to any great degree with the person's normal overall level of functioning.

Because of changes in brain function with age, older adults need more time to learn new tasks, but given *adequate time* to do so, they are able to learn and retain information just as well as younger persons. Older adults may also need more time to "retrieve" information from memory. They may not remember something immediately, but will remember it after a few minutes. Thus, there is some slowing down in mental processes with age, but again, this should not interfere with the person's general level of functioning. It is also not uncommon for older adults to notice minor problems with balance, coordination, and reaction time; these should not automatically be interpreted as disease. Nevertheless, an underlying disease may be the cause of any persistent symptoms and must be ruled out by careful medical examination. Normal changes of aging may also be affected by disease or medications (either prescription drugs or over-the-counter medications).

Psychological and Social Changes. Older persons do not ordinarily experience great changes in their personalities or interests as they age. Personality characteristics tend to remain stable from middle age onward. The older person who was outgoing and extroverted in young adulthood will likely continue to be so as she grows older. Likewise, the introverted and socially phobic younger person will likely have these traits when he is older. If anything, personality traits become more accentuated with age. Older persons will continue to enjoy the same things they enjoyed when they were younger, whether work, hobbies, social relationships, or sexual activity.

Sadness, loss of energy and interest, and withdrawal from a previously enjoyed level of social activity do *not* occur with normal aging. More than likely, these are symptoms of treatable illnesses. The same is true for sleep disturbances. While older persons normally experience a reduction in the deep type of sleep and consequently have more frequent awakenings during the night, their need for sleep remains only slightly less than when they were younger (about seven hours per night). If older adults do not get adequate sleep at night, they will feel tired and fatigued during the day; unfortunately, sleeping aids are not very helpful and may lead to memory loss and cognitive impairment. Some older adults also experience an advancement in their sleep cycle, such that they will tend to go to bed earlier in the evening and wake up earlier in the morning.

Besides normal aging, several sleep disorders (insomnia, hypersomnia, sleep apnea—cessation of breathing evidenced by loud snoring) are common in later life, and must be suspected when daytime somnolence or nighttime insomnia is present. Such symptoms may herald emotional or physical problems, including depression, heart disease, endocrine disease, or side effects from medication. If no disorders of any type are identified on complete medical and psychiatric evaluation, then changes may be due to normal aging or to undiagnosed disease that has not sufficiently pro-gressed to be clinically evident.

Any complaint that interferes with the quality of life of an older person should be taken seriously and that person monitored carefully. Nevertheless, many older adults will worry excessively about these problems because of a relative or friend who had similar symptoms and was diagnosed with an underlying disease. Once disease has been carefully ruled out, education about the normal changes of aging and reassurance by the counselor can be helpful in relieving patients' unnecessary anxiety.

Chronic Physical Illness

Chronic health problems, many of which are treatable, are common in older adults and can markedly interfere with daily life. Among persons age sixty-five or over, approximately one-half have at least two chronic medical conditions. These medical conditions, particularly when disabling and asso-ciated with other uncomfortable symptoms, often create emotional stress in the person's life. Symptoms related to chronic illness often interfere with sleep, appetite, and recreational activities. They also interfere with social relationships and can lead to isolation and a sense of alienation from others. Even the patient's family members may not really understand, particularly if they must take on extra burdens to care for the chronically ill person. Thus, older adults with chronic health problems often feel misunderstood, lonely, and at times, helpless (along with angry and frustrated).

Many older persons with health problems are struggling with loss—loss of physical vigor, strength, and the ability to do the things that give their lives meaning and purpose. For that reason, older adults tend to talk a lot about their health problems. This can be misinterpreted by the counselor as simply complaining or as a preoccupation with health (*hypochondriasis*). Many times, however, older adults simply need to talk about and work through their health losses as a way of mourning or grieving those losses. An important phase in the normal grief process is talking about the loss with someone else. The pastoral counselor who actively listens to the patient, expresses empathy and understanding, and validates the person's loss will help facilitate the grief process and speed the patient's recovery.

Religious belief and activity are powerful resources that can help chronically ill elders overcome negative feelings and experience a return of purpose and meaning to their lives. Unfortunately, religious resources are frequently underutilized—even by pastoral counselors, who may have learned to prefer traditional psychotherapeutic techniques. In a recent study of eighty-seven elderly patients at Duke Hospital who had multiple chronic medical illnesses and were in great psychological distress, we found that patients who scored highest on intrinsic religiosity (or personal faith in God) recovered significantly faster from depression than did persons with less faith (Koenig et al. 1998). Degree of intrinsic religiousness had a particularly strong effect on emotional healing in patients whose physical health problems were not responding to medical treatments (the chronically disabled). Interestingly, psychotherapy and even drug treatments for depression did not speed recovery as quickly as intrinsic faith did. Pastoral counselors should take advantage of the person's religious faith in helping her adapt to and cope with chronic changes in her health. How can this be done?

How Religion Helps Elders to Cope. We asked older persons with chronic health problems how they utilized their religious faith to cope with health problems. We received a tremendous variety of responses. The most common response was placing trust and faith in God. Many said that they simply turned their situation over to God and let God deal with it. This helped them to stop worrying and obsessing about the problems and move on to more important things in life, which provided meaning and purpose. Emotional disorder develops when people become preoccupied with or ruminate over a situation they cannot change. Releasing the problem to God can break the vicious cycle of worry and preoccupation. Unfortunately, many elders try to take the problem *back* from God and struggle with it once again. The counselor must gently remind them of what they are doing and help them once again to give the problem to God. This involves a process of mental discipline that must be learned and practiced. (I am assuming, of course, that the person has done everything possible to relieve the chronic health problem by seeking medical care and is complying with medical treatments.)

The second common way that elderly subjects reported they coped with health problems was through personal prayer—*conversational* prayer with God. They indicated that praying to God somehow brought them comfort, and in particular, hope. Even though they did not have control over their situations, the belief that God did have control and would respond to prayer brought great relief. Praying to God also relieved their loneliness and sense of isolation; even if their caregivers or family members didn't understand them, God did, and would give them strength to make it through.

A third way that religion brought comfort was through the Bible or other inspirational literature. Interestingly, many could not describe why reading scriptures made them feel better; it just did. Some said they sang religious hymns to lift their spirits. Others mentioned that religious rituals such as taking communion or saying the rosary were very helpful. Many chronically ill persons remarked how visits and prayers from clergy and church members gave them strength to cope with health problems. Knowing that their names had been mentioned during church services or had been placed on a prayer list often brought comfort. Despite serious disability and health problems, going to church was very important for many elderly patients, but they often needed assistance and transportation.

Why mention these spontaneous responses of chronically ill persons about how religion help them cope? These responses give clues about how pastoral counselors can help persons use their faith to help them cope with chronic health problems.

- Elders need a relationship with God, know that they can communicate with him as their closest personal friend, and know that they are not alone in their struggle nor in the hands of aimless fate.

- Elders need to believe that God is on their side, has their best interests at stake, and has a plan for them—a good plan. If there is some purpose and greater design for humanity, then our continued presence on Earth—even when sick and disabled—can have meaning and purpose. We as counselors must help elders find out what role they play in God's plan *given their current health circumstances* (see following).

- Elders need to realize that God is steadfastly present and willing to help. Having done everything they can to solve their problems, elders must learn to stop struggling with those problems and let God take over. If elders cannot do this, they may need help working through trust issues, which often relate to how they communicated with their own parents. Explore in an open and accepting manner their doubts and difficulties believing in or trusting God. Many may feel embarrassed and guilty about having such doubts, but verbalizing them to a concerned and respected listener can often facilitate problem resolution and development of trust.

- Elders often need to be reminded of the power of prayer. Prayer is a ready tool that can be used at any time of the day or night, and is certainly more accessible than the one or two hours per month spent with the pastoral counselor. When asked how they prayed, our chronically ill subjects said they talked with God as if the Creator were right there in the room with them. God really knew them and understood everything they were going through, a fact that reduced their loneliness and sense of isolation.

- Praying with patients and even "laying on of hands" in the traditional biblical sense can help reaffirm belief in God's healing power. This can be even more important if done within the local church, because it communicates to the chronically ill elder that he is part of a caring religious community.

- Elders may need to be encouraged to join prayer groups or prayer chains that commit to help those in need. By learning about and praying for the needs of others, the elder will be distracted from her own problems and may obtain a greater sense of purpose and usefulness.

- Elders need to be encouraged to read the Bible and other inspirational literature. Our chronically ill patients frequently mentioned that this brought them comfort. Elders may be given passages from the Bible that are particularly applicable to their situations and encouraged to meditate on these passages. Biblical figures provide role models for virtually every life situation. Consider Job, David, Jeremiah, and Paul. The pastoral counselor should discuss these passages with the older patient. Ask what these passages mean, and actively listen as the older client ponders these biblical truths. The psalms are particularly helpful for people who are depressed or anxious, since they convey comfort and security.

- Elders should be encouraged to participate in the rituals of their faith tradition. Such rituals include Holy Communion, confession, or other ritualistic blessings performed by the pastor. Mobilizing family or church members to provide elders with the opportunity to attend church and participate in these rituals may greatly facilitate their coping with illness. For example, receiving communion may remind them of how Christ suffered and died for them, reaffirming God's deep love and commitment.

- Elders should be encouraged to confess mistakes, ask for forgiveness, and give forgiveness to others. Whether confession is ritualized, as in the Catholic tradition, or more spontaneous, as in the Protestant, it is important that chronically ill elders be given an opportunity to talk about past mistakes and ask forgiveness. Real or imagined guilt over sins may prevent the elder from turning to God in his present difficulties.

These are but a few ways pastoral counselors can help older adults use their religious beliefs to cope with chronic illness. In summary, encourage elders to relate with God in a personal way; provide them with religious materials that may inspire, motivate, and give hope; and allow them to talk about and work through negative experiences with religion or guilt over past sins.

Disability and Dependency

Despite enormous improvements in health care that can extend the length of life, less progress has been made in reducing the physical disability associated with growing older. As noted earlier, during the next 30–40 years the number of severely disabled persons age sixty-five or over in the United States is expected to rise dramatically. One of the major reasons why chronic physical illness causes depression and other emotional disorders is that it results in physical disability. Indeed, one of the strongest predictors of depression in later life is disability level (Koenig & George 1998).

Being disabled and dependent on others strips a person of his identity and self-esteem. Nobody wants to be a burden on others, particularly on beloved family members. Many elders, however, have no other choice but to rely on others for their basic care needs. It is not surprising that a large proportion of older adults would rather die than live for the rest of their lives under such conditions, nor is it unexpected that elders try to numb their pain with drugs or alcohol. Adjustment to disability is particularly difficult when the disability occurs suddenly in an elder who has previously been independent and self-sufficient. Even when disability occurs more slowly, as seen in Parkinson's disease, Alzheimer's dementia, or arthritis, adjusting to dependency can be one of life's greatest challenges.

What can the pastoral counselor say to the elder who is struggling with dependency? Following is a list of practical suggestions for facilitating adaptation to chronic disability and dependency:

- Provide the elder with adaptive devices to maximize their independence and self-sufficiency.

- Listen carefully, learn about his situation, and try to put yourself in his shoes and empathize with him.

- Encourage elders to verbalize their feelings, and give them the time to do so without interrupting. Validate these feelings. You may be the only one in this person's life with whom she can share what her disability means to her, how it has affected her hopes and dreams.

Perhaps most important, gently and sensitively help the disabled elder discover and use the special gift that God has given him for his particular situation (see following).

Depression, Grief, and Suicide

Depression is the most common and treatable of all psychiatric ill-nesses in later life. It affects up to 15 percent of persons age sixty-five or older in the United States, increases to nearly 25 percent of elders in nursing homes, and explodes to nearly 50 percent of older adults hospitalized with acute medical illness (National Institutes of Health, 1991; Koenig et al. 1997). It is unfortunate that primary care physicians identify only about 10–20 percent of elders with depression, and even fewer receive adequate treatment for their depression. Many older adults, however, seek out clergy and religious professionals for help in dealing with depression and related emotional disorders.

It is important to remember that depression is a treatable emotional dis-order, *not a normal consequence of aging.* Depression is a persistent and enduring mood disturbance that interferes with a person's ability to carry out normal activities at home or pursue relationships with others. Depression has a lifetime mortality rate of 15 percent from suicide, and suicide among older adults is increasing in the United States. The causes of depression in later life are many. An older adult may be vulnerable to depression because of heredi-tary or genetic influences, because of poor nurturing or traumatic experiences in childhood, or because of biological changes in the brain brought on by ill-ness or medication. Severe brief stress or long-term moderate-to-severe stress can precipitate depression in a susceptible person, and the greater susceptibil-ity to depression, the less stress is needed to precipitate depression. Everyone has a stress threshold above which they will experience depression.

Treatment for Depression. The three types of treatment for depres-sion are psychotherapy, antidepressant medication, and electroshock ther-apy (ECT). Milder forms of depression respond well to brief counseling, whereas more severe depressions require medication and sometimes even electroshock therapy. Four types of psychotherapy are used to treat depression in older adults: cognitive-behavioral therapy (CBT), interper-sonal therapy (IPT), reminiscent therapy (RT), and supportive therapy (ST). In CBT, the most common psychotherapy used today to treat depres-sion, the therapist attempts to change dysfunctional beliefs and attitudes that are generating negative emotions. These negative cognitions are transformed into more positive, realistic ways of thinking that promote mental health. The behavioral part of CBT encourages and rewards activi-ties that produce pleasure and fulfillment. IPT is a form of brief psychody-namic therapy that helps the elder explore present and past relationships and rework conflicts in them. In RT, the elder is encouraged to perform a "life review" in order to come to terms with experiences in the past that are contributing to present difficulties.

Supportive therapy (ST) is the most effective treatment when an older adult has recently experienced severe trauma or loss, and needs support and nurturance from others to cope with the experience. Because most depression in later life is a result of loss, supportive therapy can be very helpful, especially in the short term. When depression persists over many months, however, then re-educative therapies (CBT, IPT, or others) become necessary. Persistent or severe depressions, especially those associated with suicidal thoughts, weight loss, sleep disturbance, and other "endogenous" symptoms of depression, may also have biological origins. In that case, treatment of depression requires the combined use of antidepressant medication and psychotherapy, and possibly ECT.

Antidepressants are often rapidly effective in the treatment of depression. These drugs act by affecting brain levels of serotonin and norepinephrine, chemicals that become depleted when depression strikes. Significant improvement may occur in sleep and mood during the first week of treatment, although many persons do not notice improvements until after six to eight weeks of treatment. There are many different types of antidepressants, and several may need to be tried before the "right" drug is identified for the person. The type of antidepressant that is best for a particular individual depends on drug side effects, the type of depressive symptoms the person is having, and the person's physiological makeup. Persons do not become "addicted" to antidepressants like they do to minor tranquilizers, sleeping pills, or narcotics for pain. However, if persons stop an antidepressant suddenly, they may experience a withdrawal reaction that can be quite severe in some cases.

Persons who do not respond to antidepressants or who have life-threatening symptoms of depression (serious suicidal impulses or weight loss that threatens survival) need immediate treatment. Electroshock therapy (ECT) is rapid, effective, and safe in treating severe late life depression, particularly when accompanied by paranoia or delusions. ECT may actually have fewer adverse complications than antidepressant medication when used in frail, medically ill older patients who cannot tolerate the side effects of drugs. New methods of administering ECT have completely revolutionized this form of treatment compared to older methods dramatized in *One Flew over the Cuckoo's Nest.*

The Pastoral Counselor. For older adults with more severe or persistent forms of depression, referral to a psychiatrist is often the best course of action. Primary care physicians seldom know how to adequately treat severely depressed older adults, particularly elders with multiple, complex health problems. Many milder forms of depression exist that pastoral counselors can and should treat. These depressions are often related to the process of grief.

Supportive therapy and listening, followed by re-educative therapies after several weeks or months, is often sufficient to effectively treat depression in these patients. Recall that successful grieving requires that a person talk about and work through their loss. Working through grief always requires time, so don't be surprised if it takes longer for older adults to work through their grief. Elders are often grieving for many losses all at once—loss of health, loss of independence, loss of family members and lifelong friendships, loss of former lifestyle, and loss of position in the family and/or society. A major loss may require six months to a year to complete grieving, and for some losses (death of a spouse of fifty years), it may take many years, possibly even the rest of the person's life. Nevertheless, if after the first six months grief remains severe and disabling, then treatment must be sought.

Religion and Depression. Psychotherapy that utilizes the religious beliefs of the patient has been shown to be more rapidly effective in relieving depression than secular psychotherapy in religious clients (Propst et al. 1992; Worthington et al. 1996; Koenig & Pritchett 1998). Pastoral counselors, then, have a powerful tool at their disposal to help treat depression and hopelessness that secular therapists do not have.

Depression itself can make it much harder for religious elders to access spiritual resources. The depressed person may cry out for relief to God, who appears not to be listening (as in the psalms). The religious elder may feel deserted by God and angry over her pain, even questioning her beliefs. Depression makes it difficult for people to read the Bible, pray, or make the effort to attend church services. I try to go slowly with these patients, realizing that it is very important for them to be able to express these feelings and frustrations toward God in a supportive, understanding atmosphere. These feelings almost always pass away, and if successfully worked through, will lead to a strengthening of religious faith, not its dismissal. It is also important not to arouse any further guilt in depressed patients if they are not engaging in religious practices; self-condemnation is usually already overwhelming at this stage.

Referral to Psychologist or Psychiatrist. When grief deepens to the point that therapy does not seem to be progressing, or if the elder appears stuck in a particular phase of grief (anger, bargaining, denial), then referral to a mental health specialist with advanced training should be considered. Below are symptoms suggesting that referral to a psychiatrist is necessary:

- Severe despondency or inability to experience pleasure that shows no signs of improvement after 3–4 weeks of counseling
- 5 lbs. or more of weight loss, or 10 lbs. or more of weight gain
- Severe problems with sleep (insomnia or hypersomnia)
- Severe fatigue or psychomotor retardation

- Marked irritability, agitation, or restlessness
- Bizarre ideas or paranoia (delusions)
- Suicidal thoughts or desire for death

How to Prevent Suicide. Being alert for the signs and symptoms of suicide is the best way to prevent it. Nearly 75 percent of suicides occur in people who have seen their doctor within the previous month. Interestingly, the older adult is even more likely to have contact with their pastor or pastoral counselor prior to attempting suicide (Weaver et al. 1996). Unfortunately, clergy are among the least likely professionals to recognize signs of impending suicide (at about the same level as educated lay persons) (Domino 1985). Be alert for the following:

- An older white male who is divorced, separated, or bereaved
- Concurrent physical illness or disability, especially if accompanied by chronic pain
- Cognitive impairment, reducing threshold for impulsive actions
- Alcohol abuse
- Extreme hopelessness, sense that there is no way out, and tiredness
- Prior history of suicide attempts
- Restless, agitated, or anxious type of depression (with energy to plan or carry out suicide)
- Few supportive relationships
- Possession of the means to commit suicide
- Family history of suicide

There is a cardinal rule that all counselors must follow, and there are no exceptions. *Always* ask a depressed person about suicidal thoughts, no matter how mild symptoms may appear. I have been surprised by the frequency of suicidal thoughts among those with seemingly the mildest depressions. While a bit embarrassed, most patients feel relieved to talk about this. Remember that you do not need to worry about "giving the person an idea" by asking about suicidal thoughts. Nevertheless, it is best to approach the topic slowly and gently, giving the patient permission to reveal their secret. I often ask the patient if he or she wished the Lord would just take them or end their life. If the answer is Yes, then I move slowly to determine whether or not the person has a plan and the means to carry out the plan. If so, I suggest the counselor not try to discourage or argue with the person, but rather to simply listen, try to understand their pain, communicate to them that you really care, and get information.

If the elder has persistent thoughts about harming himself, or has thought of a plan, this requires that you take action to ensure the person's safety. If the elder is unwilling to cooperate with your plan, and your level of concern is great enough, then it is necessary to contact family members. You may wish to urge family to fill out commitment papers at the magistrate's office that will direct the sheriff to bring the person for psychiatric evaluation against their will. You the counselor may also fill out commitment papers if there are no family members available. If the elder decides to leave your office and you are losing control of the situation, call 911 or the sheriff's office.

Anxiety and Fear

As people get older, there are many things to worry about—safety and vulnerability to assault or robbery, health problems of oneself or loved ones, increasing dependency, declining finances, need to sell one's homes, need to move to a nursing home, loneliness. Among these many worries, fear of death is often lower down on the list.

Approximately 6 percent of older adults have diagnosable anxiety disorders that require psychiatric treatment, including panic disorder (severe anxiety lasting a few minutes associated with racing heart and breathlessness), generalized anxiety disorder (GAD; often associated with a lifelong history of feeling anxious or nervous much of the time), and obsessive-compulsive disorder (OCD). For patients with these disorders, which are thought to be at least partly biological in origin, medical treatments are extremely effective in relieving symptoms. Medications, particularly benzodiazepines, can be habit forming and have numerous side effects in frail elders, including cognitive impairment, disturbance of balance, oversedation, and interactions with other medications. The best long-term biological treatment of anxiety disorders in older adults is antidepressant therapy. These drugs, particularly the newer ones, are much safer, are not habit forming, and are equally effective. The only problem is that antidepressants take longer to work, and may take as long as 4–6 weeks, and even 8–12 weeks for OCD, before benefits are evident. I usually combine treatment with both a benzodiazepine and an antidepressant during the first couple weeks of therapy, and once the antidepressant begins to take effect, the benzodiazepine can be gradually withdrawn. Concurrent counseling and psychotherapy is not only helpful, but often is necessary to ensure compliance with medical treatments.

The majority of older adults with less severe anxiety do not require drug therapy. For these more minor fears and worries, cognitive-behavioral therapy (CBT) is often very effective. CBT for anxiety often involves teaching the elder problem-solving strategies, correcting skill deficits, modifying ineffective communication patterns, and changing the physical environment in which problems arise. CBT is particularly effective for anxiety because it discourages "catastrophic thinking" and worry about the disasters that "might happen." CBT is a re-educative therapy that trains elders to monitor their thoughts and challenges negative thinking that arouses anxiety. Several popular books now describe how people can learn these techniques on their own. *Telling Yourself the Truth* (Backus & Chapin 1980) uses a Christian approach to CBT that challenges pessimistic and disaster-type thinking and promotes healthy thought patterns that reduce anxiety and fear.

Religion and Anxiety. Freud emphasized the neurosis-producing effects of religion in many of his writings. Surprisingly, however, there is little evidence from scientific research that devout religiousness is associated with greater neurosis or anxiety. In fact, our research studies in both older and younger adults have documented the opposite. Anxiety symptoms and disorders appear to be less common among persons actively involved in religious community and those with strong religious faith (Koenig et al. 1993; Koenig & McConnell 1999). Scriptures contain many references to anxious persons who received great comfort from God and were victorious over difficult circumstances (Isa 26:3, Gal 5:22, 2 Tim 1:7, to name just a few).

Pastoral Counseling Interventions. I have had success with having older patients memorize these scriptures and repeat them during times of anxiety. Studies have shown that repeating verses of religious scripture and saying repetitive prayers can reduce anxiety faster than the use of traditional psychotherapy and drug therapy alone (Benson 1984; Azhar et al. 1994). I have also seen group prayer, especially with laying on of hands, be effective for relieving symptoms of panic attack. Many anxiety disorders require multi-modal therapy that includes prayer, repeating religious scriptures, medication, and cognitive-behavioral therapy, which may work synergistically in the healing process.

Alzheimer's Disease

Alzheimer's disease (AD) is one of the most feared diseases of later life. AD is a progressive brain disease that increases in frequency with increasing age. While only 5–10 percent of persons over age sixty-five have the disease, some surveys report a prevalence of almost 50 percent among persons age eighty-five or older. Many people are surprised to learn that Alzheimer's disease is the fourth leading cause of death in adults, after heart disease, cancer, and stroke. AD is characterized by a gradual, insidious loss of memory and disturbance of higher cognitive functioning that has a course lasting from two to fifteen years. More specific symptoms of the disorder include the following:

- Memory loss (misplacing objects, repeating stories, missing appointments, difficulty learning new information)
- Language problems (difficulty finding the right word, naming objects; may advance unintelligible speech and muteness)
- Declining visuospatial skills (may report difficulty cooking, setting the table, fixing or manipulating objects in the home)
- Impaired cognition (problems handling and manipulating information, performing calculations, making rational judgments, or performing other higher cortical tasks)
- Personality changes (decreased motivation, indifferent, impulsive, irritable, increasing self-centeredness, preoccupied, and socially withdrawn)

Cognitive Impairment Not Related to Alzheimer's Disease. Diseases other than Alzheimer's disease cause confusion and memory loss. While Alzheimer's disease is the most common cause of "dementia" (about two-thirds of dementias), other diseases have similar signs and symptoms. About 15–20 percent of dementias result from mini-strokes (also called multi-infarct dementia) and another 5–10 percent are caused by chronic alcohol abuse (called alcoholic dementia). It is important to distinguish among the various types of cognitive impairment, because the treatments are different. The pastoral counselor may need to educate the patient and his family about the need to seek medical attention in order to make the correct diagnoses. For patients with Alzheimer's disease, there is now medical treatment that may help delay progression of the disorder, particularly if treatment is begun during the early stages. For patients with multi-infarct dementia, treating blood pressure and taking an aspirin once a day may help prevent further strokes and worsening of memory loss. Studies have shown that cessation of alcohol intake may not only halt the progression of alcoholic dementia, but may actually reverse some changes.

It is particularly important to differentiate *dementia* (which is largely irreversible) from *delirium* (which is completely reversible). Delirium is characterized by a relatively rapid onset, a decrease in level of alertness, and fluctuating level of consciousness. Delirium has many of the same symptoms as dementia and is often confused with it. Because delirium is usually reversible if the cause is identified and treated (infection, side effects of medication, metabolic disorder), it is essential to make the correct diagnosis to differentiate this transient condition from irreversible dementia. There are other conditions, called "reversible dementia," that are caused by certain vitamin deficiencies (B-12 deficiency or pernicious anemia), hypothyroidism, normal pressure hydrocephalus, or neurosyphillis. Treatment of these conditions will often improve the dementia.

Once the diagnosis of Alzheimer's disease is made, there are many things that can be done to improve the management and care of persons with this condition. Pastoral counselors can direct family members to community resources, support groups, and reading materials that make life for both patient and caregiver much easier. Patients in the early stages of AD often need counseling because of the depression and fear that memory loss arouses. Supportive therapies and positive counseling are best. Spiritual interventions can often be very helpful at this time and at later stages in the disease as well. Remember that Alzheimer's disease is a cortical dementia, often sparing those areas of the brain responsible for emotion and feeling. Even in the late stages of the disease, singing familiar religious hymns, saying familiar prayers, and participation in religious rituals (worship services, communion, and so on) are often deeply meaningful to patients. I suggest that all counselors read the book, *My Journey into Alzheimer's Disease* (Davis 1989), which tells the personal story of a prominent Protestant clergyman from Florida who contracted the disease, and how it affected his relationship with God.

Family Caregivers

Caregivers of older adults with dementia, stroke, cancer, and other chronic or disabling illnesses often experience severe emotional distress and sometimes even physical illness from trying to shoulder the heavy responsibilities involved in caring for the needs of a sick loved one. For caregivers of persons with Alzheimer's disease, the burden of care is even greater because of the prolonged course of the illness (2–15 years). In the early stages, persons with Alzheimer's disease lose their ability to perform usual household chores, transferring these additional responsibilities to the caregiver. The caregiver must now pay the bills, cook the meals, clean the house, do the laundry, take care of the yard, fix the car, all in addition to caring for the patient. In the later stages of the disease, demented persons may need to be dressed, bathed, and monitored day and night so that they do not wander out of the home, get lost, or perform dangerous activities inside the home (turn on the stove or gas). In the later stages, demented patients become incontinent of urine and stool, and may become belligerent or even physically violent toward the caregiver.

As the disease progresses, about one-half to three-quarters of patients become delusional (have fixed false beliefs that they cannot be dissuaded from—that someone is stealing from them or other paranoid ideas). Such delusions may cause agitation and cause patients to strike out at a spouse whom they no longer recognize. As the disease progresses further, patients require twenty-four hour a day supervision and cannot be left alone.

Demented persons often become active at night and sleep throughout most of the day. The caregiver may be busy all night trying to contain the patient, quickly leading to sleep deprivation and fatigue during the day (when other household responsibilities must be carried out). With little time to nurture relationships with others outside the home, it is easy to see how caregivers can easily become exhausted and socially isolated. Under this burden of stress, without relief or respite, the caregiver may easily become irritable and impatient with the uncooperative demented relative and may even physically abuse him or her. Depression, anxiety, insomnia, marital conflict, alcoholism, and physical health problems are all higher among caregivers (Cantor 1983).

What can the pastoral counselor do to help the caregiver? The primary task of the counselor is to help the caregiver obtain respite from the caregiving role, which is strangely often resisted by the caregiver. Relieving the stress associated with caregiving, then, must be a high priority for the pastoral counselor. If the caregiver can get out of the house for several hours two or three times per week to care for her or his own needs, this often provides the emotional outlet necessary to reduce stress. Other things the pastoral counselor can do to help the caregiver include:

- Encourage the caregiver to seek companionship and social activities outside the home
- Educate the caregiver on community resources that will provide him with practical help in the caregiving role
- Provide supportive counseling and spiritual support
- Provide information about the disease, its course, and options for home care and nursing home placement
- At the appropriate time, provide the caregiver with permission to place their loved one in a nursing home.

The pastoral counselor should realize that the church may also play an important role in assisting caregivers. Church members can provide respite by taking turns spending afternoons with the patient, allowing the caregiver time off to rejuvenate herself. Volunteers must be trained, and the necessary paperwork filled out that waives liability (preventing the caregiver from suing the volunteer or the volunteer from suing the caregiver). Several churches may get together to establish an adult day care that provides structured activities for demented persons for several hours per day. While private adult day cares exist in the community, it can be very expensive. The church may help provide the finances to pay for adult day care once a week, although it is likely to be less expensive to simply hire someone for an afternoon per week to sit with the patient in his home.

Depression or anxiety may often impair the caregiver's ability to carry out his responsibilities. In that case, counseling and, in some cases, referral for medical treatment become necessary. Verbalizing these stresses to a knowledgeable and interested counselor can help relieve the sense of alienation and isolation so commonly seen in these circumstances. Rather than use any particular psychotherapeutic technique, I suggest the counselor actively listen and try to understand the caregiver's situation. Because research has shown that religious beliefs are important for helping caregivers adapt to stresses of caregiving (Rabins et al. 1990), I encourage counselors to stress the person's religious faith and relationship with God as powerful coping resources. Also, be sure that the caregiver has a copy of *The 36-Hour Day* (Mace & Rabins 1981), a 250-page book that addresses many important questions that caregivers struggle with. Directing the caregiver to a support group in his community is often extremely helpful; support groups may be located by calling the National Alzheimer's Association at 1-800-272-3900 or 1-800-621-0379.

Because most family caregivers are extraordinarily committed to caring for their loved ones at home, they are sometimes reluctant to give up this responsibility even when it is clearly necessary (for their own health and for the health of their loved one). Many family caregivers feel extremely guilty about making the decision to put their loved one in a nursing home. Pastoral counselors, with guidance from the patient's personal physician, are in an ideal position to "give permission" to caregivers to place their loved one. The counselor will often need to work with the caregiver to help overcome and work through her guilt before such guilt interferes with the caregiver's ability to spend time with the relative once transferred to the nursing home. The level of care in the nursing home that the demented relative receives is heavily dependent upon how much time family spends visiting the patient.

The pastoral counselor should also encourage the caregiver to ensure that her demented loved one has the best of medical care. Nearly 50 percent of persons with dementia in the middle and later stages have delusions and other psychotic symptoms that cause them to be agitated and difficult to care for. There are effective drugs available for controlling these symptoms that are safe and effective.

Loss of Meaning and Purpose

Like persons of any age, older people need to feel useful and needed. It is in later life, however, that challenges to feelings of meaning and purpose in life occur most regularly. There is a wonderful scripture that puts this problem in perspective:

> "For I know the plans I have for you," declares the Lord, "plans to prosper you and not to harm you, plans to give you hope and a future." (Jer 29:11, NIV)

What can a pastoral counselor do to help the older person feel useful and needed? There is plenty for elders to do in this day and age, regardless of their physical health or seeming incapacities. They may need, however, to choose new roles and tasks that are different from their old ones. These new roles may then provide the meaning and purpose that old ones did earlier in life. This is possible for persons of faith who believe that God has a purpose for this world and that the elderly play a vital part in that purpose. As the elderly population increases in the United States, many older persons' basic needs will increasingly be difficult to meet by society. This will produce a tremendous opportunity for elderly congregants to engage in a powerful ministry *to each other.*

For this reason it is essential that older adults discover their unique God-given gifts and talents for the time, age, and situations they are currently in. Every situation, no matter how dismal or seemingly hopeless, contains a potential for bringing about a greater good (Rom 8:28). God has equipped every elderly person in every circumstance of life with a talent or ability that the elder can use to serve God by serving others. Some gifts or talents are more obvious than others, which may require more effort to identify. Older adults who have a relationship with God and who have committed their lives to serving God with their gifts will find opportunities all around them to be useful and needed. The pastoral counselor's job is to inspire and motivate the older adult to identify his special and unique talent and utilize that talent in service to God.

Even the chronically ill or disabled elder who is completely dependent on others and perceives that she has no abilities or talents left has a unique gift and talent that must be discovered. If that talent is used as God intended, this will create inside of the person a feeling of being useful and needed. I encourage pastoral counselors to obtain the book *A Gospel for the Mature Years* (Koenig et al. 1997), in which we outline in great detail how older adults can identify their gifts, utilize those gifts, and avoid the pitfalls that discourages many from living what can be the greatest and most meaningful stage of life.

References

Azhar, M. Z., Varma, S. L., & Dharap, A. S. "Religious Psychotherapy in Anxiety Disorder Patients." *Acta Psychiatrica Scandinavica* 90 (1994):1–3.

Backus, W. & Chapin, M. *Telling Yourself the Truth.* Minneapolis: Bethany House Publishers, 1980.

Benson, H. *Beyond the Relaxation Response.* New York: Times Books, 1984.

Cantor M. "Strain among Caregivers: A Study of Experience in the United States." *Gerontologist* 23 (1983):597–604.

Davis, R. *My Journey into Alzheimer's Disease.* Wheaton, IL: Tyndale House Publishers, 1989.

Domino, G. "Clergy's Attitudes toward Suicide and Recognition of Suicide Lethality." *Death Studies* 9 (1985):187–99.

Koenig, H. G., George, L. K., Blazer, D. G, Pritchett, J., Meador, K. G. "The Relationship between Religion and Anxiety in a Sample of Community-Dwelling Older Adults." *Journal of Geriatric Psychiatry* 26:1 (1993):65–93.

———, George, L. K., Peterson, B. L. "Religiosity and Remission from Depression in Medically Ill Older Patients." *American Journal of Psychiatry* 155 (1998):536–42.

———, George, L. K., Peterson, B. L., Pieper, C. F. "Depression in Medically Ill Hospitalized Older Adults: Prevalence, Correlates, and Course of Symptoms Based on Six Diagnostic Schemes." *American Journal of Psychiatry* 154 (1997):1376–83.

———, George, L. K., Schneider, R. "Mental Health Care for Older Adults in the Year 2020: A Dangerous and Avoided Topic." *Gerontologist* 34 (1994):674–79.

———, Lamar, T., Lamar, B. *A Gospel for the Mature Years: Finding Fulfillment by Knowing and Using Your Gift.* New York: Haworth Press, 1997

——— & McConnell, M. *The Healing Power of Faith.* New York: Simon & Schuster, 1999.

——— & Weaver, A. J. *Counseling Older Adults and Their Families: A Handbook for Pastors and Religious Caregivers.* Nashville, TN: AbingQton Press, 1997.

——— & Weaver, A. J. *Pastoral Care of Older Adults.* Minneapolis: Fortress Press, 1998.

——— & Pritchett, J. "Religion and Psychotherapy." In Koenig, H. G., ed., *Handbook of Religion and Mental Health.* San Diego: Academic Press (1998), 323–36.

———— & George, L. K. "Depression and Physical Health Outcomes in Depressed Medically Ill Hospitalized Older Adults." *American Journal of Geriatric Psychiatry* 6, (1998):230–47.

Kunkel, S. R. & Applebaum, R. A. "Estimating the Prevalence of Long-Term Disability for an Aging Society." *Journal of Gerontology* (Social Sciences) 47 (1992):S253–S260.

Mace N. L., Rabins P. V. *The 36-Hour Day: A Family Guide to Caring for Persons with Alzheimer's Disease, Related Dementing Illnesses, and Memory Loss in Later Life.* Baltimore, MD: Johns Hopkins University Press, 1981.

National Institutes of Health. *Diagnosis and Treatment of Depression in Late Life* (Consensus Development Conference Statement 9, 3), November 4–6, 1991.

Propst, L. R., Ostrom, R., Watkins, P., Dean, T., Mashburn, D. "Comparative Efficacy of Religious and Nonreligious Cognitive-Behavior Therapy for the Treatment of Clinical Depression in Religious Individuals." *Journal of Consulting and Clinical Psychology* 60 (1992): 94–103.

Rabins, P. V., Fitting, M. D., Eastham, J., Zabora, J. "Emotional Adaptation Over Time in Care-Givers for Chronically Ill Elderly People." *Age and Aging* 19 (1990): 185–90.

Smith, S., Freeland, M., Heffler, S., McKusick, D., & the Health Expenditures Projection Team. "The Next Ten Years of Health Spending: What Does the Future Hold?" *Health Affairs* 17 (1998):128–40.

Weaver A. J., Koenig H. G., Preston J. "Elderly Suicide Prevention: What Pastors Need to Know." *Quarterly Review* (Summer 1996):151–67.

Worthington, E. L., Kurusu, T. A., McCullough, M. E., Sandage, S. J. "Empirical Research on Religion and Psychotherapeutic Processes and Outcomes: A 10-Year Review and Research Prospectus." *Psychological Bulletin* 119 (1996):448–87.

Edward P. Wimberly

4. Minorities

Counseling and therapy within the American context have been described as culturally bound. In fact, counseling and therapy have been labeled as white middle-class professions that have served directly and indirectly to acculturate or assimilate persons from varied cultural backgrounds into a specific picture of mental health and wholeness without considering the unique cultural heritage of minority persons (Sue, 1981). Cultural boundness refers to values, theories, and practices rooted in and reflective of dominant American culture. Groups of persons whose historical, racial, and cultural backgrounds are different from dominant culture may experience counseling and therapy as culturally oppressive. Because of this oppression experienced in many minority persons, it is important for counseling and therapy to become cross-culturally conscious of the divergent minority groups and subcultures that exist in America. In addition to this, counseling and therapy also will have to become aware of their own culture and class-bound values and the verbal and non-verbal issues involved in counseling minorities.

Many efforts have been made by the counseling and therapy professions to address the culture and class-bound nature of their professions. This is also true of pastoral counseling. A major effort toward becoming cross-culturally sensitive took place in San Francisco in the summer of 1983 at the international Congress of Pastoral Counseling. This meeting discussed cross-cultural and international issues in pastoral counseling. This chapter is designed to continue this effort started in pastoral counseling in San Francisco with regard to cross-cultural sensitivity. This effort will focus on the cultural, racial, and historical factors that often cause problems to pastoral counselors, who have been trained in counseling and therapy models of dominant culture, when they confront counselees from minority groups.

The particular approaches employed in this discussion are the cultural variant model of conceptualizing cultural uniqueness of minority groups and the growth-wholeness practical model of pastoral counseling. These theoretical and practical perspectives will be applied primarily to Afro-Americans though a briefer treatment of other minority groups will also be included. The basic assumption is that the cultural variant model and the growth-wholeness counseling perspectives are applicable in general to all minority groups discussed in this chapter.

Definition of Minority

The term *minority* within the American context has been used to describe unmeltables in Anglo-American culture (Ethnic Minorities in the United Methodist Church, 1976). Anglo-American usually refers to white Americans of non-Spanish descent and includes northern and southern Europeans. Anglos represent the majority culture making up wider society in America. Unmeltables are primarily non-white populations whose racial characteristics have enabled them to be easily distinguishable from dominant Anglo-culture. These non-white populations include Afro-Americans, Hispanic Americans, Native Americans (American Indians), and Asian Americans. Significant numbers of Near Eastern immigrants are in America, but the discussion here will concern the four primary ethnic minorities mentioned above.

Racial differences not only distinguish primary minorities in America. Language difficulties, cultural ancestry, historical-political considerations, and in some cases surnames also serve as distinguishing elements of minority groups in America. Some minority groups cling to their cultural identity, customs, and folkways while others have been forced to modify their traditional heritages because of policy and discrimination in wider society. Moreover, the Americanization process—a process in which minority groups adopt the values, lifestyles, and culture of dominant society—has not been completed among minority groups and will probably be slowed because of racial pride and emphasis on cultural pluralism. This means that the cultural heritages out of which minorities come will have to be addressed by wider society and by pastoral counseling.

Prior to giving detailed analysis of Afro-American cultural heritage it is important to examine the other three minority groups mentioned. Primary attention will be given to census data and to unique cultural heritage factors.

Hispanic Americans are distinguished primarily by the Spanish language, Spanish surnames and ancestry, and home origins in Mexico, Puerto Rico, Cuba, and Central and South America. In 2000 an estimated 21.6 million Mexican Americans were in the United States. This is by far the largest Hispanic group with the total number of Hispanics about 34.5 million including illegal residents. As a group, Hispanics are undereducated, are overrepresented in occupations that are low paying and menial, and have high rates of unemployment when compared to the general population (Ruiz, 1981).

Hispanics are predominantly urban dwellers. Mexican Americans live primarily in the southwest; Puerto Ricans reside mostly in New York State and Connecticut, and Cubans are mostly found in Florida.

From a cultural heritage point of view Hispanics have a culture ancestry of rigid sex-role distinctions and an extended family tradition where kinfolk interact with one another across generations. There are also a rich Spanish language, religious traditions, food customs, and home medical remedies. The cultural ancestry and contemporary adherence to these traditions are distinct enough from Anglo culture to call attention to the need for culturally specific and relevant models of counseling and therapy. However, since Hispanics differ in the degree of adherence to tradition and assimilation into Anglo culture, great care is needed in choosing the correct treatment approaches with individuals and families of Spanish descent.

Hispanics who are Spanish dominant in their culture would need a bicultural approach or a Spanish culture specific program of counseling, including the use of the Spanish language and family network strengths. Those Hispanic Americans who have assimilated into Anglo culture could respond favorably to treatment programs practiced in general by the majority of counselors and therapists in Anglo culture.

Native Americans or the American Indians are an important ethnic minority group of over 2 million, including Alaskan Natives. Native Americans are perhaps the most consistently exploited and oppressed minority in America from a cultural standpoint. Very little attitudinal behavioral respect has been shown for Native American culture by wider American society historically. Moreover, the exploitive oppressive outlook toward Native American culture continues today through the activity of white professionals including counselors (Richardson, 1981).

Culturally, many stereotypical notions of American Indians exist through the media which influence how professionals behave toward Native Americans. For example, Native Americans were not nomadic hunters or fishermen as popular notions would have it. Rather they were permanent settlers in villages and communities where they farmed and fished. Their community life was well organized around social, political, and agricultural models reflecting a rich and distinctive cultural ancestry of languages, religion, music and dance expression, tribal ritual, and ornamental dress. A rich variety of social customs existed among the different tribes in diverse geographical locations. While distinct cultural ancestry and native languages existed, forced assimilation through education has eventuated in a mix of dominant culture with Native American culture. Indeed, culturally specific and relevant models of counseling could be helpful.

Economically, educationally, and occupationally Native Americans are the most oppressed minority in America. This is an often ignored fact.

Asian Americans, like the Native Americans and Hispanics, have a rich cultural ancestry. This minority group has over 10 million people whose roots are in China, Japan, Korea, India, Vietnam, Taiwan, Indonesia, the Pacific islands, and many other countries. Chinese Americans came to America soon after Europeans settled in the New World and were servants of Spaniards who settled in Mexico. In the eighteenth and nineteenth centuries many Chinese Americans settled on the West Coast because of American trade with China. American trade with Japan brought Japanese persons to America as early as the nineteenth century. Koreans also came to America as early as the nineteenth century, but the majority of them came after the Korean War in the 1950s.

Asian Americans have a cultural ancestry including language, social and family organization and customs, and complex religious heritages. The family values of loyalty and responsibility in the Asian American background are often in conflict with the value of individualism held by Anglo-oriented counseling and therapy models. Indeed, awareness of the cultural ancestry of Asian Americans by pastoral counselors is essential.

Not all minorities have assimilated completely into dominant American culture. In fact, biculturalarity exists in many minority groups in America in that there has been a wedding of distinct ancestral values, customs, and traditions with those of dominant American culture. Pastoral counselors must be aware of this biculturalarity and employ appropriate counseling and therapy models that take into consideration this cultural variance. Thus, knowledge of cultural heritages that are wedded to and are divergent from dominant American culture is an important aspect and prerequisite to counseling with the culturally different.

Afro-Americans

The writer of this chapter is an Afro-American who has become aware of the bicultural approach to counseling minorities because of his involvement with counseling black Americans. In this section an in-depth examination of the cultural heritage of black or Afro-Americans will be presented. This examination will present a conceptual paradigm that will illustrate the depth of cultural analysis needed when attempting to gain a cognitive grasp of the cultural uniqueness of minority clients when doing pastoral counseling with them. Such knowledge can be learned from cross-cultural literature and from minority clients through showing interest in cultural material when it arises in counseling.

Sensitivity of Afro-Americans to their cultural uniqueness emerged because of negative theories toward them existing in behavioral science literature. A black identity and consciousness emerged in the 1960s and 1970s through which black people sought to affirm their self-worth as whole persons in the face of negative stereotypes, racial and oppressive policies, and denied economic opportunities. Part of the efforts of black professionals and academicians has been to help black persons to reinterpret their personal and corporate identity and history in ways that affirm black pigmentation and their cultural heritage.

Also included in this reinterpretation has been an effort to help black folk accept the historical importance of black families and extended families. In addition there have been efforts to help black people to reject uncritical assimilation into white middle-class values at the expense of black folkways. Black professionals and academicians also challenged the research done by white scholars that portrayed black people as pathological living in disrupted families and communities. In short, black consciousness was an attempt to affirm the positive aspects of black life and living that had been ignored by wider society. The result of this effort to affirm the positives by black academicians and behavioral scientists has been the development of a perspective called the cultural variant model.

The cultural variant model recognizes the differences that exist between black culture and wider culture and how the cultural divergence influences individual, family, and group behavior of minority persons. This model seeks to explain individual and corporate behavior and life from within the black community context (Allen, 1978). This model counteracts the cultural deviant and pathological models that exist and describe black culture as an inferior divergence from white middle-class culture.

Moreover, the cultural variant model enables researchers to explore the normal majority of black persons and their family and community strengths rather than the convenient problem populations such as mental patients, prisoners, and welfare clients. Thus, the focus of researchers from the cultural variant model has been on the black family and extended family, male and female relationships, and values that undergird the health and growth of black persons.

What follows is an examination of the strengths of black people from the perspective of the cultural variant model. However, some statistics and vital descriptive data are essential prior to the discussion of the strengths of the black community and the implications of these strengths for pastoral counseling.

Black persons have been 12 percent of the American population since 1890. In 2000 there were 32.7 million Afro-Americans. West Africa was the origin of Afro-Americans who came to America with the original explorers and the first settlers. Afro-Americans came as bond servants from places in Africa we now call Angola, Southern Nigeria, Ghana, Senegal, Gambia, Sierra Leone, Benia, and Mozambique (Holt, 1980).

Culturally, Afro-Americans inherited diverse social systems, African dialects, and religions. However, the cultural diversity was undergirded by a common world view based on kinship ties, economic organization, and the nature of the physical and spiritual world. The corporate identity of persons, the social-wholistic contextual nature of persons, cooperation with the rhythm of nature, interaction between the here-and-now world with the spiritual realm, a present-time orientation, and the importance of the extended family were important distinctive values inherited from Africa. These cultural inherited values are reflected today among the majority of black people and have been integrated in a bicultural manner with the dominant culture. Thus, there is a significant bicultural orientation among many Afro-Americans.

Although racism and oppression of black Americans had existed historically and exists contemporarily also, the remarkable strengths of black culture to enable black people to transcend oppression and to grow with dignity in spite of racism have often been overlooked. The capacity to transcend and to live with dignity has been attributed to the African heritage of kinship ties undergirded by a spiritual world view. The historical strength producing kinship ties can be envisaged in the black family, in the black extended family, and in black male and female roles.

Research on the black family between 1750 and 1925 (Gutman, 1976) reveals the presence of stable dual-headed households in slavery and after slavery. Moreover, this research also reveals that husbands and wives as parents were central figures in the rearing of their children. Such households made up about 80 percent of the total population in southern and northern black communities during this period.

This internal dynamics facilitating the stability in black families during this period included cumulative slave experience which fashioned rules of conduct for life within the black community. Such rules included commitment to long-lasting marriages and kinship naming practices that reflected strong kinship ties. Many examples of marriages lasting more than 50 years during slavery were found by Gutman (1976). He also pointed to the record concerning the efforts of separated black families to reunite after emancipation from slavery. Moreover, examples exist of freedmen returning to slave states risking capture in order to free members of their own families who were still in slavery. Family loyalty and family commitment were the norms rather than the exceptions for the black families during the 1750–1925 period.

Following 1925 the black family began to suffer breakups. These laid the foundation for pathological models of research on the black family that have emerged since 1925. Single-parent families headed by females increased in the period after 1925. Absentee fathers also began to increase during this time. However, the breakup of the black family was reflective of a more general technological and industrial impact affecting the American family in general. It did not reflect inherent pathology within the black family itself. The breakup of black families came when families in general were under a great siege. Kinship loyalties and strong extended families are not valued in technological society as a rule.

The strengths of the black family reported during 1750–1925 have been traced to African ancestral emphasis on kinship ties (Gutman, 1976). The extended family was central to black life during this period of history and is central today (Martin and Martin, 1978). The black extended family has been a multigenerational, interdependent kinship system having rules of obligation, organized around a household, but extending across geographical lines (Martin and Martin, 1978). In the black extended family there is a built-in mutual aid system for the maintenance of the whole extended network financially and emotionally. Moreover, single-parent families fit well within the extended family network which points to the fact that the single-parent, black female-headed household is not cut off and vulnerable. The fact that the black extended family rallies around extended family members during crisis periods is a central strength of the black family.

There is also a subextended family within the black extended family (Martin and Martin, 1981). A subextended family is similar to the nuclear family in that it is composed of the husband, wife, and children. However, the difference between it and the nuclear family is that the subextended family is not cut off from relatives in the extended family. The subextended family envisages itself as part of the extended family and maintains close emotional ties with the extended family. Along with the single parent family the subextended family receives the mutual support of the extended family.

Other patterns exist which reinforce mutuality within black families. One such pattern is the egalitarian allocation of roles in black families that enables them to be more adaptive toward economic limitations placed on black males in a racist society (Allen, 1978). Because black women have traditionally had a role in employment outside the home, researchers have mislabeled this fact as a matriarchal and dysfunctional pattern in black families. That is, black women have been compared to their white counterparts who traditionally were housewives. However, black women working outside the home is not a sign of dysfunctionality or of a matriarchal pattern. Rather, it points to a cultural pattern of egalitarianism where black men and women have traditionally pulled together in order to enable the family to survive. This mutuality in black male and female relationships is supported by research that reveals that black men are more supportive of their wives' working than are white men (Allen, 1978). Also there is mutuality in sharing household chores, child rearing, and decision making.

Correlative to the egalitarian pattern is a pattern of flexibility in the assignment of roles within the black family (Allen, 1978). The emphasis is on function within black families rather than on structure, and roles are assigned so that the family survives.

There is also research that indicates that role stereotyping in black families is less severe than in wider society. Black children are raised androgynously by black parents. That is, black males and females are socialized into a synthesis of same sex-role characteristics. Aggressiveness, independence, nurturance, and emotional expressiveness are social expectations for both black male and female children.

While not all black families are egalitarian with mutual and androgynous roles, it is important for pastoral counseling to be aware of the cultural divergence existing in black families. More precisely, pastoral counseling needs to be aware of the inherent strengths of black families so that these strengths can be drawn on in the process of counseling. Extended family values, egalitarian values, and androgynous values are strengths. However, these values may clash with the nuclear family, male hierarchical, and individual values of wider society. Yet, the pastoral counselor needs to be value free enough to employ black family strengths in helping to resolve counseling problems.

In addition to paying close attention to the strengths of black families, the pastoral counselor needs to become familiar with the cultural specific patterns that directly influence pastoral counseling with black people. These concerns include cultural specific traits such as non-verbal communication, people-oriented values, views of responsibility and locus of control, and attitudes toward the profession of counseling in itself.

With regard to non-verbal communication behavior, black culture tends to be a high-context culture (Smith, 1981). In contrast to low-context cultures which place a greater reliance on the verbal part of the message, high-context cultures emphasize non-verbal aspects of communication. Black grass-roots culture, in contrast to the black middle-class and white culture, is considerably more oriented toward non-verbal communication. The non-verbal communication has to do with culturally learned cues of sending and receiving messages and patterns of eye contact. It has been pointed out that black people are keen in their ability to read non-verbal cues of both white and black people (Smith, 1981). Also it is not necessary for black people to look you in the eye at all times when communicating. Also many black persons do not nod their heads or make little noises to show the other person that they are listening. (Often white counselors interpret some of these non-verbal styles of communicating as lack of interest and fear.)

High-context cultures tend also to emphasize group identification as opposed to low-context cultures that are more individually oriented (Smith, 1982). This is related to the kinship cultural orientation discussed earlier. Thus, black people tend to be more people-oriented than thing-oriented. Service vocations are emphasized over thing-oriented technological vocations, for example. Concern and service to family and community are central and are viewed as a natural part of life rather than as a burden.

Another important factor specific to the counseling context is that black people tend to be more relationally oriented than analytically oriented in cognitive style (Hale, 1982). In the analytical mode abstraction is emphasized and logic is organized in a linear way. That is, time is a continuum and authority and responsibility are hierarchical. Black people, in general, tend to be meaning-oriented, global and whole-picture focused, and not geared to the analysis of parts. They infer conclusions from relationships more than deriving knowledge from abstract thought. Emotional involvement and participation, immediate responses and action are more important ways of learning than abstract concepts. In short, black persons, as a general rule, tend to be gestalt learners.

The gestalt relational-cognitive style and non-verbal orientation of black people mean that pastoral counseling needs to be more participatory and action-oriented when working with black persons. High verbal, nonparticipatory, passive, and interpretive models of therapy may not be culturally specific enough for many black counselees. However, such a conclusion may reflect the needs of white counselees also, but who tolerate more cognitive approaches to counseling in order to get the help they need.

Other important issues for pastoral counseling with black persons are the concern for locus of control and locus of responsibility. Locus of control relates to cultural world views where a person envisages his or her life as controlled internally by one's own values and choices or externally controlled by outside influences (Sue, 1981). Locus of responsibility refers to where a person places the blame or responsibility for what has happened to him or her (Sue, 1981). Counseling and therapy as professions tend to emphasize the internal locus of control and personal responsibility for individual behavior. However, the reality of racism and oppression with regard to black people tends to coerce them into envisioning themselves as pawns of fate. Pastoral counselors need to be sensitive to this external orientation in order to help the black person to focus on the goal of establishing realistic internal control in one's life and to take realistic responsible steps toward resolving wider community-lined problems affecting his or her life without the counselor's denying the validity of external problems.

Attitudes exist in the black community that may not facilitate the use of many models of counseling and therapy (Smith, 1981). For example, discussing family matters with outsiders is often considered a violation of family ethics. Personal problems are often carried to kinship members and especially to the mother. Moreover, a general feeling exists that it is in church where one's deepest thoughts and emotional stresses should be addressed. Other attitudes hindering the use of counseling include not seeing the value of childhood experiences as the cause of poor mental health, viewing mental health/illness as environmentally determined, and the rejection of the intrapsychic model of counseling and therapy (Smith, 1981). Often the role of the counselor is viewed as alien, and many do not see how counseling can help the fight for survival. Counselees want specific advice on matters and tend to see white counselors as irrelevant to black contexts because of the menacing social and economic problems that black people face.

The final counseling concern for this section has to do with the issues of transference and countertransference. For some white counselors, black counselees stir up unconscious feelings that must be addressed in the counselor's personal supervision and therapy (Wimberly, 1976).

On the other hand, black clients may consciously or unconsciously subject white counselors to a series of racial tests to ascertain whether or not the pastoral counselor is racially prejudiced. It is important that racial issues be confronted early in the initial counseling in facilitative ways so that the way becomes clear for helping the client with his problem. Overreacting or underreacting (countertransference) by the pastoral counselor to the tests of the black client (transference) is not facilitative to the counseling process. Rather, the white pastoral counselor should address racial concerns in ways that the counselor's competence for handling the presenting problem is demonstrated. The counselor should take the racial suspiciousness of the client as a serious concern that needs to be treated with exploration. The attitude often communicates to the client openness on the part of the counselor, and counseling can begin after the rapport is established.

This section on Afro-Americans has presented some basic cultural issues unique to Afro-Americans that are essential to know and understand when counseling with black minority persons. Attention to cultural biases of the counselor and unique cultural facets of black culture can improve the ability of the pastoral counselor to be facilitative and effective in helping black persons and their families to grow.

The Growth Model of Pastoral Counseling

The previous section focused on the unique cultural orientation of Afro-Americans which seemed to come into conflict with commonly held assumptions undergirding many models of counseling and therapy practices in wider culture. For example, extended family values, the values of androgyny and egalitarianism, non-verbal communication styles, active and participatory involvement, relational cognitive styles, external locus of control and responsibility, the need for concrete advice, and the rejection of intrapsychic models of counseling and therapy all seem to suggest that counseling and therapy models that emphasize individualism, abstract verbal behavior, intrapsychic interpretation, and one-to-one counseling are at variance with some segments of Afro-American culture. What this variance means is that an alternative model of counseling and therapy is needed—one that can utilize the strengths of Afro-American culture. Such a model is the growth counseling model (Clinebell, 1979, 1981).

The growth counseling model is a human wholeness approach to the helping process developed in the theorizing and practice of pastoral counselor Howard Clinebell. Its basic goal is to facilitate the maximum development of a person's full possibilities at each stage of the life cycle in ways that enable the growth of others and contributes as well to the development of society. It is growth-oriented in that it draws on whatever methods and resources are necessary to liberate blocked growth. It draws on resources in traditional and contemporary psychotherapies and growth-oriented psychologies and relates them with the growth-wholeness resources of the Hebrew Christian tradition. Moreover, it draws eclectically from a variety of behavioral-science therapeutic models for its growth-wholeness orientation including the resources from the human-wholeness movement, relational systems and radical therapies, and spiritual growth models. It emphasizes growth-health-systems values in contrast to individualistic, hierarchical, pathological, and medical orientations. It seeks to focus on a person's strengths rather than on weaknesses. Finally, the social network is utilized whenever possible to facilitate growth.

The value of the growth counseling model for counseling black people and the culturally different needs some exploration at the risk of redundancy. Its emphasis on the inherent strengths of persons, the importance of the natural social network of systems for healing, the constructive aspects of behavior, and the facilitative role of the community, education, and action/participation methodologies and therapies enables the growth model of pastoral counseling to address the needs of many minority persons and their families. Its rejection of hierarchical and power models of the client/counselor relationship makes it possible for the counselor to learn from the culturally different client. Moreover, growth counseling also recognizes the impact of injustice and negative social forces on personality development and takes seriously a person's struggle with injustice. The model, when applied appropriately, has the potential for affirming the role of the unique cultural resources of African Americans for growth and wholeness.

In addition to the philosophical orientation of the growth model, which is foundational for pastoral counseling with minorities, there are key skills, processes, and issues which must accompany the application of the growth model. The specific skills of empathy, immediacy, self-disclosure, respect, and challenging seem to be central. Ability to address issues of victimization attitudes emerging in transference is crucial, and the ability of the pastoral counselor to spend time educating the counselee and his or her family concerning the counseling process is key. These skills, processes, and issues need further exploration.

Empathy is an effort to be present and to give attention to the specific meaning world view of the person seeking counseling. A world view generally consists of ideas, attitudes, and feelings that inform the counselee's behavior whether that behavior is functional or dysfunctional. Seeking to understand the world view surrounding the presenting problem of the counselee helps to create an environment of care and acceptance that is essential for a successful counseling process. Such skills as being interested in what the client is saying, attending and listening posture, exploratory responses to the counselee's utterances and brief facilitative statements summarizing the world view help to build an empathic environment.

Immediacy refers to the capacity of the pastoral counselor to address the dynamics taking place between the pastoral counselor and the client when it occurs in concrete counseling situations. Usually immediacy is discussed within the counseling relationship when it arises in connection with the presenting problem. For example, the client may respond to the pastoral counselor as if the pastoral counselor represented a significant other from the counselee's past. Treating the counselor as if he or she is a significant person in the client's past is called transference, and addressing the transference when it occurs is called immediacy.

Often the counselee from a minority group will bring into the counseling relationship concerns that relate to the counselee's interaction with the majority group which need to be addressed if counseling is to progress. Addressing such issues is particularly crucial in the first stages of counseling when the counselee is testing the openness of pastoral counselor to minority group concerns. The skills of immediacy, where the concern of the counselee/counselor relationship are addressed, is important in the testing period. It facilitates a working relationship. Also disclosing one's own struggle with majority-minority group concerns in ways that convey openness and desire for learning from the client about his or her world view can be helpful in facilitating the counseling relationship. Self-disclosure can help facilitate immediacy.

Respect is another core ingredient which is an attitudinal skill usually related to accepting the counselee as a person of worth who has the right to make the major decisions concerning his or her life. Respect for the minority client is usually developed through how the pastoral counselor is empathic and responds to the racial and cultural issues when they implicitly or explicitly arise. Also respect is established when a working contract or agreement is made between the client and pastoral counselor. A contract is a firm but flexible agreement between the pastoral counselor and client concerning the goals and responsibilities of each participant in the counseling relationship. It includes the steps and responsibilities the client will exercise in resolving the presenting problem and the steps the pastoral counselor will take in helping the client to resolve the presenting problem.

With a contract defined, the hope is that the pastoral counselor will avoid the kind of paternalism that ignores the client's own strengths and capacities for resolving his or her problem. To take away the client's right to resolve his or her problem is to show a lack of respect. To allow the client to give the decision-making possibilities to the pastoral counselor is also a demonstration of lack of respect to the client. The role of the pastoral counselor with minorities is to help the minority person exercise whatever degree of decision-making capacity the person has over his or her life.

After a working relationship has been established between the counselee and the pastoral counselor, dysfunctional patterns of behavior that do not contribute to the resolving of the presenting problem can be challenged. Challenging is a counseling skill that gently brings to the client's attention ideas, attitudes, and behavioral patterns that prevent the client(s) from achieving stated goals or resolving the presenting problem. Dysfunctional ideas and behavior on the part of the counselee presuppose that a contract concerning the presenting problem has been reached. To challenge an idea or behavior without having a firm contract is to show disrespect for the client, and it allows for the introduction of culturally biased values by the pastoral counselor. However, if a firm contract is established, then the pastoral counselor can facilitatively introduce responses that challenge non-productive attitudes and behaviors related to the resolution of the presenting problem.

One general pattern I have noticed when working with minority clients is a victimization attitude. Victimization is adopting the attitude of a helpless, dependent victim in the face of real or imagined suffering at the hands of others. Acknowledging the reality of minority group victimization at the hands of wider society's attitudes and practices is important and should not be denied when the minority person raises such issues. However, the victimization attitude used to escape exercising what limited control that one has over his or her life in the oppression should be called to the attention of the minority counselee. Indeed, empathy is needed, but this empathy needs to help the person exercise the decisions needed so that the person does not see himself or herself as a helpless victim. Often the victim may try to get the pastoral counselor to treat him or her as a helpless victim, but to respond to the client as a helpless victim, by not enabling the person to do what he or she can, is to respond out of the needs of the pastoral counselor (countertransference) rather than to respond to the needs of the client. The key to helping the minority client face the victimization issue is the helping of the client to develop or formulate an action plan for resolving the presenting problem. It is important for the pastoral counselor to help the client explore what is possible in terms of action even in the most difficult circumstances.

The final consideration for pastoral counseling with the minority client is the need to educate the client concerning the process of pastoral counseling. It can be assumed that the culture from which the minority client comes will not have prepared the client for understanding the counseling process as white middle-class culture has prepared its cultural adherents. Therefore, the pastoral counselor needs to take time to explain how the process of pastoral counseling works when the opportunity arises. This should be done very early in the counseling process. For example, I point out early that the initial phase of counseling involves the exploration of the problem and that I need all the relevant information that can be given. Second, I point out that the problem needs to be understood in as broad a context as possible. That is, I introduce a variety of ways of understanding the problem so that the client(s) can grasp a picture of the problem as a whole. Third, I point to the need to set goals outlining the steps needed for the client to resolve the presenting problem once it has been understood. Such a three-step explanation alerts the client(s) to what to expect in the actual counseling as well as to know what their role will be in the counseling process itself.

Case Study

This chapter will conclude with a brief case study illustrating selected aspects of the preceding discussion of pastoral counseling with minorities. The specific case to be presented is of an upper-middle-class black family functioning as an extended family. Specific concerns to be raised include a family systems therapy approach to pastoral counseling, the integration of a black male into a central role within the family, and the counseling skills needed to carry out a counseling process with a family. The case study is designed to illustrate the practical nature of the discussion of the cultural variance and growth counseling approach to pastoral counseling with minorities.

The Johnson family is composed of the husband-father, David, who is thirty-three; a wife-mother Martha, age thirty-two; a son, James, age three; and a brother-brother-in-law, John, age fifteen. John is Martha's brother. Parents of Martha and John are named Maurice and Janice Smith. Maurice is fifty-nine and is a successful dentist, and Janice is a housewife and is fifty-five years old. Maurice and Janice have another son in addition to John who attends college in a fashionable eastern school. David works for a computer company and his wife Martha is a housewife.

The presenting problem emerged when David and Martha came for counseling complaining that John, the fifteen-year-old brother of Martha, was disruptive, unruly, and prevented them from giving attention to their own three-year-old son. As the problem was explored through the counseling skills of empathy, it was revealed that the brother John was sent to David and Martha's home because Martha's parents were having marital problems. Janice, John's mother, felt that John would be better off living with his sister in a southern city. Janice decided that John would be sent south without the consent of her husband Maurice or of her daughter Martha. Martha and her father accepted the decision passively.

After the first session with David and Martha, John was asked to accompany David and Martha to counseling. All three persons came to the second session and the problem exploration and clarification phase of counseling continued. John revealed his resentment at being forced out of his family of origin in the north. He described his dislocation as being dumped. He indicated that his disruptive behavior was an attempt to get his sister and brother-in-law to send him back home to live with his parents. He also indicated that he desired to have a closer relationship with his father.

Following the third session with David, Martha, and John a relationship of rapport had been established with each person individually so that new perspectives or enlarged ways of looking at the problem could be introduced. David and Martha had perceived the problem to be theirs rather than belonging to Janice and Maurice. The idea that they had let someone else's problem become their own exclusively was introduced by the pastoral counselor for exploration of the counselees. During the session they explored how they let this happen and began to consider the new perspective as their own. After they embraced the new perspective, the pastoral counselor suggested that they invite Janice and Maurice to come south to meet as an intergenerational extended family network to decide what would be done about the problem. Both Janice and Maurice came to the fourth and fifth sessions.

At the fourth and fifth sessions Maurice's concern for his son surfaced, and he expressed real hurt that he had been left out of the decision-making with regard to both of his sons. He also regretted that he had allowed his dental practice to take him away from his family. He resolved to become more involved with his sons and to become more active in the decision-making in the home. He said right there in the fifth session that his son John would be going home with his parents even though the marital problem had not been resolved. Janice resisted Maurice's new-found involvement in the matter with John, but she relented when she saw that John was happy. Janice and Maurice resolved to go to marital counseling when they returned north.

Although this was a black middle-class family, certain cultural dynamics were apparent. There was the extended family network where certain family obligations were expected. The daughter was expected to help out the parents in crisis situations. Second, the father experienced his exclusion from the home as abnormal, and this reflects the egalitarian orientation of black folk toward rearing children. Given the family network and the egalitarian orientations, the pastoral counselor utilized a family system therapy-growth-problem-solving orientation to help resolve the family's problem. The phases of problem exploration, clarification of the problem, introducing new perspectives on the problem, and formulating and taking action to resolve the problem were the phases of counseling. During these phases many core counseling skills were used in carrying out the counseling. Specifically, the skill of challenging was the most obvious in the case although many others were used. Challenging took place when new perspectives were introduced through which a new understanding of the problem emerged. Based on this new understanding an action plan was developed designed to use the whole family resources in resolving the problem.

By way of conclusion, it is important not to assume that all minority clients have to be forced into a cultural specific model of pastoral counseling. Indeed, each case should be treated uniquely, because there is great variety within minority groups. However, when certain culture specific characteristics appear, the culture specific model should be employed where appropriate.

Bibliography

Allen, W. R. "The Search for Applicable Theories of Black Family Life." *Journal of Marriage and the Family,* February 1978, 117–129.

Banks, W. M. "The Social Context and Empirical Foundation of Research on Black Clients." In R. L. Jones (ed.), *Black Psychology.* New York: Harper & Row, 1980.

Clinebell, H. *Contemporary Growth Therapies: Resources For Actualizing Human Wholeness.* Nashville: Abingdon Press, 1981.
———. *Growth Counseling.* Nashville: Abingdon Press, 1979.
Cortes, C. E. "Mexicans." In S. Thermstrom (ed.), *Harvard Encyclopedia of American Ethnic Groups.* Cambridge: Belknap Press, 1980.
Ethnic Minorities in the United Methodist Church. Nashville: Discipleship Press, 1976.
Fitzpatrick, J. P. "Puerto Ricans." In S. Thermstrom (ed.), *Harvard Encyclopedia of American Ethnic Groups.* Cambridge: Belknap Press, 1980.
Gutman, H. G. *The Black Family in Slavery and Freedom 1750–1925.* New York: Vintage. 1976.
Hale, J. *Black Children: Their Roots, Culture, and Learning Styles.* Provo: Brigham Young University Press, 1982.
Henderson, G. *Understanding and Counseling Ethnic Minorities.* Springfield: Charles C. Thomas, 1979.
Holt, T. C. "Afro-American." In S. Thermstrom (ed.), *Harvard Encyclopedia of American Ethnic Groups.* Cambridge: Belknap Press, 1980.
Kim, H. "Koreans." In S. Thermstrom (ed.), *Harvard Encyclopedia of American Ethnic Groups.* Cambridge: Belknap Press, 1980.
Kitano H. H. L. "Japanese." In S. Thermstrom. (ed.), *Harvard Encyclopedia of American Ethnic Groups.* Cambridge: Belknap Press, 1980.
Lai, H. M. "Chinese." In S. Thermstrom (ed.), *Harvard Encyclopedia of American Ethnic Groups.* Cambridge: Belknap Press, 1980.
Martin, E. P. and Martin, J. M. *The Black Extended Family.* New York: University of Chicago Press, 1978.
Richardson, E. H. "Cultural and Historical Perspectives in Counseling American Indians." In D. W. Sue (ed.), *Counseling the Culturally Different: Theory and Practice.* New York: John Wiley & Sons, 1981.
Ruiz, R. A. "Cultural and Historical Perspectives in Counseling Hispanics." In D. W. Sue (ed.), *Counseling the Culturally Different: Theory and Practice.* New York: John Wiley & Sons, 1981.
Smith, E. J. "Cultural and Historical Perspectives in Counseling Blacks." In D. W. Sue (ed.), *Counseling the Culturally Different: Theory and Practice.* New York: John Wiley & Sons, 1981.
Spicer, E. H. "American Indians." In S. Thermstrom (ed.), *Harvard Encyclopedia of Ethnic Groups.* Cambridge: Belknap Press, 1980.
Sue, D. W. (ed.). *Counseling the Culturally Different: Theory and Practice.* New York: John Wiley & Sons, 1981.
Wimberly, E. "Pastoral Counseling and the Black Perspective." *The Journal of Pastoral Care.* December 1976, 264–272.

Steve Sangkwon Shim

5. Pastoral Counseling with Asian Americans

Introduction

As an Asian American person myself, undertaking this study on the subject of "Pastoral Counseling with Asian Americans" is felt as an enormously risky task and effort for me, personally, for a number of reasons.

A key reason is my own keen awareness of who Asian Americans are: they are an enormously diversified group in the United States. Another is that I, as a Korean American therapist, feel unqualified and extremely reluctant to counsel with other Asian American persons, for instance, with Chinese Americans, Japanese Americans, Filipino Americans, or others, simply due to the drastic differences in our languages, race, and cultures, historical backgrounds, and worldviews. Another important reason is my personal disbelief in so-called Asian American psychology, even though the literature in the field of psychology and human behavioral sciences overwhelmingly advocates such ideas and theories, ever since Asian American Studies emerged in American academics in the early 1970s. It is also my personal contention that stereotyping Asian Americans, or for that matter, stereotyping any racial or ethnic group, is one form of American racism and dehumanization. Especially in the field of pastoral counseling, stereotyping a client of any group by his or her counselor or therapist is taken as a "sin" against the client because of its dehumanizing effect on the client.

In my personal perspective, it seems virtually impossible to address the subject of *counseling Asian Americans* without committing the sin of grossly stereotyping Asian American clients.

Thus, it seems reasonable to first limit as much as possible the scope of the Asian American populations for the purpose of this study to reduce the possibility of grossly stereotyping them.

It is long overdue that the field of pastoral counseling pay attention to the care and counseling of Asian American clients. This study attempts to address the issues and concerns of counseling with Asian Americans, especially from a pastoral counseling or therapy perspective.

The chapter is arranged into three parts, along with an introduction and conclusion. The first part describes three Asian American groups: Chinese, Japanese, and Korean Americans; the second part deals with the clinical issues in counseling or therapy with these three groups; and the third part deals with clinical approaches in procedures, therapeutic strategies, interventions, methods, and referrals.

Asian Americans or Pacific Islanders/Asian Americans: A Myth of Asian American Psychology

It is my contention that *Asian American* is a politically oriented term invented in the racially diversified society of the United States. My personal belief is that "Asian American" is not a psychological reality. Thus, in my view *Asian American psychology* is a myth invented under the influence of American racism, and we as counselors and therapists need to be extremely careful about its application in our work.

It is also my hope that further discussion on the Asian American will exemplify the danger implicit in the term *Asian American psychology*.

First of all, *who are Asian Americans?* In the literature, we find mostly two designations for Asians and their descendants in the United States, namely, *Pacific Islanders/Asian Americans* or *Asian Americans*. Depending on the author, Asian Americans would include descendents from the geographical continent of Asia in the widest scope, including more than twenty nationalities from the middle east, southeast, southwest, and northeast areas of Asia.

Historically, Asian Americans in American society had been limited to Chinese Americans, Japanese Americans, Filipino Americans, and Korean Americans until the 1960s. Even among these four groups, Chinese Americans and Japanese Americans had once been the most visible and predominant in numbers; the other two groups had been relatively invisible and hidden in American society.

Beginning in 1965, due to the liberalization of immigration laws by the U.S Congress, Asian American communities, except for the Japanese American community, have drastically increased in number and size and scope by the influx of new immigrants. The Asian American communities in the United States have expanded from the four early major groups to more than twenty national groups from Asia since 1965. For example, they now include immigrants and refugees of the Taiwanese, the Hong Kong Chinese, the Vietnamese, the Laotians, the Cambodians, the Hmongs, the Thais, the

Indonesians, the Malaysians, the Pakistanis, the Indians, and the Bangladeshis, just to mention the major ones.

As already alluded, some authors would include the Pacific Islanders from Guam, Fiji, Samoa, and the Hawaiian Islands in the Asian American communities under the rubric of Pacific Islanders/Asian Americans. Numerous authors have been trying to make a case for Asian American communities in light of the demographic growth among the Asian American populations, based on the U.S. census.

In my judgment, it is fruitless to quote the U.S. census in this chapter to validate the demographic growth of Asian American communities in the United States as a way of rationalizing the importance of the needs of Asian Americans. Nowadays, a general consensus is that Asian American communities in the United States are visible and sizable enough to deserve the attention of the American society, specifically those of the human care service providers.

Although I once trained in Asian American Studies and Psychologies, like other Asian American authors and researchers who often worked from their own ethnic perspectives in their writings and research, my perspective and approach to this study is intentionally toward Korean American experiences. My rational for this is due to the fact that the literature in Asian American Studies and Psychologies has predominantly been written by Chinese American and Japanese American authors. For example, most of the research and descriptions about the Korean American experience have largely been done by Chinese American or Japanese American authors, or non–Korean Americans, for Korean American authors had been, for many different reasons, very scarce in the field of the Asian American Studies and Psychologies

In fact, this study on *counseling Asian Americans* is one of the first attempted by a Korean American author, or for that matter, any Asian American author in the literature of pastoral care and counseling in the United States. In a final analysis, even through I have explicitly stated my intentionally biased perspective on this study, it is also my hope that the Korean American perspective may be applicable to understanding and counseling the Chinese Americans, Japanese Americans, or others in a limited way.

I. The Asian Americans: Three Groups

For the focus of our discussion here, I am arbitrarily limiting the Asian American communities to the major groups of the Chinese Americans, the Japanese Americans, and the Korean Americans because of the similarities of their worldviews, beliefs, and attitudes, as influenced by Buddhism and Confucianism and their geographical affinity in the northeast zone of the Asian continent.

In dealing with Asian Americans, non–Asian Americans need to know and understand the vast diversity in language, race, culture, and historical backgrounds among the different Asian American communities in the United States. Although Chinese Americans, Japanese Americans, and Korean Americans have historically held similar worldviews and beliefs from Buddhism and Confucianism, these three groups are vastly different in their language, race, culture, historical experience, and background.

In view of their acculturation levels into American society, Asian American communities may be divided into three subgroups, namely, (1) *American-born* Asians and their descendants, (2) *Asian-born* immigrants and their children, and (3) *newly arrived Asian refugees*. The subgroups may be characterized as *American Asians, Asian Americans,* and *Asian immigrants*. This differentiation will help us understand the levels of their acculturation and adaptation into American society.

The Asian-born immigrants mostly include the Chinese (Hong Kong included), Taiwanese, Koreans, and Filipinos, Indonesians, Malaysians, Thais, Asian Indians, and others. Refugees from Asia are primarily Vietnamese, Laotian, Cambodian, Hmong, and similar. The *immigrants* have entered into the United States by voluntary choice, looking for their destiny in the new homeland of America, whereas the *refugees,* mostly from Southeast Asia, are in the United States by involuntary choice, political victims with war-torn scars and the loss of their homelands and family ties.

Chinese Americans

Historically, the Chinese Americans were the first Asian American settlers in the United States. They first arrived on the west coast in the 1850s as railroad laborers. Since these first settlers in the mid-nineteenth century, Chinese Americans have undergone severe racial discrimination, resulting in establishment of separate Chinatowns for over a century in the United States.

Those first Chinese settlers have continued their descendants for three to five generations. Their descendents are *American-born Chinese,* or *Chinese American.* These Chinese Americans are all well versed in the English language and have a true sense of biculturalism. They are well acculturated into the dominant culture of America and are very active in the mainstream of American life.

However, since the late 1960s, as already noted, the Chinese American community has been rapidly expanded by the influx of immigrants from Hong Kong and China. In addition, the influx of immigrants from Taiwan has added to the size of the Chinese American community in American society, although the Taiwanese immigrants themselves have tried to claim and maintain their own racial and ethnic identity in the United States.

In the Chinese American community, its subgroups are the *American-born Chinese* and their descendants, who have bilingual and bicultural backgrounds, and the *China-born immigrants* and their children, who are monolingual and have a monocultural orientation of Chinese language and culture, with varying degrees of acculturation and a minimal level of bilingualism, largely determined by the length of their stay in the United States.

Sue and Sue (1999, p. 268) have postulated to delineate the Chinese American community into four types: *Type A* (high in assimilation, low in ethnic identity), *Type B* (high in assimilation, high in ethnic identity), *Type C* (low in assimilation, high in ethnic identity), and *Type D* (low in ethnic identity, low in assimilation). This typology may help identify acculturation levels of other Asian American communities in the United States, although it is very questionable whether Type D exists in the Asian American communities.

In the wake of the influx of recent immigrants, the Chinese American community, once dominated by the American-born Chinese population, is now dominated by the immigrants or newcomers from China and Hong Kong.

In terms of community dynamics, the influences of mainland China, Taiwan, and Hong Kong have exerted an extraordinary impact on Chinese Americans' psyches and their community dynamics. Until the ideological modification of Communism in mainland China in the early 1990s, the intra-community dynamics were severely divisive and conflictual within the Chinese American community in the United States, fueled by the ideological division between supporters of pro-Communist China and pro-Nationalist Taiwan. Although the tension and division between these two groups within the community have been relatively relaxed and easy since the political change in China, residual effects are still felt among the Chinese Americans in the sectors of the older generation. Although the Chinese American community is gradually overcoming the old wounds caused by the ideological division in their motherland China, the impact of the motherland China is imposed upon the Chinese American community and upon their ethnic identity by American racism. In short, the international image of mainland China has directly affected the image of the Chinese American community in American society.

By and large the Chinese Americans, especially the new immigrants, are heavily influenced in their worldviews and lifestyles by Confucianism and Buddhism, along with their superstitious practices. The Chinese Americans are relatively religious in general. Also, Protestant faiths of Christianity have influenced Chinese Americans, through active Christian churches in their communities. In general, their religious practices are based on the conservatism of their faiths.

All in all, the Chinese American community is the oldest Asian American group in America, and it has become an acculturation and adaptation model for the rest of the Asian American groups in American society.

Japanese Americans

Japanese Americans are the second-oldest group in the United States. The Japanese American community is distinctively different from the Chinese American community in composition and characteristics. Their language, race, culture, and historical background are further different from the Chinese Americans.

In its composition, the Japanese American community was begun by the *Issei* (the first generation), who as farm laborers arrived on the west coast from Japan in the 1870s. Later, the community was succeeded by the *Nissei* (the second generation), the *Sansei* (the third generation), the *Yonsei* (the fourth generation), and so forth. The Issei was known as high in ethnic identity and low in assimilation; the Nissei was high in assimilation and low in ethnic identity; the Sansei was known as high in assimilation and high in ethnic identity, and the Yonsei are the similar. The Japanese American community in general is far greater assimilated into American society than the Chinese American community has been. Historically, the Japanese American (the Issei and Nissei) were once incarcerated and suffered in the war camp during World War II as a result of the racial policy of the American government. Much of this incarceration experience had pushed the Nissei to accelerate their assimilation into the mainstream of the American life.

Unlike the Chinese American or other Asian immigrant communities, Japanese American communities did not grow in number because of new immigrants from Japan to the United States in the 1960s or thereafter. The size of the Japanese American community has remained relatively the same for decades. Instead, the community has been faced with an increasing number of transits to the United States of businessmen and their family members who are relatively distant in affinity from the Japanese American community. The average length of their stay in the United States is three to five years. These transits are generally low in assimilation and very high in ethnic identity.

Another characteristics of the Japanese American community is the fact that the Japanese Americans in the Hawaiian Islands, unlike those in the mainland, feel a sense of being part of a majority ethnic group rather than a sense of being a minority. The Japanese Americans tend to perceive them-selves as a part of the mainstream of the Hawaiian Islands.

In addition, the Japanese American community in the United States had historically maintained a relatively homogeneous community until WW II. It was WW II that severely divided the Japanese American community. Hostile international relations between the United States and Japan caused the incarceration of and discrimination against Japanese Americans by the American government. In the post–WW II era, as Japan has emerged as one of the world superpowers because of its economic empire, the public image and interracial relations of the Japanese American community have been improved and upgraded in American society. The Japanese American image has been altered from that of an enemy to a friend and an economic super-power in the interracial view of the American public.

On the other hand, the Japanese American community in general is influenced by Christian churches and Zen-Buddhist temples. Japanese Americans tend to manifest less religious activity than Chinese Americans do, in terms of numbers of organized religious institutions or churches found in the Japanese American community in America. These religious institutions or churches are often found to have religious practices of two separate congregations—namely, the English-speaking congregation and the Japanese-speaking congregation, respectively—under the same roof of one church or temple.

Korean Americans

Of the three groups from the northeast area of the Asian continent, the Korean Americans were the last arrivals to the soil of the United States. The Korean American community, begun as early as 1903, was numerically too small to noticed by the dominant racial groups in the United States until the 1970s. Before then, Korean Americans were often mistaken or stereo-typed as Chinese Americans or Japanese Americans by the members of the majority group in America.

It was in the 1970s and 1980s, due to the increase in new immigrants from Korea, that the Korean American community first emerged visible in its size and its interracial relations as a racial ethnic group distinct from the Chinese American or the Japanese American communities. Actually, it was in 1992, when the interracial conflict between the African American com-munity and the Korean American community in the Los Angeles Riot was nationally exposed to the American society by the major news media, that the Korean American community was acknowledged as a racial ethnic iden-tity by the mainstream American society.

Although the Korean Americans are historically heavily concentrated in metropolitan areas such as Los Angeles, they are scattered in cities throughout the United States and have established Korea-towns in their areas, following the footsteps of Chinese American models of Chinatown.

Characteristically, Korean Americans are economically active in "mom and pop" stores operating predominantly in the African American and the Hispanic communities, or in their own Korea-towns, while their residence is mostly found in middle-class white American communities. Even though their residence pattern has taken an assimilated mode, and their children are highly assimilated into the white community by the American education system, the parents are very low in assimilation and very high in ethnic identity. As a whole, the Korean American community is the least bilingual, bicultural, and interracial of the three Asian American groups for a few reasons.

First, as already observed, the Korean American community is predominantly first-generation immigrant and fairly new in comparison with the Chinese American and Japanese American communities in the United States. Thus they have assimilated themselves much less into the multicultural and multiracial society of America.

Second, culturally, the Korean Americans (especially, the first generation), rooted and grounded historically in the racially homogeneous society of their motherland, tend to be socially reluctant and less skillful in mingling and interacting with other racial or ethnic groups or persons.

Within the Korean American community, a group of second-, third-, or fourth-generation descendents of the first generation who had arrived in the United States in the early 1900s are called *American Koreans* to distinguish them from the new arrived immigrants. The number of these American Koreans is low, and they are very high in assimilation and low in ethnic identity, with only a monolingual ability of English language. These American Koreans are mostly assimilated into the white American community. In all, the American Koreans are generally perceived as outsiders by the predominantly immigrant-centered Korean American community in America. In fact, they suffer from double rejections from white Americans and from Korean Americans at the same time.

Beginning in the late 1980s, an increasing number of the one-point-five (1.5) generation and a small number of the new second generation are reaching adulthood, providing a special impetus and impact by their community leadership and interethnic advocacies. The 1.5 generation is differentiated from the second generation in that the 1.5 generation was born in Korea and migrated in their early childhood to the United States with their parents. The new second generation is generally very high in assimilation and low in ethnic identity, with a monolingual ability of English, whereas the 1.5 generation is high in assimilation and high in ethnic identity, with thorough bicultural and bilingual abilities. The predominant group of the first generation is least low in assimilation and very high in ethnic identity, with an exclusively monolingual ability of their mother tongue.

Historically, the Korean American community had first suffered as being "nameless" and "faceless," without a racial ethnic identity until the 1970s. It was during the 1970s that the Korean American community began to be socially visible and to appear with its own "Korean American" identity. Further, the Korean American image was hurt by the "poverty and backward" images of Korea, a stereotype that was for a long period accepted by the racially biased American public. Similarly, the image of North Korea is still held in such a manner by the American public.

In another aspect, the Korean American community had been suffering for many decades, pained by the occupation and colonization of the Korean peninsula in the pre–WW II period; further, in the post–WW II period, the Korean American community has further been suffering because of the national and ideological division of the Korean peninsula between South and North for the last half-century. Its intracommunity dynamics have been until today extremely divisive and conflictual due to the national division of their motherland.

Nowadays, the images of the Korean American community have been positively enhanced by the impact of the unprecedented economic progress of South Korea in recent decades. Further, the economic network and support of the megacorporations from South Korea have become another important factor influencing the development and enhancement of the Korean American community in the United States.

Among the Asian American communities at large, the Korean American community is known for its religious practices within Christian churches in America. In fact, the outgrowth of Christian churches in their community has surpassed that of all other major racial ethnic and minority groups in the United States. Thus, it is critical to understand and assist Korean American individuals and their families through their religious practices in Christian churches in their communities. And, their religious practices are generally conservative ones, tending to reinforce their ethnic identity.

Thus far, I have tried to depict a framework of the Asian American communities using the purposefully selected groups of the Chinese American, the Japanese American, and the Korean American communities. Their groups may be summarized in Tables 1 and 2.

Table 1
Intragroup Diversities of Chinese Americans, Japanese Americans, and Korean Americans

The Chinese Americans	The Japanese Americans	The Korean Americans
1. **The First Generation** Low in Assimilation High in Ethnic Identity 2. **The Second Generation** High in Assimilation Low in Ethnic Identity 3. **The Third, Fourth, and Fifth Generations** High in Assimilation High in Ethnic Identity 4. **The New Immigrants** Low in Assimilation High in Ethnic Identiy 5. **The New Second Generation** High in Assimilation/ Low in Ethnic Identity High in Assimilation/ High in Ethnic Identity	1. **The Issei (First Generation)** Low in Assimilation High in Ethnic Identity 2. **The Nissei (Second Generation)** High in Assimilation Low in Ethnic Identity 3. **The Sensei and Yonsei (Third and Fourth Generations)** High in Assimilation High in Ethnic Identity 4. **The Transits of Businessmen and Families** Low in Assimilation High in Ethnic Identiy	1. **The Early First Generation** Low in Assimilation High in Ethnic Identity 2. **The Old Second and Third Generations** High in Assimilation Low in Ethnic Identity 3. **The New First Generation** Low in Assimilation High in Ethnic Identity 4. **The New Second Generation** High in Assimilation Low in Ethnic Identity High in Ethnic Identity 5. **The 1.5 Generation** High in Assimilation High in Ethnic Identity

Table 2 Other Nationalities of Asian Americans/Pacific Islanders	
Southeast Nationalities	**Southwest Nationalities**
1. The Vietnamese 2. The Laotians 3. The Cambodians 4. The Hmongs 5. The Thai 6. The Indonesians 7. The Malaysians	1. The Indians 2. The Pakistanis 3. The Bangladeshis
Northwest Nationalities	**Pacific Islanders**
1. The Hong Kong Chinese 2. The Taiwanese 3. The Filipinos 4. The Singaporeans	1. The Samoans 2. The Fijians 3. The Guam 4. The Hawaiian Islanders

II. Clinical Issues and Concerns in Counseling Asian Americans

In this section, we shall deal with some important clinical issues and concerns in counseling Asian Americans. These include (1) Asian American common cultural values, (2) ethnic-oriented issues and concerns, and (3) the working/therapeutic alliance.

Asian American Common Cultural Values

Asian Americans with the racial or ethnic backgrounds of the Chinese Americans, the Japanese Americans, and the Korean Americans who have been influenced by Confucianism and Buddhism share their common cultural values and beliefs in a certain way. In this regard, Sue and Sue (1999, p. 263) provide a useful comparison of Western and Asian American values in Table 3.

Table 3 Comparison of Cultural Values of Asian Americans and Westerners	
Asian American Values	**Western Values**

Collectivism
Family and group focus
Interdependence
Hierarchical relationships
Restraint of emotions = Maturity
Counselor should provide
   solutions
Mental illness as shame and
   family failure
	Individual focus
	Independence
	Equality of relationships
	Emotional expression = Healthy
	Clients to develop solutions
	   through introspection
	Mental illness as "personal
	   problem"

Table 3 illustrates that the three groups of the Chinese Americans, the Japanese Americans, and the Korean Americans share some common values with Westerners. My brief explanation of each value listed may clarify their meanings for our further understanding.

Collectivism versus Individual Focus. Asian Americans are generally reared and taught their personal identity and maturation in light of the family or group identity and relations. Thus, Asian American individuals are generally oriented to subjugating one's personal need to the family's or group's need and expectation. For this reason, Asian American individuals are apt to comply with or be submissive to their families and groups instead of seeking self-assertion. In a sense, the Asian/American personality is matured in terms of the relational self in the family or group life rather than in seeking ego gratification or self-realization. The Asians/Asian Americans value a collective self-identity rather than individual or ego-identity.

Familism versus Individualism. Asian American clients value familism over Western individualism. Asian American clients view their individual needs as subject to the needs of their families. Individual needs must be resolved in light of one's own family needs and expectations. The family need supercedes the individual's need in Asian American family life. To the Asian Americans, the family comes first.

Interdependence versus Independence. Asian Americans tend to be interdependent rather than independent in their interpersonal relationships. In Asian American families, independence is perceived as selfishness or egoism. Asian Americans want to be mutually dependent each other in all human relationships. The Asian American sense and behavior of interdependence are often perceived and misinterpreted as dependent behavior by Westerners.

Hierarchical Relationships versus Egalitarianism. The Asian American person will perceive all human relationships in a hierarchical way, namely one up and one down. The factors of age, social class and status, order of birth, and gender will determine one's relationship with another person or group in a hierarchical relationship. Especially, in this regard, the Japanese Americans and the Korean Americans would reflect their senses of hierarchical relationship with their mother tongues *in an honorific form.* Also, this hierarchical relationship is usually manifested in either a submissive or an authoritarian manner. The egalitarian gesture by an older person to a younger person is often perceived as undignified and improper behavior by Asian American persons.

Emotional Restraint versus Emotional Expression. Asian American persons were reared in their childhood by their parents to restrain or suppress their emotions in public and in the presence of older persons. To Asian Americans, expressing one's emotions to strangers is considered to be immature and improper. It is important to note that Asians value a suppressive, closed culture, whereas Westerners value an expressive, open culture. The Asian Americans tend to be less expressive in themselves, especially in their feelings and emotions. They tend to express themselves cognitively rather than emotively.

In addition to the values listed in Table 3, I would add the following important values.

Filial Piety versus Self-Realization. Asian Americans also share the importance of veneration and obedience to their parents. It is an utmost duty and virtue of an Asian American person to be subservient to his parents' needs and expectations. The parents remain the unquestionable authority over the individual rights of their children. The sense of being dutiful to the parents' needs and expectations supercedes the need of self-realization of the children. Usually, this sense of duty to parents is felt mostly by the oldest child, especially by the oldest son in the Asian American family. The children of Asian Americans who tend to be high in acculturation and low in ethnic identity tend to create inevitable intergenerational conflicts with their parents regarding this value of filial piety over their need of self-realization.

Shame versus Guilt. Asian American persons tend to behave in the name of shame rather than guilt. Shame is a determining factor that motivates Asian American persons in their interpersonal relationships. For Asians or Asian Americans, to "lose face" means to lose a sense of self-esteem and dignity in the presence of others. For the Westerners, guilt is oriented within an individual's intrapsychic dynamics and motivation. To them, guilt motivates one to behave in both private and public manners. To the contrast, Asian Americans tend to feel less guilt and much more shame over the same matter the Westerner would feel an enormous sense of guilt over.

For the Asian Americans, shame is usually activated and directed in their interpersonal or group relations. To them, shame is felt in reaction to their perceived perception of other individuals or group. In a sense, shame is understood as other-directed dynamics, whereas guilt is understood as self-directed dynamics. Shame is focused on the sense of one's being harmonious and conformity with others in individual or group relations, while guilt is much focused on the sense of one's being right or wrong or achieving *justice* in light of one's inner values and external norms. Because of shame dynamics, the counselor or therapist makes an effort to help her client to "save" face instead of focusing on the sense of justice in the client's interpersonal or group conflicts and relations. Counseling or therapy with Asian Americans requires on the part of the counselor or therapist skills in helping the client to save his (or the group's) face when applying conflict resolution in human conflict situations.

Harmony versus Justice. Asian Americans tend to value the importance of harmony over the right of justice in their public and group life. For these Asian Americans, one's sense of being right or wrong or a sense of justice is less critical than a sense of one's being harmonious in the public or group behaviors. To them, they would give up their own sense of right and wrong and maintaining justice in the name of harmony and conformity with the group. In point, an individual voice with a sense of justice is disvalued or disrespected by the group when it breaks or disrupts the harmonious atmosphere of the group. In a sense, they tend to value a group consensus behavior rather than independent or self-centered behavior out of one's own conscience. For this reason, it is hard to expect an Asian American individual to express his or her own independent voice in the midst of his or her family or group members.

Although the three groups share common values as already noted, these three groups distinctively carry their own ethnic values. Their distinctive ethnic values need to be further delineated for counseling or therapy with members of these three groups. I have inevitably limited this study without including further study of their distinctive ethnic values.

Ethnic-oriented Issues and Concerns

The Chinese Americans, the Japanese Americans, and the Korean Americans tend to face certain patterns of clinical issues and concerns. There is one set of clinical issues for the American-born Asians and another set of problems for the Asian-born immigrants and refugees.

American-born Asians are usually concerned about the problems and issues of racial discrimination in working places, mental health, family discords, and individual's self-actualization or realization. Because of their high level of assimilation and relatively low ethnic identity, the American-born Asians are more concerned with their needs of self-actualization and self-realization, including their own individual mid-life crises, career goals, marital and family discords, intergenerational communications, egalitarian relationships, and so on.

Asian-born immigrants are confronted predominantly with the issues and concerns of economic survival and jobs, social and cultural adjustments, and living skills in their new homeland of America. In addition, they tend to face marital and family discords, intergenerational conflicts, issues of interracial dating and marriage, homesickness and cultural uprootedness, and separation from their motherland ties. Issues of mental health care among the children of the first generation are increasingly predominant in the Asian American families and communities.

The Therapeutic/Working Alliance

In general, it has been observed by Asian American researchers that Asian American clients tend to underutilize mental health care services for many different reasons (Sue & Sue, 1999).

America-born Asians without cultural and language barriers don't have difficulty encountering a counselor or therapist of the majority group in America. Linguistically, they can encounter a counselor or therapist who comes from outside their own community.

On the other hand, Asian-born immigrants are extremely limited in their ability to meet a counselor or therapist from outside their own ethnic community. Among many different reasons are the language and cultural barriers that prevent them from receiving help from outsiders. It is critically important for an Asian-born immigrant to match herself with a counselor or therapist from within her own ethnic community. Other alternatives may be a counselor or therapist from one Asian American community meeting a client from a different Asian American community. In this case, a match between a Japanese American person and a Korean American person for counseling or therapy would be most strenuous and stressful due to the countries' historical background of enmity.

Next to a stressful match of inter-community dynamics may be a match between an Asian American person and a person of another major racial or ethnic minority, namely an African American, Hispanic American, or Native American person. The language and cultural variance may be a barrier to this match, even though Asian Americans commonly share the burden of American racism with other racial ethnic minority groups in the United States.

Sometimes, those Asian Americans who are bilingual and bicultural would prefer to seek a white counselor or therapist rather than one of their own kind out of fear of shame and self-disclosure to their own ethnic community. The Asian American clients would perceive self-disclosure to their own community as losing face and a shameful act. In light of the power hierarchy, the white counselor can be unexpectedly helpful to the Asian American clients in spite of cultural and language barriers. The white therapist would be able to exert his social power effectively to enable the Asian American clients to get through any structural and racial barriers to organizational assistance.

In sum, in counseling or therapy with Asian American persons, a realistic match in terms of racial, cultural, language, and historical background between the client and the counselor or therapist may become a critical factor to the success and effectiveness of the work.

III. Clinical Approaches with Asian Americans

At the dawn of the third millennium, cross-cultural counseling and therapy is emerging and taken as the "Fourth Force" in psychology, as observed by some cross-cultural theorists (Pedersen, 1991; Sue & Sue, 1999).

In recent decades, the concept of *cross-cultural counseling or therapy* is often used interchangeably with the term of *multicultural counseling or therapy,* as contemporary American society is being described as a multiracial and multicultural society. And the literature in the field of multicultural counseling and therapy becomes increasingly abundant in light of the rapid demographic growth of racial and ethnic minority groups in the United States.

However, the field of pastoral care and counseling, which traditionally has relied heavily upon the resources and methodologies of counseling psychology, psychiatry, psychotherapy, and behavioral sciences, also began to show its interest in cross-cultural/multicultural counseling or therapy in the recent decade, too, on a token level (Augsburger, 1986, 1992; van Beek, 1996).

The literature in cross-cultural or multicultural counseling or therapy all address issues of clinical approaches and methodology for the racial or ethnic minority group clients that should be different from the traditional approaches and methods used with clients of the racially culturally dominant and majority group in America (Sue & Sue, 1999, pp. 51–73).

Here we need to consider issues particularly related to Asian American clients. In so doing, this section includes issues of procedures, intakes and termination, methods, approaches, and referrals in counseling or therapy with Asian American clients.

Clinical Procedures

On one hand, the so-called *American Asians* (the descendents of first-generation immigrants) easily adapt to the traditional standard procedures of practice and administration in counseling and therapy because of their high level of assimilation and bicultural and bilingual abilities.

On the other hand, *Asian-born Americans* (the first-generation immigrants) are relatively less adaptive and are resistant to the standard procedures of therapy, primarily due to language and cultural barriers.

Further, as the Western concept and mode of counseling is a totally foreign notion to *Asian-born immigrants,* self-disclosure to a stranger and an outsider of one's own family would be considered losing face and inflicting a sense of shame by the Asian American clients. Because of this reason, the counselor or therapist needs to match with a member of his or her ethnic community if all possible, in order to reduce tension and anxiety on the part of the Asian American client.

Also, prior to completing a formal intake form, it would be more effective to take a verbal interview to establish a rapport and structure the procedures in the first session, if all possible. The less formal the procedures are, the more the Asian American client would feel comfortable and relaxed about her in-depth self-disclosure. Especially, effective structuring would be a critical factor to enhance the effectiveness of counseling and therapy with Asian American clients.

Further, the notion of a termination session is very unfamiliar to the Asian-born immigrants. They tend to initiate and terminate their sessions at their own wish and will. Even though there may be a very clearly explicit agreement with the client, she may drop or stop counseling at any time. In other words, the premature termination rate for Asian immigrant clients may be very high and should be expected. Thus, this high rate of premature termination may indicate that a short-term or brief counseling or therapy may be more feasible for Asian American clients.

Clinical Methods and Approaches

As previously observed, in counseling with Asian American clients, the methods and approaches should be culturally and racially sensitive and adaptive to the Asian American persons.

In order to be culturally responsive, the clinical methods used with Asian American clients should be carefully selected and adapted. Depending upon the nature of symptoms and personality of the clients and the levels of their acculturation, selective methods should be applied to therapy with Asian Americans.

Overall, the Asian American clients are relationship-oriented and thus are apt to solve their conflicts by correcting or modifying the relationship or emotional bonding rather than through rational intervention techniques. (For instance, among Asian American males, an interpersonal conflict is often resolved by having social drinks.) Because of this cultural mode, establishing a rapport and therapeutic relationship with the Asian American client in the initial session may be a key factor to the success and effectiveness of counseling. In so doing, an emotive approach is more effective than cognitive approach to Asian American clients in establishing an emotional bonding. In terms of building up therapeutic relationships, Rogerian methods of therapeutic qualities, including unconditional positive regard, empathy, and congruence, may be useful and effective to the Asian American clients in the initial stages and sessions.

Further, Asian Americans are goal-oriented and tend to be responsive to an action-oriented approach with a problem-solving focus, rather than talk therapy with insight and interpretation techniques.

In terms of intervention skills, behavioral techniques, including a self-help approach and various types of homework, may be effective with the Asian American clients, especially with immigrant clients. Additionally, in the intervention stage, insight approaches for relatively educated clients, behavioral approaches for less intellectually sophisticated clients, transactional analysis and cognitive-behavioral approaches for average intellectual persons, and so on, may be applied to Asian Americans.

In view of cultural factors, Sue, Ivey, and Pedersen (1996, p. 39) suggest for the multicultural counselor or therapist four cultural factors, including respect for authority, subtlety and indirectness, and well-defined role relationships, practiced by Asian American clients. In my judgment, these cultural factors are helpful for understanding the Asian American clients culturally, as they (Asian American clients) tend to behave passively and compliantly toward their counselor or therapist.

Further, Sue and Sue (1999, pp. 263–65) offer useful treatment strategies, including the following culturally related strategies for the counselor with Asian American clients:

1. Use restraint in gathering information;
2. Do a through analysis of current environmental concerns;
3. Assess the worldview of the client, the way they view their problem;
4. Focus on the specific problems;
5. Take an active or directive role;
6. Deal with the immediate future;
7. Pay attention to intergenerational conflicts, differences in acculturation, and hierarchical structure of family;
8. Be aware of refugees for family history in home country.

These eight strategies may also be applicable to Asian American clients besides the three groups discussed here. In fact, these strategies are considered general enough to be applied to non–Asian American clients, too.

In general, theorists in multicultural counseling or therapy advocate competencies in three ways: (1) the counselor's awareness of his own cultural values and biases, (2) the counselor's awareness of the client's worldview, and (3) the use of culturally appropriate intervention strategies (Sue & Sue, 1999, pp. 224–27). Again, these three cultural competencies are also applicable to all cross-cultural/multicultural counseling or therapy with Asian American clients.

Further, it is important for the counselor or therapist to heed the three common clinical errors that Sue and Sue (1999, pp. 221–24) note, namely, (1) using appropriate process with inappropriate goals, (2) using inappropriate process with appropriate goals, and (3) using inappropriate process with inappropriate goals. Undoubtedly, it is most effective when the counselor or therapist applies an appropriate process with an appropriate goal. To match an appropriate process with appropriate goals with an Asian American client would require cross-cultural/multicultural competencies and skills on the part of the counselor.

The importance of cross-cultural communication skills in dealing with Asian American clients is stressed as essential by the cross-cultural/multicultural counseling and therapy theorists (Sue & Sue, 1999, pp. 74-96: Augsburger, 1986, pp. 27–32; Klopf & Park, 1982, pp. 59–123; van Beek 1996, pp. 27–37).

In point, these theorists stress the importance of verbal and nonverbal communication skills, especially in light of the emotional restraint and indirectness of the Asian American clients in their communication styles.

Resources for Supportive Networks and Referrals

Counseling with Asian American clients would require a variety of clinical approaches and skills of the counselor or therapist. Additionally, the therapist is required to utilize a variety of resources surrounding the clients.

The resources of Asian American clients generally include the family or extended family network, the social support network, especially intimate friends, and the religious institution or church, which often functions as an extended family in the Asian American community.

It is critically important to treat the Asian American client in light of his relationship with his family relations and expectations. Thus, the counselor is often required to approach a significant member(s) of the family for assistance for his client.

In addition, intimate friends are another important resource for assistance in therapy with the Asian American client. The intimate friends are often identified as the playmates acquainted in adolescent or younger ages.

The Asian American client often tends to confide her private secrets (thoughts and feelings) to her intimate peers, not necessarily to her spouse. In this context, the intimate peers often play a very important, supportive role as well as a peer-counselor role during crisis or critical times. Therefore, it is advisable for the counselor to utilize intimate friends as resources for assistance to the Asian American client, if at all possible, with the permission of the client.

Another important resource for the Asian American client is the religious temple or church in the Asian American community. As noted already, the religious temple or church often plays an extended family role in its supportive network for the Asian American individuals and families. For this reason, utilizing and connecting with the leaders of the temple or church often becomes a critical therapeutic strategy for intervention or referral in counseling with the Asian American client.

As previously observed, in many cases, counseling or therapy with the Asian American client requires a single-session approach or a brief counseling approach because of the goal-orientation of the Asian American client. In case of a single or brief session, counseling with the Asian American client requires referral skills of the counselor or therapist.

Referring an Asian American client also requires culturally sensitive skills. For instance, the Asian American client is interdependent with the counselor or therapist in session. Thus, the Asian American client can easily mistake the referral as a professional rejection unless the referral is approached with cross-cultural communication skills. At times, the referral needs to be directly arranged by the counselor in a caring manner, perhaps with a personal note written on the counselor's calling card on behalf of the client.

In most cases, counseling and therapy with Asian American clients would require that a referral be made in one form or another, largely due to the frequency of single or brief counseling or therapy sessions with them.

Conclusions

It must be clear to readers that counseling or therapy with an Asian American client is not an easy matter but rather a complex and complicated effort.

It is so first of all because of the vast diversities among the Asian American communities, with more than twenty nationalities with different race, cultures, worldviews, and historical backgrounds. Realistically, it is virtually impossible for any one author to attempt to define the Asian American communities without gross overgeneralization and stereotyping.

In an attempt to minimize the risk of overgeneralization and stereotyping, I have intentionally confined this study to only the three groups of Chinese Americans, Japanese Americans, and Korean Americans. Even an effort to limit the Asian American communities to these three groups does not guarantee that we will be free of overgeneralization and stereotyping.

It must be further clear to readers that the three groups of Chinese Americans, Japanese Americans, and Korean Americans are different in race, culture, language, and historical background, and thus need to be approached in different ways with different methods. It is most desirable and effective to match the Asian American client with a counselor or therapist from the same racial or ethnic community if all possible. It must be emphasized that utilizing and collaborating with counselors and therapists from within the Asian American communities is an essential strategy that anyone from outside of the Asian American communities needs to pay attention to.

Further, this chapter raises the issue of the rest of the Asian American communities that are excluded from this study; they need to be studied one by one, with each nationality approached by a person from within the same community. The Asian American communities in the United States are too vastly diversified to include them all under the name of "Asian Americans." Each ethnic group must be dealt with in a careful manner by an author from the same community.

And, a culturally sensitive counselor or therapist would be able to apply wisdom and skill to utilize and collaborate with the resources within the Asian American communities for the sake of the treatment and well-being of the Asian American client. To outsiders, the good news is that Asian

American counselors and therapists are rising in number within each Asian American community in the United States.

It is my personal optimism that these Asian American caregivers and therapists will undoubtedly increase in number enough to meet the needs of the Asian American clients in the fields of pastoral care and counseling, as well as in the field of mental health and human care services, in the third millennium.

References

Abel, Theodora M., Metraux, Rhoda & Roll, Sammuel. *Psychotherapy and Culture* (rev. & expanded ed.) Albuquerque: University of New Mexico, 1987.

Augsburger David W. *Pastoral Counseling across Cultures.* Philadelphia: Westminster, 1986.

———. *Conflict Mediation across Cultures: Pathways and Patterns.* Louisville, KY: Westminster/John Knox, 1992.

Axelson, John A. *Counseling and Development in a Multicultural Society.* Monterey, CA: Brooks/Cole (1985), 89–111.

Bemak, Fred et al. *Counseling and Psychotherapy with Refugees.* In Paul B. Pedersen et al., eds. *Counseling across Cultures.* Thousand Oaks, CA: Sage (1996), 243–65.

Carter, Robert T. *The Influence of Race and Racial Identity in Psychotherapy: Toward a Racially Inclusive Model.* New York: John Wiley and Sons, 1995.

Chin, Lau Jean et al., eds. *Transference and Empathy in Asian American Psychotherapy: Cultural Values and Treatment Needs.* Westport, CT: Praeger Publishers (1993), 15–29.

Doi, Takeo. *The Anatomy of Dependence.* Tokyo: Kodansha International, 1973.

Dyrness, William A. *Invitation to Cross-Cultural Theology: Case Studies in Vernacular Theologies.* Grand Rapids: Zondervan, 1992.

Espin, Oliva M. & Gawelek, Mary A. *"Women's Diversity: Ethnicity, Race, Class and Gender in Theories of Feminist Psychology."* In Laura S. Brown and Mary Ballou, eds. *Personality and Psychotherapy: Feminist Reappraisals.* New York: Guilford (1992), 88–110.

Feltham, Colin, ed. *Understanding the Counseling Relationship.* London: Sage, 1999.

Frank, Jerome D. & Frank, Julia B. *Persuasion and Healing: A Comparative Study of Psychotherapy* (3rd ed.) Baltimore: Johns Hopkins University, 1991.

Ho, Man Keung. *Family Therapy with Ethnic Minorities.* Newbury Park, CA: Sage (1987), 24–68, 230–72.

Hsu, Francis L. K. *"The Self in Cross-Cultural Perspectives."* In Anthony J. Marsella et al., eds. *Culture and Self: Asian and Western Perspectives.* New York: Tavistock (1985), 24–55.

Hu, H. C. *"The Chinese Concepts of Face."* In D. G. Haring, ed. *Personal Character and Culture Milieu.* Syracuse: Syracuse University, 1975.

Ivey, Allen E., Ivey, Mary Pradford & Simck-Morgan, Lynn. *Counseling and Psychotherapy: A Multicultural Perspective* (3rd ed.). Boston: Allyn & Bacon, 1993.

Kazarian, Shashe S. & Evans, David R., eds. *Cultural Clinical Psychology: Theory, Research, and Practice.* New York: Oxford University Press, 1998.

Kim, Jin Young. *A Son's Search for Identity Through Relationship: A Cross-Cultural Venture in Psychoanalysis and Confucianism.* Ph.D. diss., Drew University (1998), 235–44 (Confucian Values in Korean American Families).

Kim, Thaddeus Chang-Sok. *"Korea."* In Robert J. Wicks & Barry K. Estart, eds. *Pastoral Counseling in a Global Church: Voices from the Field.* Maryknoll, NY: Orbis Books (1993), 113–22.

Kitano, Harry H. L. *"Counseling and Psychotherapy with Japanese Americans."* In Anthony J. Marsella & Paul B. Pedersen, eds. *Cross-Cultural Counseling and Psychotherapy.* New York: Pergamon (1981), 228–42.

———— & Maki, Mitchell T. *Continuity, Change, and Diversity: Counseling Asian Americans.* In Paul B. Pedersen et al., eds. *Counseling across Cultures* (4th ed.). Thousand Oaks, CA: Sage (1996), 124-45.

Kleinman, Arthur. *Patients and Healers in the Context of Culture.* Berkeley, CA: University of California Press, 1980.

Klopf, Donald W. & Park, Myung Seok. *Cross-Cultural Communication: An Introduction to the Fundamentals.* Seoul: Hanshin, 1982.

Leong, Frederik T. L. *"MCT Theory and Asian American Populations."* In Derald Wing Sue, Allen E. Ivey & Paul B. Pedersen. *A Theory of Multicultural Counseling and Therapy.* Pacific Grove, CA: Brooks/Cole, 1996.

Marsella, Anthony J. & Pedersen, Paul B., eds. *Cross-Cultural Counseling and Psychotherapy.* New York: Pergamon (1981), 228–42.

McGoldrick, Monica, Pearce John K. & Giordano, Joseph, eds. *Ethnicity and Family Therapy.* New York: Guilford, 1982.

Mezzich, Juan E. & Berganza, Carlos E., eds. *Culture and Psychopathology.* New York: Columbia University, 1984.

Pedersen, Paul B. et al., eds. *Counseling across Cultures* (4th ed.). Thousand Oaks, CA: Sage, 1996.

Saba, George W., Karrer, Betty M. & Hardy, Kenneth V., eds. *"Minorities and Family Therapy."* In Lee, Evelyn, *Assessment and Treatment of Chinese American Immigrant Families.* New York: Haworth (1990), 99–122.

Shim, Steve S. *A Clinical Case Study of "Haan" Experiences among Korean Immigrants in Southern California: A Cross-Cultural Pastoral Counseling.* Unpublished Ph.D. diss., Claremont School of Theology (1990) UMI Dissertation Services: Order No. 9034164.

Shon, Steven P. & Ja, Davis. *"Asian Families."* In Monica Mc Goldrick, John K. Pearce & Joseph Giordano., eds. *Ethnicity and Family Therapy.* New York: Guilford (1982), 208–28.

Sue, Derald Wing, Ivey, Allen E. & Pedersen, Paul B. *A Theory of Multicultural Counseling and Therapy.* Pacific Grove, CA: Brooks/Cole, 1996.

―――― & Sue, David. *Counseling the Culturally Different: Theory and Practice* (3rd ed.) New York: John Wiley & Sons (1999), 255–71.

Sue, S. & McKinney, H. "Asian Americans in the Community Mental Health Care System." *American Journal of Orthopsychiatry* 45,1 (1975), 111–18.

van Beek, Aart M. *Cross-Cultural Counseling.* Minneapolis: Fortress, 1996.

Walsh, Roger. "Asian Psychotherapies." In Raymond J. Corsini & Danny Wedding, eds. *Current Psychotherapies* (5th ed.) New York: F. E. Peacock (1995), 387–99.

Wicks, Robert J. & Estart, Barry K., eds. *Pastoral Counseling in a Global Church: Voices from the Field.* Maryknoll, NY: Orbis Books, 1993.

Rebeca M. Radillo

6. Pastoral Counseling
with Latina/Latino Americans

Pastoral counseling focuses on relationships, meaning, and symbols. It refers to a counseling in which spirituality is taken seriously or is carried out within a theological context that promotes attention to the broader scope of the psychological, ethical, and social realities of our clients. A well-established theoretical footing, including these elements as well as an understanding of the socio/political/economic knowledge of persons seeking our counsel, is essential for our relationships with our counselees.

There is an inherent danger in presenting and formulating theories and specific treatment approaches with respect to a particular group. In so doing, a writer runs the risk of stereotyping, thus fostering detrimental generalizations and conclusions and compromising the counseling process. One must be aware that within each racial, ethnic, or cultural group there is a multiplicity of variances and one risks the needs of a client with the assumption that culturally appropriate counseling embraces all members of his or her particular group.

To evade comprehensive observation and responsible research on the subject undermines the importance that an informed sensibility has in the counseling process and minimizes its effectiveness, since all counseling must be contextual and mutual. A very important contribution in this area was formulated by Berry (1993) and is reflected in Stephen Quintana's work on "Acculturative Stress: Latino Immigrants and the Counseling Professional" (1995):

> We cannot hope to understand the situation of an "ethnic minority" in a plural society unless we also understand the "ethnic majority," and their mutual relationships. Such an exclusive focus on the "ethnic minorities" gives us only part of what we need to know, and perhaps reinforces the implicit view that it is "they" who need fixing rather than "us."[1]

Latin Americans are a diverse and complex population. We are speaking of Whites, Blacks, Mestizos, Mulattos; we are talking about multiple levels of educational backgrounds and social status. We are speaking of recent immigrants with legal status and undocumented persons; naturalized citizens, and those whose roots are in any of our Spanish-speaking countries, whose culture remain very much Latin American and whose first language is English. Latin Americans come from the Caribbean, from South and Central America. Each group has a complex social and political history and a rich cultural heritage that has contributed to their personal development and their worldviews.

As a Latina pastoral psychotherapist, I am often asked about the need for the study, the understanding, and the integrating of a cultural perspective in counseling. Others of my colleagues take an absolutist position in their work with Hispanic and other racial or ethnic clients. Such approach supports the notion of a psychological understanding and treatment void of cultural, racial, and ethnic influences. The editors of *Cross-Cultural Psychology: Research and Applications* make us aware that this particular construct comes closer to nurturing ethnocentric behavior by implying that differences point to less intelligent people, those dishonest, primitive, and incapable of engaging in an in-depth counseling and psychotherapeutic process.

The term *ethnocentric behavior* refers to a person's understanding of others as inferior, as emotionally, mentally, and intellectually deficient. Because of the inherent arrogance in this concept, "there exists a strong tendency to use one's own group's standards as the standards when viewing other groups, to place one's group at the top of a hierarchy, and to rank all others as lower. This tendency may even be a universal feature of cultural group relations."[2]

Ethnocentrism is a manifestation of the elitist behavior demonstrated by the culturally encapsulated therapists who, on the basis of culture, ethnicity, or race, deem persons analyzable or not based upon a client's contextually appropriate behavioral patterns. Further detrimental outcomes of ethnocentrism have to do with treatment and diagnosis of clients. Psychoanalysis has been biased since its genesis by excluding an integral element in human development, the social, cultural, economic, spiritual, and political context in which a person was formed.

In her chapter, "What Is a Multicultural Perspective for Psychoanalysis?" Rose Marie Perez-Foster clearly summarizes the bias of the psychoanalytic profession as follows:

> Psychoanalysis has a very defined view of life and how it should be lived, and it is this perspective that determines who is to be treated, who is analyzable, who has adequate ego strength, who

can meaningfully relate to objects and who is capable of exploring his or her deep inner self. We see those who do not fit our life program as "simpler people" who have limited or narrower life goals, "poor people" who are too consumed with the reality-based problems of daily survival, or "foreign people" who come from alien cultures or alien neighborhoods and simply do not fit the picture of self-actualization as we define it in our psychoanalytic culture.[3]

This reflects some of the psychoanalytic core premises that may in fact predispose a practitioner to think that an immigrant, a poor person, or a member of another racial or ethnic group is incapable of self-understanding, self-direction, and insight-oriented work. Often lack of empathic affirmation and understanding of the culturally different world of the counselee accounts for early treatment termination and the underutilization of mental health services by Latin Americans.

A biopsychosocial approach to care and counseling with Latin Americans provides caregivers with a wider perspective and knowledge of the internal and external forces and dynamics that are present in the formation of personality and in behavior. Racism, political powerlessness, and poverty, among others, have direct consequences in the development of a person's intrapsychic development. Environmental forces shape the thought patterns of a person and provide a system of meaning and symbols that must be taken into account in order to provide a professional and ethical counseling experience to the counselee.

This chapter will address several concepts, understandings, and dynamics essential to counseling Latin American counselees, in an attempt to provide an informed framework or guideline containing the cultural, social, and psychological realities of this growing population as it has major implications in the treatment and the chosen modality for therapy.

As with any other counseling situation, it is of the utmost importance that the pastoral counselor or therapist be aware of the existing variances in the treatment of an individual or family. In working with persons from different groups, it behooves the practitioner to be knowledgeable about the conceptualization of health and illness as well as the understanding of the cure acceptable to each group. This knowledge will afford the counselor the insight to develop a treatment plan and the best modality to maximize a mutually effective counseling experience.

Sociopolitical and Economic Profile
of Latin Americans and Hispanics

In the Latin American kaleidoscope of people of cultural and value differences, the family is the most important institution. The family system must be understood in its extended context. When we think of the Latin American family we are including relatives and others beyond that kinship, including any person who lives in the household, as well as *compadres, comadres,* and the *compadrazgo:* God-parents who are responsible for the children's well-being in the event of the death of the parents.

The concept of *family* includes both blood relatives and close and significant friends; therefore, a nuclear family perspective will not be useful in understanding and treating Latin Americans. Family ties can be construed as either codependent or as pathological, hence negating this cultural behavioral pattern of Latino families.

In their extensive research into the areas of families, McGoldrick, Garcia-Preto, Hines, and Lee (1991) found that among Hispanic families, loyalty, unity, and family commitment and responsibility were most often emphasized. These authors noted that commitment to family took precedent over individual family members. This strong family focus is expressed through the concept of *familismo,* that is family loyalty over individual self-interests (Baruth & Manning, 1991).

In working with Latin American or Hispanic families a counselor or therapist must be aware that *familismo* is not to be construed as pathological or a family considered enmeshed. Family boundaries are flexible; security and emotional support are essential factors in the family group. *Familismo* is ever-prevalent when a family member is vulnerable or facing a serious problem. Many years ago, as I began my own therapeutic process, my nephew contracted meningitis. I called my therapist to cancel my session the night before the scheduled time due to this emergency. My next visit was an unending probe as to why I had missed the session and what unconscious material or resistance to treatment this could represent. I was bewildered, angry, and hurt by what I perceived to be the therapist's insensitivity to our family crisis.

Cultural attitude as well as family values are concepts promoted by the family system. *Familismo* is protection. While *family* is equivalent to a sacred concept in the Latin American community, one must also realize that obligations to the extended family at times may induce stress. Acknowledging family stress is a painstaking reality, and family members may present deep guilt and shame in treatment.

The concept of family in our communities is understood from a hierarchical perspective. This hierarchy is to be respected and acknowledged in the counseling process. While social, political, and economic changes, including the women's movement, have forced the Latin American family to make some adjustments and reorganization in the family system, especially among the younger generations, the autocratic, disciplinarian, and demanding father still commands respect from children and the wife. At times transitions collide with the family system, and counseling becomes a necessity. In such cases, the counselor may need to do some educational interventions in order to deal with these changes.

Another concept promoted by the family system is that of *respeto*. Older adults are bestowed with a degree of respect and deference, their role in the family is one of power and authority. Respect is also held for others, and severe disputes occur when it is not honored or when people feel disrespected.

The implication of *respeto* in the relational dyad of counselor/ counselee could be misunderstood, as a practitioner may experience this *respeto* as the client's passivity or lack of motivation for the counseling process. This may indeed affect the transference and countertransference and even the development of the therapeutic alliance.

As trained counselors and therapists in the field of pastoral counseling or psychoanalytic psychotherapy, we have been taught that the ultimate signs of health have to do with autonomy, individuation, and separation. This poses a serious dilemma for Latin American counselees, for whom these ultimate goals in therapy are ego dystonic and a true denigration to the family system from whence the self emerges.

Psychologist Alan Roland's conceptualization of what he calls "the familial self" explains how the self is understood in terms of a person's relationship with others, especially members of the extended family. Furthermore, Roland (1988) notes that this construct of "familial self" is useful to understand Latino's dedication to children, parents, family honor and unity. From this perspective it is easy to see how money, objects, all possessions become family property rather than that of a single family member.[4]

Growing up in Havana, of poor family, I lived in a large room that my mother kept impeccable and very organized. The generosity of my parents in sharing with relatives and friends whatever we had to eat and accommodating anyone who needed shelter was apparent. Once one of my aunts arrived with her three grown children and their families after the sudden death of her husband. Though they arrived unannounced, they were welcomed and assisted in finding accommodation. For a week, five other family members joined us, and we shared what we had until housing was found for them. No questions were asked. The family responded to my aunt's family crisis.

A counselor may be surprised at the number of people who may share a small house and the fact that they may or may not be blood relatives. Therefore, a thorough exploration of persons living at home will reveal the power and the wide dimension of the concept of *familismo* and dismiss notions of this behavior as pathological or primitive.

Family therapy can be a treatment of choice for Latin American families. The reasoning behind the recommendation regarding treatment modality relates to the characteristics discussed regarding the prominence of family in the Hispanic culture. For instance, the extended family is a holding environment for its members, offering a secure milieu where its members had been protected and nurtured and where other crises had been dealt with and resolved through learned coping mechanisms. Structural family therapy is highly recommended due to the hierarchical structure of the family. Salvador Minuchin offers the following comprehensive statement regarding the value of family treatment:

> Family therapy can be thought of as an approach to treating human problems by bringing together members of a family to help them work out conflicts at their sources. But it is also a new approach to understanding human behavior as fundamentally shaped by its social context....Family therapy challenged the equally cherished belief in self-determination by illuminating the power of the family.[5]

The *context* and the *power* are the operative notions that serve as the basis for suggesting family therapy as a preferred modality for addressing conflicts. The structural patterns of the Hispanic family require that a counselor be aware of *respeto* in addressing the adults first, and using the formal Spanish (*usted*) when speaking to the adults as well as titles such as *Señor, señora, señorita,* and so on. The first session must be formal, addressing the structure, focusing upon resolution of conflicts, communications, and possible resolutions of the presenting problems. The family's understanding of the role of the counselor as a professional include their *respeto* for authority, and they will be hesitant to raise any issue perceived to be impolite or contradictory, since this constitutes a challenge to an authority.

Whether family, individual, or group work, it is of the utmost importance that a time of clarifying the purpose of therapy be revealed, as our populations are suspicious of the therapeutic process, which in some cases is considered antithetical to religious beliefs. Taking the time early in the process to do so can prevent premature termination. Determination as to the acculturation of the family, language, race, process of immigration, and other social, economic, and political variables are also important consider-ations for the counselor preparing to work with Latin American families.

To the aforementioned issues, a counselor must also keep in mind the "cultural particularities" of the family seeking counseling. Each family has its own system of communication, behavioral structure, values, and patterns of behaviors. Failure to take these into account may result in stereotyping, which will prove detrimental to the therapeutic process.

Another modality for treatment of Latin Americans can be a group approach. Group work can serve well the needs of these clients, because group is symbolic of a "family group." Wisely Panniagua suggests the emphasis of the group should be a *problem-focus approach.* Cultural pro-visions must be set in place: that is, the group composition from the per-spective of language, and the acculturation level of the other group members as well as the social and economic background of the group. Values and beliefs are important considerations in the group members' selection.

Immigration and the Hispanic Family

Immigration itself varies in its impact on the family because of the dif-ferent manners of entry into the United States by various Hispanic groups. It is wise to differentiate between the newer immigrants and those who have been living in the United States for several generations. The immigration process begins in the family's country of origin. Making the decision to immigrate begins to threaten the homeostasis of the family and creates a great level of anxiety.

Because this issue is vital to a counselor's understanding of the family or individual seeking counseling it is of utmost importance to "investigate" a number of issues tied to this process of immigration during the initial inter-view. For example, it is helpful to clarify the role each family member played in the immigration process, as well as the original motivation for the move and the general level of support found within the family.

It is very important to keep in mind other factors deserving careful consideration and exploration of the immigration phenomenon, for instance, the expectations with which they immigrate and whether or not these have been realized, positively or negatively. Questioning may reveal the counselee's level of stress, providing a sense of appreciation for what the person is enduring.

The illegal status of immigrants presents a serious moral and spiritual dilemma for religious persons and those who take a special pride in their honesty and integrity. Immigration in a great number of cases is an act of survival and desperation on the part of people fearing their demise and their family's safety due to political persecution in their homelands from the right or left and to devastating socioeconomic circumstances. For a person whose values are compromised by survival needs, this process can be devastating to the self and by implication to the entire family.

To the extent to which families are able to understand the complexities of their decision to migrate, and to the extent to which the family members are able to recognize their own feelings of dislocation and fears in a strange lands, they can begin to seek means of support from their own ethnic community, other family members, churches, and a counselor.

There is no doubt, however, that immigration and the reality of separation from family and friends have had a damaging impact upon the family. The very process of migration and the subsequent adaptation (e.g., finding work, learning a new language, etc.) often preempt the completion of family development tasks and interfere with the stages of family development. As a matter of fact, in my private practice, I have discovered how first- and second-generation individuals in counseling will present issues related to their migratory experience.

The process of immigration, in terms of the emotional, spiritual, and psychological health of a person, is rather costly. This is obvious in our therapeutic practices. In the introduction of the book edited by Rose Marie Perez-Foster, Michael Moskowitz, and Rafael Art Javier (1996) the authors write the following regarding the trauma caused by immigration: "Like the individual who has suffered the loss of a parent, life-threatening illness or physical or sexual abuse, so do we consider the immigrant patient who has lost his or her family homeland, and environmental surround, to be injured and potentially derailed in his or her pursuit of a full life."[6]

Sara's Story

Sara is a thirty-five-year-old woman from El Salvador. She has been living in New York for the past seven years. She left El Salvador due to an excruciating economic condition. She arrived with her oldest son Carlos, who was ten years old at the time. He is now a seventeen-year-old school dropout with long-standing disciplinary problems. Sara had divorced Carlos's father after five years of marriage due to his history of domestic violence and drug abuse.

A year following her divorce, she met Oscar. They moved in together and they parented a son, Tony, and Tania, a daughter. Once again this relationship was abusive, and the intensity of the beatings was grave enough to send Sara to the hospitals for weeks at a time. Oscar was an alcoholic, and when intoxicated he not only became violent toward Sara, but also toward his children. She moved out and went back to live at home with her parents and her children.

Sara was encouraged by a relative in New York to join her, with the assurance that she would find her adequate employment so that Sara could support her children and eventually reunite the family. To such an enticing offer and out of desperation for her rapidly deteriorating financial conditions, Sara came to the United States with her older son illegally. For almost a year, her only employment was cleaning homes while staying with the relative who had encouraged her to come to New York.

After a long wait Sara obtained legal status and found a job in a factory, working as a pattern maker. She proved to be talented and became a respected worker and one well compensated by her company. Sara began to send money for the care of her younger children, and she visited them in El Salvador twice in the seven years she was away from them.

Sara would experience the pain of a single mother working six days a week and evenings as a seamstress at home in order to provide for the children and to save enough money to bring her younger children to live with her. She was interrupted endlessly at her job by telephone calls from school for parental consultations regarding her older son. His adjustment to the new culture was dreadful. Sara was overwhelmed and aghast and tried to find help within the school system, but her efforts proved to be futile.

Regardless of her problems with Carlos, Sara was able to reunite the family, only to discover that her "dreams" had turned into nightmares. After a short-lived period of happiness and accomplishments, her younger children, too, had serious disciplinary problems in school. To add to her pain and bewilderment, she learned that her daughter Tania had been raped by two sixteen-year-old boys in El Salvador when she was ten. Tania blamed her mother, claiming she abandoned them and therefore was responsible for the rape.

I met Sara as she came to the clinic in tears and exasperation. She herself had been molested as a child and had left her home at age fourteen to work and live in a tiny food business owned by family friends. Her own mother was emotionally distant from her, and her father had been killed due to his political involvement, leaving his wife with eight children under the age of sixteen. Hunger, fear, and tragedy characterized Sara's life as a victim of social and political injustices. Sara understood her decision to migrate as a hope for her children and herself. She was experiencing chaos and uncertainty, and when she came to see me she was filled with anger, guilt, shame, and hopelessness.

Sara remained in treatment with me for a long time. We held individual and family sessions. The oldest son Carlos became entangled with the law; her daughter accused her of physical abuse, and her middle son returned to El Salvador to be with the only "mother" he really knew, Sara's mother. This case necessitated an interdisciplinary team, and I became one of the team's members, along with social workers, court personnel, and even her priest.

The immigration phenomenon is perplexing; its ramification impacts upon every aspect of individual and family life. It has a multigenerational aftermath as well, as it summons forth the health or pathology of an individual and his or her family system.

The Acculturation and Assimilation Phenomenon

Involvement on the American scene can include different processes depending on the person, his or her culture, reason for immigration, economic and political extraction. Acculturation is a conscious process that entails the acquisition of the culture, language, beliefs, and behavior of the host society. The traditional view of acculturation, while most often viewed as a one-dimensional process affecting only the migrating group, has been challenged since not only those migrating into the country are affected but so the members of the host culture. Acculturation is a coping mechanism that permits an individual to incorporate portions of the dominant culture without losing one's own cultural identity.

Acculturation can be seen as a way of adopting to the mainstream value, while maintaining some traditional values (Padilla, 1990, 1995). There is no doubt that this process creates high anxiety and inordinate stress levels. As with any stress, this process elicits loss of homeostasis and therefore is an affront to the sense of identity of the person and his or her family.

A counselor, working with a family from a culture other than his or her own, may experience different levels of acculturation among its members. This will depend not only on the date of the family's arrival, but also on the age of the different members, their levels of education, and their work experiences. Future plans are also a concern. Many are aware that their stay in the country will be temporary; others will resist any move toward acculturation as a defense against the psychological and spiritual losses of the country of origin. Others will modify some behaviors enough as to be acceptable, but will return home, where culture remains intact.

In working with this population, Stephen Quintana points out that "the tendency to focus on the problems of ethnic minorities seems to serve a function that is similar to the focus on the identified patient in a dysfunctional family system. In a dysfunctional familial relationship the systemic issues need to be addressed in order for substantive changes to be made."[7]

Acculturation is relational and systemic, impacting upon life. As counselors we must be aware of the painstaking acculturation process in order to understand the Latino dynamics and subsequent responses to this phenomenon. We must never underestimate the strength that immigrants possess to deal with the complexities of acculturation. A counselor must develop a keen ear, capable of hearing the descriptions of their clients in relation to their immigration and acculturation processes. A rather conflicting experience in such is a redefinition of self in the family, especially for older adults.

The counselor must be concerned with the importance of exploring the socioeconomic distresses endured by the Latino population or, for that matter, of those of any other immigrant group. Economics play a powerful role in the sense of self-identity. I can validate this in working with Latin American counselees: Because of language or lack of proper educational documentation, even professionals and persons with highly technical training have been forced to take menial employment, resulting in feelings of inferiority and inadequacy and threatening their ego-identity.

In working with immigrants, a counselor must realize the monumental task of acculturation. We tend to place all responsibility of this process on the newcomer, with limited if any responsibility without interaction on the part of the host society. There is a sense that newcomers will immediately internalize the new culture and that the psychological adaptations will ensue without any difficulty or trauma. A word of forewarning is appropriate at this juncture: Generalizations may occur through the assumption that this process is equal for all. Acculturation, like any other process, is to be understood individually as well as collectively. Individuals will respond to this process according to their ego strength, their emotional health, their intellectual abilities, and their economic status. In the process of acculturation, another significant factor is the historical and political relationship between a person's country of origin and the host culture.

Assimilation can be a negative process that works to the detriment of a person. It must be understood that our identity emerges in the cultural milieu in which we are born and reared. Our cultural surroundings inform our value system; our emotional and psychological life is molded by the family traditions into which we are born. The cognitive and spiritual development of the self emanate from experiencing the philosophical and religious context of our countries of origin.

The process of assimilation, which is by definition the blending of the self with members of the dominant culture and the *relinquishing* or *total conscious abandonment* of one's culture of origin for the sole purpose of "being accepted," is detrimental to the emotional, psychological, and spiritual health of the individual. A person who is marginalized or impoverished by racist or discriminatory practices may feel that the only way to survive and thrive is by becoming totally immersed in the mainstream culture and in some cases negating any connection with his or her culture.

When an individual uses assimilation as a process of becoming accepted by members of the dominant culture, self-identity and self-concept are jeopardized. Both are the result of the person's membership in his or her ethnic group. The work done by Van Oudenhoven and Willemsen (1989) indicates that reviewing the evidence from intergroup relations in Europe, concluded that "some form of pluralism is to be preferred over complete assimilation. One of the negative consequences of full assimilation is that a cultural vacuum among minority group members may develop. The second generation of immigrants in particular may lose their ethnic, linguistic, or religious roots, while not being rooted in the majority culture either."[8]

Religion and Spirituality

The Latin American community is a very religious one. This community is largely influenced by the Catholic religion, yet there is a significant diversity emerging from within our populations. A recent phenomenon in our communities is the conversion from Catholicism to Protestant traditionalist or conservative groups. There is a shift to storefront churches. David Maldonado, Jr., understands this transition in the following manner: "Storefront congregations' styles, forms and rhetoric very often reproduce those of a congregation in the originating country. Life in these communities of like-minded individuals is patterned after the old country precisely to provide the meaning and community that has been lost. It is a way to retain the past in the new context."[9]

It is consequential to a pastoral counselor or therapist that religion (spirituality) is not overlooked. As a matter of fact, to ignore this aspect is to miss a quintessential element that has true implications in understanding the counselee and in treatment. The church is still the center of the Hispanic/Latino family. Virgilio Elizondo, in his book *Christianity and Culture,* emphasizes, "No aspect of life was separated from religion. Numerous rites, prayers, rituals and ceremonies accompanied not only every moment of each day, but also the seasons and yearly cycles."[10]

To imply that only Roman Catholics and Protestants make up our religious communities is to ignore persons from the Jewish faith, Buddhists, spiritualists, santeros/as, and others. Latin Americans are not a religious monolithic people. Because of the high emphasis placed on religion and folk healers, it is essential that practitioners have an understanding of how the belief system of Latin Americans influences their concept of pathology and health. On occasions a therapist, pastoral counselor, or folk healer all may share in the healing process. Consultation may be joint and must be tolerated and understood by a clinician. In the appendix of the *Diagnostic and Statistical Manual,* this issue has been included as a cultural syndrome.

Many of our clients and patients come to us referred by their clergyperson. For a Latino/a person, counseling and therapy are viewed with suspicion. Seeking treatment is a sign of failure and the admission that one is defective or even demented. This perception is intertwined with the concept of family as the context for healing and support. In her chapter on "Culturally Relevant Issues and Treatment Implications for Hispanics," Lillian Comas-Diaz makes the following remarks: "The sense of family is so vital for the Hispanic patient that Canino and Canino (1982) have argued that mental illness among Hispanics is a family affair and not an individual situation."[11]

To seek help from a stranger is a major traumatic experience for the individual. A clergyperson however, becomes the "trusted authority" and a sort of deeply respected family surrogate from whom a person may accept his or her referral to enter into a counseling relationship. The concept of health and illness is jointly understood from biological social, spiritual, emotional, and psychological perspectives.

Language

Language plays a crucial role when working with multilingual or monolingual persons from another culture. When we speak, we are reflecting words laden with affect, symbols, and values that have been brought into existence within a cultural context. Language incorporates cognition and affect as extracted from particular worldviews and social constructs, as well as from psychological and emotional acceptance of a people and a group.

Extensive work on language has revealed that language reflects how a person organizes his or her thoughts and an expression of affects. Luis Marcos, M.D., and Leonel Urcuyo, M.D., were prolific writers concerning this subject. In their 1979 paper in the *American Journal of Psychotherapy,* they thoroughly discussed two dimensions: the language barrier and the language independence of bilingualism.

Concerning the language barrier, they show that clients process information in the non-dominant language. They explain the difficulty and "additional mental operation of constant translation from or into the dominant tongue."[12] To be aware of this reality is a way for a practitioner of preventing making an erroneous hypothesis which may have serious implications for diagnosis and treatment. This process can be frustrating for both the counselee and counselor. Language also may be used as a defense against repressed psychic pain. Several years ago, a young and bright religious Colombian woman who was attracted to a married man in the congregation sought help for her dilemma. They did not have intercourse, but had engaged in heavy petting and other sexual activities. Our sessions were conducted in English. She talked about guilt according to her values and her own faith tradition. As treatment proceeded, I noticed that although she expressed her regrets and guilt about this relationship, her affect was not analogous to the situation. On a particular day, she began speaking Spanish in the session as she commented on a gathering she had attended. During the session she mentioned his name as he, too, was at the gathering. Then she burst into tears. She had used English all along in order to ward off her feelings of guilt and shame. Language had served as an ego defense and had operated as a resistance to deal with such a painful and opprobrious behavior.

In her chapter on "Functions of Language in the Bilingual Patient," Rose Marie Perez-Foster states:

> The bilingual speaker possesses not only dual sets of symbols for referring to internal states and the external world, but two different chains of meaning producing self-objects interactions and developmental contexts. Whether a second language has been acquired in a different environment or in a different developmental period (in school, upon migration), or whether a second language has simply been taught in early life by another caretaker, each code system will represent a separate composite of unique relational-contextual experiences.[13]

This particular understanding is fundamental to the practitioner when insight-oriented work and dreams are brought into the session. Symbolism is critical in language. It behooves the counselor to engage in a thorough exploration of symbolic meanings since these reflect a mode of being and perception of the world and the self. Symbols as expressed in the spoken language are indisputably religiously and culturally biased. In working with bilingual persons, considerable attention must be paid to language and how this connects with ego defenses, splitting and experience of the self, formation of ideas, and defensive functions, among others.

Pastoral Counseling with Latin American Clients

This chapter has accented several basic dynamics that have direct implications in the counseling and treatment of Latin Americans. In the past five years significant research and publications have presented myriad aspects to underscore the necessity of responding to the spiritual, emotional, and psychological needs of the increasing Latin American population in the United States. The number of publications emerging in the past five years are an indication that we can not be dormant or delude ourselves that we can continue business as usual in pastoral counseling or psychotherapy.

In the past, counselors encapsulated in the dominant culture believed that it was the counselee's sole responsibility to adapt to the counselor's expectations and to accommodate a process that ignored the client's fundamental cultural values. Multicultural counseling has made inestimable contributions to the field as it delves into methodological and skill development to respond to the complex needs of racial, ethnic, and culturally diverse communities.

Multicultural counseling reminds practitioners that contextual treatment, which takes into account the biopsychosocial and spiritual context of a client, is integrative. At the same time this approach fosters healing for the counselee and challenges the counselor to reevaluate his or her own context, including ethnicity, culture, and spirituality.

There are some paradigm shifts that must be in place in order to provide appropriate treatment to Latin Americans as well as to other racial or ethnic cultural diverse groups. There is a certain amount of elitism that is palpable among many practitioners. Szalita (1968) commented that "analysis is an aristocratic method. It is meant for a few by a few."[14]

As responsible practitioners, our task is to engage in a personal ongoing continued education process in order to develop new skills and acquire knowledge that will allow us to be more proficient in our field of endeavor, resulting in a more effective treatment to those whom we serve. If a person engages in multicultural counseling, it is expedient to secure theoretical frameworks that inform work with a particular group and evaluate the treatment modalities that will best suit the clients. Processes and goals in treatment must adhere to and be genuine to the identity and context and spiritual values of the counselees. The conscious effort to establish professional dialogue with professionals from different cultures is imperative.

In working with multicultural clients, one must begin the task of deconstructing the rigid Euro-American model and incorporate new dimensions that will birth a new paradigm, one that is more integrated and true to the experiences of our communities. A reconstruction will reflect a biopsychosocial and spiritual dimensions. Some orthodox practitioners fear and resist a deconstruction, in the belief that to do so will dilute theoretical frameworks. This, however, is a fallacy, since in multicultural counseling, as in any other therapeutic processes, working alliance, transference, countertransferences, resistance, and so on are very much at the core of the work we do with our clients. The pivotal issue is how we understand these dynamics at play in the specific context of the client.

One illustrative example is taken from "Psychodynamic Treatment with the Working Poor," written by Rafael Art Javier, referring to a session conducted with a patient:

> What added to the strength of this working alliance was the constant focus of the sessions on helping the patient to differentiate between what he needed to do for his survival—secure shelter and food and confront the socioeconomic and sociopolitical limitations of his reality—and the view of himself as inadequate and degraded. His self definition derived directly from, and reflected, the prejudicial and negative quality of his environment. However, these qualities also became a convenient occasion for the projection of his negative introjects.[15]

In working with individuals, families, or groups, the quality of work must not be diminished. Instead it must be augmented and integrated by the use of a biopsychosocial spiritual approach.

Some of our clients' behavior will intrude on our sterile psychoanalytic training, which frowns, for instance, on receiving gifts from clients. This particular behavior is understood as having deep-rooted dynamic implications for Latin Americans. Culturally, we have been taught that at Christmas, regardless of the recipient's faith, one must show appreciation to those persons who make a difference in our lives; therefore, in most instances we must honor Freud's adagio, "Sometimes, a cigar is just a cigar." To delve in an ongoing exploration of this action is to convey unappreciation for a "true expression of gratitude" and may lead the giver to feelings of shame and possible acting out. Shaking hands with a therapist is not crossing boundaries; it is a sign of deference and respect.

A bias that I have encountered among some colleagues when working with Latin Americans and especially with those poorer and with limited formal education has to do with the erroneous perception that such clients are unable to do insight-oriented work due to their socioeconomic conditions, that the egos of these clients have been transformed by poverty.

Experience has proved that many clients who are poor and lacking formal education, if given a good holding environment, a strong alliance, and an interpersonal approach, begin to experience self-understanding, personal power, and self-direction, which point to objectives of insight-oriented work. Spiritual restoration and a decrease in a fatalistic perception of life result in the emergence of a liberated and empowered individual through this counseling process.

In summary, working with Latin Americans and other racial or ethnic groups has provided counselors with the opportunity to expand their own knowledge of themselves, widen their theoretical framework, and develop a sense of creativity and flexibility that will benefit their dominant-culture clients as well as members of diverse cultures. "Cross-cultural counseling has been recognized as the 'fourth force' in counseling, co-equal in its relevance and impact to the three traditional 'forces of psychoanalytic, behavior modifications and humanistic counseling.'"[16] Cross-cultural counseling has stimulated the therapeutic field to become sensitive to the total person and therefore strengthen the healing and wholeness that solid therapeutic work can foster.

Notes

1. Quintana, S. M. "Acculturative Stress: Latino Immigrants and the Counseling Profession." *Counseling Psychologist* 23:1 (1995).

2. Berry, J. W., Poortinga, Y. H., Segall, M. & Dasen, P. R. *Cross-Cultural Psychology: Research and Applications* Levine, R. A. & Campbell D. T. (1998) *Ethnocentrism*. New York: Wiley, p. 8.

3. Perez-Foster, Rose Marie, in *Reaching across Boundaries of Culture and Class: Widening the Scope of Psychotherapy.* R. M. Perez-Foster, Moskowitz M., Javier, R. A. (eds.). New Jersey, London: Jason Aronson, 1996.

4. Roland, A. "In Search of Self in India and Japan." In Folicov, C.J., *Latino Families in Therapy: A Guide to Multicultural Practice.* New York, London: Guilford Press, 1988.

5. Minuchin, S., Nichols, M. P. *Family Healing.* New York: The Free Press, 1993, 35, 36.

6. Perez-Foster, et al. *Reaching Across Boundaries of Culture and Class.*

7. Quintana, "Acculturative Stress."

8. Van Oudenhoven and Willemsen (1989). In Berry et al., *Cross-Cultural Psychology,* 299.

9. Maldonado, D. *Protestantes/Protestants: Hispanic Christianity within Mainline Traditions.* Nashville, TN: Abingdon Press, 1999.

10. Elizondo, Virgilio. *Christianity and Culture.* Huntington, IN: Our Sunday Visitor, 1975.

11. Comas-Diaz, L. "Culturally Relevant Issues and Treatment Implications for Hispanics." *Crossing Cultures in Mental Health.* Roslow, D. R., Pathy, Salett (eds.). 1989, 31–48.

12. Marcos, L. R. and Urcuyo, Leonel. "Dynamic Psychotherapy with the Bilingual Patient." *American Journal of Psychotherapy* XXXIII:3 (July 1979).

13. Perez-Foster, et al. *Reaching across Boundaries of Culture and Class.*

14. Szalita, A. "Reanalysis." *Contemporary Psychoanalysis* 14 (1968):88-103.

15. Javier, R. A. (1996), in Foster et al. *Reaching across Boundaries of Culture and Class,* 104.

16. Pederson, P. B., Dragus, J.G., Lonner, W. J., Trimble, J. E. (eds.). *Counseling across Cultures,* 4th ed. Thousand Oaks and London: Sage Publications 1990, 1991, vii.

References

Baruth, L. G., Manning, M. L. *Multicultural Counseling and Psychotherapy: A Lifespan Perspective.* New York: Merrill. 1991.

Bernal, M. E., Saenz, D. S., Knight, G. P. Ethnic "Identity and Adaptation of Mexican American Yourths in School Setings.' In A. M. Padilla, ed., *Hispanic Psychology: Critical Issues in Theory and Research.* Thousand Oaks, CA: Sage, 1982.

Berry, J. W. "Ethnic Identity in Plural Societies." In M. E. Bernal & G. P. Knight (eds.). *Ethnic Identity: Formation and Transformation among Hispanics and Other Minorities* (271–96). Albany, NY: SUNY Press, 1993.

Berzoff, J., Melano, L., Flanagan & Hertz, P. (eds.). *Inside Out, and Outside In: Psychodynamic Theory and Practice in Contemporary Multicultural Context.* New Jersey and London: Jason Aronson, 1996.

Cancelmo, Joseph A., Millan, Fred, and Vazquez, Carmen I. "Culture and Symptomatology: The Role of Personal Meaning in Diagnosis and Treatment: A Case Study." *American Journal of Psychoanalysis* 50:2 (1990).

Garcia-Preto, N. "Puerto Rican Families." In M. McGoldrick, J. Giordano, J. K. Pearce, eds., *Ethnicity and Family Therapy* (164–86). New York: Guilford, 1982.

Garza, Raymond T. & Gallegos, Placida I. *Environmental Influences and Personal Choice.* Thousand Oaks, CA: Sage, 1995.

Goldberger, N .R., Bennet-Veroff, J. (eds.). *The Culture and Psychology Reader.* New York and London: New York University Press, 1995.

Goleman, Daniel. "*Making Room on the Couch for Culture.*" New York Times, 1995.

Locke, C. D. *Increasing Multicultural Understanding: A Comprehensive Model*, 2nd ed. Thousand Oaks/London/New Delhi: Sage, 1998.

Marcos, Luis R. *"Understanding Ethnicity in Psychotherapy with Hispanic Patients." American Journal of Psychoanalysis* 1988. Padilla, A .M. ed. Acculturation, Biculturism and Adjustment Among Cuban Americans. J. Szapocznick and W. Kurtins, Boulder, Colorado. 1980.

Myers, David G. *Psicologia.* Madrid: Editorial Medica Panamericana, 1988.

Organista, P. B., Chun, Kevin M., Marin, G. (eds.), *Reading in Ethnic Psychology.* New York & London: Routledge, 1998.

Panniagua, F. A. *Assessing and Treating Culturally Diverse Clients.* Thousand Oaks & London: Sage, 1994.

Pedersen, Paul. *A Handbook for Developing Multicultural Awareness,* 2nd ed. Alexandria, VA: American Counseling Association, 1994.

Phinney, Jean S. *Ethnic Identity and Self-Esteem.* Thousand Oaks, CA: Sage, 1995

Sotomayor, Marta. ed. *Empowering Hispanic Families: A Critical Issue for the 90s.* Milwaukee, WI: Family Service America, 1991.

Stavan, Ilan. *The Hispanic Condition.* New York: Harper Collins, 1995.

William C. Gaventa, Jr.

7. Pastoral Counseling with Individuals with Disabilities and Their Families

Introduction

There are three basic premises for this chapter on pastoral counseling with individuals with disabilities, all of which point to both the challenges and the opportunities afforded to pastoral counselors and clergy as they work with people with disabilities and their families.

First and foremost, pastoral counseling with individuals with disabilities cannot be examined without looking at issues of family, context, environment, and community. Many of the life issues faced by people with disabilities relate to issues of support, access, and participation. Having a disability and dealing with its consequences can impact an individual, family, community, and congregation. As pastoral care and counseling grows in its awareness of the importance of context and community, this is one area where those issues are clearly evident, and, in this chapter, will bear close attention.

Second, pastoral counseling with individuals with disabilities may not be different in kind than any other form of pastoral counseling. People with disabilities struggle with the same questions and issues that impact others, and may bring to the counselor the same issues or questions about faith, loss and grief, addiction, relationships, transitions, or family dynamics as anyone else does. One of the gifts that a pastoral counselor can offer a person with a disability is that of ministering with, or treating, the person first and refraining from the assumption that the presenting issues or concerns may be caused by the disability. Many life issues addressed by clergy and by pastoral counselors can certainly be magnified or hidden by a disabling condition, but the disability in and of itself may not be the main issue. To state that premise another way, the skills and issues in pastoral counseling addressed in the other chapters in this volume are also applicable to people with disabilities and their families.

Third, as if the first two premises did not make broad enough the scope of this chapter and the issues faced in pastoral counseling with people with disabilities, the arena of "disability" is a huge one. There are many types of disabling conditions and many possible times of onset. This chapter will not try in a comprehensive way to deal with specific issues facing people with various kinds of disabilities, but it will try to point you in the direction of sources and resources that can provide disability-specific information.

Thus, we will begin with a look at the statistics and what is meant by *disability*. Then the chapter will focus on some of the specific challenges to pastoral counselors and clergy and the ways in which time-honored pastoral roles can support people with disabilities. The latter part of the chapter will draw attention to specific times within life journeys of people with disabilities that beg for pastoral intervention and support, and to some general trends in the "disability arenas" with which pastoral counselors need to be familiar. It will close with a list of sources for more information and resources on collaborating with other avenues of support, services, and ministries for people with disabilities and their families.

People with Disabilities: Who Are They?

The statistics on the numbers of people in the United States varies, but U.S. Census statistics state that there are approximately 54 million citizens in the United States with some form of disability. Another statistical lens cites a percentage of 17 percent of the population with some form of disability. When a person with a disability is viewed in context—that is, the disability impacts and is impacted by others—the numbers of people impacted by disability is staggering. One might reframe the question as, "Who is *not* impacted by disability?" at least at some point in their lives. Or, said another way, the question is not whether but *when?*

The official definitions of *disability* also vary. One can describe the 54 million to include people with physical disabilities, sensory (hearing, visual, and environmental (that is, chemical sensitivity) disabilities, intellectual or cognitive disabilities, emotional disabilities, learning disabilities, psychiatric disabilities, and disease-related disabilities; for example, multiple sclerosis, HIV and AIDS. Or the description can convey whether a disability is developmental (that is, occurred sometime in the prenatal or post-natal process up to age twenty-one; for example, cerebral palsy or Down Syndrome) or acquired through an accident, such as spinal cord injury or traumatic brain injury, or through aging.

There are several operative definitions written into public legislation and policy that are important descriptors. The ADA (Americans with Disabilities Act of 1990) defines *disability* as a physical or mental impairment that substantially limits a major life activity. The act protects three classes of people with disabilities: (1) those who have a disability, (2) those with a record of having a disability, and (3) those regarded as having a disability if that perception results in some form of discrimination.

The Developmental Disabilities Act defines a disability as a severe, chronic disability of a person that:

- Is attributable to a severe mental or physical impairment or combination of mental and physical impairments;
- Is manifest before age twenty-two;
- Is likely to continue indefinitely;
- Results in substantial functional limitations in three or more of the following areas of major life activity: self-care, receptive and expressive language, learning, mobility, self-direction, capacity for independent living, and economic self-sufficiency.

Developmental disabilities include but are not limited to mental retardation, autism, cerebral palsy, epilepsy, spina bifida, and other neurological impairments that meet the stated criteria.

It is important for pastoral counselors and clergy to know something about the legal and public definitions of disability because of the counselor's potential role in advocacy. For the purposes of pastoral care and counseling, the most helpful definition may be that of the World Health Organization (WHO). The WHO defines disability in three levels:

1. A physical or mental impairment, that is, a description of the physical or psychological cause of the condition. That could be genetic, a disease, an accident, a chemical imbalance, or many more.
2. A disability that results from the impairment, that is, a change in functioning or adaptive capabilities that results from the impairing condition. The "disability" may then result from an interaction between an impairment and an environment. For example, a person who uses a wheelchair may not be "disabled" in some environments or life activities, but will be so in others, including, possibly, getting in to see a pastoral counselor or clergy person.
3. A handicap is the value judgment placed on the disability, that is, as in golf or a race, a socially imposed value judgment about the impairment, disability, or difference. What do I think about my difference or disability? What do others think? What are assumptions, expectations, and judgments made on the basis of the label? What kind of stigma is involved?

One of the trends in definition and classification is away from seeing *disability* in medical terms and toward seeing it simply in terms of difference and diversity. A person with a disability may or may not be sick. A healthy person also has limitations, or, frequently, some form of impairment and disability. A second is the move away from terms like *resident, patient,* or *client* to an economic model like *consumer* or a political definition such as *self-advocate.* Another is that some definitions have moved explicitly toward defining a disability as a characteristic that results from the interplay of inherent abilities, environments around an individual, and the kinds of supports needed. Thus, for the AAMR (American Association on Mental Retardation), a person who used to be described as "profoundly retarded" is now a person with "pervasive support needs."

One of the main reasons to be careful about the ways definitions, terms, and labels are used is precisely because of the stigma often associated with disability and the long history of discrimination, neglect, and abuse against people with disabilities. When confronted with the confusing array of terms and labels, there are two basic counseling strategies. First, use what is called "people first" language. Phrase the disability as a descriptive adjective, not a noun. Use phrases like "a person with a physical disability" rather than "the disabled." Stated in relation to one of the premises of this chapter, a person "has a disability," not "is disabled." A disability, like any other personal characteristic, may be a major part of someone's life, but it does not define him or her totally unless that definition is imposed. Second, if you are not sure how someone with a disability wants to be described, ask him or her rather than making assumptions. There are a wide variety of opinions and preferences in both personal and professional arenas. In my experience, most people with disabilities dislike euphemisms such as "physically challenged" as much as they dislike old and stigmatizing labels such as "cripple," "retard," or "dumb." When in doubt, ask. Even the question shows sensitivity, and may be a helpful pathway for a counselor into the issues of self-understanding and personal identity.

Challenges to Pastoral Counseling

Thus, the first challenge to pastoral counselors is the immediate immersion into both real and symbolic issues of definition, classification, diagnosis, and terminology. There are a number of others, including:

Personal Experience. Many professional caregivers, clergy included, have had limited personal experience with people with disabilities. Thus, a counselor may bring socially inherited attitudes and assumptions, or simply fear and uncertainty, into a possible relationship with a person who has a disability. The paradox is that a counselor may feel "incapable," or more directly, "disabled" in his or her capacity to relate to a person with a disability.

Training. Most training in seminaries and/or human services has not included many issues related to people with disabilities, at least in ways that address them directly. Conversely, training programs for people who provide services to and with people with disabilities have often built on the premise that people need "special training" to work in such a "specialized area" with "special people." Both personal experience and training impact issues like personal comfort with different styles of communication.

The "Chronic" Nature of Disability. Many caregivers have received training in acute care settings and/or bring assumptions and expectations about being able to resolve issues, fix problems, and promote healing. Most pastoral counselors know that personal and relational issues that bring people to a counselor are not easily, if ever, fixed, but that is certainly true about most disabling conditions. In addition, there may be very different issues for a person who is born or grows up with a disability as compared to someone whose disability comes later in life as a result of injury, illness, or aging.

The Complexity of the Interaction between Person and Environment. In light of the three-level WHO definition, a counselor has to assess whether and/or how the presenting issues are related to the impairing conditions, the "disability" those impairments cause in a person's daily life and environment (which may also be a source of the disability), and/or the value judgments by the individual and by others about the impairment and disability. That complexity is heightened by the fact that different cultural traditions and social classes may interpret disability in different ways.

All of those challenges are also opportunities for learning, and, for pastoral counselors, clergy, and pastoral caregivers, opportunities for dealing with fundamental theological questions that almost leap out and grab pastoral caregivers who are willing to listen carefully to people with disabilities, their families, and their caregivers. People with disabilities are first of all people, who may struggle with any psychological, spiritual, or theological question or issue, but there are at least four issues that get magnified through the lens and experience of disability.

First, what is a counselor's doctrine of personhood? What does it mean to be human? What does it mean to be "whole" and/or "disabled"? A focus on wholeness or holistic healing without careful thought can quickly exclude and discriminate against a person with a disability. Labels and terms raise complex issues concerning the ways that people identify and define themselves and others. One of the particular dimensions of this issue has to do with value judgments about different forms of disability. People with some forms of disability refuse to identify themselves as such. For example, for many in the deaf community, deafness is a culture, not a disability. Others see and define disability as difference. Others get caught in comparative judgments, for example, "He has a physical disability but at least he is not retarded." The phenomenon of a "pecking order" in disabilities has many ramifications, but one of its tragic sides comes from the impetus to "prove oneself" as "more normal." Another is the way that advocacy groups have sometimes been forced to compete with one another for public support and funding.

If, as one would hope, a pastoral counselor can first see a person with a disability as a child of God, or created in the image of God, however one defines that in a particular religious tradition, then the second theological question follows quickly. What is one's image of God as reflected in the person with a disability? How does the experience or social construct of disability impact one's image and understanding of God? Nancy Eiesland (1994) explores this in depth in her book *Is God Disabled? Towards a Liberatory Theology of Disability.* A related question is, What is the meaning of faith? Does it depend upon intellectual understanding, and, if so, how is that affected by intellectual disabilities that impact traditional understandings of knowledge?

Third, a counselor has to confront what he or she believes about the importance of community and the collective identity of God's people. If we believe that participation in the community of faith is crucial for human and faith development, how do we assist people with disabilities and their families who may have felt or experienced isolation and exclusion? Does a counselor see a presenting problem by a person with a disability as a failure to "accept" or adjust to the disability? Or is the problem coming from the community that, in the terms of the ADA, does not want to make accommodations for the person with a disability, much less be welcoming and inclusive? This is not the only area of ministry and counseling where pastoral counselors are representatives of the faith community. A counselor's welcome and capacity to receive the projections of past and/or current experience may be crucial issues for a person with a disability. It is certainly not the only area of pastoral counseling where a key role is dealing with spiritual abuse, pain, or wounds that may have been caused by the faith community rather than by the disability. Henri Nouwen, in his movement into the L'Arche Daybreak Community during the last decade of his life, brought many of these issues to his writing, as did his mentor Jean Vanier.

Fourth, a pastoral counselor moving into relationship with a person with a disabling condition may be pushed quickly to experience his or her own feelings of vulnerability and limitation as well as his or her understandings of power and capacity to help others change. One dimension of this issue, as already stated, is the struggle with how to help with issues or problems that are not "fixable" or easily resolved. It is an area where the questions of pastoral care and counseling around "doing" and "being" are quickly encountered. I once heard psychologist and counselor Dan Gottlieb, the moderator of public radio program *Voices in the Family,* describe his quadraplegia as a symbol of "everyone's living nightmare." Thus, paradoxically, a gift that a person with a disability may bring to a counselor is a renewed awareness of limitation, vulnerability, mortality, and loss.

The frustration of "What can I do?" or "How can I help?" may be magnified by feelings of impotence in relation to the vast number of helping services and advocacy groups in the "worlds" of disability, and the lack of attention in those systems to spiritual needs, issues, and gifts in the lives of persons with disabilities. Again, the paradox is that a counselor may indeed "dis-empower" himself because he has the skills to address fundamental spiritual and theological questions that are often not addressed in service systems for people with disabilities. The question may be as fundamental and unspoken as "Whom do people with these kinds of problems belong to?" That pushes a pastoral counselor's understanding of and capacity to relate to other disciplines and services. The irony is that clergy and pastoral counselors may rule out their own capacities to help or support a person with a disability, just as in the secular service systems there is growing "faith" in the potential of generic community supports for people with disabilities, and growing attention to the power of spiritual supports in the secular research arena.

Related to all four of these theological assumptions and issues is the fact that people with disabilities raise two of the oldest and most primal of theological questions, that is, "What is the meaning of suffering?" and "Why did this happen?" There are at least four ways this issue gets raised frequently in the lives of people with disabilities and their families. The first dimension is around questions of "responsibility." Who caused it? What caused it? Whose fault was it? Again, one encounters a paradox: at the same time as many clergy and pastoral counselors would not endorse or condone a theological position that disability is a punishment, or that the "sins of the parents are visited upon the child," we are becoming increasingly aware of the ways in which human actions do have direct relationships to some forms of disabling conditions, for example, birth defects caused by environmental pollution or fetal alcohol syndrome, or injuries caused by failure to wear seat belts or helmets.

The second dimension of the theistic questions is that of purpose. For people with disabilities, this is too often a move from being seen as "cursed" or "punished" by God to being a blessing, or a special person, or, as some disability advocates would say, a "super crip." Being a special person, super-parent, or symbol of faith and dedication may be just as much a burden as being an outcast. Does one understand her experience as God's will, and, if so, how? As in any transforming event or encounter, the pastoral question is how one learns to interpret that event and its implications for someone's understanding of their life's call, vocation, and purpose.

The third dimension of the questions is that of healing and the role of faith. At one extreme are those who believe that lack of healing is a result of lack of faith, an attitude that people with disabilities and their families too frequently encounter and that they can experience as blaming the victim. More subtly, the question pushes clergy and pastoral counselors to explore their own understandings of the role of faith in healing, what is meant by healing in relation to cure, and, as stated earlier, what people mean when they talk about holistic approaches and "whole persons."

Finally, the "Why?" question often gets encountered and raised by people with disabilities and their families when they come face to face with environmental barriers, prejudice, and exclusion by others. "I had to fight for my child everywhere else," parents may say, "but I did not expect to have to fight when it came to church." Or the question may come in the form of "Why did my friends, pastor, and community disappear shortly after the onset of my impairment or disabling condition?" The question here is not the one framed classically by Harold Kushner in his book about his experience with a son with a disability, *When Bad Things Happen to Good People*, but rather, "When or why do bad things come from good people?"

The goal of this first part of the discussion has been to outline the clinical, social, and pastoral context that a minister or pastoral counselor may encounter in his or her work with a person with a disability and that person's significant others. My first assumption is that the reader, whether counselor, chaplain, minister, priest, or rabbi, comes to this discussion because of a current or potential professional relationship with a person with a disability or a caregiver to such a person. My second is that you, the reader, have very significant gifts to offer in your pastoral or counseling role. The primary issue may not be that you have to learn new skills and capacities in order to relate to people with disabilities, but that you may simply have to expand the boundaries of your understanding of the ways your gifts may impact and assist others. Those understandings of pastoral skills and identity vary greatly, as you know, but let's turn to some fundamental roles of pastoral care and counseling and the ways you, and those tools, can be powerful sources of support and ministry.

Pastoral Roles and Gifts

Each clergyperson and pastoral counselor will have her own vision and understanding of the gifts she brings to those with whom she ministers or counsels. The first assumption should be that those skills could be offered to and used by people with disabilities and their families, who are, after all, people. That offer reveals that the counselor has moved beyond the feelings of fear, anxiety, avoidance, or pity that people with disabilities so often encounter in others (Gaventa, 1986, 1997).

In my experience, the multiple possibilities in pastoral care and counseling have jelled into four basic roles: presence, guide, advocate or shepherd, and community builder (Gaventa, 1997). For the purpose of this discussion, I want to examine the implications of these roles for the pastoral counselor or clergyperson who faces the opportunity of providing a counseling ministry with people with disabilities, their families, and perhaps others who support them.

Presence

The basic rule of pastoral care and counseling is, of course, *be there.* Be present. Go there. Offer a presence of hospitality and welcome. Your relationship with the person, and the place it occurs, are a symbolic *presence* whose power is amplified by your capacity to listen, to hear the personal stories, to touch and hold the struggles and journeys of another's personality and soul.

The most obvious issue for a person with a disability, particularly a physical disability, is whether or not that relationship is architecturally possible. Can a person with a physical disability get into your office or place of ministry? Are there accessible bathroom facilities? Have you looked at the environment in which you work in terms of its hospitality and welcome to people with varying forms of disabilities, for example, the ways that furniture is placed and lighting is used? If you work in an inaccessible place, are you willing to go and how will you get to where a person is or a place where they feel comfortable? That, in fact, may be the more frequent option, since many people with disabilities are not able to get in, or feel comfortable in, places where they have not been welcome. If there are staff personnel working at your office, what kind of awareness training have they had?

There are several strategies that you as a counselor can use to move your presence and your physical space toward hospitality and, theologically, sanctuary—that is, a safe and welcoming place where one's soul may be bared.

First, if you have not had much experience with people with various forms of disabilities, get hold of some basic guidelines for relating to people with disabilities—*Disability Etiquette: Tips on Interacting with People with Disabilities* (Cohen, 1998) or *That All May Worship* (Thornburgh, 1997). These provide basic, common-sense tips, that include things like not presuming that others (for example, people with visual impairments) need help but offering it; speaking directly to people with hearing impairments; recognizing that a person's wheelchair is an extension of his body; treating an adult with mental retardation as an adult, not a child; not pretending to understand someone with speech impediments when you don't; and many more. There are videos, books, and booklets that explore these guidelines. If they are not readily available, contact an advocacy group, support group, or agency that serves people with the particular form of disability in which you are interested. And, finally, if you are unsure how best to help a person feel welcome, ask her.

Second, take a close look at the physical environment in which you do ministry. Are there architectural changes, listening devices, large print resources, and other ways that your working space can be adapted to increase a person's sense of welcome, ease of access, and utilization of the gifts your ministry offers? Architectural changes, such as ramps, may be expensive, but remember that increased ease of access may benefit many more people than those with an obvious disability.

Third, the most important part of your presence is your capacity to hear the questions and stories that an individual brings to you as minister and counselor. Most people with disabilities can tell whether you are genuinely interested in them as people, see them as people with gifts as well as limits, are willing to deal with your uncertainty, want to hear their story and questions. Even a simple opening—"Tell me your church (synagogue) story"—will often elicit amazing stories of faith and support or neglect and exclusion. You, as counselor, need to be prepared to hear the depths of lamentation and anger, the dreams that are real, the daily frustrations of dealing with barriers of access and attitude in others. Your place of ministry, the person you are, and the person (with gifts and limits) you see in the one labeled *disabled* will be key elements in the establishment of a safe and hospitable place where hope can become possible and ministry may happen.

Guide

Each counselor will have his or her own understanding of the ways they use their faith traditions and pastoral and professional skills to *guide* another in their journey. In using your counseling gifts with people with disabilities and their families, first see that the issues they bring to you are not different in kind from those of other people, but may differ in degree and intensity. That intensity may come from the stark ways that feelings, values, and beliefs are felt in coping with impairments, disabling conditions, or social barriers and stigma. It may also come from the fact that disability is not usually a short-term phenomenon, but rather, usually, a long-term journey.

The issues that a particular person brings to you for counsel and guidance may or may not be related to their disability. A counselor's sensitivity to that possibility is a gift, for one of the struggles faced by people with disabilities is others' interpretations of everything in their lives through the lens of their label or disability.

As already noted, though, a person with a disability may be coming to you with real questions about responsibility, purpose, faith, healing, and stigma. When an individual or parent notes that "this must be God's will," are they saying, "There must be a purpose here, and I will keep working till I find it"? Or, are they hinting at real anger and resentment at God, so that your role becomes that of allowing the emotions to be verbalized and heard? When people struggle with issues of cause and responsibility, blaming others or themselves, the counselor's gifts in mediation, forgiveness, and reconciliation are paramount. When the presenting issues are ones of faith and its relationship to cure or healing, your personal theology, and your role as teacher, may come to the fore. What may be crucial is your capacity as counselor to see another as whole, to see their gifts, rather than as a person defined only by a disability. When you help people deal with the ways they are treated by others, your guiding skills help them deal with anger, recognize discrimination, and work toward reconciliation.

There are several "guiding" skills used in pastoral counseling when supporting people with disabilities and their families. One goes back to the fact that this may be a lifelong journey for the person seeking counseling, and the counselor needs to be aware of key transition points at which old issues may re-emerge. (We will explore some of the life stage issues for people with disabilities and their families later in the chapter.)

A second skill involves the need for guides to serve as sources of information. Information can enlighten and empower, and at times many people with disabilities and their families may not have the information they need about available resources and services, people who are struggling with similar issues, and strategies for support. Many counselors these days have access to the Internet in addition to written information and knowledge about how to access networks to find information. There has been an explosion of resources (especially technological aids), services, and support networks in the last decade. In your role as guide, if you are not familiar with these resources, help find them. Helping a person with a disability find a support group or community where they can move from feeling isolated and alone may also open up an opportunity for you as counselor or minister with others.

Third, a key counseling skill for a "guide" is helping people reframe issues and problems they bring to the counselor. Your reframing as counselor begins the minute someone with a disability walks or rolls in to your office, with your capacity for hospitality and your ability to see both the gifts and struggles in a person with any form of disability. But it also involves your ability to help the person you are counseling see their issues in light of similar questions, answers, or journeys of others in the communities or traditions of faith without obvious disabilities. People with disabilities, because of their difference from the norm, often draw questions that reveal the anxiety or uncertainty of individuals or communities who are raising the question. So the guiding role here is to reframe by reversing the question and, possibly, the answers. How do people without disability deal with the same issues or questions that are being asked of or around the person with the disability?

One reframing strategy may come from exploring the issues brought by the person along the lines of the three-level WHO definition discussed earlier in this chapter. Does an issue come from the impairment, a "disabling" environment, or value judgments and attitudes about the disability? In helping anyone learn to accept and cope with something that has happened to them, does "accepting" a disability mean having to accept the limitations of the environment or the discriminating attitudes of others? If presenting issues are the relationship between faith and healing, how might a pastoral counselor help a person to see the issues of healing in terms other than "fixing" or "curing"? What needs to be fixed or cured may be, in fact, barriers in the environment and/or discriminating stigma or attitudes in others. One of my favorite reframing stories is that of the person with a disability who was approached by a stranger on the street (a too-frequent occurrence in the disability community) and told, "If your faith were strong enough, you could be healed." The person with the disability immediately shot back, "If your faith was strong enough, you could cure me."

Finally, as guide, a pastoral counselor may have a key role in helping other service providers see and understand the spiritual dimensions of issues that may be impacting a person with a disability. The importance of spirituality and spiritual supports is receiving more attention in the worlds of secular services and supports for people with disabilities and their families, but not to the extent of other areas of health and human service. There may be a number of reasons for that, including the over-objectification of services with people with disabilities (that is, not seeing their internal lives), the lack of welcome and support experienced by many with disabilities in the religious community, the equating of intellectual ability with faith (thus impacting people with mental retardation or cognitive disabilities), and/or the equation of faith or interest in spirituality with psychological disease or delusion.

At one retreat I gave for people working in the area of supported employment, this latter issue was poignantly expressed by a woman with a psychiatric disability who was also working as a job coach. She noted that her interest in faith and spirituality made her feel like an outcast in the psychiatric community and that her history with mental illness made her feel like an outcast in the faith community. The guiding role of a pastoral counselor may thus include helping other service providers and caregivers to see the spiritual dimensions of the needs and gifts of a person with a disability with whom they are working. As the example points out, the role of the pastoral counselor as guide may also include working with the religious community, a role that should not be unfamiliar to pastoral counselors who often work with people "in between" religious and secular supports and/or with people whose faith journey has disenfranchised them from congregational life.

Advocate or Shepherd

The role of guide, when moved from the sanctuary of an office or counseling space into the public arena, quickly becomes the pastoral role of *advocate,* or, to use a biblical symbol, *shepherd.* In the imagery of the 23rd Psalm, a shepherd helps to provide the sanctuary (the place beside the still waters and in the green pastures, and the table in front of my enemies). The shepherd accompanies in the journeys (through the valleys of the shadows of death), and, with a rod and staff, takes an active role in defending and in clearing the way (through red tape as well as wildernesses). She also helps find the place of peace, and of gratitude and abundance ("My cup runneth over") for the person with whom she is advocating.

As stated earlier, the advocacy or shepherding role may be in relation to secular services such as health-care systems, employment programs, or schools. It may be in relation to congregations and clergy. Or it may be in relation to the general community, assisting an individual to deal with public attitudes or stigma about disability. The key task for a counselor working with persons with disabilities and/or their families, as with anyone being counseled, is working *with* them so that a therapeutic/pastoral partnership is established in which the counselor empowers others to advocate for themselves and develop their own leadership skills.

What are some of the particular advocacy roles that may present themselves to a pastoral counselor or minister? First, be informed. Learn something about the public laws like the Americans with Disabilities Act or Individual Development and Education Act (IDEA), which impact services and supports for adults and children with disabilities. All states in the United States have state and national offices that can provide information and assistance; in other countries, service and advocacy groups can do the same. You may be in the position of helping a person advocate for, or fight for, their rights and deal with real discrimination.

Second, do not underestimate the power of your role as an advocate. Many educational, health, and service systems are committed, in theory, to assisting a person with a disability and their families to use "natural," "generic," or "community" supports. A pastoral counselor and the faith community he or she may represent are prime examples of natural community supports. In practice, many people with disabilities and their families feel less than powerful in the face of interdisciplinary planning processes, categorical services, and complex systems. Your contact or presence on behalf of, or with, a person with a disability is a real and symbolic expression of the fact that this person has allies and supports in the community.

One humorous yet poignant story I often cite in this regard came from a mother of a child with Down Syndrome. When asked to share her "church story," she said, "We took our minister with us to the IEP (Individual Education Plan) meeting at their daughter's school...often an intimidating process for children and families in the face of numerous professionals). It was wonderful. We got everything we wanted....They thought he was our lawyer."

Third, your role as advocate may be public, addressing issues in communities or service systems. Think of how you would envision your role if a person you were counseling was slated to move into a group home or other residential support in your community, and the community erupted into a fit of "Not in My Back Yard." Think of how the issues faced by a person with a disability may lead you to lend your meeting space, organizing capabilities, and name to the establishment of a new community service or support organization. One of the hardest issues faced by people with disabilities is their underemployment. (Over the past decade, the basic statistic of 67 percent unemployment for people with disabilities has held constant, even in a booming economy.) Think of how you might use your networking skills and your capacity to see the gifts in a person with a disability to encourage employers to give someone a chance.

Fourth, when you are called upon to advocate with the religious community on behalf of, or with, a person with a disability and their family, remember the irony that the community that might have led the way in acceptance and hospitality is usually exempt from public laws that support inclusion and accommodations. Therefore, your advocacy role may move

into that of the guide or coach who can help a minister or congregation realize the significance of what they can offer a person with a disability, and conversely, the gifts that individual may offer to them.

Community Builder

While many counselors may see themselves as working in one-to-one
relationships in pastoral counseling, the roles of guide and advocate lead into
pastoral roles of facilitating participation and inclusion in a community of support. Many of the problems or issues a person with a disability may present to
you may be related to issues of isolation or exclusion rather than issues inherent in the disability itself. This means, as with other counselees, helping individuals address issues in their own communities or networks, finding new ones
as necessary, dealing with the boundaries you establish in counseling relationships, and working with someone, in your own style, on ways to empower or
facilitate their connection to supportive communities and networks.

The temptation may be for counselors to see the issues presented by a
person with a disability or their family member as a personal rather than systems or community issue. I remember clearly a mother of a child with a significant disability who went to a pastoral counselor, and, after a short time, quit.
She told me the counselor wanted to talk about her relationships with her
mother and parents, and, what she needed, she realized, was some time of
respite care away from the day-to-day (24/7) demands of caring for her child.

There are a number of community-building skills that have already
been mentioned. They include:

- Good information and referral, so a counselor can connect people
  with appropriate services and supports. The Internet is a huge
  resource for counselors.
- The capacity to collaborate with public service providers, advocacy
  and support groups, and clergy and congregations.
- The willingness to model the kind of hospitality and welcome you
  hope other community supports will provide to people with disabilities and their families.

There are, in addition, three key strategies that pastoral counselors
may utilize in effective community-building activities that enhance the
opportunities for inclusion, participation, and support for people with disabilities and their families.

First, be sure that planning, advocacy, and community-building activities include the person himself. Don't do it for someone. Make sure he is

included and has a place at the planning and networking table. In disability matters, he is the expert.

Second, community building may be counterintuitive for counselors, because it begins not with needs and issues, but rather with a recognition of gifts and capacity. One role you may have as counselor is helping counselees and others to see the many dimensions and interests of a person's life, beyond, along with, or in spite of her disability. You might encourage connections around that interest, skill, and gift rather than around the need or disability. People with disabilities are so often put in the position of being helped, of having to receive, that a crucial reframing and community-building skill may be helping them, and others, to be connected around their other interests, gifts, and capacities. It can be as simple a process as helping a person with a disability discover her interests and gifts and helping her think of places where she can be a giver and contributor as well as a receiver. It can be more complex, as you may need to assist her. Your role as counselor may be crucial in helping make introductions and open doors of possibilities. Would you make a call, for example, to a pastor and say, "I know a woman with cerebral palsy who uses a chair and wants to sing in the choir. Can you help me?" Or might you say, "One of my counselees is Mary Smith. She has given me permission to call you. She loves to sing, loves music, but has never had the opportunity to express those interests and gifts. That has been partly impacted by her disability. Would it be possible for me to introduce you to her, or to your music director, and explore ways she could make a contribution?" The skill in community building is helping to discover the gift or interest, or, as some have said, the "third thing" around which a person can connect with others, and thus move the focus away from the disability to an area where all feel connected and empowered. (Schwartz, 1996) The parallel to the famous pastoral care maxim of "The place where one meets another in the presence of a Third" is perhaps glaringly obvious.

Third, while there is a growing literature on the skills and strategies of community building (Gaventa, 1998), one strategy that has come out of the world of education and developmental disabilities has a natural affinity to pastoral care and counseling. It is called by various names, but most commonly it is known as the development of a "circle of support" for a person with a disability. The circle of support can involve family, friends, community members, and service providers, and usually begins with "person-centered planning," a process that focuses on a person's gifts, dreams, relationships, and quality of life as much or more than his or her needs and limitations. The role of the circle is to tap into the skills and love of others, in an intentional yet non-overwhelming way, so that people can work together in any number of ways to assist access, participation, inclusion, and supports.

One of the first intentional circles of support was developed by Judith Snow, a woman with multiple physical and health-related disabilities, who was trapped in a system of services that did not offer the quality or vision of life she wanted. She called her circle the "Joshua Committee," an obvious reference to band of supporters who helped her through a wilderness and into a promised land (Pearpoint, 1992; Snow, 1996). One of the members of that circle was Fr. Patrick Mackan, a priest who worked with others to begin the use of circles with children with disabilities to help them be included in schools and community life. Some faith groups, such as the Mennonites, have developed useful circles of support models in congregations (Bartel, 1998).

One key premise of a circle of support is that it helps people break out of the embarrassment of asking for support and assistance, and, for others, wanting to help but not knowing how. A key role, as you might imagine, is the facilitator of the person-centered planning process and the circle of support. Knowledge of the strategies for establishing a circle of support and the option of serving as a facilitator are two skills that a pastoral counselor or minister could bring to a pastoral or counseling relationship with a person with a disability and their family. It is also a community-building strategy that a counselor could help initiate and then, in time, turn over to another facilitator.

As a final note in this exploration of pastoral roles of presence, guidance, advocacy, and community building with people with disabilities, a reader may in fact be saying that these roles and skills do not differ that much from what they already do when counseling others. The manifestations and strategies may differ, along with the words and helping languages, but these roles of pastoral care and counseling and the process of helping a person discover a welcoming and safe place where the counseling relationship can assist the person to find internal and community supports for his life is really no different. That is just the point. The other is that these roles and skills, developed in response to the unique needs and gifts of persons with disabilities, may be useful and helpful for many other people as well.

Transitions and Trends

As pastoral counselors and clergy grow in their capacity and experience to include people with disabilities in their practice and ministry, we will also grow in our awareness of some key transition points in the life journeys of people with disabilities and their families. As a pastoral counselor or clergyperson becomes known and trusted, he or she may become a pastoral or spiritual support that others in the "disability networks" turn to for counsel and guidance. Thus, it is important that counselors be aware of these key life transitions as well as the key trends emerging from the wider arena of services, advocacy, and supports.

Transitions: A Life-Cycle Perspective

Clergy and pastoral counselors are already familiar with the importance of pastoral care, counsel, faith, and ritual at key life-cycle transitions. Those may vary in different religious and cultural traditions, but presence, ritual, and tradition are crucial parts of the faith and life journey when navigating those transitions.

People with disabilities and their families may or may not have the opportunity, invitation, or welcome to use those traditions and rituals, just as they may or may not have a connection to pastoral care or guidance at key life-cycle transitions.

Birth/Diagnosis/Onset

The birth of a child is full of spiritual themes, ritual, and celebrations. The birth of a child with a disability is often a shock, disappointment, and, at minimum, an event that causes a radical adjustment of expectations and plans and introduces a huge influx of new questions and issues. Many stories and accounts by families and caregivers compare the process to a death and grieving process, or certainly to a radical readjustment by families and others. The same may be true for a young child whose impairment is not immediately apparent, but becomes obvious over time (for example, autism), resulting in a search to find out what's wrong and what can be done. Or, the crisis may be at the time of onset, the discovery of a chronic and disabling disease, the aftermath of an accident that causes spinal cord or brain injury, or a stroke that leads to paralysis.

The importance of the pastoral roles of presence, guidance, advocacy, and community building is perhaps evident, but too often they are not present. It may be because pastors do not know what or how to respond, or it may be that families and others do not know how to ask. It can also be that supports are available for the short term, but disappear over time, as a disability becomes more chronic and life changing.

The importance of pastoral care and counsel at these points is crucial, for there are many personal, family, spiritual, and theological issues involved. If the pastoral response is committed to being with a person and family on that journey, perceptive enough to know that disability does not mean one cannot have a great quality of life, and knowledgeable enough to connect individuals and families with sources of information and support, the role increases in power and impact. It can also involve the commitment to welcome a child into the religious community with the rituals appropriate to the faith tradition, the organizing of congregational supports for the long haul, and the promise to assist individuals and families to do what it takes to include them in the circle of pastoral and congregational care and support. It may also involve a pastoral modeling of the capacity to see the strengths and gifts of a child, young person, or adult at the points at which their families or significant others may be caught in their experience of loss and grief.

School and Education

In spite of huge changes in the public laws and supports in educational services for children with disabilities, families still often face real struggles in finding the appropriate educational services for a child with a disability, or end up feeling like they are fighting eternal battles to get the kinds of opportunities, services, and supports they want. As the difference or disability becomes more apparent or evident, in some cases there is a corresponding re-living of the sense of grief and crisis. As a parent once said to me, "I was fine until the Sunday School superintendent said, 'We are going to have to leave your child back.'"

When that happens in the context of religious and spiritual development, the result is both powerfully real and symbolic. Many children with disabilities have not been offered the opportunity to participate in rituals of transition and growth, such as confirmation or bar and bat mitzvahs. Intentional work by clergy and counselors in the religious community, with the resources and examples now present around the country and world, points to the enormous value of inclusion in religious education and the value of developmental rituals for their own sake and for the sake of keeping and enhancing relationships. Moreover, pastoral presence, sensitivity, counsel, and guidance can be a significant resource at the points of adolescence when sexual questions arise, along with typical teen struggles with self-esteem, belonging, and direction. Those issues are magnified and/or intensified by the presence of a disability.

From School to Work

For many young people and families with disabled members, in spite of issues with educational systems and services, the school process still provides a framework for supports that can disappear when the student "ages out" of the school system. There are growing numbers of young adults with disabilities who go on to college, but when that is not an option, the transition to the world of work and adulthood may often mean movement to a waiting list for adult services and supports and/or simply to nothing other than increased reliance on family caregivers.

Again, there are numbers of possible ways for clergy and pastoral counselors to be involved if they are sensitive to this transition. They could include vocational counseling, advocacy with adult services, using networks (in and out of congregations) to find job opportunities and supports, or assisting with planning and circles of support. It is a crucial time, and just as clergy assist young people in finding their own sense of call and the paths by which they can make their own ways in the world and find ways to make contributions, so can counselors assist young people with disabilities and their families.

This is also a time in which many young people are leaving home. If that does not happen, as is often the case for families with disabled members, then there may be a pastoral role for helping find ways for both the young person and the families to be apart as well as supporting the family as primary caregiver. If the person with a disability moves to independent living or to supported living in a group home or other program, it is huge time of transition, in which the disability may magnify issues involved in independence and letting go. It is also a time when many young people are forming lifelong partnerships in marriage. A young person with a disability may be faced with all kinds of barriers to his or her own relationships with persons of the opposite sex, and/or with the experience of seeing his siblings grow up, go to school, marry, and move out. Again, this is a transition time when the old coping skills and supports may not be present, and both individuals and families may feel like they are starting all over again.

What Happens After I'm (We're) Gone?

That is the crucial question faced by many families with disabled members. Who is going to care for my son or daughter, brother or sister, husband or wife, after my death, or after the point I can no longer do so? This is a transition point that raises all kinds of family dynamics and points to the importance of pastoral guidance in long-range planning with individuals and families. It can involve information and referral to appropriate resources, collaboration with other services and supports, mobilization of friends and congregation through tools like the circles of support, and issues of guardianship and care. If, as one would hope, the faith community is a trusted and stable support, there can be significant ways for pastoral support stepping in to say, "We will help watch and support" (Bartel, 1998).

A second pastoral role in this area is helping families and individuals deal with anticipatory grief as well as the experience of death or loss. If a person with a disability has been living at home with family all of his adult life, the death of a parent or parents can cause two radical adjustments—one in the loss of parent, the other in loss of place and home. People with cognitive disabilities such as mental retardation are also too frequently seen by families and caregivers as not able to deal with death or as capable to cope with grief (Luchterhand, 1998). Conversely, a key pastoral role may be ministering or counseling with families and caregivers when a person with a significant disability dies. The dynamic they may face is a community that interprets the death as insignificant, while the primary caregivers and support providers may be dealing with deep personal and vocational commitments to the person they loved. Or, when a disability is acquired in adulthood, the grief process may be experienced very differently. For example, a person with a traumatic brain injury may need to grieve for, but have difficulty articulating, the skills and abilities that have been lost as a result of the injury.

Trends

While the array of spiritual and pastoral issues arising from the "worlds of disability" is complex and varied, and one has to be very careful making any generalizations about "people with disabilities," there are some key trends that have been touched upon in this chapter but which need specific highlighting. They include:

1. The move away from seeing disability as a medical issue to one of diversity, citizenship, and community membership. With the Americans with Disabilities Act, many other laws, and a huge variety of service and advocacy supports, one can indeed talk about the disability movement as a civil rights movement. Pastorally and theologically, how can the discussions around minorities, diversity, gender, and difference be expanded to include people with disabilities?

2. With that civil rights movement comes the importance of empowerment, self-advocacy, and community contribution. People with physical, cognitive, sensory, emotional, learning, and psychiatric disabilities all have national networks and supports in which people are asking for more choice, enhanced citizenship, the power of self-determination and control over their own supports, and the opportunity to contribute to the community rather than simply be seen as objects of charity.

3. Technological advances, in both micro and macro ways, in electronics, computers, engineering, and architecture are making major advances in helping to "level the playing field" for people with disabilities, all the way from computers that work from the blink of an eye to wheelchairs to climb

stairs and terrain to concepts of universal design that make life more manageable for everyone, not just people with disabilities.

4. With those technological advances and successful strategies that demonstrate the capacity of people with disabilities and highlight the barriers of environment and attitude, there is increasing attention to questions of ethics and belief. Those are perhaps highlighted most explicitly in debates about abortion, right to life, and the ethical controversies around intensive supports or active euthanasia for infants with multiple disabilities, or in issues at the other end of life, exemplified by the protests in the United States of groups like Not Dead Yet against assisted suicide and euthanasia, because of the ways the quality of life of people with disabilities is so often determined by a lack of opportunities and supports and/or by the views of others, not the persons themselves.

5. Finally, to come full circle back to earlier discussions of the definition of disability in its interaction with the environment, there is growing awareness of the ways that some disabilities, particularly ones like "challenging behaviors," are a manifestation of restrictive environments and opportunity rather than disability unto themselves. This has particular implications for pastoral counselors and clergy who may be called upon to help deal with a person whose behavior is the real issue, not the impairment. In a system of services and supports that may too quickly push an individual to behaviorally adapt to the norms or use medications as a way to eliminate behaviors, the ability to listen and to hear the message in the behavior within the contexts of the life and community of the person involved is a key skill that pastoral counselors and clergy may bring to that situation. "Positive behavioral supports" is a body of literature and practice that is receiving growing attention, but one may note, involves new ways of applying ancient skills of listening, understanding, loving, and supporting in ways that help both the individual and his or her community to learn and grow (Lovett, 1996).

You Are Not Alone

The offer of presence, guidance, and community by a pastoral counselor to a person with a disability and his or her family is the therapeutic and spiritual foundation on which the helping relationship is built.

For clergy and pastoral counselors, the reverse is true. There are outside resources available, many of which can support you in your ministry and counseling with people with disabilities. There is no way to list them all without being immediately out of date, but, in this section, we will point to some sources you can contact or use for state-of-the-art information and resources.

Local

Check both with agencies that serve and support people with disabilities and their families, and/or with local chapters of advocacy and service organizations, such as the Arc, Easter Seals, United Cerebral Palsy. Your city or community may also have a Center for Independent Living, a cross-disability support and advocacy organization that is part of a national network of CILs. CILs often assist community organizations that need accessibility audits and plans for making buildings more accessible.

State and Publicly Funded

In local areas, there may be offices of statewide programs, such as vocational rehabilitation and services for people with developmental disabilities. Many advocacy organizations also have statewide organizations. In every state, there are four federally and state-funded organizations that cross disability areas to provide support to individuals, families, professionals, and communities. They are

1. Parent Training and Information Centers, many of which focus on educational issues, but many also that support chapters of the Parent to Parent network, a national network that connects parents to other parents who are dealing with similar kinds of disabilities. The national number is 888-248-0822. Web: *www.taalliance.org*
2. University Affiliated Programs, with different names, but which provide training, resources, information and referral, and technical assistance in a variety of areas. National AAUAP number is 301-588-8252. Web: *www.aauap.org*
3. Protection and Advocacy Offices, whose role is to support people with disabilities who are dealing with discrimination, violations of rights and due process, and other issues related to rights and laws.
4. Developmental Disability Councils, federally funded offices and programs whose advisory boards bring together representatives from disability organizations, parent groups, and state agencies to guide and develop state-focused projects in public education, advice, empowerment, and policy.

National

All of these programs have national offices and associations. There are also national advocacy and support networks for almost every type of disability. The Internet is a wonderful resource that has assisted any number of people to connect with each other and with sources of information. *Exceptional Parent* magazine also publishes an annual organizational resource directory listing many of these national and state based organizations (Phone: 877-372-7368; Web: *www.eparent.com*)

Pastoral Care and Counseling/Religious

There is a growing awareness of and interest in the role of spirituality, pastoral care, and congregational inclusion in many of the organizations. But for specific resources in pastoral care and counseling and congregational ministries, contact:

1. National offices of your faith group or the one of the person you are assisting. Many have specific offices related to resources and support for individuals, families, and congregations. Many of these offices in Christian denominations are connected through the National Council of Churches Committees on Disabilities and through Ministries with Persons Who Are Deaf.

2. National ecumenical and/or interfaith organizations focused on people with disabilities and their families. They include:

- The Religion Division of the AAMR
- National Catholic Office for Persons with Disabilities
- Christian Council for Persons with Disabilities
- Pathways to Promise (focus on mental illnesses)
- Religion and Disability Office, National Organization on Disability
- Jewish networks
- Rehab Chaplains Network

A Final Note

The goal of this chapter on pastoral counseling with people with disabilities has been to introduce the reader to an area of ministry and service that, under one label, is vast, diverse, at times complex, but also full of frequently unrecognized opportunities to assist people with disabilities and their families as well as untapped opportunities to learn from them and enable their gifts and graces to make a contribution to community and congregational life. People with disabilities and their families are as different and unique as we all are different and unique. Be careful with assumptions that come from labels, and, when in doubt, or even when you think you are certain, be willing to learn from the individual, family, or group with whom you are working. Your capacity to see strengths as well as needs, the accessibility and hospitality of your attitude and relationship, and your commitment to do what it takes to include and assist them in your ministry and service are all the foundation for a pastoral relationship that may do little about the impairment, but may do wonders for the person.

References

Bibliographic resources in this area of ministry and service have grown tremendously in the past decade. The Religion Division, AAMR publishes a quarterly newsletter that lists new resources, and, in collaboration with the Boggs Center on Developmental Disabilities, a resource guide with sections on all areas of ministry, religious services, and related resources for families, community building, and more (Gaventa, 1998). There is also a *Journal of Religion, Disability, and Health* published by Haworth Press.

Bartel, D. *Supportive Care in the Congregation* (rev. ed.) Elkhart, IN: Mennonite Developmental Disabilities Office, 1998.

Cohen, J. *Disability Etiquette: Tips on Interacting with People with Disabilities.* Jackson Heights, NY: Eastern Paralyzed Veterans Association, 1998 (1-800-444-0120).

Eisland, N. *Is God Disabled? Toward a Liberatory Theology of Disability.* Nashville: Abingdon Press, 1994.

Gaventa, W. "Religious Ministries and Services with Adults with Developmental Disabilities." In Summers, J. (ed.) *The Right to Grow Up: An Introduction to Adults with Developmental Disabilities.* Baltimore: Brookes Publishing Co., 1986.

————. "Pastoral Care with People with Disabilities and Their Families: An Adaptable Module for Introductory Courses." In *Thematic Conversations Regarding Disability within the Framework of Courses of Worship, Scripture, and Pastoral Care.* Dayton: National Council of Churches Committee on Disabilities, 1997.

————. *Dimensions of Faith and Congregational Supports for People with Developmental Disabilities and Their Families: A Resource Guide for Clergy, Laity, and Service Providers.* New Brunswick, NJ: The Boggs Center-UAP, 1998.

Lovett, H. *Learning to Listen: Positive Approaches and People with Difficult Behavior.* Baltimore: Brookes Publishing Co., 1996.

Luchterhand, C. *Helping Adults with Mental Retardation Grieve a Death Loss.* Philadelphia: Taylor and Francis. Synopsis also available in booklet, *Mental Retardation and Grief Following a Death Loss: Information for Families and Other Caregivers.* Washington, DC: Arc US, 1998.

Pearpoint, J. *From Behind the Piano: The Building of Judith Snow's Unique Circle of Friends.* Toronto: Inclusion Press, 1992.

Schwartz, D. *Who Cares? Rediscovering Community.* Denver: Perseus Westview Books, 1996.

Snow, Judith. *What's Really Worth Doing and How to Do It.* Toronto: Inclusion Press, 1996.

Thornburgh, G. *That All May Worship: An Interfaith Welcome to People with Disabilities.* Washington, DC: National Organization on Disability, 1997.

Gail Lynn Unterberger

8. Counseling Lesbians: A Feminist Perspective

A call comes into the pastoral counseling center. The caller, who describes herself as a white woman in her 40s, asks for a woman counselor to help her make an important decision. The secretary triages the intake to me. At the time of our meeting the client appears, having just come from the office, dressed in a business suit with a lace ruffled blouse, clasped by a cameo at the neck. During the first half of the counseling session, Lisa [not her real name] tells me that she works as a top manager, a job not without its stresses, but one in which she is comfortable and challenged The problem lies in her personal life. She has been dating a man for several months, and he has asked her to marry him. Her parents, with whom she has always lived, are encouraging her to accept the offer, as they don't want her to be "an old maid." Her three other siblings have long since moved out, gotten married, and had children. She has chosen to stay with her parents, she says, in order to take care of them as they age.

Upon further discussion she divulges the information that she is not attracted to her present "beau"; indeed, though she likes him as a friend, she is "revolted" by his physical advances. In her Christian belief system she feels it would be sinful for her to have premarital sexual relations with him, or anyone else for that matter. Pressed for further details she admits that she has never had any romantic feelings for men, but she has felt strong longings for women. In fact, she feels she may be in love with a woman who works in a neighboring office. They are good friends, lunching together regularly. But Lisa does not want to let her friend know her heart beats so fast whenever she is in her presence. Lisa relates this last with great apprehension, apparently worried about my response.

It turns out that she has been aware of these "longing, loving feelings for women," in which she yearns to be "close to the woman in every way," since she can remember. Yet she has been taught that such "queer" feelings are not only sick but also sinful. So she has tried to ignore them and channel them into relationships with men. For two years she regularly attended a *local Christian self-help group for lesbian and gay people who want to become heterosexual. She states that they and she have prayed "day and night" for Christ to change her feelings but, she says, apparently "Jesus has not seen fit to heal her of this disease, this evil part" of her. She wonders if she would get over this problem if she just married her current beau. She suggests she might be able to become cured if I, as an ordained minister, would continually pray for her and would remind her weekly that her homosexual longings are not only sick, but also sinful.*

Introduction

Homosexuality has been compared to a fishbone caught in the throat of Protestant, Roman Catholic and Jewish congregations—an obstruction that can neither be swallowed whole nor ejected and forgotten (Rashke 1976, p. 28; Nugent and Gramick 1989). From time to time various denominations attempt to update their formal statements in response not only to calls for civil rights and inclusivity raised by the gay liberation movement itself, but also to requests by religious homosexuals for equal opportunity to serve the church and synagogue in both lay and ordained positions. In the meanwhile pastoral care givers have had to find ways to respond with love and integrity to the pastoral concerns and theological questions presented to them by lesbian and gay constituents. Such pastoral counselors have had to minister to the families and friends of gays and lesbians, as well as to address the issues of concern brought by the increasing number of heterosexual church members who are moving into solidarity with the goals of the gay and lesbian movement.

There can be no doubt that religious institutions have played a powerful role in the oppression of lesbians to a greater or lesser extent throughout history. The religious community's acceptance of male homosexuality has paralleled variance within Western culture from New Testament times to the present (Boswell 1980). Even so, religion has given theological, biblical, and doctrinal arguments to undergird homosexuals' status as social pariahs, sexual deviants, loathsome, and the worst of all sinners in the eyes of God. And religion has depicted lesbians as more degraded, depraved, promiscuous, and damnable than heterosexual women.

While most denominational policy statements stop short of endorsing the denial of civil rights of homosexuals, they often do not grant full acceptance to them either, specifying for example that homosexual activity, if not the orientation itself, is incompatible with Christian teachings. Progress is being made toward greater acceptance. Scholars of religion, sociology, anthropology, and psychology representing a wide range of denominations are challenging the traditional church stances based on new understandings from the fields of psychiatry, biology, biblical exegesis, theology, and ethics. Several mainline denominations are currently in the process of reevaluating their statements. Yet with the exception of the Moravian Church, the Friends, the Unitarian Universalists Association, and the Metropolitan Community Churches, presently most Christian denominations refuse to ordain self-affirming (self-avowed), practicing (as opposed to celibate) homosexuals. However, the American rabbinate for Reform Judaism has recently voted to admit acknowledged, sexually active homosexuals into its ranks (Wall 1990, p. 1189). But the problem is not confined to the clerical side of the church. Many lesbian and gay church members report that they must hide their sexual orientation from fellow congregants for fear they would not be welcome in the congregations should the truth be known.

Defining Lesbian

While there is no single authoritative way of defining who is lesbian, care must be taken concerning the methodology of definition, since it is of utmost importance that lesbianism be a self-defined orientation. This is not because every lesbian knows and acknowledges, at once consciously and unconsciously, her sexual orientation. Indeed, many lesbians and bisexual women block out any same-sex romantic longings or sexual desires due to the terrible dread of acknowledging in themselves such feelings, which dominant society defines as loathsome. Lesbian history, like the history of many secondary-status groups, is not widely known (Vicinus 1989). Since self-identified lesbians often choose to "pass" for straight women, there are few well-known healthy role models for lesbians. Lesbians as portrayed by the dominant literature, media, culture, and narratives are usually not sympathetic personalities but are stereotypically depicted as unattractive, butch, bull-dykes, man-haters, "witches," and more.

In fact, lesbians are single, married, happy, sad, angry, complacent, well-adjusted, and maladjusted. They dress in stereotypically feminine as well as stereotypically masculine clothes along with any mix of the two, and they have an equally diverse sets of mannerisms. They are in every walk of life, every culture, every society, and they pursue all careers open to women. As adults, lesbians look back and recognize they were "different" from other girls, at least insofar as they expressed their assumption that they would be economically self-sufficient as adults and to varying degrees rejected stereotypical female roles (Saghir and Robins 1973). Lesbians are teenagers, young adults, middle-aged women, and elderly. They comprise about 10 percent of all women, and they sit in the church pew, preach from the pulpit, say prayers on the Sabbath, and hold responsible offices in all levels of ecclesiastical hierarchy. Most of all they are in various stages of acknowledging their lesbianism, that is, of being "out of the closet" within ever-widening circles of their immediate relationships and the larger society.

Often lesbians distinguish themselves from bisexual women, who are able to entertain the possibility of having a sexual/romantic/emotional relationship with a male as well as a female. To be labeled bisexual is safer in heterosexual society, though in the lesbian community a bisexual woman is often either despised as one who implicitly denies her exclusive lesbianism or is tolerated as a lesbian who is simply on the journey to realizing exclusive lesbianism. She may be viewed as even more of a traitor to the lesbian community than straight women by certain lesbian communities. A bisexual woman, following the Kinsey continuum model, might see herself as positioned more or less in the middle of a continuum of human possibilities of attraction and sexual involvement. At one end of the continuum are persons who are attracted to and sexually involved with same-sex partners exclusively. The other end of the continuum includes those whose exclusive attraction and sexual involvement is with partners of the other sex (Scanzoni 1978, pp. 74).

There are numerous definitions of lesbianism, the least complex being a woman who "has taken a woman lover" (Grahan 1978, p. 67). This definition is based predominantly on sexual-genital contact, which does not address the situation of the pre–sexually active or celibate female, nor does it exclude bisexuals or the straight woman who has previously experimented with a lesbian relationship. Alternatively, problems arise if the definition of lesbianism is made on the basis of emotional, mental, or spiritual attraction, since that might then define as lesbians all women who have a fleeting sexual fantasy or an idle sexual thought about a possible sexual affair with another woman. All definitions are problematic in that even the act of labeling can bring up the very real fear of individual harassments or "witch hunts." However, for the purposes of discussion a five-part model, taken from a feminist theological perspective, may offer the most holistic understanding for pastoral counseling purposes. Certainly a definition of lesbianism must eschew traditional patriarchal constructs as well as simplistic, reductionistic approaches of the social sciences.

Mary Hunt (1989) considers these five elements essential:

1. Context: Paradoxically, labeling becomes important in a society which calls lesbians "outsiders, outlaws and even outcasts" (p. 106). In my experience self-avowed lesbians may be in a position to claim their orientation with pride or may need to conceal it for political and professional reasons even though they personally are comfortable and at-home with their own self-understanding. All of this depends on the dangers involved in the individualized coming-out process. In the counseling setting the counselor should establish a trusting, confidential relationship in which a woman will feel safe to explore and/or discuss her own process of self-identification without fear of judgment.

2. *Eros:* This is an essential dimension of being a lesbian. "Fantasy, touch, dreams and attractions all aimed at women are part of what it means to love women in a context which tells us not to" (p. 106).

3. *Community:* Especially since the beginning of the gay rights movement, the lesbian community is being established and defined. The particulars of overlapping communities may be defined by geographical proximity, professional group, local church, denomination or faith group, or the more widely dispersed group that acts as the community to whom lesbians "are held accountable for our behavior, including sexual conduct, fidelity to friends, use of resources, etc." (p. 107).

4. *Sexual experience:* Widely interpreted as ranging from casual sexual feelings to genital sexual activity these are "active, creative dimensions of sexual expression in the context of female-female relationships, as well as the healthy orientation or openness toward such experiences in a culture which considers them taboo" (p. 107).

5. *Spirituality:* Difficult to define, but essential to a holistic pastoral counseling definition, lesbian spiritualities are just now being articulated in the theological literature, though the sources have long been found in women's literature, music, poetry, and so on. While there is not one monolithic spirituality to be delineated, feminist lesbian spirituality includes a "celebration of relationships and the goodness of our woman love...which can involve commitment or covenant ceremonies for long term relationship compasses our efforts to honor and recall the lives of our foresisters" (p. 107).

Etiology of Lesbianism

During the last century theories about homosexuality have abounded though only recently have lesbians been addressed as a population apart from gay males. While the debate continues, the current consensus is that we do not understand definitively how it is that one person is homosexual and another heterosexual; there is no single correct explanation. Scientific researchers and political advocates have argued from both sides of a rather dualistic line with social constructionists on the one side and essentialists on the other. The former prefer to focus on lesbian *desires and acts,* since the expression of these change over time and across cultures. The latter discuss lesbianism in terms of *identity,* as a human sexual orientation, probably present at birth. The homosexual rights movement of the 1970s embraced essentialism.

Guy Menard notes how "scientific" approaches to homosexuality dating from the end of the nineteenth century "featured the development of a new frame of reference which first saw homosexuality transferred from the category of 'sin' to that of one type of 'sickness' or 'disorder' or another, until one other variant appeared among the rest, a possible and legitimate one: homosexuality as a 'sexual orientation'" (Menard 1989, p. 128). Laura Reiter (1989) differentiates between sexual orientation, which is determined in the childhood years, and sexual identity as it changes over time. She discusses how identity may or may not be congruent with orientation and how these affect self-labeling. Other researchers debate the functions of repression and denial and their role in subsequent self-labeling.

In any case *homosexuality* is actually a fairly new Western word connoting a new construct in terms of lifestyle, the discussions and studies of which have been dominated by male experience. Only very recently have lesbians become engaged in delineating the parameters of the discussion and naming the issues. Therefore it may be too early to determine whether arguments from social constructionist and essentialist theories elucidate or obscure lesbianism, or even whether they matter at all. But for many religious constituents, the matter of causality is paramount in terms of dictating the appropriate ethical response. For example, some well-meaning Christians breathlessly await definitive scientific evidence that would prove homosexuality to be a matter of genetics or prenatal hormones so they could then categorize the condition as a kind of chronic and immutable "disability" rather than a sinful predilection over which one has choice or a perverted illness that can be cured by psychotherapy or even (barring miracles) prayer. Alternatively, the Quakers have long since described homosexuality as no more inherently sinful or diseased than left-handedness, which occurs about as often in the population. Still, misinformation, myth, and a cloak of silence dominate in religious circles, with long-standing psychoanalytic viewpoints preferred over essentialist theories. In the meanwhile some Christians settle the issues with the well-known cliche, "love the sinner but not the sin," which sentences lesbians to lifelong celibacy in order for them to achieve acceptance. Otherwise intelligent and informed persons have been heard to espouse the idea that one can "catch" lesbianism from a teacher, parent, or mentor, though it is clear that most lesbians grew up in a heterosexual environment (Corley 1990, p. 4).

In summary, given the state of knowledge of psychology, therapists cannot look definitively to the woman's past or dwell on the intrapsychic structure to fix the "blame" for the woman's sexual orientation. Most lesbians are not interested in blaming anyone, and religious lesbians often are heard to proclaim, "If you have a problem with it, take it up with my Maker." However, it is crucial to note that in a hostile and predominantly heterosexual world, lesbians' feelings of anger, rejection, and hurt can exacerbate whatever situational, emotional, or developmental crises arise during the life cycle.

Pastoral Counselors: Caught in the Middle

Illness or Variation

Pastoral counselors, more than "secular" therapists, are often caught in the middle between the predominant assessments of the psychological sciences and the prevailing opinion of their religious group affiliations. For example, certain church groups, while they may not characterize homosexuals as sinful, resort to the label of "psychologically disturbed." This commonly occurs despite the fact that in 1974 the American Psychiatric Association removed homosexuality from the index of psychological pathology on the basis that most psychiatrists no longer considered homosexuality in and of itself a pathological adaptation. The American Psychological Association took similar action the following year. Or religious officials or concerned lay people may recommend that a lesbian seek counseling, though studies have shown that no psychotherapy has been successful across the board in transforming a person's exclusive sexual orientation to the opposite one on the continuum. While behavior change may result, usually only for a short period, a lesbian's deepest longings and passions remain with same-sex individuals. As Reiter notes in the post-1973, literature it has been shown how the so-called cures really were "instances of the suppression of homosexual behavior in bisexual people" whose behavioral changes "usually were not accompanied by a fundamental shift in underlying erotic preference" (Reiter 1989, p. 144).

The clinical pastoral education movement was influential in helping many clergy move from the earlier medical model to the essentialist model through exposure to increasing scientific evidence. Nugent and Gramick (1989) note:

> CPE was a more professional attempt to equip pastoral ministers with better skills to undertake direct helping relationships in a variety of human problems and situations. One of these areas was the reality of homosexual people encountered by clergy in every denomination and religious group....Whether individual clergy personally undertook the counseling of homosexual clients or made referrals to other professionals, they soon acknowledged the apparent fixity of a genuine homosexual orientation and identity in certain individuals. Seeing that even

intense and prolonged psychotherapy would not alter a true homosexual orientation, many were faced with the personal decision of having to adopt a kind of prophetic stance in their churches about homosexuality or else to remain silent (p. 13).

Sin or Part of Rich Diversity of Creation

Pastoral counselors are also caught in the middle of the theological debates between official church statements and contemporary scholarship. For example, faith groups may make certain declarations about the inherent sinfulness concerning either the nature (identity, orientation) or the sexual practice (acts) of lesbians, usually determining to what extent they can be barred from baptism, church membership, lay office, or ordination. Professional specialists in pastoral counseling have often taken extra courses or workshops on human sexuality, sexual ethics, and biblical exegesis, educating themselves concerning current scholarly debate and becoming informed as to the complex issues involved as opposed to making sweeping statements about sin or broad ethical judgments concerning homosexuality.

In particular, having undertaken studies in these areas of theology and sexuality, pastoral counselors often find themselves in diametric opposition with the prevailing denominational authorities, who have not become similarly informed. In other words, a counselor may be moving in the direction of greater acceptance of lesbians as persons with a minority sexual orientation. Indeed, one study (Hochstein 1986, p. 162) of a sample of pastoral counselors in the American Association of Pastoral Counselors showed that around 70 percent scored in the non-homophobic (high or low grade) range on the Hudson and Ricketts' *Index of Attitudes toward Homosexuals* (IAH). Such counselors may have integrated one of the liberation theologies, such as feminist, womanist Latin American, or Asian, as a basis for theological understanding of the praxis involved in the liberation of minorities. Or perhaps the counselor has utilized the specific literature on lesbian and gay spirituality emerging presently. In so doing the counselors find themselves faithful to their theology of liberation but at odds with the doctrinal or official faith statements of their governing religious authorities. Like the Roman Catholic priest who is asked by his parishioners in premarital counseling sessions about the ethical and practical issues of using birth control, pastoral counselors often answer with another question: "Do you want to know what the church thinks or do you want to know what I think?"

This latter possibility—categorizing oneself simplistically in opposition with the formal statements of one's own faith group—does not offer a quick and easy out for pastoral counselors. This is due to the fact that such a position lacks integrity unless it is also clear that the counselor is teaching, working, and/or writing to make changes in the religious institutional structures. An activist stance gives evidence that counselors are in solidarity with the aims of religious lesbians, because in so doing, pastoral counselors expose themselves, albeit only in small part, to the very dangers that the lesbian confronts every day of her life on a much grander scale. In turn, this deepens counselor empathy for lesbians.

In most ecclesiastical and theological communities it is ostensibly no longer tolerable to express racist views. It is also increasingly less fashionable to exhibit sexist beliefs and behaviors (despite political retrenchment on both fronts). Yet homophobia and heterosexism are rarely discussed, confronted, or confessed in the pulpit or Sunday School. The liberal churches have failed utterly to take heterosexism seriously, and therefore have failed to do justice to women's lives "whether lesbian, heterosexual, bisexual, genitally active, genitally inactive, or celibate" (Heyward 1987, p. 37).

This makes counseling for liberation that goes on behind the closed doors of the pastor's office even more estranged from the life of the church when it comes to issues of homosexuality and heterosexism. The topic is silenced and lesbians remain invisible. Time and time again when I was serving as a parish minister, parishioners would tell me there were no gays in our congregation, that it was not an issue for our local church. Pastoral counselors are caught in the middle when we choose to counsel ethically and effectively while remaining silent on the subject in the pulpit; when we join in the quiet consensus on the part of many specialized ministers while not opposing those who proclaim that lesbianism is a threat to family values or against natural law.

Finally, there is a certain amount of fear within some denominational circles that if one's personal viewpoint as a clergyperson were known to be "gay affirming," ecclesiastical endorsement could be jeopardized. This leads to rampant paranoia on seminary campuses on the part of gay and lesbian ministerial candidates and prospective religious educators. But it is also a fear for straight people who are sympathetic to the cause of religious gay and lesbian movement.

"Neutral" Silence or Prophetic Endangerment

This dilemma is even more exacerbated for well-known pastoral counselors than for other scholars of religion. Certainly a number of systematic theologians, biblical scholars, and ethicists have been "silenced," threatened, or ostracized by religious constituents or authorities because they have made public through their writings, lectures, or preaching their call for greater acceptance of gays and lesbians by religious groups. But it is a very real danger for pastoral counselors to speak out on this as a justice issue since their tenure and ordinations are more firmly linked to their clinical practice and academic careers. For example, pastoral counselors certified by the American Association of Pastoral Counselors must be endorsed by their own faith groups. Their accreditation, hence their clinical pastoral ministry, is threatened should their ordination or endorsement status be revoked by their faith group, for whatever reason.[1]

Key to Effective Pastoral Counseling: Conscientization Through an Integration of Psychology and Religion

Given the previous understandings, certain assumptions follow concerning effective pastoral counseling of women minorities in general and lesbians in particular.

1. *Effective pastoral counseling of lesbians mandates counselor genuineness.*

Counseling is not a value-free enterprise. Every school of therapy prescribes empathy and genuineness as important counselor attributes. Competent counseling requires that one be able to relate empathically and exhibit genuineness since these, along with respect for the client, are at least the necessary if not sufficient conditions for establishing therapeutic alliance leading to client change (Rogers 1961). As Kohut wrote: "Empathy, the accepting, confirming, and understanding human echo evoked by the self, is a psychological nutrient without which human life, as we know and cherish it, could not be sustained" (Kohut 1978, p. 705). Basic helping manuals, such as Carkhuff (1987) and Egan (1990), stress the ability to respond empathically. But empathy, along with unconditional positive regard, must be genuine.

> Homophobic therapists can't help homosexuals. It's ridiculous to imagine entering into the spirit of a gay person and truly understanding their experience from the inside if you are uncomfortable with or revulsed by homosexuality....If therapists do not, in fact, feel or think that homosexuality "just is," that it is neither bad nor good, healthy nor sick, but is simply a part of the cosmos, they will never be able to love gay patients (*all* of them) and help them grow (Fortunato 1982, p. 118).

It may be unreasonable to expect pastors and other pastoral counselors totally to have eradicated their personal homophobia before they can effectively counsel lesbians. However, it seems crucial that they be genuinely moving in the direction of more and more open-mindedness, confronting and transforming homophobic and heterosexist attitudes in themselves as a process of their personal spiritual and political journey.

Rigid, anti-gay viewpoints *will eventually* come through in the counseling process, just as misogynist or racist attitudes do. If one has not become sufficiently educated and conscientized to the psychological and religious implications in terms of justice for homosexual persons, then the viable ethical response is to refer lesbian parishioners or clients to a counselor who has. Comparisons can be made to the military chaplain who believes strongly that Jesus is the *only* way to salvation, not simply as a confessional statement for herself but as a universal truth applying to everyone. There are definite limits to how effective such a chaplain would be in counseling Jews or others in an interfaith context.

Self-knowledge is the starting point for the process of conscientization. As Egan writes, "Like everyone else, helpers are tempted to pigeonhole clients because of gender, race, sexual orientation, nationality, social status, religious persuasion, political preferences, lifestyle and the like....The importance of self-knowledge...includes ferreting out the biases and prejudices that distort our listening" (Egan 1990, p. 118).

2. *Effective counseling with lesbians mandates adequate cross-cultural counseling skills.*

Counseling with minorities, including sexual minorities, is often a cross-cultural issue. Fortunately more and more pastoral care curricula are beginning to acquaint theological students with the basic skills of cross-cultural counseling in general and pastoral counseling across cultures specifically (Augsberger 1986). One need not be homosexual oneself to work successfully with lesbian parishioners or clients (Hall 1985). Rather, effective counseling not only involves capacity for empathic response but also involves affirming certain values important to cross-cultural counseling theory. It concerns cultural sensitivity, understanding, and skills competency. In this case understanding of gay and lesbian differences is important. For example, while gay males sometimes choose to work with lesbian therapists, the reverse is seldom the case. This may be because there are more cultural and psychological affinities among women, straight or gay, than there are between lesbians and gay men, though the latter certainly share the experience of heterosexist and homophobic discrimination.

3. *Effective pastoral counseling with lesbians requires utilizing the wider lenses of family systems and cultural analysis.*

Utilizing a family systems lens for understanding lesbians and their problems is critical, especially to determine to what extent problems and pain are exacerbated by societal stigma—the process by which certain groups, such as racial minorities, physically challenged people, and lesbians are considered unworthy or discredited. The problem worsens for lesbians to the extent that people view lesbianism as a moral failing. Still, to be "gay affirming" is similar to being feminist; that is, the women's liberation movement showed that the universal problem for women was not women but the problem of sexism and misogyny. Similarly, the civil rights movement brought to consciousness that the problem for African Americans was not their blackness but the surrounding climate of racial prejudice and bigotry. So also the "problem" for lesbians is dominant culture's homophobia and heterosexism.

Homophobia can be described as the dislike, hatred or fear of gay men and lesbians, as well as discrimination against lesbians and gay men (*Bulletin* 1983, p. 1). Heterosexism is a predominant universal assumption that everyone's experience is heterosexuality. It also means a lack of support for any relationship that is not heterosexual. The practical problems include what Roth calls "direct invasion of the lesbian couple boundary by the heterosexual surround" which takes form in various ways:

> ...as not including the partner as a relative at holidays and other major family-of-origin events, giving the partners separate rooms during visits to families of origin, depriving one partner of access to the other and/or of decision-making power in time of serious illness, and depriving the partners of legal protection in mutual ownership of property and in survivorship unless they take special action (Roth 1989, p. 290).

This climate makes it very difficult to affirm one's own experiences either as a single person or as a lesbian in a relationship, especially since whatever sensitization goes on around the subjects of homophobia or heterosexism are targeted at adult population and rarely involve children's literature and education. Few children learn about how prejudice functions with regard to homophobia and heterosexism. Some journals, such as *Open Hands,* help parents learn how to raise or educate children concerning homophobia, but it is difficult when the rest of the society, including the schools, do not participate in such liberating efforts. One has to constantly reteach emancipatory attitudes. Perhaps a personal story will illustrate:

> In raising my son, age 8, and daughter, age 6, to guard against prejudice in all of its forms, I endeavored to acquaint them early with the fact that some people happen to be able to fall in love with people of their own gender, while more people happen to be able to fall in love with people of the opposite gender. They

seemed both clear and comfortable about this. One day we were invited to a Holy Union, a celebration of commitment between two lesbians at a local Metropolitan Community Church. Once again I reminded the children about sexual orientations and told them all I knew about the particulars of an MCC liturgy. My son, who gets very excited about going to any kind of celebration, was playing at a neighbor's house on the afternoon before the service. When his dad picked him up, he said enthusiastically, "I have to get going, we're going to a lesbian wedding tonight." "That ought to be interesting," said the friend's dad. My husband came home and remarked that he guessed he might not be asked to be den leader of the Cub Scouts any more.

Later that evening at the service my daughter expressed dismay that the two participants weren't dressed in the traditional bridal regalia. I assured her that they could have worn such gowns, but perhaps they chose sparkling New Year's dresses because of the season. She seemed satisfied. My son, having been told about eucharist MCC style participated with an open attitude, receiving communion as a family at the altar and sharing embraces and kisses with the pastor. But after partaking of the wafer and cup, when we returned to our pew, he stated loudly, "Now *that* was weird." Alarmed, I shushed him up quickly, whispering, "What was so weird?" His reply was, "Why was it with those little crackers anyway? Don't they serve bread in this place?"

Sexism, which also is not sufficiently addressed in our educational systems, plays a major part in homophobia.

Sexism lays the ground work for homophobia. As women we are assumed to be asexual if we are not involved with men. Women are not seen as having an independent, aggressive sexuality of their own" (Loulan 1984, p. 10).

Once certain women are viewed as lesbian by the larger culture, they are seen as purely sexual beings, defined only by their genital contact with other women. This makes it difficult for some women to identify themselves as lesbians if they are celibate, infrequently sexual, or "primarily companionate." Therefore internalized homophobia makes a lesbian doubt her own reality.

Homophobia and heterosexism, rampant in Western culture across racial, ethnic, and class boundaries, are perpetrated through socialization and cemented through institutionalization. This socialization is so powerful that it affects not only heterosexuals but lesbians as well. Just as women hold sexist and misogynist viewpoints "deep down" and racial minorities participate in their own oppression, so too lesbians internalize homophobia and heterosexism, effectively participating in their own self-hatred.

> Before any kind of feminist movement existed, or could exist, lesbians existed: women who loved women, who refused to comply with behavior demanded of women, who refused to define themselves in relation to men. Those women, our foresisters, millions whose names we do not know, were tortured and burned as witches, slandered in religious and later in "scientific" tracts, portrayed in art and literature as bizarre, amoral, destructive, decadent women. For a long time, the lesbian has been a personification of feminine evil....
>
> ...Lesbians have been forced to live between two cultures, both male-dominated, each of which has denied and endangered our existence....Heterosexual, patriarchal culture has driven lesbians into secrecy and guilt, often to self-hatred and suicide (Rich 1979, p. 225).

Theorists, theologians, and spokespersons differ about whether heterosexism is a subset for sexism or whether it is a analytic construct in its own right. For lesbians and for pastoral counselors it hardly matters; the oppression is compounded in either case. Through a systems viewpoint the cultural problem of exclusivist, intolerant heterosexual attitudes becomes evident. Such attitudes have become institutionalized in societal and ecclesiastical tenets and structures. They also become internalized, through social learning, in both heterosexuals and homosexuals.

   4. *Effective counseling of lesbians requires appreciation for the ways in which a variety of oppressions affect lesbians.*
   Many lesbians experience further discrimination by virtue of their color, ethnic and religious background, physical disabilities, or primary language. Lesbians of color, for example, may experience sexism and racism in their work area, only to return home to their parents and experience their family's and culture's rejection of them for their sexual orientation. Barbara Cameron (1983), a Native American, notes:

> It is of particular importance to us as third world gay people to begin a serious interchange of sharing and educating ourselves about each other. We not only must struggle with the racism and homophobia of straight white America, but must often

struggle with the homophobia that exists within our third world communities (p. 50).

Teenagers, in particular, may find there is no place that feels like "home" to them. These feelings, so acute during adolescence, never truly end, though they may lessen as adults come to self-identity and are able to claim it. As Latina Cherrie Moraga (1983) writes:

> When I finally lifted the lid to my lesbianism, a profound connection with my mother reawakened in. me. It wasn't until I acknowledged and confronted my own lesbianism in the flesh, that my heartfelt identification with and empathy for my mother's oppression—due to being poor, uneducated, and Chicana—was realized. My lesbianism is the avenue through which I learned the most about silence and oppression, and it continues to be the most tactile reminder to me that we are not free human beings.
>
> You see, one follows the other. I had known for years that I was a lesbian, had felt it in my bones, had ached with the knowledge, gone crazed with the knowledge, wallowed in the silence of it. Silence *is* like starvation. Don't be fooled. It's nothing short of that, and felt most sharply when one has had a full belly most of her life (pp. 28–29).

Like a multi-stranded cable, structures of oppression—patriarchy, racism, sexism, classism, misogyny, and heterosexual imperialism—are intertwined and interconnected under conditions of patriarchy which the church sanctions through its patriarchal structures and tenets. just as feminism could not sustain its movement for liberation of women without directly facing its heterosexism, the church cannot truly be a liberation force against sexism without also facing its homophobia and heterosexism.

5. *Effective pastoral counseling of lesbians must utilize a situation ethic of mutuality, reciprocity, and caring as moral evaluators for lesbian relationships.*
Utilizing the "full acceptance" theological position, being a lesbian and acting on one's lesbian identity is no more inherently sinful than being a heterosexual and acting out of one's heterosexual identity. The counselor cannot substitute moral absolutes for moral complexities. The standard for what is holy, wholesome, healthy, good, is not simply whether partners are same or differently gendered.

A more complex criterion on which to base ethical and moral discernment about sexual behavior is the extent to which any relational activity is life-enhancing. Sexual behavior should enhance and fulfill human beings rather than inhibit, damage, or destroy them. Any sexual activity that is selfish in expression, cruel, impersonal, or obsessive is unhealthy. Therefore effective ethical criteria may be concerned with the degrees by which any relationship is characterized by caring and concern, tenderness, mutuality, trust, and respect toward each other. Other values center around nonoppressive, non-coercive, non-hierarchical, consenting, loving adult acts expressed through shared commitment.

6. *Effective pastoral counseling is not the same as secular psychotherapy with lesbians.*

Pastoral counseling must not simply defer to secular psychotherapeutic and sociological research and formulations over against theological stance. The distinguishing marks of pastoral counseling are not limited to the fact that it is concerned with a holistic view of the person, although often lesbians come to pastoral counselors because they mistrust secular counselors.

> Jane, 43 years old, sought out a pastoral counselor because she had become terribly frustrated with her former therapist, who happened to be a psychologist. He did not take her seriously, she said, when she discussed the depth of her commitment to her personal spiritual journey. He seemed cavalier about her wish to integrate a "new" sense of morality into her relationships with women partners. She was searching for a way of living her life openly and with integrity. Her identity as a Christian woman was very important to her, and she wished her counselor would take it seriously as well.

In our culture, religion and spirituality have much to do with individual functioning, and the making of values of meaning throughout the lifespan. With confusing values all around, clients seek counselors who will take seriously their sense of spiritual depth, their hunger for meaning, and their sincere desires to make moral choices within the fullness of God's creation and blessings. In counseling lesbians, fortunately, we are not left only with the God of liberal theology, who is all too often imaged by lesbians as indifferent to them and their sexual orientation at best. That theology is not to be deemed completely negative; after all, it is based on the very same liberal theology, at least in part, on which pastoral counselors have centered their stance of quiet affirmation. Nevertheless, we may now move ahead because specific theologies, which are gay-affirming, articulated by gay and lesbian theologians, activists, clients, and other writers, are now becoming more available. Keeping theology and spirituality central to our perspective, we also have had for some time the resources emerging from the liberation theologies in general. These are widely accessible and are foundational to inform our work with parishioners and clients so they can make spirituality a central part of their healing journey as well, a journey which involves affirming rather than fighting their consonant experiences of identity.

Lesbian Psychology

With a few exceptions lesbians bring to counseling the same issues straight women bring. Such problems, however, may be more or less compounded by their sexual orientation, the social stigma of being lesbian, social ostracism, downright hatred and violence against them. As Gordon Allport (1954) noted, victims of prejudice may express certain symptoms related to their status as persecuted groups. Struzzo (1989) lists these briefly as

> ...excessive concern and preoccupation with minority or deviant group membership; feelings of insecurity; withdrawal; passivity; neuroticism, strong in-group ties coupled with prejudice against out-groups; slyness and cunning; acting out self-fulfilling prophecies about one's inferiority; secrecy; and self-hatred (p. 198).

Anthony (1981–1982) mentioned among special areas of concern for lesbians the following: 1) establishing and maintaining lover relationships; 2) alcoholism; 3) certain life-cycle issues of lesbian adolescents and older lesbians; 4) bereavement; 5) unique issues related to parenting; and 6) problems of being a woman who is not associated with a male. This last should not be seen as simply an issue of living as a "single person." It has to do with major issues of what it means not to have access to males' money. Heterosexual privilege usually means greater status for women who "marry up." Often the poorest of the poor are lesbian couples who may bring in less total money because there is no male wage earner.

Several other factors interlaced with issues of oppression make it difficult for lesbians to form congruent and healthy self-identities.

Invisible History

As mentioned before, little has been written about lesbian history, and that which has is not widely disseminated as yet through the population. In part, the problem has been that early theorists disagreed about whether a biological background assumed its "naturalness" or whether homosexuality was an "acquired" condition. This confusion, according to Carole Vance (1989), meant that before 1960 medicine, biology, psychology, and sexology created "a new frame of reference, converting same-sex behaviours into biologically or psychologically based dispositions and subsuming all sexual arrangements between members of the same sex under them" (p. 7). In addition such writings focused solely on the studies about men. Further, as Vicinus (1989) points out, histories that have been recorded have not necessarily been done by trained and practicing historians. She traces a history of how sexual identity came to be the overarching issue for modern Euro-American lesbians over the past three hundred years. The historical suppression of female sexuality is at the heart of any process of tracing lesbian history.

For lesbians in counseling the lack of lesbian history and the invisibility of lesbians has meant not only a dearth of self-affirming role models, heroes, and mentors, but also the lack of knowledge that such a lifestyle even exists. A 56-year-old grandmother, when asked why she had just come out as a lesbian, responded, "I simply did not know there was any other way to live than heterosexual. I knew I was pretty miserable, but I just accepted that as part of the way things had to be" (Lewis 1979, in Groves, p. 17).

Trouble with the Church of Their Childhood

Heyward notes that liberal churches have "always displayed some measure of tolerance toward those women and those homosexual people whose *public* presence has been strictly in conformity with patriarchal social relations" (Heyward 1987, p. 37). This is, in part, due to liberal religions making false dualisms of being and act, of person and eros, the body and soul. The problem comes about for the ecclesiastical organizations when lesbians no longer pass as straight women, when they begin to break the silence about their own orientation and the church's sexism and heterosexism.

We cannot minimize or discount the experiences of prejudice, oppression, and discrimination lesbians feel by categorizing sexual orientation as a compartment of human experiencing. Gay people often hear (especially from well-meaning, kind-hearted "liberal" religious people), "What you do in your own bedroom between mutually consenting adults is of no concern to me and no business to anyone else." Usually such a statement is followed by the admonition stated aloud or added implicitly, "Besides, we don't *want* to know." This reduces lesbians to sexual objects. Lesbianism is more than sexual activity, and as feminism has so long admonished, the personal is political. Sexual orientation is experienced as a lifestyle that is all-encompassing whether a person is gay, straight, or bisexual. Compartmentalizing is problematic with regard to sexuality. This is why it is so incomprehensible for lesbians to understand good-hearted church people who say, "I don't condemn you, I just condemn your sexual activity." This obvious variation of "love the sinner but hate the sin" becomes unbearable for most lesbians, who consider their sexual orientation to be as much a part of their constitution as their femaleness or the color of their skin.

The church has not been healthy place for lesbians. But many lesbians have been raised in the church, and while many have left the religion of their childhood and youth, it is hard to leave religion completely behind. This is especially true since biblical standards permeate Western society, and Jewish and Christian belief systems undergird much of our cultural symbols, rituals, and mindset. Most lesbians who have stayed in the congregation remain in the closet. Sometimes the very last place a woman will come out is to her church or synagogue.

When a lesbian comes to her pastor, it may be at the very beginning of a process of coming out to the church. Education in terms of the wide range of theological viewpoints on the subject of homosexuality may be an important aspect of her emancipation from parochial religious views. She can be alerted to the writings of biblical scholars, ethicists, and theologians whose works have helped lead individuals and church groups through the complex issues of Bible, traditions, human knowledge, and human experience to an affirmative stance on homosexuality from one of the traditional faith positions.[2]

Multiple Oppression

Excluding issues of heterosexual relationships, lesbians have all the same issues other women do, only more so, because their lifestyle is not appropriated by society. Lesbians have more in common with straight and bisexual women because of issues of common womanhood than they have with gay men (though there are some important affinities such as the fact that gay men and lesbians experience heterosexism and homophobia in all their contextualized and varied forms). But Gloria Anzaldua, one of the editors of *This Bridge Called My Back*, reports that while white lesbians are invisible, the lesbian of color is considered nonexistent. "Our speech, too, is inaudible. We speak in tongues like the outcast and the insane" (Moraga and Anzaldua, p. 165).[3]

Desire to Conform

Lesbians tell of desperately wanting to please their parents and to fit into "normal" society. Even though they may have been aware since early childhood of their sexual preference, they try to fit in with heterosexual teens, dating and having sex with young men. They may deliberately or inadvertently marry and bear children, sometimes in part to prove to themselves and others that they are no different from other women. It is only later that they come to the full realization of their primary orientation toward attraction to women.

Problems with Self-Esteem

Furthermore, as Miller (1986) has noted, self-esteem for women is largely defined by their relationships, particularly familial ones, whereas men tend to relate their self-esteem to their work (p. 103). If society defines a woman's primary emotional and romantic attachment with another woman as tabu it is hard for a lesbian to feel good about herself. If her true self is unacceptable to herself and others, and the false self is at odds with her authentic feelings and understanding of her own reality, self-hatred occurs. In addition, depending upon her family of origin's degree of homophobia, she may have a strained relationship with her primary affiliations from childhood and youth. Disownment and rejection may occur. If that is compounded with a work place where lesbians are ignored, feared, or have to live in the dread of being found out, healthy self-esteem may be a difficult, seemingly impossible, achievement. The path to self-esteem may be the arduous and costly process of living more and more openly as a lesbian.

Counseling Lesbians

Emerging Literature

Our work with lesbians in pastoral counseling has been hampered by the dearth of literature on the subject of pastoral counseling of homosexuals in general and of lesbians in particular. The Jewish and Christian religious communities (of which most pastoral counselors are a part) have been mistrustful of sexuality, and often homosexuality has not even been seen as a legitimate concern. The literature on pastoral care and counseling of lesbians is sparse; only a few articles are available. Struzzo's "Pastoral Counseling and Homosexuality" (1989) describes how he utilizes transpersonal psychology and creation spirituality to help gay men or lesbians "appreciate the basic goodness of all creation, including their sexuality, without becoming possessive and addictive" (p. 199). Topper (1986) shows how the gay or lesbian spirituality journey deepens through a complex search for meaning, which must be addressed in the pastoral counseling setting.

However, in the secular fields much more has been written, including the publication of journals (*Journal of Homosexuality, Women Changing Therapy, Women & Therapy,* for example) that regularly address issues of lesbian psychology, psychotherapy, mothering, and so forth. Due to the gay civil rights and feminist movements, increasing numbers of women are making their sexual orientation a matter of public knowledge, and a circle of professionals who take an interest in minority psychology is growing. Rather than review all the psychological literature, the reader is referred to such works as *Lesbian Psychologies* (Boston Lesbian Psychologies Collective 1987), which discusses issues of identity, diversity, bisexuality, intimacy, relationships, socialization, families, child-rearing, lesbian community, alcoholism, eating disorders, and a host of other clinical issues in doing therapy. Another important book is *Lesbian Studies* (Cruikshank 1982), which includes chapters on lesbians in academics and in the classroom, new research/new perspectives, and an excellent list of resources (books, journals, articles, and groups) for and about lesbians of color, lesbians with disabilities, elderly lesbians, lesbian mothers, and so on.

Similarly, there are many models for doing psychotherapy from the viewpoint of a variety of schools, such as family therapy (Roth and Murphy 1986), cognitive therapy (Padesky 1988), sex therapy (Nichols 1987), and treating alcoholism and eating disorders (Nicoloff and Stiglitz 1987; Brown 1987). Similarly much has been written about couples therapy for lesbians (Carl 1990; Berzon 1988; Roth 1989).

It is possible that one of the main reasons lesbians turn to their pastors or pastoral counselors is because they need help and wish for affirmation in the process of coming out Roth (1989) speaks of the need lesbian couples have for the therapists to "witness and validate" the coming together of their relationship, a "social role performed by ministers, rabbis and others in the heterosexual world" (p. 290). It seems to me that lesbians need support and pastoral care not only in their coming together as partners, but also at life's critical points. In general, each of these points is affected most by the degree to which the woman or couple is "out of the closet"; therefore, this section will focus on that issue.

In and Out of the Closet

Coming out in lesbian feminist terminology has come to mean the "process of self-labeling, self-acceptance, and sharing one's lesbian identity with others" (Groves 1985, p. 17). For most females, unlike males, the discovery of a love relationship often precedes awareness of sexual orientation. Although sexual orientation is usually fixed by the age of five, it is not uncommon for a woman to come out after she is in her middle years. Aside from totally closeted lesbians (who may not even be self-identified), lesbians are "more or less out," that is, a fewer or greater number of persons know about their lifestyle. The process of coming out goes on for a lifetime; indeed much time can elapse between personal awareness and open acknowledgment to family and friends.

The tradeoff for coming out is honesty in place of safety. Because lesbianism by nature implies sexual, emotional, and economic freedom from men (Abbott and Love 1972), patriarchal society is threatened by its very presence. In upsetting the "natural order" or structures of hierarchy, the status quo, lesbians pose a serious threat to the patriarchal notion that women exist for men. Therefore, a woman who comes out as a lesbian incurs the wrath of patriarchal society for upsetting the status quo, for reminding it of the hidden awareness that "the emperor has no clothes." Specifically, she may encounter a lack of support, loss of close friends, family rejections, loss of job, or loss of a possible romantic relationship. The therapist who works with lesbians must be knowledgeable about the issues involved in coming out and the contemporaneous issues of identity formation (Groves 1985, p. 18).

Paradoxically, some heterosexual women may envy lesbian women simply because of the greater connectedness lesbian women have with other women, in general. Straight women may envy that lesbians "get to sleep with their best friend." In heterosexual circles a high percentage of women widely acknowledge that their husband, partner, or lover is not, in fact, their best friend. Since collegiality is so difficult between men and women, a longing for a primary woman-woman relationship is often mentioned by straight women when open discussion is made possible.

While straight women may have a real or imagined romantic notion of what lesbian relationships are like, the fact is that lesbians have to give up their wish for real or imagined heterosexual privilege, which takes the form of access to male status, power, class, and economic privilege (earning power or accumulated wealth).

> Judy, a 32-year-old mother of two, got married right after college. She put her husband through medical school and residency by working as a legal secretary. Her hours were long and hard, but so were his. Later, Judy quit her job to take care of two daughters. At one point it was necessary to take in a boarder to help pay the mortgage and to give Judy some time away from the house. Over several months, Judy found herself attracted to the boarder, Sandra, and began to have an affair with her. It reminded her of her last relationship before she married her husband, one in which she was with her best friend in college. At

one point, her husband became a little suspicious about the growing closeness he noticed between his wife and Sandra. By now, he had a growing family practice, though he still continued to work long hours. He took Judy aside and said, if she wanted to "explore" her sexuality, if she wanted to find out whether or not she was gay, then he would allow her to do it. But she would have to leave the house and the children to do so. Judy came into counseling terrified that she would lose her children, and her very identity in life, were she to make a choice concerning leaving her husband to be with Sandra. Not only that, but she had grown accustomed to her lifestyle as a doctor's wife and with all the amenities just now coming into being after so many years of scrimping and getting by.

In general, greater health is established the more a woman is able to define her own identity and realize and embrace the fullness of her personality. For the lesbian, however, this may mean becoming more publicly self-affirming and self-declaring, which exposes her even more to the very oppression by which she is already victimized. Yet with support, as Gloria Anzaldua writes, "our vulnerability can be our power—if we use it" (Moraga 1983, p. 195). A supportive community is of utmost importance, as well as few negative beliefs about lesbian lifestyles.

The first coming out process is often to oneself. This involves an awareness of lesbian feelings that have, usually through some precipitating event, broken through the denial system concerning lesbian identity. Perhaps the woman has read some literature which has placed lesbianism in a better light, such as the current periodical *Outlook*, an upscale magazine for gay men and lesbians. Perhaps she has seen an educational movie which addressed her situation or has met an "out" lesbian who has broken all the stereotypes. As such, "the woman finds herself in the position of choosing between societal abuse if she lives openly as a lesbian and the self-alienating experience of living a lie if she continues the denial pattern" (Groves 1985, p. 18).

Groves (1985) notes that positive coming out experiences are related to the development of a self-esteem with regard to newfound identity and orientation, relinquishment of investment in the patriarchal system (which has been the source of her survival), the finding of positive lesbian role models, and the ability to overcome significant feelings of loss (p. 19). Feminist psychology notes that for women—straight or lesbian—to develop a positive sense of self, they need to define themselves outside patriarchal expectations. This situation is doubly precarious for lesbians, however, who must also define themselves beyond heterosexist expectations. Leaving the legitimacy of (even the possibility of) a heterosexual lifestyle is a major step.

As a client or parishioner works through her own self-definition, it is crucial that she experience her therapist as not interjecting heterosexual or homosexual bias into the counseling, for she may then feel pressure to adopt a lifestyle contrary to her own nature. While eschewing the use of labels themselves, counselors can encourage clients to explore their feelings, thoughts, and fantasies, and they may try out various labels in the process (Moses and Hawkins 1982). Groves writes, "The therapist must be careful not to determine the client's identity for her, but to validate lesbianism as an acceptable lifestyle" (Groves 1985, p. 21). For the pastoral counselor and the religious lesbian working through to self-definition, this often means integrating spiritual with psychological understandings. The pastoral counselor needs to make it clear to the parishioner or client that whatever identity she understands herself to be is the crucial issue.

Once a woman has begun to achieve a positive self-image as a lesbian, she may be ready to come out to her family. A pastor or pastoral counselor may be consulted with regard to this process. Often lesbians come out first to siblings. Then they may write a letter to both parents, or each parent individually, before discussing their sexual orientation with them in person. Many lesbians are particularly relieved to know that their mothers, at least, have guessed the situation for quite a while. Others are threatened with being cut off, emotionally and/or financially. If parents do not know better, they may "blame themselves" for their daughter's orientation. Groups such as Parents and Friends of Lesbians and Gays (PFLAG) can be very helpful for parents in coming to a deeper understanding of their children.

Another critical time for counseling is when a lesbian mother considers coming out to her children. Do the children have a right to know about their mother's sexuality? Some researchers say yes. Corley (1990) discusses all of the possible issues, explaining that children of all ages can be told in age-appropriate language. Children can understand, for example, that this "family secret" is not a secret because it is something shameful, but because some people will not understand, will not agree, or are not educated about lesbian lifestyles. The most important issue for children is the modeling of a positive lifestyle and relationship. Unless there are overarching reasons for nondisclosure (such as an ex-husband's using the information to prohibit the mother's visitation or custody rights), it may well be in the best interests of both mother and child to keep their relationship honest. "A child told nothing about her mother's homosexuality can only relate to a fantasized image based on deceit and misinformation, even though her mother's intentions may have been the best in the world" (Corley 1990, p. 10). The process of coming out to a child is greatly facilitated if the grandparents are supportive; then the child won't have to carry the information alone in the family system.

A pastoral counselor can be very helpful in this process by helping the mother, perhaps also in counseling with her partner or with her ex-husband, to discern the right timing for disclosure and the right phrasing. If the family undergoes especially disruptive experiences, the pastor can mediate through family counseling.

In terms of coming out in the work place, some careers are relatively safe, for example, certain types of self-employment, segments of the art world and literary world, performance arts, modeling, sports, areas of science, and others. But for some vocations it can mean virtually automatic firing, such as in most denominations of ministry, in the military, and in teaching children and youth. People in politics, along with many other highly visible public persons, live in great fear because their careers are in jeopardy if they are "found out." There are variations in terms of level of safety in work places in terms of the consciousness of the work place and overall community (for example, whether it is a rural or urban area), and the prevailing political climate.

Other Life Passages

Myriad other issues may arise as the pastoral counselor works with lesbians. These include determining commitment to a relationship, mothering, co-parenting, and so on. These issues can be addressed through individual, couples, or family counseling as needed. Religious lesbians may need help in deciding about making a commitment to a long-term relationship, with or without benefit of the holy union services available in some Jewish and Christian circles, and therefore may call upon the pastor for couples counseling when they are making a decision about the future of their relationship.

Being lesbian does not exclude women from the ability or the desire to mother. Therefore many lesbians, within or outside of a long-term relationship, may ask for help in deciding whether or not to have children (through adoption, artificial insemination, or self-insemination). As a single parent, an "out" lesbian can adopt children, from infants to teens, depending upon the part of the United States and the laws. A closeted lesbian may find it easier to adopt children. As same-sex partners, lesbians cannot legally adopt children together. Since laws differ from state to state, a pastoral counselor can often help most by referring parishioners or clients for legal advice or steer them toward educational material such as legal guides for lesbian and gay parents or to self-help groups such as a nearby chapter of Gay Parents. In the same vein it is important for lesbian couples to define their relationship through legal documents that allow the partners to make certain decisions concerning the other's health care if one were to become incapacitated as well as with regard to wills. In short, though parenting is never an easy task, there is abundant research that happy, healthy gay parents in happy, healthy relationships will not have bad effects on their children (Corley 1990, pp. 12–13).

Since it is often the case that women come to recognize a lesbian identity after they have experienced a heterosexual marriage and already borne children, co-parenting is an important issue that comes up in therapy. One or both of the partners may be birth parents from previous heterosexual relationships. In this case the new partner may take on the role of "helping" parent, although she does not take the place of the father. Legally, responsibilities go to the natural custodial parent, then to the noncustodial partner, and only then, by special arrangement, to the lesbian partner. In any case, the new partner along with the children should have a major voice in determining how they want to relate to one another within the blended family. Counselors can help by normalizing this procedure in the ways of new family structures.

Lesbian couples may request counseling not only at the beginning stages of the relationship with issues of coming out, but also as they learn more and more how to live in egalitarian relationship with the right mix of intimacy and separateness in a society where few role models are available. Couples may sometimes worry unnecessarily about frequency of sexual contact. Sexual desire, which is strong in gay male couples and less in heterosexual couples, may be even less in lesbian couples (Loulan 1984; Loulan and Nelson 1987). Similar to gay men, many lesbians remain friends with their ex-lovers much longer than heterosexual persons, sometimes for a lifetime. Pastors should be aware of this, especially in the contexts of hospital visitation, holy unions, funerals, or other developmental or situational events of the life-cycle where a host of ex-lovers may be present because they still hold deep friendships with the parishioner.

Other Pastoral Counseling Issues

Religious Lesbians

Lesbians have always been members of our congregations, tithing, ministering, providing outreach, holding church positions. Parishioners who come to their pastors for counseling often have an idea that the pastor will be open to their particular area of concern, so lesbians usually have sensed it is "safe" to approach the pastor or pastoral counselor. For example, if a United Methodist church is a part of the "Reconciling Congregation Program," lesbians will feel more free to join or to approach that pastor with issues of their deepest concern. The same is true for pastors of Presbyterian "More Light Churches."

Alternatively, many of the major denominations have organizations that exist for groups of self-affirming gay and lesbians, such as Dignity for Roman Catholics, Integrity for Episcopalians, Affirmation for United Methodists. Olson (1984) lists thirty-six Christian organizations that relate to homosexuals mostly in affirming ways, though a few of the groups noted are dedicated to "transforming" homosexuals to at least act as if they were heterosexual through prayer, peer support, and counseling. Pastors can become involved with their faith group's gay-affirming ministries, or they may refer their parishioners to such settings for support.

There are gay and lesbian clergy and rabbis in virtually every faith group. Unfortunately, the church often encourages dishonesty and secrecy about sexual orientation in order to become ordained. It is a terrible thing to be forced to lie about one's sexual orientation in order to be permitted to fulfill one's call to ministry. Pastoral counselors who are known to be gay-affirming are often called on by lesbian and gay clergy for pastoral care if not counseling, especially in the coming out process. An important support group for lesbian clergy and lay women is CLOUT (Christian Lesbians Out Together). Ecumenical, multiracial, and multi-cultural, CLOUT addresses church policies on ordination and networks with Jewish lesbians, postchristian, profeminist, and prowomanist gay men and other organizations of marginalized women and men.[4]

Once it becomes apparent within the lesbian community that a particular pastor is empathic and non-judgmental, lesbians who may not be affiliated with any congregation but are searching for a faith community may seek pastoral counseling. In the process they can be referred to a faith community which is most open and welcoming for them. Besides "reconciling" or "more light" churches, the MCC, and other denominations that take an welcoming stance, a local woman-church group is another place for ritual, community, and feminist liturgy. In any case, parishioners and other interested clients should be informed about the various gay and lesbian groups affiliated with many of the denominations.

Emerging Lesbian Theologies and Spiritualities

The goal of reformist feminist Christian and Jewish women scholars and activists is to seek ways to redeem the tradition, practices, and structures of the organization from patriarchy. For Christians, this involves a critical examination of the ways in which patriarchy, anti-Judaism, and exclusivism go to the core of the religion. A hermeneutic of suspicion is utilized to discover the images, traditions, and dogmatics which can be seen as messages for justice and wholeness. Recently attempts have been made to articulate a critique of heterosexist theology and to begin to articulate a theology, spirituality, and ethic from the perspective of the experience of religious lesbians. Carter Heyward, an Episcopal priest, has published numerous works (see Heyward 1982, 1984, 1987, 1989a, 1989b). Roman Catholic lesbian women have begun the effort (Zanotti 1986; Grammick and Furey 1988) as have Jewish lesbians (Balka and Rose 1989). Women in general, and lesbians in particular, may find their own experience articulated best in theologies that describe God as present in relationships characterized by mutuality and empowerment (Heyward 1982). As Virginia Mollencott (1987) has expressed it,

> God's presence is known in those relationships that are mutually sympathetic, helpful, and interdependent rather than in hierarchical one-up, one-down relationships. The goal here is…to grow intentionally toward the recognition of God's image in everyone and in everything, and toward the mutual respect that such responsibility entails (p. 4).

Just as any competent pastoral counselor should be familiar with the variety of faith symbols and religious resources involved in ecumenical and interfaith counseling, so also it is imperative that the pastoral counselor be knowledgeable about, or at the very least cognizant of, the resources of gay and lesbian theologies (Glaser 1990; Fortunato 1982; Heyward 1989a and b; Hunt 1991). Such theologies challenge the liberal traditions and call into question—as do Latin American, Asian, African-American, and feminist theologies—the supposition that there is any theology free of bias or ideology. In content, the God described in gay and lesbian theologies appears as one who is primarily relational, neither distant nor "above the fray…unaffected by the clamor and clutter of human struggle, including the passions, problems, and confusions of human sexuality" (Heyward 1987, p. 34).

By assisting a parishioner or clergywoman to find access to these emerging theologies and organizations, pastoral counselors help lesbians realize they are not alone in their search for identity and in their yearning for a respectful place within their own religious tradition. It may relieve them greatly to realize they have choices in the manner and ways of relating to their root faith or to discover new possibilities for faith and community beyond their heritage. Organizations and writings are available to let a lesbian know she need not necessarily make a choice between affirming her sexual orientation and growing self-esteem, on the one hand, and her religious tradition on the other. And it always helps to know she is not alone in the struggle.

Orthopraxis: Social Justice Issues

To do pastoral counseling with lesbians is to help individual clients and parishioners experience through the counselor's mediation the accepting, redeeming, and loving presence of God. While this is an important activity, it is not enough. Pastoral counselors who are involved in the life of the church can be involved in many areas of ministry to help bring about change, through preaching, lecturing, and workshops. Educational events must address issues of heterosexism and homophobia. We must work to confront the structures in church and society that perpetuate this violence against sexual minorities; we cannot be solely engaged in treating the victims, important as that is for the individuals. Prejudice is learned; it can be unlearned, especially as people come into dialogue with those they fear, those who are the "stranger." Anxiety subsides and stereotypes lessen as people become more and more acquainted with "real life" people who call themselves lesbians. Many lesbians report that people get to know them first as women who are assumed to be straight. As the bond of friendship grows, they feel safe to come out to such friends, causing them to confront their own stereotypes and prejudices. This is perhaps the best way for people to learn about others, though it puts an inordinate amount of pressure on the minority individuals to play such an immense role as central instigators for change. Now that so much literature is available, people can begin to educate themselves by reading about the lives and struggles of lesbians and their emerging theologies. Such theologies, incidentally, have a lot to teach the church in general about healthy sexuality, new images of God, and mutual friendship.

Pastoral counselors work for justice on all fronts; we must not step aside on this particular issue. It is critical to work within one's own denomination and faith stance as well as ecumenically to educate parishioners, local churches, and larger groups wherever possible to begin to eradicate the violence of gay-bashing, which takes form physically, emotionally, intellectually, and spiritually. We cannot be satisfied to work in a smaller scope to help people who come damaged by the church without also working to change the church's attitude and behavior toward the marginalized people. Religious institutions need to repent of sexism and heterosexism and move beyond their institutionalized homophobia. When they do, then the issues of counseling lesbians will change, because such women will finally feel at home in their congregations, free to live their lifestyle openly with integrity.

Consequently, counselors must denounce homophobia and heterosexism just as fervently as they condemn racism, sexism, classism, and other structures of societal injustice. In so doing they present the good news of love and justice. Women's well-being must be an important hermeneutic for judging all things pastoral and prophetic. This means not just heterosexual women but lesbian women as well. To work to free the "least of these," the disabled, working-class lesbians of color, is to work to free us all from all oppressions. Not only that, but we all gain from learning from lesbians how we can be a faithful community. As black lesbian Cheryl Clarke has written,

> If radical lesbian-feminism purports an anti-racist, anti-classist, anti-woman-hating vision of bonding as mutual, reciprocal, as infinitely negotiable, as freedom from antiquated gender prescriptions and proscriptions, *then all people struggling to transform the character of relationships in this culture have something to learn from lesbians* (Clarke 1983, p. 134).

Summary

This chapter is written from the point of view of feminist liberation theology as integrated into sound psychological theory, research, and practice currently available. In so doing, it takes a gay-affirming stance, prevailing in the psychological and sociological literature, which determines that lesbianism per se is not a disease; rather it is a minority sexual orientation. As members of a minority group lesbians become the object of subjugation by the majority. All lesbians are subjected to the oppressive forces of sexism, heterosexism, and homophobia. Most lesbians also experience the debilitating effects of racism, classism, and/or ethnic and religious discrimination. Competent pastoral counseling requires that counselors be aware of the systemic effects of discrimination and oppression upon the overall health and well-being of the lesbian parishioner or client.

In terms of determining the morality of lesbianism—both orientation and acts—the chapter assumes the historic "full acceptance" position, considering that lesbian expressions may be ascertained to be moral or immoral by the extent to which they express authentic human loving. Feminist theory has discussed the values upheld and enacted by authentic loving. I do not assume human freedom to be value-free from a moral perspective, but consider the valuing of anyone's personal agency to be set first and foremost in the context of just social relations.

It is inconsistent within the feminist liberation theological stance to concern oneself only with furthering heterosexual women's physical, emotional, psychological, and spiritual health and flourishing. Therefore heterosexual pastoral counselors must recognize the epistemological privilege of the voices and writings of the experiences of lesbians within and outside the religious community. In fulfilling the mandate to put experience of the oppressed first, understanding the experience of lesbian women is the foremost criterion for the formulation of theological and ethical view-points which feminist pastoral counseling affirms concerning same-sex orientation. The authoritative nature of scripture, tradition, and reason are not discounted; rather their role in contributing to the historical stances of rejecting-punitive, rejecting-nonpunitive, and qualified acceptance can be critiqued and their content reevaluated and reinterpreted in light of further research, historical analysis, and biblical exegesis.

A feminist liberation theology affirms women's freedom in the context of just social relationship to express their natural right to sexuality. It therefore affirms lesbians' right to develop their sexuality within their understanding of their context of spirituality, mutuality, and reciprocity. It is the nature and quality of the relationship itself, rather than the gender of the persons involved, that is important. Therefore, a gay-affirming feminist pastoral counseling stance 1) denies the moral superiority of genital sexual activity for procreation; 2) rejects as unjust requirement of imposing upon all lesbians a lifetime of sexual abstinence; and hence 3) cannot use the criterion of marital bonding to apply to a group of women for whom this is not a legal or, in most cases, an ecclesiastical possibility. Any sexual activity is then judged by a complex set of criteria, ideally suggested first by the lesbian community itself, regarding such issues as mutuality, equality, level of commitment, and reciprocity.

It is not outside the pastoral counselor's role to be prophet of traditionally unpopular religious viewpoints, especially with regard to speaking out against injustice perpetrated by the majority upon minority groups. Pastoral counselors also have a mandate, insofar as they participate in the ecclesiastical circles, to call their religious groups to accountability for perpetuating such injustice. A systemic analysis shows the links among all the structures of oppression: sexism, racism, classism, and heterosexism. All oppressions are thus interconnected through patriarchy, which the church sanctions through being itself a patriarchal structure as well as through holding patriarchal tenets. Just as feminism could not sustain its movement for liberation of women without directly facing its heterosexism, the church cannot truly be a liberation force against sexism without also facing its homophobia and heterosexism. I acknowledge that such public proclamation and actions directed toward eradicating sexism and thus heterosexism within traditional religions comprise a dangerous and subversive activity, as lesbians well know. It is, although to a lesser extent than for their lesbian parishioners and clients, dangerous for pastoral counselors who nevertheless must choose between integrity and the personal duplicity of affirming privately while remaining silent in public.

In terms of diagnosis, it is crucial that a self-definition of *lesbian* be achieved by the client or parishioner who has sought pastoral counseling. This is best achieved when the pastoral counselor is gay-affirming and can help the person in the coming out process with neither naive and hollow reassurances about the response of society nor a blame-the-victim reaction. To come out as a lesbian in a homophobic and heterosexist society is to endanger oneself and one's loved ones in physical, emotional, and spiritual ways. At the same time, the counselor must eschew participation in dominant religious traditions' judgmentalism and blanket disavowal of either the orientation or the acts. Lesbians, no less than straight women, may need help with holistic self-definition in a patriarchal society and in finding ways to express themselves in mutual, responsible, and loving relationships with their partners, families, and friends. Only when pastoral counselors minister genuinely, respectfully, and with unconditional positive regard for lesbians as well as for heterosexuals can we effectively participate in God's healing and justice-making activity. As with other theologies of liberation, where minorities become agents for calling the faith communities to greater faithfulness, so lesbians have much to teach the church about how to *be* the church.

Notes

1. This situation is exemplified by the difficulty in finding a scholar and clinician with a Ph.D. in pastoral counseling who is "out" professionally and publicly to the extent that she would not feel her position compromised through being recognized as the author of such a chapter as this. Though I cannot write *as* a lesbian, my hope is to write *on behalf of* lesbians due to my personal and political stance, my experience in counseling lesbians, and my research methodology. The latter includes 1) interviewing members of lesbian communities on both coasts; 2) extensive review of the literature; and 3) remaining accountable to the communities through their kind and careful reviewing of the drafts. However, this should not in any way be seen as a simple substitute for having one or a group of lesbian pastoral counselors write on this subject for the pastoral counseling field, the religious groups, and the wider public. It is hoped that the urgency with which this chapter is written will make room for lesbians to do such writing more and more in the future.

2. See, for example, the writings of Lisa Cahill, Charles Curran, John McNeill, Norman Pittinger, Margaret Farley, James Nelson and Robin Scroggs, Beverly Harrison, James Spong, among a host of others. For a brief though certainly not exhaustive overview of the history of the progression toward acceptance which also references some of the major writers, see Nugent and Grammick 1989, pp. 7–46.

3. *This Bridge Called My Back* not only contains writings about the struggles of lesbians of color, but includes a bibliography of some writings of lesbians of color. Other articles, such as Greene (1986), address issues of

interracial counseling in the lesbian community in comparison with the straight community.

4. For a description of CLOUT (P.O. Box 460808, San Francisco, CA 94146-0808), see *More Light Update* (February 1991).

References

Abbott, S., and Love, B. 1973. *Sappho Was a Right-on Woman: A Liberated View of Lesbianism.* Briarcliff Manor, N.Y.: Stein and Day.

Allport, G. 1954. *The Nature of Prejudice.* Reading, Mass.: Addison-Wesley.

Anthony, B. 1981–1982. "Lesbian Client-Lesbian Therapist: Opportunities and Challenges in Working Together." *Journal of Homosexuality* 7, 2/3: 45–57.

Augsberger, D. 1986. *Pastoral Counseling Across Cultures.* Philadelphia: Westminster.

Balka, C., and Rose, A. eds. 1989. *Twice Blessed: On Being Lesbian, Gay, and Jewish.* Boston: Beacon.

Berzon, B. 1988. *Permanent Partners: Building Gay and Lesbian Relationships that Last.* New York: Dutton.

Boston Lesbian Psychologies Collective. 1987. *Lesbian Psychologies: Explorations and Challenges.* Urbana: University of Illinois Press.

Boswell, J. 1980. *Christianity, Social Tolerance, and Homosexuality.* Chicago: University of Chicago.

Brown, L. 1987. "Lesbians, Weight, and Eating: New Analyses and Perspectives." In Boston Lesbian Psychologies Collective, *Lesbian Psychologies,* pp. 294–310.

Cameron, B. 1983. "Gee, You Don't Seem Like an Indian from the Reservation." In Moraga and Anzaldua, *This Bridge Called My Back,* pp. 46–52.

Carkhuff, R. 1987. *The Art of Helping VI.* Amherst, Mass.: Human Resource Development Press.

Carl, D. 1990. *Counseling Same-Sex Couples.* New York: W. W. Norton.

Clarke, C. 1983. "Lesbianism, an Act of Resistance." In Moraga and Anzaldua, *This Bridge Called My Back,* pp. 128–37.

Corley, R. 1990. *The Final Closet: The Gay Parents' Guide for Coming Out to Their Children.* Miami: Editech.

Cruikshank, M., ed. 1982. *Lesbian Studies: Present and Future.* Old Westbury, N.Y.: Feminist Press.

Egan, G. 1990. *The Skilled Helper: A Systematic Approach to Effective Counseling.* Pacific Grove, Calif.: Brooks/Cole.

Fortunato, J. 1982. *Embracing the Exile: Healing Journeys of Gay Christians.* San Francisco: Harper & Row.

Glaser, C. 1990. *Come Home! Reclaiming Spirituality and Community as Gay Men and Lesbians.* San Francisco: Harper & Row.

Grahan, J. 1978. "The Common Woman." In *The Work of a Common Woman.* Oakland: Diana Press.

Grammick, J., and Furey, P. eds. 1988. *The Vatican and Homosexuality: Reactions to the "Letter to the Bishops of the Catholic Church on the Pastoral Care of Homosexual Persons."* New York: Crossroad Publishing Company.

Greene, B. 1986. "When the Therapist Is White and the Patient Is Black: Considerations for Psychotherapy in the Feminist Heterosexual and Lesbian Communities." *Women and Therapy* 5, 2–3 (Sum/Fall).

Groves, P. 1985. "Coming Out: Issues for the Therapist Working with Women in the Process of Lesbian Identity Formation." *Women & Therapy* 4, 2 (Summer): 17–22.

Hall, M. 1985. *The Lavender Couch: A Consumer's Guide to Psychotherapy for Lesbians and Gay Men.* Boston: Alyson.

Hasbany, Richard, ed. 1989. *Homosexuality and Religion.* New York: Harrington Park Press.

Heyward, C. 1982. *The Redemption of God: A Theology of Mutual Relation.* Lanham, Md.: University Press of America.

———. 1984. *Our Passion for Justice: Images of Power, Sexuality and Liberation,* New York: Pilgrim Press.

———. 1987. "Heterosexist Theology: Being Above It All." *Journal of Feminist Studies in Religion* 3 (Spring): 29–38.

———. 1989a. *Speaking of Christ: A Lesbian Feminist Voice.* New York: Pilgrim Press.

———. 1989b. *Touching our Strength: The Erotic Power and the Love of God.* San Francisco: Harper & Row.

Hochstein, L. 1986. "Pastoral Counselors: Their Attitudes Toward Gay and Lesbian Clients." *Journal of Pastoral Care* 40, 2 (June): 158–63.

Hunt, M. 1989. "On Religious Lesbians: Contradictions and Challenges." in D. Altman, et al., *Homosexuality, Which Homosexuality?* 1989, pp. 97–113.

———. 1991. *Fierce Tenderness: A Feminist Theology of Friendship.* New York: Crossroad.

Kohut, H. 1978. "The Psychoanalyst in the Community of Scholars." In *The Search for Self: Selected Writings of H. Kohut,* edited by P. H. Ornstein. New York: International Universities Press.

Lewis, S. 1979. *Sunday's Women.* Boston: Beacon.

Loulan, J. 1984. *Lesbian Sex.* San Francisco: Spinsters Ink.

———, and Nelson, M. B. 1987. *Lesbian Passion: Loving Ourselves and Each Other.* San Francisco: Spinsters/aunt lute.

Menard, G. 1989. "Gay Theology, Which Gay Theology?" In D. Altman et al., *Homosexuality, Which Homosexuality,* pp. 127–38.

Miller, J. B. 1986. *Toward a New Psychology of Women,* 2d ed. Boston: Beacon.

Mollencott, V. 1987. *Godding: Human Responsibility and the Bible.* New York: Crossroad.

Moraga, C. 1983. "La Guera." In Moraga and Anzaldua, *This Bridge Called My Back,* pp. 27–34.

———, and G. Anzaldua, eds. 1983. *This Bridge Called My Back: Writing by Radical Women of Color.* New York: Kitchen Table.

More Light Update. Monthly journal by Presbyterians for Lesbian and Gay Concerns. Elder James Anderson, P.O. Box 38, New Brunswick, N.J. 08903.

Moses, A., Hawkins, Jr., E. Hawkins, Jr., R. 1982. *Counseling Lesbian Women and Gay Men.* New York: Mosbey.

Nichols, M. 1987. "Doing Sex Therapy with Lesbians: Bending a Heterosexual Paradigm to Fit a Gay Life-Style." In Boston *Lesbian Psychologies* Collective, *Lesbian Psychologies,* pp. 242–60.

Nicoloff, L., and Stiglitz, E. 1987. "Lesbian Alcoholism: Etiology, Treatment and Recovery." In Boston Lesbian Psychologies Collective, *Lesbian Psychologies,* pp. 283–93.

Nugent, R., and Gramick, J. 1989. "Homosexuality: Protestant, Catholic and Jewish Issues; a Fishbone Tale." In Hasbany, *Homosexuality and Religion,* pp. 7–46.

Olson, M. 1984. "Christians and Homosexuality," a booklet of reprints from the January, February, and April 1984 issues of *The Other Side.*

Open Hands. Quarterly Journal of the Reconciling Congregation Program in the United Methodist Church, P.O. Box 23636, Washington, D.C. 20026.

Padesky, C. 1988. "Attaining and Maintaining Positive Lesbian Self-Identity: A Cognitive Therapy Approach." *Women & Therapy* 8, 1–2: 145–56.

Rashke, R. 1976. "Dignity Like a Fishbone Lodged in the Church's Throat." *National Catholic Reporter,* 6 April 1976, p. 28.

Reiter, Laura. 1989. "Sexual Orientation, Sexual Identity, and the Question of Choice." *Clinical Social Work Journal* 17, 2 (Summer): 138–50.

Rich, A. 1979. "The Meaning of Our Love for Women Is What We Have Constantly to Expand." In *On Lies, Secrets, and Silence: Selected Prose* 1966–1978. New York: W. W. Norton.

Rogers, C. 1961. *On Becoming a Person*. Boston: Houghton Mifflin.

Roth, S. 1989. "Psychotherapy with Lesbian Couples: Individual Issues, Female Socialization and the Social Context." In M. McGoldrick et al., *Women in Families*, New York: W. W. Norton.

————, and Murphy, B. 1986. "Therapeutic Work with Lesbian Clients: A Systemic Therapy View." In *Women and Family Therapy*, edited by Marianne Ault-Riche, pp. 78–89. Rockville, Md.: Aspen Systems Corporation.

Saghir, M., and Robins, E. 1973. *Male and Female Sexuality*. Baltimore: Williams and Wilkins.

Scanzoni, L., and V. Mollenkott. 1978. *Is the Homosexual My Neighbor?: Another Christian View*. San Francisco: Harper & Row.

Struzzo, J. 1989. "Pastoral Counseling and Homosexuality." In Hasbany, *Homosexuality and Religion*, pp. 195–222.

Topper, C. 1986. "Spirituality as a Component in Counseling Lesbians-Gays." *The Journal of Pastoral Counseling* 21, 1 (Spring-Summer): 55–59.

Vance, C. 1989. "Social Construction Theory: Problems in the History of Sexuality." In D. Altman, et al., *Homosexuality, Which Homosexuality?* pp. 13–34.

Vicinus, M. 1989. "They Wonder to Which Sex I Belong: The Historical Roots of the Modern Lesbian Identity." In D. Altman et al., *Homosexuality, Which Homosexuality?* pp. 171–98.

Wall, J. 1991. "Faith, Tribe, Nation: Top Story of 1990," *Christian Century* 107, 37: 1187–1190.

Zanotti, B., ed. 1986. *A Faith of One's Own: Explorations by Catholic Lesbians*. Trumansburg, N.Y.: Crossing Press.

For Further Reading

Altman, D. et al. 1989. *Homosexuality, Which Homosexuality?* London: GMP Publishers.

Council on Interracial Books for Children. 1983. "Homophobia and Education," *Bulletin* 14, nos. 3 and 4.

Edwards, G. 1984. *Gay/Lesbian Liberation: A Biblical Perspective*. New York: Pilgrim Press.

Grahan, J. 1984. *Another Mother Tongue: Gay Words, Gay Worlds*. Boston: Beacon.

Hoagland, Sara. 1988. *Lesbian Ethics: Toward New Value*. Palo Alto, Calif.: Institute of Lesbian Studies.

Scroggs, R. 1983. *The New Testament and Homosexuality*. Philadelphia: Fortress Press.

Richard Byrne

9. Pastoral Counseling of the Gay Male

The Shaping Contexts of Culture and Church

The Culture in Transition

Any reflection upon a Judeo-Christian approach to pastoral counseling of the gay male must take into account the powerful shifts in attitudes toward homosexuality that have been taking place in the culture and churches during the past twenty-five years. The gay male comes to the pastoral counselor shaped by these often ambivalent and changing attitudes toward his situation. In turn, many pastoral counselors are undergoing change in their attitudes toward gay persons as a result of shifting cultural and ecclesial climates.

The Stonewall riots of 1969 in New York historically represent the emergence of gay culture from its closet of fear to an open posture of dialogue and debate with the normative heterosexual community. The dialogue insists upon recognition of the dignity of homosexual persons and the effective promotion of their political, legal, religious, and social rights by the culture as a whole and by its representative institutions in particular. While bigotry still exists in the majority of the population, great gains have been made in legislation protecting the rights of the homosexual population and in the promotion of more positive social attitudes toward gay people.

Like other movements of reform and revolution, gay liberation has employed many different strategies. Chief among them has been a consciousness-raising effort that makes people aware of the omnipresence of gays and lesbians in the culture. Gay people are everywhere, in all walks of life, in every profession, in each extended family structure. They embrace all temperaments and lifestyles, and hence can never be reduced to the traditional stereotypes of the effeminate, the queer, the faggot, the bull-dyke, or the sick invert. As part of the raising of consciousness, the media—film, television, literature, visual arts—have been much freer about treating gay themes and thereby helping the public become more aware of the prevalence of the gay population and the patterns of gay and lesbian life. Historians have uncovered the creative contributions of leaders of Western civilization whom gays today would number among their confreres—in-so-far as these leaders seem to have displayed an erotic and affectional preference for members of their own sex: Michelangelo, Leonardo da Vinci, Tchaikovsky, James Baldwin, W. H. Auden, Samuel Barber, Benjamin Britten, Willa Cather, Gertrude Stein, Michel Foucault, and an endless list of others (Duberman, Vicinus, and Chauncey 1989). Finally, the arrival of the AIDS virus has further revealed the face of the gay community to the wider population, which is witnessing the courage of those who live and suffer with the disease, as well as the overwhelming outreach of compassion and advocacy on their behalf.

There has indeed been a movement toward more humane and accepting attitudes toward gay persons in many segments of American culture. And yet, except on some streets in San Francisco and Manhattan, can two men walk down the street holding hands and express other ordinary signs of affection in public without ridicule? Most gays are still afraid to do so. This is because, despite gains of tolerance and acceptance within the culture as a whole, there still lurks a profound, instinctive fear of and distaste for homosexual persons in the hearts of a vast majority of the population. Despite the fact that the American Psychiatric Association removed homosexuality from its list of emotional disorders and sexual perversions in 1973, many persons think there is something wrong with the gay person, something wrongfully different. Whatever the cause of this deepseated antipathy and fear, simple observation attests that it exists everywhere in our culture. The movement of gay liberation has helped modify prejudice; it has not eradicated it.

The Churches in Transition

The Judeo-Christian traditions in Western culture have a similar record of condemnation of homosexuality, although recent scholarship has documented that prior to the thirteenth century Christian churches often had a more tolerant and accepting approach (Boswell 1980). Christian prejudice against gay persons is partly rooted in a fundamentalist interpretation of certain biblical texts—and this on the part of scholars and readers who interpret the rest of scripture with well-informed hermeneutical understanding and flexibility. These texts are well-known: Genesis 19:1–29, the Sodom and Gomorrah story which in fact is an indictment of inhospitality and social injustice; and the Holiness Code in Leviticus 18:22 and 20:13, which was a condemnation of the sacral prostitution and sexual orgies in Canaanite fertility worship. The New Testament records no words of Jesus about homosexuality, either as act or orientation. The key references in the

Christian scriptures are from St. Paul in Romans 1:18–32, 1 Corinthians 6:9–10, and 1 Timothy 1:8–11. Scholars have documented that none of these texts represents what we today would call a gay orientation or the responsible expression of intimacy between two persons of the same sex (Nelson 1978, p . 181–88 McNeill 1976, pp. 37–66). In fact,

> The central biblical message regarding sexuality seems clear enough. Like every other good gift, it can be misused. The idolatrous dishonoring of God inevitably results in the dishonoring of persons, and faithfulness to God will result in sexual expression which honors the personhood of the other. Our sexuality is not a mysterious and alien force of nature but part of what it means to be human. It is a power to be integrated fully into one's selfhood and to be used in the service of love. That message, I am convinced, applies regardless of one's affectional orientation (Nelson 1978, p. 188).

A literalist reading of the scriptures and a convergence of sociopolitical, economic, and other factors resulted in the centuries' long story of Christian culture's persecution of gay persons. The story has been largely ignored because until recently there has been no gay history. Stoning, burning, exile, sexual mutilation, and the death penalty were common punishments for homosexuals (Crompton 1974).

The church approved of some of these brutalities, yet tended to be less physically violent. Nonetheless, the church was spiritually even more severe (Nelson 1978, p. 189). The homosexual was a sinner. The unrepentant gay person was ostracized by the community and refused participation in its sacramental life.

The situation in the churches today is in a state of transition, both on official and informal levels. The official teaching of most Christian churches still proclaims that homosexual activity represents objectively sinful behavior, while the homosexual orientation as such is not sinful. Churches tend to see the orientation as either morally neutral or a "disorder of nature."

For example, the Roman Catholic Congregation for the Doctrine of the Faith in its *Letter to the Bishops of the Catholic Church on the Pastoral Care of Homosexual Persons* (1986) states that a former Roman document, *Declaration on Certain Questions concerning Sexual Ethics* (1975) may have led to an "overly benign interpretation given to the homosexual condition itself, some going so far as to call it neutral or even good. Although the particular inclination of the homosexual person is not a sin, it is a more or less strong tendency ordered toward an intrinsic moral evil; and thus the inclination itself must be seen as an objective disorder" (par. 3). The text goes on to say that "special concern and pastoral attention should be directed toward those who have this condition, lest they be led to believe that the living out of this orientation in homosexual activity is a morally acceptable option. It is not" (par. 3).

This same document, as well as any number of pronouncements issued by church authorities since the early seventies, advocates compassion and pastoral outreach to gay persons as well as advocacy for social justice on behalf of the gay community (Nugent and Gramick 1982). A careful hermeneutic of these documents could demonstrate how positive they are and that, given the essentially conservative nature of church authority, not much more can be expected at this period of history. But the typical gay Christian does not concern himself with this level of hermeneutical sophistication. All he hears is that he is "disordered," that something is wrong with him, that he may not express his love in sexual intimacy. All he tends to see are some church leaders actively opposing city ordinances that protect the rights of the gay community against discrimination in housing and employment. Sitting in the midst of a family-centered, heterosexual congregation, he has never heard a sermon affirming the value of his way of loving. And hence he sits alone, alienated in the midst of the Christian assembly.

As in the culture, advocacy and support groups have been formed in recent years to offer a context of healing, reconciliation, and mission to gay and lesbian Christians. Dignity in Roman Catholicism, Integrity in the Episcopalian tradition, Affirmation in the Methodist church, Lutherans Concerned, and so forth, are barely tolerated by the governing bodies of these denominations, yet they exist and sometimes flourish as contexts where people can worship, support each other, and minister to the wider community as both gay and Christian persons.

As a summary of the experience of gays in our churches and culture, one can survey the range of contemporary moral and theological positions that prevail in Christian churches and by extrapolation in Western "Christian" culture. Nelson (1978, pp. 188–99) provides four helpful categories for this overview.

The first position is the *rejecting–punitive* motif, which has prevailed in Christian history. While few but the most fundamentalist leaders hold this position theologically today, it may still be the approach most favored by a large percentage of Christian people. At base, it is a vindictive prejudice, rooted in centuries of conditioning and fear of the "other," who is the gay person. The rejecting–punitive disposition may also be an expression of the classical defense mechanism of projection whereby sections of the population "scapegoat" a minority because they are unable to accept the hated quality—in this case, their own homosexual tendencies—in themselves.[1] Among more educated persons this prejudice rarely takes the form of physical violence. It is, however, expressed in modes of social exclusion, inequities in the work place, sarcastic humor about gay people, prejudicial attitudes handed on to children around the dinner table in the form of bigoted remarks, and so on. Why do most parents dread the prospect of having a gay son? Why do they look for signs that the child is a "regular guy" from earliest infancy onward? Somehow, being gay represents a tragedy and a stigma for most people. Some would even prefer a child who grows up a criminal to one who turns out to be gay.

The second position presented by Nelson is the *rejecting–non-punitive* motif. This is represented by one of the greatest theologians of our century, Karl Barth. Barth holds that humanity comes into its fullness only in relation to persons of the opposite sex. To seek one's fulfillment in a person of the same sex is "physical, psychological and social sickness, the phenomenon of perversion, decadence and decay" (Barth 1961, p. 166). Yet, convinced that the central theme of the gospel is grace and forgiveness, Barth advocates the condemnation of homosexuality but the acceptance of the gay person. This approach seems close to the official positions adopted by various Christian denominations that make a distinction between "orientation" and "activity" in the lives of homosexual persons. In other words, hate the sin but love the sinner.

A third approach is *qualified acceptance.* This option holds that while homosexuality is in some way against the order of creation, there are homosexually constituted persons who have no choice regarding this sexual orientation. The ideal for these is sublimated abstinence. If this proves impossible, then they should "structure their sexual relationships in an 'ethically responsible way' (in adult, fully-committed relationships). They should make the best of their painful situations without idealizing them or pretending that they are normal" (Nelson 1978, p. 196). This opinion has become fairly common among moral theologians and church leaders. A caricature of it would run: "If they have to be that way, then let them at least model their relationships on the Christian heterosexual norm and not flaunt their gayness as good."

The fourth possibility from the ethical point of view is that of *full acceptance.* Those who adopt this position accept fully the conclusions of medical and psychological research that the gay orientation is a simple given. Although no common agreement exists about the etiology of homosexuality, major theories cluster around either genetic or psychogenic explanations. All concur that subjects discover rather than invent their homosexuality. Christian theologians who advocate full acceptance interpret this "given" as "grace" (McNeill 1976; Pittenger 1977; Whitehead and Whitehead 1984). It is part of the mystery of divine creation according to which God created each person in God's image. Since God *is* love (1 Jn 4:8), then the human being in God's image *is* also love. Love is the deepest ontology of the human:

> To say that I am made in the image of God is to say that
> love is the reason for my existence, for God is love.
> Love is my true identity. Selflessness is my true self.
> Love is my true character. Love is my name (Merton 1961, p. 60).

In this view, sexual attraction and its loving expression are intrinsic to the mystery of personal identity—that is, to the "love" that each person is in the depths of his or her being where a person images God who is love. Homosexual love, then, becomes a way of imaging God, just as heterosexual love images God.

The slogan "gay is good" is thus more than just a cry for liberation or an expression of ego self-esteem. It articulates the deepest spiritual reality of gay persons. Far from having something wrong with them (their gayness), they in fact have something altogether right with them: the gift of a unique dignity, a unique way of loving, a unique mission to live their homosexual orientation as a way of imaging God. God's creative and redemptive love is less present in the world when individuals, aided and abetted by culture and church, deny their homosexual orientation or loathe themselves because of it.

Which of the four approaches—rejecting–punitive, rejecting–non-punitive, qualified acceptance, full acceptance—is morally "correct" is not the concern of this chapter. Theologians will continue to debate them. The focus of this chapter is the psychological maturity and spiritual growth of the gay male who approaches the pastoral counselor for help in facing the "problem" of his homosexuality.

As defined by the Association of Pastoral Counselors, *pastoral counseling* is "a process in which a pastoral counselor utilizes insights and principles derived from the disciplines of theology and the behavioral sciences in working with individuals, couples, families, groups, and social systems toward the achievement of wholeness and health" (Wicks, Parsons, and Capps 1985, p. 15). In light of the goal of pastoral counseling, the assumptive presupposition of this chapter is that the fourth theological option of full acceptance will best promote the gay male's movement toward wholeness and health.

Justification for the counselor's adoption of this most positive of the four approaches lies precisely in the adjective *pastoral* that describes his or her counseling ministry. Pastoral counselors are not moral theologians engaged in debate over ethical issues. Neither in their role as counselors are they official representatives of the current authoritative teachings of their denominations. They are always and above all *pastors,* that is, fellow Christian charged with the ministry of shepherding the depth dimension of human life, which is the "soul" or true self created in the image of God. Pastoral counselors draw upon whichever insights from the theological or human sciences seem best to foster the emergence of the unique person toward wholeness and health. They root their ministry in the long tradition of the "primacy of conscience," which is the freedom and duty of the individual to follow the voice of God speaking in the depths of his or her responsibly formed conscience, even if this may seem to go contrary to the current teachings or demands of religious institutions. Pastoral counselors try to help their clients listen to this "voice of God" as the primary directive for guidance in and through whatever problems are being faced in the counseling sessions.

In view of these considerations the full acceptance of homosexuality within the framework of the gospel imperative to love can thus form the basic assumption of our approach to pastoral counseling of the gay male.

For the effectiveness of this approach, however, counselors must recognize the extremely complex and ambiguous situation that obtains during a time when churches and cultures are in a crisis of transition in their valuation of homosexuality on all levels—moral, psychological, spiritual, and cultural. As this transition occurs, all the uncertainty and insecurity that accompany major attitudinal shifts are at least preconsciously present in the psyches of most people, including the client and the counselor. For instance, the death of their best friends' son from AIDS recently plunged a prejudiced couple into the throes of this transition. The couple love their friends, who had to struggle to accept and affirm their son's gay orientation upon learning about it through his illness. This caused the formerly prejudiced couple to question their negative attitudes, to read some enlightened literature on the subject, to respond to the special demands of AIDS bereavement within the wider context of supporting their friends, who had hitherto kept their son's gayness a secret, even from themselves. Stories like this—of passage from a rejecting-punitive stance to at least a posture of qualified acceptance—are occurring all the time as a part of the more positive cultural and ecclesial scene that has been described. Yet, the old stories of prejudice, fear, and rejection also remain in force as part of the shadow (in the Jungian sense) side of a culture and churches that cannot deal in distinctly human and Christian ways with the gay expression of God's creative love in this world.

The gay male who comes for pastoral counseling emerges from the lived context of secular and religious culture, not from a solipsistic record of individual experiences. Philosophers like Hans Georg Gadamer (1975) have protested the Enlightenment's rejection of tradition as profoundly explanatory of human behavior and understanding. Following them, psychologists have emphasized the necessity of understanding the contemporary climate and its lived traditions in the therapeutic encounter.

In this regard Adrian van Kaam, existential psychologist and spiritual author, postulates an aspect of the self called the "sociohistorical" dimension (van Kaam 1983, pp. 57-59), which is the matrix of all the other dimensions of the personality: the organismic-emotive, the egoic-functional, and the transcendent-spiritual. All of our organismic, egoic, and spiritual interactions with reality are at least partly shaped and colored by the sociohistorical dimension of the self. Van Kaam calls the dynamics of this dimension "pulsations" (pp. 260–61). Pulsations are often unconscious or preconscious. They represent values, attitudes, uncritical judgments, feelings that have been blindly introjected from family, culture, and church since earliest childhood.

Risking generalization, one could conjecture that in relation to homosexuality these pulsations are still most often negative among the majority of the population, including the gay client and his counselor. This negative sociohistorical conditioning has often been partly reformed by more humane, Christian approaches adopted later in life. Nonetheless, however enlightened one's attitudes may later become, residual deformative pulsations continue to affect the deepest self-estimation of gay clients as well as the attitudes of their pastoral counselors.

Counselors of gay males must, therefore, first of all have an educated awareness of the complexities and ambiguities of homosexuality in today's churches and culture. They will recognize that both they and their clients are in a period of transition in their perceptions and responses toward the facts of homosexuality. Counselors will examine their own consciousness, either in private reflection or with the aid of a supervisor, as to their own internalized pulsations on emotional, moral, and spiritual levels. They might recognize that in truth they retain a level of rejecting-punitive moral judgment; or that they are in fact afraid of gay men; or that they look prejudicially at homosexuals as "people with a problem" rather than as images of God endowed with a unique way of loving.

Whichever pulsations predominate in pastoral counselors' minds and hearts, it seems imperative that they acknowledge them so that these preconscious or unconscious reactions do not interfere with their mission to guide gay people toward wholeness and health, to ward psychological maturity informed by a religious value horizon. If in this honest self-examination some counselors detect the presence of hidden or obvious prejudice and negative judgments about homosexuality that are difficult or impossible to reform before receiving the gay client, they are best advised to refer the client elsewhere. There are sufficient gay counseling centers and gay-related church organizations that can recommend or provide competent assistance.

Toward a Positive Gay Identity and Integration

Having surveyed the ecclesial and cultural climates from which the gay male comes for pastoral counseling, we are in a position to reflect more specifically upon the purpose, structures, and dynamics of a sequence of pastoral counseling sessions with a gay male. While it is impossible to characterize the gay male under general stereotypes, one may offer some informed general patterns of approach that may apply, at least in some instances, to the growth of gay males toward psychological and spiritual integration.

Two Working Hypotheses

Two convictions or working hypotheses undergird this approach to pastoral counseling of the gay male. The first is that the counselor's task is the evocation and support of the gay client's radical self-affirmation as one uniquely created in the image of God precisely as a gay person. Second, the counselor's work involves assisting the client's responsible choices in integrating his affirmed identity as a gay person in the context of his everyday life.

These statements of purpose correspond to the underlying dynamics in all human growth: disclosure and incarnation rooted respectively in consciousness and freedom, or intellect and will, or knowledge and love, cognition and behavior. There is always something and something more to be discovered about the mystery of the self within the horizon of divine mystery. Based on new disclosure, there is always something more that can be "done," incarnated, or integrated in order to approximate more deeply the true self or divine image that each of us already is and is on the way toward becoming.

In practice, this journey of disclosure and incarnation of the client's deepest identity is the core issue in all pastoral counseling, perhaps in a special way for homosexual persons who are necessarily preoccupied with issues of identity and integration because of constant challenges to them. To trace the inner dynamics of the journey, we shall examine what van Kaam calls the "intraspheric formation powers" of apprehension, appraisal, affirmation, and application (van Kaam 1985, pp. 66–78; 1987, pp. 140–43).

From the perspective of formative spirituality, whose conceptual paradigms have potential for use in pastoral counseling, the intraspheric formation powers are the primary tools of growth. They represent the counselor's and client's capacities of mind and will on both the transcendent/spiritual and functional/egoic levels. These primary interior capacities are aided by the auxiliary powers of imagination, memory, and anticipation that foster their insightful and free use at the service of human formation, reformation, and transformation (van Kaam 1985 pp. 108–64).

Overview of the Intraspheric Powers

From a Christian perspective, God speaks and communicates in and through life experience. History is the context of grace. The "life-field" of clients refers to the whole context of their life experience: their experience of self, others, situation, wider world, and, ultimately, their experience of the divine Mystery that both permeates and transcends these other dimensions of experience. Formative spirituality calls this context the "formation field" of the client (van Kaam 1983, pp. 286, 296). It is the integrating or disintegrating total context of one's life. The life-field is an interwoven network of directives or influences that shape and are shaped by the client. This approach is based on the assumption that all reality "speaks," that the matter of our life is not inert but is in fact brimming over with directives, meanings, messages, calls, promptings, inspirations, and clues. Some of these directives mediate God's call for the client; others do not.

The pastoral counselor's task is to help clients face and transcend, insofar as possible, those obstacles and problems that prevent the disclosure and incarnation of the true self of the client. In practice, this often means the counselor helps clients to discover and incarnate consonant directives in the context of their life-field. This assistance has traditionally been called the art of discernment, discretion, prudence, or appraisal. Although these terms derive from the tradition of Christian spirituality and the practice of spiritual direction, they are an integral part of the pastoral counselor's role insofar as the counselor is concerned ultimately to help clients discern and do the will of God in their lives.

Like spiritual directors, pastoral counselors must follow the scriptural admonition:

My dear friends,
not every spirit is to be trusted,
but test the spirits to see whether they are from God
(1 Jn 4: 1, *NJB*).

Life experience is full of "spirits" or dynamics—both conscious and unconscious—that motivate our perceptions and behaviors. The pastoral counselor will help clients appraise whether these are consonant or dissonant in relation to human and Christian growth. Once a judgment is made as to the relative consonance or dissonance of a particular directive, the counselor encourages and supports the client's freedom in letting go of the negative options and embracing the positive directive.

This whole process at the core of the counseling situation involves four major steps that engage the transcendental operations of the human spirit, as indwelt, illumined, and empowered by the Holy Spirit: apprehension, appraisal, affirmation, and application of consonant directives for growth.[2]

APPREHENSION

In apprehension, counselor and client pay attention to the life-field of the client in as many of its dimensions and ranges as seem pertinent. This is the process of getting in touch with actual life experience and enabling the client to listen to it. The client is encouraged to narrate "what is going on" physically, emotionally, functionally, and spiritually in his self-experience and his relations to others, situation, wider world, and the mystery of God. The counselor evokes this narration, and receives it with empathic listening and helpful reiteration. It is a process of attention, contemplative seeing, making explicit the directives that are shaping or misshaping the client's growth. It can be called the process of conscientization, whereby relevant directives—conscious, preconscious, or unconscious—are raised to focal attention so that they can be evaluated (van Kaam 1983, p. 299). This is similar to the first step in social transformation advocated by pedagogues and theologians of liberation who encourage the raising to explicit consciousness of oppressive elements in the political and social situation, as well as awareness of the gifts that persons and communities bring to the task of social change (Freire 1982, pp. 27–56).

APPRAISAL

Following apprehension, the task of appraisal occurs. This parallels directly the central process of the traditional art of discernment, discretion, or prudence. Client and counselor together sift through the directives that have been uncovered, Their goal is to attain tentative but sound judgments about which are consonant and conducive to growth—in religious language, which directives might represent God's call to the client. Having received the client's narration of experience, the counselor now confronts with gentle and firm care the client's story. He or she engages the client in the appraisal process, which is an interpretive reading of the client's field of directives in order to seek the truth that will foster the client's growth in freedom (Jn 8:32). Questions of congeniality, compatibility, compassion, and competence form the heart of the interpretative dialogue (van Kaam 1985, p. 67 et passim).

Congeniality asks whether a particular directive, course of action, decision, feeling, or disposition (any aspect of experience) seems in harmony with my deeper self or my true nature as I glimpse it at this time of my life. For example, as an educator I have been invited to accept a promotion to an administrative position. Does this really fit? Would I find meaning behind a desk, doing paper work, confronting other personnel? Or am I a teacher who simply must teach to find some measure of contentment in life?

Compatibility addresses the life situation, our commitments, family life, and other responsibilities and asks whether the proposed directive at least does not offend the situation. Ideally it will foster greater harmony, peace, and justice within it. The administrative post will bring a salary increase, which will help my family. On the other hand, if I am miserable as an administrator, my family and others will suffer.

Compassion examines the limits and vulnerabilities in both self and significant others to see whether the proposed course of action takes these into account in compassionate ways. I will look to each member of my family and to possible future employees, trying to imagine how my decision will affect them. I will examine my energy level, my needs for privacy, and other areas of life to discover which is the more compassionate of the choices that face me.

Finally, there is the obvious question of *competence*. Do I have the training and expertise necessary for administration? Can I learn on the job? Or is my competence more confined to the space of the classroom where students have consistently rated me a good teacher?

The questions represent four criteria that may help one come to sound judgments in the appraisal process. They are ways into life experience and its meaning; they help us disclose the direction of our life. They are in no way exhaustive, but give some hints that enable us to listen with our clients to the fullest possible range of their life experience—and not, for example, just to their interior feelings or dysfunctional family history—in the adventure of disclosure of God's call and our true self. In the end, after all our questioning and careful appraising, the moment of insightful judgment usually comes as gift. It comes to me, for example, that I should take the risk of accepting the administrative position. This represents an "affinitive or affective" appraisal more than a strictly reasoned one. It is in the end more a judgment of the thinking heart than of the analytical mind (van Kaam 1987, pp. 195–96).

AFFIRMATION

The next step in the logic of the pastoral counseling process is affirmation. This act represents the client's decision to embrace directives that have been judged consonant and to let go of those discerned to be dissonant. The act of affirmation is an expression of the spiritual will. This is our deepest freedom to surrender to what we perceive to be the claim, will, or call of God upon our lives. Once the educator sees and judges that he should accept an administrative post, he integrates this judgment into the broader horizon of his life within the kingdom by the act of obedient surrender to God. This is the most authentic act of human and Christian existence. Through it we move toward health and wholeness, for we integrate our deepest freedom with God's purposes for the world insofar as we perceive these purposes, albeit through a glass darkly.

APPLICATION

Application represents the final structure of the counseling encounter. Under the influence of the spiritual will that has said yes to a perceived manifestation of God's direction, the more functional egoic dimensions of the mind will begin to plan and execute the decision taken and to apply it within the daily reality of the life-field. In this attempt at incarnation clients may make many mistakes. They must realize that functional willing is secondary to growth and transformation in which spiritual willing, our deepest freedom, has primacy of place. The counselor's task is to encourage the trying and the testing of new behaviors. Even more it is the counselor's mission to support the very act of affirmation and surrender by various modes of encouragement and challenge.

Two things must be noted in conclusion about the structures of apprehension, appraisal, affirmation, and application. First, they are logical rather than chronological operations. That is, they do not pretend to be a four-step method for an effective series of counseling sessions. They are rather perspectives on the logic or meaning-structure of the counseling engagement. Although seldom a predictable situation, analysis of many forms of pastoral counseling and spiritual direction reveals that they have these four structures in common. They are balanced and ordered according to the demands of the problems presented and the individuality of the client.

Second, both counselor and client engage in these four operations together in a coformative dialogue. The steps form the process to which both parties are committed in appropriate ways. For example, the counselor hears the apprehensions of the client and challenges him to widen them. The counselor raises questions that move the client toward the act of tentative judgment, which the counselor may or may not explicitly support. The accent in affirmation is, of course, on the client and his or her freedom, which may have to be evoked and encouraged by the counselor; likewise for the task of application.

In terms of these structures, one could say that the entire aim of pastoral counseling is to evoke and sustain the art and discipline of apprehension, appraisal, affirmation, and application in the lives of the clients so that they become capable of living their own lives under the direction of the Spirit (see Gal 5:25).

Using the structure of the four "A's" as a point of departure, we will look more closely at the purpose, structures, and dynamics of pastoral counseling of gay males. We shall examine the progression of experience that might occur in a typical series of pastoral counseling encounters, recognizing all the while that the "typical" gay male does not exist except as a figment of a prejudicial culture's imagination. We shall first discuss disclosure of a positive gay identity as integral to the processes of apprehension and appraisal. Second, we shall address the authentic integration of gay identity through the structures of affirmation and application. To focus our discussion, we shall take a crucial period of every gay male's experience—the process of "coming out." It is at this developmental juncture that many gay persons seek pastoral counseling.

Apprehension and Appraisal: Toward Positive Gay Identity

As a guest in a parish house for dinner one evening ten years ago, I recall the pastor telling of his meeting that day with "a homosexual" who dropped into his office. The pastor went on, "It was very simple. I told him all he had to do to overcome his problem was to be silent and meditate for half an hour each day. Too much fuss is being made today over this 'gay thing.'" I asked timidly, "Did you invite this man to return for further pastoral conversations?" The pastor replied, "Of course not, there was nothing more to talk about."

While fairly typical ten years ago, such a conversation is less likely to happen today. What does occur in practice? Word gets around the gay community that Reverend Joan or Pastor James is a "good person to talk to." Or the prospective client will go to a pastoral counseling center, trusting that the professionalism encountered there will not be marked by discrimination. Or, attending church, the gay man will intuitively size up, correctly or incorrectly, the presider at worship and ask for an appointment. In each case the presenting problem has something to do with a suspected or clearly recognized homosexuality that the client perceives as problematic, as an impairment to his faith life, his family and social life, his professional occupation, his emotional health, and so forth. Clearly the client is in conflict, sometimes in desperation, over this problem and how to solve it.

Peter, age twenty-three, is the eldest of four siblings in a middle-class Methodist family. A college graduate, he lives on his own and works for an insurance company. He had a number of sexual encounters with men in college, but dismissed these as locker room antics. He has dated women since high school but has never fallen in love. A gnawing suspicion that "I might really be gay" has been eating at him for over a year. It throws him into fear and indeed panic.

Three months ago Peter and a buddy from the office went out drinking on Friday night. The evening ended in bed, which Peter ascribed to intoxication. The friend, however, pursued the relationship. He invited Peter for dinners and other social occasions. The attraction between them grew. Soon it dawned on Peter that for the first time in his life he was really in love and falling more deeply into it each day. He felt he couldn't handle the situation on his own. He sought the help of the pastor of a neighboring Methodist church, Howard. Peter had heard Howard was a good listener, a caring person, and "liberal" in orientation.

What was the focus of their first few sessions? In Rogerian terms, Howard gave Peter a quality of attention marked by "unconditional positive regard" (Hall and Lindzey 1978, p. 288–89). Howard evoked Peter's story in as many of its facets as possible. He encouraged him to explore as many aspects of his life-field as seemed relevant to the presenting problem of conflict due to perceived or suspected gay orientation. Through evocative questions and empathic listening, Howard gradually acquired some of Peter's "internal frame of reference" (Hall and Lindzey, pp. 303–4). At this point Howard's main intentionality was not explanation, advice-giving, or interpretation. He wanted to co-listen with Peter to all the interwoven directives in Peter's life-field that played a role in his present conflict—on the personal, interpersonal, situational, and religious levels.

For example, Howard evoked and heard the directives of attraction and excitement emerging from Peter's vital-sexual self in relation to his friend; spiritual longings for partnership with a beloved other; fears of what his family would think about the relationship; great anxiety about the work situation should the relationship become known; dread of divine judgment and the possible need of self-imposed exile from the church community; an uneasy sense of ostracization from normal and normative culture as he has always known it. Through these and many other directives woven into the conflict lurked Peter's ultimate question: "Is there something really wrong with me, and what can I do about it?"

This first stage of apprehension is crucial for growth. The counselor cannot pass lightly or quickly over Peter's life-field with its ranges of conflicted experience by suggesting or imposing his own positive interpretations of homosexuality. As Howard evokes and listens to Peter's story in all its relevant pathways and chapters, Peter is given to himself through his act of narration. He comes home to the truth of his own experience in all its ambiguity and conflict, but with some hope that, because the counselor seems to accept him, his story may also be one of hope and opportunity.

There are three levels going on all the time in the apprehension process: the co-listening and apprehension of Peter and Howard together of the dynamics and directives in Peter's life-field; the concomitant internal processing of Peter within his own psyche and spirit; the ongoing self-apprehensions of Howard, who must remain congruent with his evolving experience of the client. (In this regard, in relation to the gay male, pastoral counselors must be highly self-critical, as noted previously, about their actual feelings and dispositions toward the client. These may range from unconscious fear or repugnance for homosexuality that gradually surfaces to consciousness all the way to countertransferences such as falling in love with the client. The latter is more probable for counselors who have not dealt with the homosexual component of their own personalities.) Through the convergence of these three levels of apprehension Peter and Howard move together toward the best possible apprehension of Peter's situation, the best *understanding* that is available to them of Peter's experience. The client often experiences this phase of the process as a homecoming. This may be the first time in years that a client has been helped to "be himself," to come home to the truth, to allow the real self rather than the ideal self to prevail, at least in the counseling session (Horney 1950, pp. 17–86).

After evoking and hearing Peter's story in a process of co-apprehension of the conflicting phenomena in his life, the pastoral counselor directs Peter toward a more interpretative mode of exchange. Together he and Peter seek the deeper meanings of his situation so that Peter will come to mature insight and judgment about his life direction as a gay man. In the actual dynamics of the counseling session, this will involve a movement from a phenomenological (disclosing structures of experience) to a more hermeneutical stance (interpreting the underlying dynamics at work in the life-field). This hermeneutical process is the work of appraisal or discernment, using guidelines and norms for appraisal such as congeniality, compatibility, compassion, and competence.

The appraisal process is a conversation that aims to foster the client's mature assessment of his situation. Integral to the process is the counselor's ability to propose questions in a creative and noncontrolling way. In *The Analogical Imagination* theologian David Tracy, following Gadamer, notes that hermeneutical understanding is best fostered by authentic conversation. About this type of conversation Tracy writes:

> Real conversation occurs only when the individual partners move past self-consciousness and self-aggrandizement into joint reflection upon the subject matter of the conversation. The back-and-forth movement of all genuine conversation (an ability to listen, to reflect, to correct, to speak to the point—the ability, in sum, to allow the question to take over) is an experience which all reflective persons have felt....Real conversation occurs only when the participants allow the question, the subject matter, to assume primacy. It occurs only when our usual fears about our own self-image die: whether that fear is expressed in either arrogance or scrupulosity matters little. That fear dies only because we are carried along, and sometimes away, by the subject matter itself into

the rare event or happening named "thinking" and "understanding." For understanding *happens;* it *occurs* not as the pure result of personal achievement but in the back-and-forth movement of the conversation itself (Tracy 1981, p. 101).

The conversation of appraisal or discernment will thus be a back-and-forth movement about the truth of the negative voices apprehended in the life-field that incline Peter toward self-loathing and rejection, as well as about the more positive directives that hold out hope and wider horizons for Peter's life. The criteria proposed for appraisal of congeniality, compatibility, compassion, and competence may be helpful in this conversation.

CONGENIALITY

The first and most significant matter for appraisal is a congeniality issue; namely, Peter asks, "Am I really gay?" Many gay men have no doubts about their predominately homosexual orientation. They have known it since childhood. Others are profoundly disturbed by the question and have great difficulty in accepting themselves as primarily gay. The pastoral counselor may have to offer pointed questions to help assess whether gayness is congenial for the client, in harmony with his true self. Usually some simple questions aimed at disclosing the spontaneous pre-reflective orientation of the client's sexual and affective energies will promote the necessary self-knowledge. For example, "You see an attractive male/female couple walking down the street. Are you spontaneously drawn to the male or the female in your 'first look.'" "Is the primary content of your sexual fantasy life and your dreams more male or female-oriented?" These and similar questions can help the client appraise the actual direction of his sexual orientation.

The deeper congeniality question comes down to this: "If I am gay, is there something really wrong with me, and what can I do about it?" This is a pivotal question for the gay male at this stage of his development. The pastoral counselor cannot arbitrarily dismiss it or give a positive pat answer that does not take the anguish and depth of the question seriously. Instead, through the back-and-forth of the conversation (in which both parties open themselves to the subject-matter and let it hold sway) the counselor will help the client struggle his way toward the answer. There are many directives, for example, in Peter's life-field from church, family upbringing, and male culture that tell him: "Yes, there is something wrong with you. It is your sexual orientation. And all you can do is hide it, suffer it, and try not to make a fool of yourself. You can even try 'passing' as a heterosexual man. Maybe even get married; it might work. At least you'll have a respected position in society, and who knows, you may be capable of a loving and sexual relationship with just the right woman." These directives have long reinforced unconscious and conscious feelings of self-doubt and loathing in Peter's life.

Howard can offer other questions that may point Peter toward a more positive direction. He can appeal to their shared faith tradition, which appraises all that God has created as very good (Gn 1:31), especially humanity created in God's own image. Being gay, therefore, is not only a sexual attraction; it is a profound orientation of one's deepest embodied soul, created to image God by loving as a gay person. Howard can appeal to the vitality and lifting of low-grade depression that Peter is experiencing in his new relationship with the friend from work. He can stress that each of us has only one life to live, and that the greatest tragedy is never to be one's self. Holiness and wholeness consist in disclosure and incarnation of one's true self. Being gay is part of being one's true self. Howard can point to positive gay role models in the church, the wider culture, and in history. He can counsel that there is a world of relationships, an alternative religious and secular culture, for example, church groups for gays and lesbians, in which Peter could find spiritual and social support for his personal quest.

COMPATIBILITY

Another strand of the pastoral conversation will focus upon issues of compatibility for Peter. How will being gay relate him differently to others? Should he inform his family of his newfound identity? What about the work situation? Should he be open, discreet, or completely secretive about being gay? Especially in a pastoral counseling context, the issue of compatibility with the church may be a serious question. Can he remain a practicing Christian since he may be living in contradiction with his church's official teachings? Is it honest to do so? A significant number of gays have left their churches precisely because of this question and the refusal or inability to distinguish the institutional churches from the reality of God's kingdom of justice, peace, and mercy.

Other compatibility questions will focus upon more immediate and long-range bonding issues. What about the relationship with his new friend? Shall he pursue it? Should they live together? If they continue to grow in love, should they make a formal or informal commitment to one another—and what shape could the commitment take? Or, perhaps he is not the "marrying kind," either as a gay or straight person. Would he be better off living alone as a single person, even embracing a celibate life as an expression of gay loving?

COMPASSION

Taking into account one's own and others' limits and vulnerabilities is integral to the client's task of appraisal with the pastoral counselor. The questions of compassion help temper inappropriate expressions of the newly found gay identity and self-affirmation. Peter, for example, is temperamentally a private person with extreme sensitivities to the opinions of others. Compassion for his own vulnerability, therefore, might suggest he be most discreet about self-disclosure. He would not have the inner stamina to go public as a gay person, but could "come out" to a few trusted friends. Peter's family members have always been liberal in their views and committed to social justice issues. They have always insisted that their children live their own lives. Thus, Peter assesses that they will probably accept his gayness without too much conflict or suffering, and tentatively judges that he will come out to them in the near future.

COMPETENCE

In order to maintain and enhance their self-esteem, all humans seek to maintain the conviction that they are competent to give and receive shape, love, and direction in their everyday lives. Plagued by a history of self-doubt, many gay men suffer a lifelong history of diminished self-esteem, which sometimes leads to self-abusive activity in thoughtless promiscuity, alcohol and drug addiction, and self-defeating behaviors in other realms of life, such as the work place. All of this amounts to self-fulfilling prophecies based on a deep sense of incompetence.

In their shared assessment of Peter's situation, Howard and Peter may want to explore Peter's deeper feelings about his basic sense of potency in life. Does Peter generally feel that he "can do," so that he can identify with Paul's "There is nothing I cannot do in the One who strengthens me" (Phil 4:13, *NJB*)? Can he accept failure and defeat with the conviction that "It is, then, about my weaknesses that I am happiest of all to boast, so that the power of Christ may rest upon me....For it is when I am weak that I am strong" (2 Cor 12:9–10, *NJB*). This sense of biblical competence is important for gay males, whose sense of self-esteem must be deeply internal in a culture and society that so often withhold their approval.

Affirmation and Application: Toward Wise Integration

Peter and Howard have had ten counseling sessions over a three-month period. Howard has helped Peter become present to the truth of his experience, to express himself freely as together they explore the many directives shaping Peter's life and make tentative but sound judgments about which directives are consonant with his life call—that is, congenial with his true self, compatible with his situation, compassionate toward self and others, and competent. Peter's overall judgment is that it is all right to be gay. In fact, it is a gift of God. From the judgment that "something is really wrong with me," he has moved toward the judgment that being gay means that "something is right with me." There has been a transformation of consciousness, an experiential shift in perspective. This new judgment articulates Peter's interior passage from the closet of fear to the open space of freedom. Peter has come out of hiding from himself, from the protected place of false security where the truth of his being never finds the light of expression (Whitehead and Whitehead 1984, pp. 134–35).

The next task for pastoral counselor and client is the engagement of the client's freedom through the spiritual capacity we call the "will." Peter has grown in awareness. For a mature integration of homosexuality into his human and Christian life, there must now occur the interior assent of his freedom to the truth he has disclosed. Second, he must start incarnating his assent in daily life. These are the operations of affirmation and application.

As we have seen, affirmation is an expression of the spiritual will, which is that depth of our freedom where we are always able to say yes to the divine mystery, even when we cannot incarnate this assent immediately in our behaviors. Van Kaam (1979) calls it "intentional wholeness" and the "wholeness of good will" (p. 133). It is the foundation for further psychological and spiritual growth. Without this firm and free engagement of the spiritual will, the client runs the risk of mere behaviorism or voluntarism in his attempts to apply new directives in daily life.

In the context of Judeo-Christian pastoral counseling Peter has discerned that God seems to will his gayness, that God calls him to love as a gay person. While such a judgment is only probable, it is all we can achieve in our search for the unfathomable mystery of God's will, which always remains ultimately hidden in light inaccessible (1 Tm 6:16). Placing Peter's new judgments about his gay experience within a religious horizon and encouraging a response to the divine mystery in light of this horizon seem to be the characteristics that distinguish pastoral counseling from secular therapies.

Howard will encourage Peter to say yes to God by saying a profound and free yes to his graced sexual orientation. In that yes the dichotomy between sexuality and spirituality is overcome at its root. This yes is the only radical antidote to the internalized homophobia from which many gay men suffer. This assent is truly an exodus from the bondage of self-depreciation to the freedom of self-affirmation and celebration of Peter's essential goodness as a gay man.

Saying yes to one's gay identity and its Source is the foundation of subsequent integration for the gay male. The movement is from awareness (apprehension and appraisal) through acceptance toward integration (affirmation and application). No client can authentically integrate a new perspective or disposition in his or her life without the prior moment of a free assent in which the client radically affirms the appraised directive as "for me" in relation to the gracious and meaningful Mystery we name God. Without this affirmation, the new disposition or perspective is built on sand; it becomes a willful striving or a new behavioristic conditioning.

Only Peter can say this yes. The counselor cannot do it for him. Howard, however, can suggest the motivations of religious meaning that can support Peter's surrender. Howard can encourage Peter as he wrestles with this angel throughout the night of crisis (Gn 32:26–29). He can stand by Peter in this hour of decision so crucial for the rest of his life journey toward spiritual wholeness and psychological health. The choice is Peter's. It must not be assumed that because he sees gayness as a positive identity that he will assent to and assume this identity. The new identity is still largely in the realm of the unknown. To choose it freely is to risk the unknown, and risk generates fear. It is possible that, having ventured two steps toward freedom, Peter can walk three steps back into self-depreciation. He can reject the new directive of self-goodness or, more typically, experience paralysis in relation to it. That is, he will never really embrace and assent to it. The challenge for the pastoral counselor in this moment of the process is to shepherd the freedom of the client, to encourage conscious choice, and to offer his support as Peter surrenders to the divine mystery.

For wise integration of a newly affirmed gay identity into the whole context of one's life and commitments, the process of application must occur. This is often a long search and struggle. Usually only the first steps of it take place within a formal pastoral counseling situation.

In a sociohistorical situation charged with conflict and ambivalence in regard to homosexuality, positive and life-giving incarnation of one's affirmed gay identity will never be easy. Part of Howard's task is to help Peter realize and accept this so that he will not suffer disillusionment and consequent regression when he confronts the obstacles to integration in his own life and culture. He can encourage in Peter the conviction that no human or spiritual integration is possible without taking our share of "hardships for the sake of the gospel, relying on the power of God" (2 Tm 1:8, NJB).

Central to the task of application will be a cycle of strategic appraisals as to how Peter can best live as a gay man. Many of the issues involved in this movement toward integration will already have been explored in previous sessions, but now they take on a more urgent focus: "Fine, I'm gay and I'm okay, but now what do I *do* about it?" A host of questions present themselves. For instance, what about gay culture as such in its heterogeneous shapes? Like any culture, gay culture is both fallen and graced. The mature person participates in it with discrimination. Does being gay mean I will frequent places of gay socialization like bars, discos, gay community centers?

Should I join Affirmation, the gay outreach group of the Methodist church? Again, how public shall I go? There are various stages of coming out that Peter may go through and probably should start trying while still in counseling. There is coming out to oneself, to a few trusted others, to family and all or most of one's friends. Finally, some gay people are called to a more public coming out, for example coming out as both gay and Christian in public forums such as writing, public speaking, public leadership in gay organizations, and so on. Each gay man is unique in this regard. He must find modes of application that are congenial, compatible, compassionate, and for which he is competent.

The criteria for application parallel those for the act of appraisal. The difference is that there is the "trying." Peter tries out different behaviors and strategies in his attempts to incarnate his identity as a gay man. Ideally, he does this within the stratum of values represented by his faith commitment. In practice, however, the counselor may have to stand by and witness behaviors he does not understand or agree with—casual and uncommitted sex, for example. The educated counselor will realize that this is common among gay men for many reasons. Chief among them are the alleviation of loneliness and protest against the oppressive dictates of the normative culture of heterosexuality. The counselor will not condemn or disapprove of such behaviors. His or her task is to challenge the client toward integration of sexual identity with the client's deepest values and commitments, especially the vocation to love that each human has received in the core of his or her being. No one is perfect in loving. The pastoral counselor shepherds the client's attempts to test and apply his newly affirmed gay identity. The counselor walks with the client in this process. As parents do not scold children for stumbling as they learn to walk, so the counselor does not disapprove when inappropriate behaviors are engaged in. The counselor continues to walk with the client and helps him stand up again when he stumbles or falls into inauthenticity or dissonant applications.

Pastoral counselor and client thus move together through the interpenetrating cycles of apprehension, appraisal, affirmation, and application. These structures and dynamics of the counseling session must always be kept in balance in a climate of freedom and disciplined spontaneity. It is all too easy to fixate on one or two at the expense of the others. For instance, Peter and Howard could spend many months getting in touch with Peter's experience (apprehension) and never think carefully through (appraisal) the meaning of the experience for human and spiritual growth. Or, they could gloss lightly over the range of Peter's experience and do all kinds of interpretive work before Peter has fully explored and come home to the truth of his experience. The subtle and deep act of affirmation or surrender might be passed over in favor of fixated attention on Peter's attempts to apply his new identity in functional behaviors. What matters in the pastoral counseling setting, as always, is mature balance on the part of the counselor, who must make wise decisions about when to engage in each of the four processes in service of the psychological and spiritual growth of the gay client.

Conclusion

We have attempted to portray the cultural and ecclesial situation from which the gay male comes for pastoral counseling. We saw that it is a conflicted context both objectively and subjectively for the gay man himself. For an accurate understanding of the gay male, the counselor will see him as embedded in this wide sociohistorical conflict.

Pastoral counselors will educate themselves in regard to the possible theological and ethical assumptions about homosexuality. They will be in touch with their own intellectual and emotional assumptions about persons with homosexual orientations. If they cannot counsel the gay male toward acceptance, affirmation, and positive incarnation of a gay identity, counselors ought to refer the gay male to someone who can serve his wholeness and health. There is no shame here, no accusation of incompetence. There is the simple recognition that pastoral counselors cannot counsel everybody. They should be aware of both their gifts and their limits and humbly accept them.

Once undertaken, the pastoral counseling contract with the gay male has at least a twofold purpose. First, the counselor will assist the client in the movement toward a radical self-affirmation as a gay man whose gayness is part of his creation in the very image of God. Second, counselors of gay men commit themselves to foster the wise integration of the affirmed identity in the total context of the client's life-field, including his relationship with the mystery of God that permeates this field.

Finally, we explored basic structures and psycho-spiritual dynamics that serve the purposes of pastoral counseling of gay men: apprehension of directives from the life-field, mature appraisal of the meaning of those directives concerning gay experience, support for the affirmation, and application of consonant directives for human and spiritual growth.

For the gay male, pastoral counselors can be midwives of a new identity and integration. It may seem shocking that part of their pastoral mission, which the Christian tradition has called the *cura animarum* or "the care of souls," may include helping bring homosexual persons out of the closet. But that is only because the theory and practice of ministry have been in part misshaped by cultural prejudices for centuries. The light of the authentic Judeo-Christian tradition invites all believers to come out of the closets of oppression and fear into the freedom of grace, wherein all people have been created to love with their unique orientations and gifts. Being gay is a graced orientation and a gift to church and society. Pastoral counselors stand in awe of this particular vocation as they assist gay people in their passage from darkness into light.

Notes

1. Freud, for example, taught that all humans are inherently bisexual; each sex is attracted to members of the same sex as well as to members of the opposite sex. This is the constitutional basis for homosexuality, although in most people the homosexual impulses remain latent. Whether hetero- or homosexuality gains ascendancy depends to some extent upon early conditioning factors in family and society (Hall and Lindzey 1978, p. 57). Denial of one's homosexual capacities often leads to *homophobia*, which is irrational fear of and consequent prejudice toward persons who are primarily homosexual. Often homophobia implies unconscious rejection or loathing of one's own latent homosexual tendencies and potential.

2. See the parallel with Bernard Lonergan (1972). Lonergan discusses "transcendental method" in theology and relates it to the exercise of the transcendent operations of the distinctively human spirit through its faculties of mind and will: experiencing, understanding, judging, deciding, and communicating.

References

Barth, Karl. 1961. *Church Dogmatics.* Vol. 3. Edinburgh: T. & T. Clark.

Boswell, John. 1980. *Christianity, Social Tolerance, and Homosexuality.* Chicago: University of Chicago Press.

Congregation for the Doctrine of the Faith. 1986. "The Pastoral Care of Homosexual Persons." Rome: 1 October 1986. Origins: *NC Documentary Service,* vol. 16, no. 22 (November 13, 1986).

Crompton, Louis. 1974. "Gay Genocide: From Leviticus to Hitler." Address delivered to the Gay Academic Union. New York University (November 30).

Duberman, Martin, Vicinus, Martha, and Chauncey, Jr., George, eds. 1989. *Hidden from History: Reclaiming the Gay and Lesbian Past.* New York: Penguin Books.

Freire, Paulo. 1982. *Pedagogy of the Oppressed.* Trans. Myra Bergman Ramos. New York: Continuum.

Gadamer, Hans Georg. 1975. *Truth and Method.* Trans. Garrett Barden and John Cumming. New York: Seabury.

Hall, Calvin S., and Lindzey, Gardner. 1978. *Theories of Personality.* New York: John Wiley and Sons.

Horney, Karen. 1950. *Neurosis and Human Growth.* New York: W. W. Norton.

Lonergan, Bernard. 1972. *Method in Theology.* New York: Herder and Herder.

McNeill, John J. 1976. *The Church and the Homosexual.* Kansas City: Sheed, Andrews and McMeel.

Merton, Thomas. 1961. *New Seeds of Contemplation.* New York: New Directions.

Nelson, James B. 1978. *Embodiment: An Approach to Sexuality and Christian Theology.* Minneapolis: Augsburg.

Nugent, C. Robert, and Gramick, Jeannine. 1982. *A Time to Speak: A Collection of Contemporary Statements from U.S. Catholic Sources on Homosexuality, Gay Ministry and Social Justice.* Mt. Rainier, Md.: New Ways Ministry.

Pittenger, Norman. 1977. *Gay Lifestyles: A Christian Interpretation of Homosexuality and the Homosexual.* Los Angeles: The Universal Fellowship Press.

Tracy, David. 1981. *The Analogical Imagination: Christian Theology and the Culture of Pluralism.* New York: Crossroad.

van Kaam, Adrian. 1979. *The Transcendent Self.* Denville, N.J.: Dimension Books, 1979.

———. 1983. *Fundamental Formation.* New York: Crossroad.

———. 1985. *Human Formation.* New York: Crossroad.

———. 1987. *Scientific Formation.* New York: Crossroad.

Whitehead, Evelyn Eaton, and Whitehead, James D. 1984. *Seasons of Strength: New Visions of Adult Christian Maturing.* New York: Doubleday.

Wicks, Robert J., Richard D. Parsons, and Donald E. Capps, eds. 1985. *Clinical Handbook of Pastoral Counseling.* New York: Paulist Press.

For Further Reading

Conn, Joann Wolski. 1989. *Spirituality and Personal Maturity.* New York: Paulist Press.

Fortunato, John E. 1983. *Embracing the Exile: Healing Journeys of Gay Christians.* New York: Seabury.

Gonsiorek, John C., Ed. 1985. *A Guide to Psychotherapy with Gay and Lesbian Clients.* New York: Harrington Park Press.

Moses, A. Elfin, and Hawkins, Robert O., Jr. 1982. *Counseling Lesbian Women and Gay Men: A Life Issues Approach.* St. Louis: C. V. Mosby.

Tripp, C. A. 1975. *The Homosexual Matrix.* New York: McGraw Hill.

SECTION II
SPECIAL CHALLENGES
AND OPPORTUNITIES FOR PASTORAL
COUNSELORS IN THE THIRD MILLENNIUM

The chapters in section II address the issues, concerns, and trends that appear to be taking center stage as both challenges and opportunities for pastoral counselors in the third millennium. From the opportunities and support provided by hospice to the sadly increasing need to minister in the age of AIDS and addiction, each chapter, while discussing some of the more devastating threats to human existence, provides hope in the form of a pastoral counseling response.°

In chapter 10 "Pastoral Counseling with Those with Sexual Addictions," Stephen J. Rosetti draws upon the research and his own extensive clinical experience to provide a comprehensive view of the long road to recovery faced by those with sexual addictions. Rosetti provides the reader with a clear understanding of the assessment process, the addictive cycle, and the treatment approaches used to break the cycle. Rosetti makes it clear that the word *cure* is neither appropriate nor helpful when dealing with sexual addictions. Neither the question nor the answer is one of cure, according to Rosetti, but is one of hope and an ability to live a healthy, productive life free of sexually deviant behavior.

In chapter 11, "Hospice, Pastoral Counseling, and Care in Response to Death and Dying," Constance M. Mucha takes a sensitive and challenging look at pastoral counseling and care's response to those who are dying. Mucha posits that with proper training the pastoral counselor can provide invaluable support in preparing the client for the journey. However, it is essential that prior to offering this support the pastoral counselor be

---

° The reader should be aware that, while an editorial effort has been made to update statistics in places, some outdated statistics have been kept in order to respect the theses of the original articles. In each case, it was determined that the pastoral content of the article is still valuable and relevant for contemporary pastoral counseling.

prepared for the journey. Through a wonderful blending of theory, research, and clinical illustrations, Mucha offers that preparation.

In the next chapter (chapter 12), "Suicide Survivors: Moving Beyond Intervention and Postvention," Richard D. Parsons provides an in-depth analysis of the socio-psychological forces that exist and that encourage suicide survivors to deny and repress their grief, thus creating a pathogenic response to mourning and establishing the possible fertile soil for additional suicidal attempts. The chapter presents a model for diagnosing pathogenic grief and steps to take not only to remediate and intervene but to do so in ways that have a primary prevention impact.

Chapter 13 presents a pastoral view of post-traumatic stress disorder. The authors, David W. Foy, Kent D. Drescher, Allan G. Fitz, and Kevin R. Kennedy, provide a model for discriminating normal adjustment to trauma from pathological adjustment. Further, these authors offer specific guidelines for appropriate pastoral responses. A very special contribution of this chapter for counselors currently working with those who have been victimized is the authors' depiction of vicarious victimization. The authors highlight the potential for all who work with this population to experience vicarious victimization. They offer strategies for reducing the risk of vicarious victimization that are essential for the health and well-being of all pastoral counselors.

The final essay in this section addresses one of today's most devastating phenomena: AIDS. In "Embracing Pastoral Ministry in the Age of AIDS" (chapter 14), Walter J. Smith provides the clinical data on AIDS in a very real and personal manner. Through the sharing of a story of a young man named Matthew, Smith not only highlights the importance of unconditional love for these patients but also the opportunity to experience it from these patients in return. Smith challenges pastoral counselors not to depersonalize the syndrome, but to address their own personal and professional limitations when working with AIDS patients.

Stephen J. Rosetti

10. Pastoral Counseling with Those with Sexual Addictions

Case Study: John Doe, a long-time member of the parish and a member of the parish council, calls one evening and asks to schedule an appointment for the next day. He sounds tense and worried. He is an attorney, husband, and father of three children. He enters the office and says that a neighbor saw him go into a pornographic theater and informed John's wife, who insisted that her husband speak to a counselor.

No one would never have guessed that John would be engaged in such behavior. He informs the counselor that he has been under a lot of stress lately and admits that he did, indeed, go into the theater. However, he says that this has never happened before; he stayed for just a moment and then, realizing the mistake that he had made, left quickly. At this point in the conversation, John is clearly distressed and begins to tear up. He promises that it will never happen again.

During the course of the conversation, John also mentions that the neighbor who witnessed him going into the theater has serious emotional and family problems himself. John then becomes visibly angry and says that the person has been trying to smear his character for years. He goes on to say that this man is not a practicing member of the community and is hostile to the faith.

John finishes the conversation by speaking of how frightened he is about his marriage. He admits, somewhat sheepishly, that he and his wife have not gotten along sexually for many years. Nevertheless, he loves his wife and is hoping that the counselor will speak to her and ask her to forgive him.

The first inclination of a counselor in such a situation might be to do exactly as John Doe wishes. The counselor could opt to be an empathic listener, consoling John in his distress and fear. He or she might speak to him of the

211

mercy and compassion of God. And, since the couple is well known to the parish and the pastoral counselor, the counselor might be tempted to speak to John's wife, assuring her that she has spoken to John and is confident that this was a momentary lapse due to stress and that it is unlikely to happen again. Further, the counselor might refer them to a marriage counselor to address the fact that they "have not gotten along sexually for many years."

Such a pastoral response might, indeed, be an appropriate one. However, it is very likely that it is not. In fact, the counselor who takes such an approach, without further probing, is probably being manipulated by Mr. Doe and unwittingly colluding in his psychological defenses.

Even if the counselor has no experience dealing with sexual addictions, he should be skeptical about aspects of John's account. For example, it is highly unlikely that this was the first time John entered a pornographic theater. People are not usually caught by friends the first time they enter. It is more likely that they are apprehended after dozens, if not hundreds, of times.

Second, it is probably more than a coincidence that John was seen in a pornographic theater and also has been having sexual problems with his wife. There are probably underlying, long-standing issues around intimacy and sexuality that have plagued John, and thus his marriage.

Third, John seems to be steering the guilt and blame away from himself. He complains of stress at work and at home, suggesting that the stress is the cause of his aberrant behavior. He also tries to blame his neighbor. John is angry at his neighbor for turning him in, and John acts as if he is a victim. John tries to manipulate the pastoral counselor by speaking of his neighbor's lack of faith. And, he further tries to manipulate the counselor into smoothing things over with his wife. Clearly, John has not taken full responsibility for his behavior, nor is he trying to face himself and do whatever is necessary to change himself and his behavior.

If pastoral counselors are to be of assistance in such cases, they will need to understand some of the dynamics of sexual addictions and the appropriate means of dealing with such issues.

What Is a Sexual Addiction?

There are some clinicians who do not support the term *sexual addiction* and would rather use a phrase like *sexual compulsion*. Indeed, the term *addiction* is not a diagnostic label found in the American Psychiatric Association's DSM-IV, even for alcohol and substance problems. Rather, the DSM-IV speaks of "abuse" and "dependence." Also, the term *addiction* is in danger of being over-used today and applied to a variety of normal behaviors that are not seriously compulsive or destructive.

Nevertheless, *addiction* is a popular term that is often descriptive of a specific type of problematic situation. And thus the term *sexual addiction* can be helpful in many cases. It suggests that there are people for whom repetitive sexual acting out is an increasingly destructive behavior over which these people have little or no control. Most sexual addicts are males, and thus the male gender will be used in speaking of sex addicts. However, occasionally, there are women for whom this label seems appropriate.

Examples of sexual addicts might include the person who compulsively masturbates several times a day, or the man who has had hundreds of anonymous homosexual partners, or the adult who has befriended and molested dozens of eleven- to thirteen-year-old boys, or the college professor who has seduced scores of female students. Increasingly common is the person who spends a growing amount of time each day viewing Internet pornography.

The sexual addiction is often, but not always, hidden as a secret part of their lives, split off from their "normal" selves. Usually, the sexual acting out is done in a destructive cycle that has much to do with shame, isolation, damaged self-esteem, frustrated needs for intimacy, and unhealed childhood traumas.

Just as alcoholics, without assistance, are powerless over their drinking, so too sex addicts are usually incapable of breaking the destructive cycle without reaching out to others and to God. Also, sex addicts, like alcoholics who have begun to live a life of "sobriety," should not view themselves as completely "cured," but living "one day at a time" instead.

In his landmark work, *Out of the Shadows,* Patrick Carnes suggests a simple formula for determining whether someone's sexual behavior might be accurately described as compulsive or addictive. Dr. Carnes uses the acronym "SAFE." A sexual addict's behavior is usually a *Secret* that covers the shame of a double life; the behavior is *Abusive* either to one's self or to others; the sexual behavior is used to avoid painful *Feelings;* and it is *Empty* of a loving, caring relationship (Carnes, 1992).

Certainly, there are people who have sexual problems who are not sexual addicts. The man suffering from an erectile problem or the women with anorgasmia are obviously not sex addicts. Also, there are people who have engaged in deviant sexual behaviors that appear to be only transitory. For example, it is not uncommon for a few males who have had a passing use of pornography or interactions with prostitutes or who have engaged in sexual contact as adults with adolescents to move beyond such problematic behaviors. However, the counselor should be wary of being deceived. Denial is a powerful reality in most sex addicts.

Denial

One of the greatest obstacles to counseling sexual addicts effectively is their ubiquitous use of the psychic defense of *denial*. Denial may used in such subtle and convincing ways that inexperienced counselors are very likely to be deceived and manipulated by sexual addicts. In fact, it is not uncommon that experienced clinicians will occasionally be "conned" into believing a deceitful tale spun by a sex addict. This is why doing assessment and treatment of sex addicts is most effective when using a team of experienced clinicians; one person may be fooled, but it is highly unlikely that an entire team will be misled.

Dealing effectively with the sex addict's denial is particularly important in today's society. It has happened many times that professional clinicians have been deceived and manipulated by sex addicts, with damaging and possibly legal implications. Future victimizations that might have been avoided can occur, and counselors who are conned by the addicts may find themselves at the other end of a civil lawsuit, their reputations tarnished.

As an example of denial in the case cited, John Doe asks the counselor to accept John's personal belief that his behavior is not of serious concern. He also wants the counselor to try to convince his wife of this. John wants to be "let off the hook" with his wife, and he does not want to face the truth of his behavior or its consequences. Thus, he is asking the counselor to collude in his denial. Many counselors do collude with sex addicts because the addicts can be very persuasive (including the tears in John's eyes simulating a repentance that is probably not yet genuine). Only through competent training and experience do counselors have a chance of seeing through such defenses.

John's description has several tell-tale signs of denial. In addition to blaming the neighbor, John said that his entering the porno theater has never happened before and that he left the theater quickly. While theoretically possible, it is highly unlikely. Also, John said his behavior was due to stress; however, most people do not go to porno theaters under stress. Again, he is shifting the focus away from his behavior and his own responsibility, and denying the significance of what took place.

A more subtle denial is John's denial of his real inner psychic state. Both his tears and his anger are part of his defenses. His tears during the counseling session are probably either a manipulation and/or possibly tears of remorse that he was caught, but they are not likely to be tears of true repentance or real remorse for his behavior. His anger is in service of maintaining his stance as a "victim," and the intensity of this anger suggests that there is an inner rage, probably directed at himself, inside him. John is not yet in touch with the fear, guilt, overwhelming shame, internal devastation, and inner rage that are likely to be buried deep within his psyche.

The long road to recovery will necessarily include facing the inner shame, conflicts, and rage. It will be painful process of re-integrating his inner self and his emotions. In the beginning, however, his pervasive denial keeps such truths at a long arm's length.

Initial Assessment

The beginning of any effective pastoral counseling and/or referral is an initial assessment. What precisely are John's problems, and how best can these difficulties be addressed? In the case of assessing sexual addicts, it is very likely that what is revealed in the first session is only the beginning of a much more extensive and complex psychosexual history. Even if the counselee loudly protests that he has revealed everything and remains the innocent victim of people who are out to defame his reputation, the counselor should reserve personal judgment.

I believe that one of the reasons that some sex addicts are so convincing in their denial of the truth is that they themselves, at least on a conscious level, believe what they are saying. They are able to maintain this inner psychic split because there is often some degree of dissociation in sexual addicts. They consciously live in the "good" self and have split off from consciousness this "despicable" self that has such an abhorrent problem. In essence, their psyches tell them, "It is not me. I am not the person who does such awful things."

A clear example of this is the counselee who is encouraged to attend a group for recovering sex addicts. He attends one session and returns to tell the counselor that he does not belong in such a group. After listening to their stories, he might say, "These people are really terrible and disgusting people. I have nothing in common with them." However, the counselee's sexual behavior and acting out is similar to those of the people in the group. He does not identify with them because he is not yet ready to own the part of himself that is very much like them.

The pastoral counselor should not precipitously engage in dislodging the sex addict's denial. Psychic defenses perform a valuable function and can only be dissolved when the counselee has developed the psychic strength to face the truth. John Doe, the lawyer who is a pillar of the community, a husband and father of three, may not be ready in the beginning to face the full truth. The shame could be overwhelming. More than a few sexual addicts have attempted suicide when the truth of their behavior has come to light, particularly in the public forum. The revulsion expressed in the community is usually less devastating than the inner self-revulsion felt by the sex addict himself.

Rather, it would be healthier for the sex addict, in a psychically safe environment, to slowly and piece by piece reveal the full truth. One reported visit to the pornographic theater may eventually become three, then ten, then scores. And the alert counselor will recognize that sexual addicts many times have multiple addictions. The man who is visiting pornographic shops may also be engaged in phone sex, voyeurism, exhibitionism, and/or compulsive masturbation or cruising. Addictions may spread to other sexual behaviors and may increase in frequency. Rather than being a static reality, the addiction often absorbs increasingly more of the addict's time and energy.

Thus, in an initial assessment, the counselor should directly inquire about other sexual behaviors as well as the frequency of the referred behavior. The counselor may want to ask questions like: How often do you go to pornographic theaters? When did you first start? What do you do in these theaters? Have you ever had sexual experiences while in such theaters? Have you ever engaged in other sexual behaviors that some people would call deviant? Have you ever had phone sex? Made obscene phone calls? Bought or used pornographic materials? Viewed sexual materials on the Internet?

It will take some time to do an initial assessment of the person's sexual behaviors. If the counselee has an extensive sexual history, he may be willing to reveal inklings of other deviant behaviors in an initial session. However, the counselor should be aware that the addict may parse his words carefully to confuse or to deceive. For example, an addict might be asked, "Have you ever visited a prostitute?" The addict may say, "No." However, when subsequently asked if he ever had sex with someone he had not met until that day, he might then say "Yes." He will admit that he paid the person upon completion of the sexual act. When you bring up the contradiction, he may defend his answers by stating that he considered the paid sex partner to be a friend, even though he will never see that person again. It is shameful to admit that one is frequenting prostitutes; it is less shameful to the psyche to admit that one had sex with someone and then offered the person money, perhaps as a gesture of "kindness."

The initial assessment will help the counselor to understand the client's behavior and make appropriate referrals.

Childhood Sexual Traumas

It is almost always true that adult sex addicts have had significant traumas during their developing years. For example, a high percentage of those who sexually abuse minors will themselves have been sexually abused as a child. In one clinical case, a man had sexually abused a fourteen-year-old boy in the shower. When asked if he himself had ever been sexually abused, he said, "No." However, he was then asked if he, as a child, ever experienced an unwanted sexual advance by an adult. He responded, "Yes." The client was asked to describe the event; it turned out to be an exact replica of the abusive act that he himself had recently perpetrated. He had been a fourteen-year-old boy who was abused in a shower by an adult male using the same physical touches. When asked if he saw any connection between the two events—his own victimization and its replica—he replied honestly, "No." In this case, one might hypothesize that he was engaged in a "repetition compulsion" of a psychically disturbing childhood event. His eventual recovery will necessarily include coming to grips with his own childhood victimization and its powerful yet unconscious effect on him as an adult.

Other sexual addicts may have been sexually overstimulated as children, having engaged in such behavior as excessive and deviant childhood sex play. These might include oral sex or group masturbation circles that are beyond the normal exploratory experiences of children who may look and touch each other and themselves. Some sexual addicts grew up in sexualized households in which interpersonal boundaries were blurred or nonexistent. Many others grew up in rigidly repressive sexual environments; their sexual histories are marked by an almost complete lack of any discussion of sexuality and a stigmatization of sexual desires as unacceptable and dirty, or perhaps frightening and uncontrollable.

Part of an extensive healing process for sexual addicts sometimes includes "working through" these childhood sexual traumas. This would be particularly important for those sex addicts who are compulsively and unconsciously re-enacting their own childhood traumatizations. In these cases, the unhealed childhood trauma is "crying out" for resolution and driving the adult dysfunctional behavior.

The first task in working through early traumas is recognizing that the abuse experienced was harmful. Fully half the adult perpetrators of child sexual abuse that I have worked with do not initially identify their own childhood sexual contact with an adult as abusive. Many times the victims as adults will continue the perpetrator's seductive, manipulative belief that the sexual contact was consensual and an act of love. In direct contradiction to this erroneous belief, there may be body language and an affective response as the story of the abuse is told that clearly indicates its traumatic effect. For example, I recall one man who said that his childhood contact with an adult did not affect him negatively. However, his body stiffened as he spoke and his face tightened. Upon deeper inquiry, he said he felt frightened and confused by the experience.

As the perpetrator of sexually abusive behavior begins to recognize how personally destructive his own abuse was as a child, he is then much more likely to be able to recognize the damage his abusive behavior as an adult is causing to others. He begins to develop empathy for his victims when he can develop empathy for his own abuse.

In addition, raising to consciousness and working through the childhood sexual traumas of adult sex addicts can help the adult make sense of the seemingly "spontaneous appearance" of his destructive sexual compulsion. The sex addict learns that his compulsion did not mysteriously and magically arise, but rather grew out of an identifiable series of behaviors, experiences, and ideas that can be addressed and treated concretely and directly. While individually he feels powerless over his addictive behavior, with God's help and the help of others he can find healing and recovery.

This re-empowering of the adult sexual addict is important. One of the most destructive aspects of childhood sexual traumas, particularly sexual abuse by an adult, is the imprint of powerlessness left on the victim's spirit. Recalling the powerlessness of his own victimization, the person moves into adulthood feeling disempowered and perpetually a victim. This victim stance makes the adult much more prone to continuing to be victimized. Reaching out for help and understanding one's childhood traumatization are ways to reverse the imprint of powerlessness and to choose the path of empowerment and recovery.

The Addictive Cycle

As noted previously, not everyone who engages in deviant sexual behavior would be considered a sex addict. Rather, there is an identifiable pattern in the sex addict that results in an ever-tightening addictive cycle and deterioration of the addict's life.

The first stage is a *mismanagement of emotions*. The sex addict's life is not a healthy, well-balanced emotional existence. Rather, he is not getting his essential needs met in functional ways, and, in particular, he often has difficulty dealing with "negative" emotions and conflictual situations.

For example, the addict is likely to be emotionally isolated, even though some may be externally affable and seemingly very sociable. But true emotional intimacy almost always eludes the sex addict because such intimacy requires vulnerability, openness, honesty, and an ability to work through the hard times in relationships.

The sex addict, on the other hand, is likely to have few social skills to deal with anger or conflict. He may be easily shamed and is likely to carry large deficits in his self-image. Whenever conflicts arise and his inner shame surfaces, he is at a loss for a healthy response.

Exacerbating this inability to deal with such emotions and conflicts, sex addicts do not know how to reach out to others for support, either during their routine daily lives or especially during times of particular need. They believe they must "go it alone," and their own tools for dealing with these crises are the deviant tools they learned in childhood. Through this recurring mismanagement of emotions, the sex addict is in a state of vulnerability to engaging in deviant behavior.

As the addict becomes increasingly more vulnerable to acting out, he will display a number of "budding signs." In the lore of addiction recovery, these budding signs can be clues to the addict that he is on the road to a relapse. Budding signs are particular to each individual addict, but can include such things as isolating one's self from others, engaging in negative thinking, surfacing old angers, or wallowing in self-pity. Recognizing one's budding signs and taking immediate steps to deal with one's emotional life in more positive ways are keys to recovery for a sex addict.

The second stage is the *trigger*. The addict's emotional mismanagement and resulting vulnerability become activated and taken up into an active addictive cycle through an event or emotional situation called a "trigger." Each addict has a typical shaming type of event or emotional situation that will send him into a tailspin and activate his sexual fantasies. For some it will be the shaming comments of a spouse or a belittling comment at work. For others it will be the surfacing of old angers through the innocent remarks of a neighbor. The trigger for others will be a pervasive sense of loneliness and the perceived rejection by an acquaintance.

Whatever the trigger is, each sex addict has his own set of vulnerabilities and triggers. The healing process helps the addict recognize these vulnerabilities, budding signs, and triggers and assists him in learning to recognize immediately and deal with these in more effective ways. The goal is to help the addict stop the addictive cycle in its earliest stages. The farther into the cycle the addict goes, the more overwhelming it is, and the less likely he will be able to stop it.

Unless the cycle is stopped, the sex addict will then respond to his vulnerability and trigger by a rapidly intensifying surge in sexual fantasizing and ritualized behavior. This is the third phase: *fantasizing and sexual preparation*. Some addicts will drive toward anonymous pickup places and start cruising for a sex partner. Others will begin to stake out a favorite voyeuristic site for possible victims. Others will search out pornographic bookshops or places where prostitutes hang out. Once this phase has begun, the addict is well into his deviant sexual cycle.

It is important to note that this fantasizing and sexual preparation are an integral part of the sexual experience itself. The preparation and fantasizing about the illicit sexual event are actually part of the thrill. The illegal and furtive nature of these deviant sexual behaviors adds to the excitement and sexual stimulation. This surge is sometimes described as an emotional high that can be every bit as intense as the drug addict's high. One sex addict described it as being "on fire." Once the fire had begun, he was out of control and unable to stop the cycle. This emotional high is different and more addicting than the orgasmic response of normal sexual behavior, which is why some addicts are loathe to give up their exciting but often dangerous deviant behavior.

The fourth phase is *sexualized behavior.* This could take dozens of forms, from compulsive masturbation and obsession with pornography to necrophilia or child sexual abuse. "Unfortunately," the sexually deviant behavior does not bring the connection and fulfillment that all human beings desire. Rather than satisfying and affirming, the sexually deviant behavior is denigrating and destructive.

The sexual thrill is quickly replaced by feelings of self-loathing and disgust. These lead to the fifth and final phase of the addictive cycle: *shame and remorse.* The sex addict is often profoundly shamed by his own behavior. The deviant act becomes one more sign that he is unlovable and disgusting. He is filled with remorse and promises himself that he will never do it again.

If he is found out and confronted by family members, he is likely to deny the allegations, or he may break down in tears of sorrow. This was John Doe's response: he cried and admitted that it was true. However, this is probably part of the addictive cycle itself and is not yet a sign that the addict is truly on the road to recovery.

The shame and remorse reinforce his devastated self-image and self-loathing. These feelings exacerbate his inner dysphoria and heighten his inner conflicts. Since the addict does not know how to manage such emotions effectively, he moves back into his mismanagement of emotions, and the addictive cycle is re-engaged with even greater intensity and destructiveness.

Having experienced this destructive cycle again and again, the sex addict is likely to despair of ever getting out of his "pit" of shame and self-disgust. As more than one sex addict has said, "There is no hope for me."

Treatment of Sex Addicts

Some have suggested that sex addicts are not treatable. Almost like a mantra, popular publications have often repeated the sentence: "Sex addicts cannot be cured." The implication is that sex addicts are beyond hope. Ironically, this is one of the core beliefs of the sex addict himself. And the more we echo such hopelessness, the more we reinforce the pathology of the sex addict.

The word *cure* is not a helpful one when dealing with mental illnesses in general, and it is often misleading to use it in such contexts. Would one say that a person suffering from depression could be cured? The real question for the depressed person, as well as the sex addict, is, Can I be successfully treated? Can I live a healthy and productive life? For the sex addict, we would add, Can

I stop sexually acting out? The answer is clearly "Yes." There have been many sex addicts who have benefited greatly from treatment and have gone on to live healthy lives free of sexually deviant behavior. There is hope.

Nevertheless, such treatments need to be comprehensive and expertly focused on the cognitions, behaviors, and dynamics that prevent healthy living and feed the addictive cycle. Typically, treatment modalities for sex addicts might include some or all of the following: training in victim empathy, anger management, adjusting cognitive distortions, identifying and intervening in one's addictive cycle, social skills training, management of emotions, healthy sex education, and working through one's personal victimization.

Common treatment goals for the sex addict are to:

- Admit one has a problem and take responsibility
- Develop victim empathy and recognize the damage one has caused to others (if appropriate) and to self
- Undo some cognitive distortions
- Heal some of the inner anger and learn to manage one's anger better
- Develop social skills and peer relationships
- Learn one's addictive cycle and develop skills to intervene
- Commit to a lifelong process of recovery.

The pivotal place of anger management in the treatment might be a surprise to some. Many sex addicts do not seem to be angry and may have a rather passive, dependent demeanor. However, the traumatic hurts of their childhood coupled with a feeling of their own powerless victimization often combine into a pervasive anger, sometimes rage.

Robert Stoller, M.D., in his important book *Perversion: The Erotic Form of Hatred,* put forth the notion that all sexual perversions, at their root, are actually hatred and hostility that have become eroticized. While such a sweeping hypothesis might be an overstatement, it has been my clinical experience that buried anger is an integral part of a significant percentage of sex addicts' pathology. And the sex addict who walks out of treatment without having dealt with his anger is someone who will have serious problems in the future.

The Pastoral Counselor's Role

One-on-one counseling sessions by themselves may have little impact on the sexual addict in the throes of an addiction. The preferred treatment is an intensive and comprehensive program that includes a combination of verbal and nonverbal therapies in individual and group sessions. Unfortunately, such programs are not always available or possible for many people caught up in sexual addictions.

If the pastoral counselor, of necessity, is providing individual care to the sex addict, the counselor should determine whether she has the requisite training and experience to provide such care. If not, competent supervision will be important. Individual counseling sessions with sex addicts can be complex, and the counselor who works alone is open to manipulation and a discouraging powerlessness.

Countertransferential issues will be important for the counselor to acknowledge and constructively face. It is normal to feel some revulsion for deviant sexual behavior, especially for child sexual abuse, rape, and other sexual crimes. Working with the perpetrator of sexually deviant behavior will probably raise in the counselor issues of anger, sexual conflicts, power, shame, and one's own childhood traumas. The counselor who has not faced these issues and come to some internal resolution is likely to be affected strongly when facing the sex addict for the first time. There will likely be several kinds of subtle tendencies evoked in the counselor, including punishing and shaming the sex addict verbally or through nonverbal behaviors. Providing a consistently nonjudgmental, compassionate yet challenging presence to the sex addict takes a considerable degree of integration in the counselor. Before agreeing to such an undertaking, the counselor should take stock of his readiness to engage in this work. Again, competent supervision, and one's own therapy, may be indicated.

It will be very helpful, perhaps essential, to complement individual counseling sessions with group sessions. A therapy group for sex addicts might be available, especially in a metropolitan area. Also, there are several different kinds of twelve-step groups for sex addicts throughout the United States and abroad. These groups are free and provide much support and challenge for the sex addict.

Some of them are

Sex Addicts Anonymous (SAA)
PO Box 70949
Houston, TX 77270
713-869-4902
800-477-8191
Web site: www.saa-recovery.org

Sexaholics Anonymous (SA)
PO Box 111910
Nashville, TN 37222-1910
615-331-6230
Web site: www.sa.org

Sex and Love Addicts Anonymous (SLAA)
PO Box 338
Norwood, MA 02062
781-225-8825
Web site: www.slaafws.org

Sexual Compulsives Anonymous (SCA)
West Coast:
PO Box 4470
170 Sunset Blvd. #520
Los Angeles, CA 90027
310-859-5585

East Coast:
PO Box 1585
Old Chelsea Station
New York, NY 10011
212-439-1123
Web site: www.sca-recovery.org

Each group is slightly different, but all deal with sexual addictions from a twelve-step fellowship model. The pastoral counselor will have to make a prudential judgment whether to see the sex addict in individual sessions if the addict is not willing to attend some form of group therapy, especially twelve-step groups, which are free and readily available in many areas.

In the first session, the counselor will want to discern the sex addict's motivation for seeking counseling. In John Doe's case, he was caught and his wife was informed; she then insisted her husband go into counseling. As soon as the motivation disappears, the client may leave counseling. The task will be to encourage the client to begin to realize himself that the addiction is destroying his life and that he needs to change. If the client comes in with at least some willingness to look at his destructive behavior, then this small opening may be all the counselor has to work with in the initial stages. However, the counselor should be cognizant of the client's real motivation. It is unusual, although it happens occasionally, that a sex addict will present himself freely and without pressure for counseling. Ultimately, the client who does not eventually become fully invested in overcoming his addiction will not do so. There is no amount of hard work on the counselor's part or prodding by John Doe's wife that can replace John Doe's own motivation to change.

Attendance at twelve-step groups or other group therapies for sex addicts can help the sex addict become aware of the need for change. Underneath the ambivalence to give up the sexual behavior is a despair that such change is even possible. Witnessing years of sexual sobriety of others in these group settings can give a strong consolation to the addict that he is not alone and that recovery from sex addiction is possible.

Breaking Through the Denial

In the initial stages of the counseling, the following statements or similar variants are sometimes heard from sex addicts and should be viewed with suspicion: "It's the first time I ever did it"; "I was under a lot of stress; it's not really a sexual problem"; "It was just a momentary lapse; I'll never do it again"; "She was coming on to me; I am the real victim here." Each of these typical statements is used in service of the client's denial and is intended to deflect the counselor's, and the client's, attention away from the seriousness of the sex addict's problem and the responsibility of the addict for his behavior.

In the initial stages of counseling, it will be important to probe in detail the history and details of the client's addiction. When did it first start? How often do you do it? Describe the sequence of events when you act out. Are you involved in any other kinds of sexual behavior? When was the last time you did it? Sex addicts are notorious for not volunteering important pieces of information that reveal the extent and seriousness of the sexual acting out. Also, as mentioned previously, they will often parse their words to mislead the counselor. Thus, the counselor will want to ask the same questions several different times and in several different ways. It is likely that, even after doing an initial thorough assessment of the sexual behavior, the counselor will continue to learn about more deviant sexual behavior as the sessions progress. The counselor should expect the addict to reveal slowly and over a significant length of time the full nature of his addiction. "Breaking through the denial" usually continues throughout the course of counseling. Some addicts may never tell you everything.

Integrating the "Bad" Self

When initially telling the "story" of his addiction, the sex addict is likely to profess a genuine ignorance of any pattern or cycle to his acting out. He will probably say, "It just happens"; or "I found myself doing..." as if he is a passive victim of a strange and powerful force that overcomes his will and blots out his consciousness. Indeed, some "trance-like" qualities reflecting a psychic dissociation are often present when the sex addict has entered into his addictive cycle. He often "splits off" his sexually addicted self from his consciousness. So, whenever the addict is engaged, it does not feel like himself who is acting but some strange and disgusting person.

Thus, it is not unusual that when sex addicts first attend twelve-step meetings, they do not recognize themselves in other people's stories. They may say things like, "I don't belong here," or "I am not like these people, they are really sick and disgusting," even when the account of sexual behavior to which they are listening is identical to their own.

Splitting off one's addictive self protects the person from the overwhelming shame and self-loathing the addict feels. During the course of treatment, he will need to begin acknowledging and owning this part of himself and the deviant behavior. In the beginning, as the reality of his deviant behavior comes directly into his consciousness, the sex addict can be overwhelmed by the "bad" side of himself. He may lose touch with the fact that there is any good to himself at all; he may feel like his entire life has been a lie. The counselor will want to be a balancing force, reiterating the message that he is both a child of God and a sinner as well. It will not be an easy or quick task for the sex addict to come to a balanced acceptance that he is created by God and thus is "very good," and yet he also is a sinner. For any adult, this is a difficult task, but for the sex addict, it is daunting.

The tendency of the sex addict is to want to obliterate the "bad" self, the self that is engaged in this despicable sexual behavior. However, like all "split-off" selves, the addict cannot be obliterated. This is fortuitous, because the split-off self that is the addict invariably has some important human qualities that are essential for full recovery and a passionate life. For example, I recall one sex addict who vehemently stated that he would not give up the anger that propelled him into his sexual behavior. Upon further exploration, it became clear that it was this anger that kept him alive emotionally during his traumatic childhood years. He believed that if he let go of his anger, he would succumb to the lurking traumas of his childhood.

It would not have been advisable, nor possible, to attempt to strip away the anger that informed his sexually addictive self. Rather, he needed to learn to harness and manage this passion of anger in a productive way. While not rejecting the emotion, this sex addict needed to learn some healthy anger management, a common therapeutic modality for sex addicts.

Likewise, the counselor will *not* seek to obliterate the sexuality or the striving for intimacy that are inherent in the sex addict. The counselor should assist the addict in recognizing that his efforts at finding intimacy and sexual fulfillment have been misguided. The counselor will then assist the sex addict in developing more nurturing peer relationships and a resulting healthier expression of his sexual desires.

To assist in emotional management and developing peer relationships, some kind of assertiveness training is often used with sex addicts. Many forms of sexual deviancy, such as rape and child sexual abuse, are also abuses of power. Thus, learning to use one's power in assertive rather than destructive ways is essential. Sex addicts often find themselves on extremes of the power spectrum: they either act in passive or in aggressive ways, or alternately in both. Empowering sex addicts may sound like a counterintuitive treatment goal, but it is an integral part of the recovery process.

A sex addict who has ceased acting out but has not replaced the deviant behavior with a healthier assertiveness, more positive relationships, and the beginnings of true intimacies is unlikely to remain in recovery for long.

Intervening in the Addictive Cycle

As the sex addict begins to face and integrate his "bad" self, he can begin to identify in some detail his addictive cycle. Instead of believing that "it mysteriously just happens," he will want to identify those conditions under which he is more vulnerable to engaging in his sexual behavior. For example, he may find that he is most vulnerable when he is feeling angry, lonely, or depressed. Helping the addict to recognize when he is in such vulnerable states will be an important therapeutic task. Sex addicts are often *alexythymic,* that is, seriously unaware of their own emotional states, thus the emotional mismanagement inherent in the early stages of the addictive cycle. It may require significant work for addicts to become aware of their emotions.

Once the addict can recognize the early stages of the addiction, he can learn more productive ways of dealing with the dysphoric condition. For example, to deal with loneliness, the addict can learn to rely upon a network of friends or twelve-step companions. He might learn to reach out to family members, or he can talk about his loneliness with the counselor during their next session. Early recognition of one's budding signs and quick, appropriate intervention are keys to stopping the addictive cycle.

Should the dysphoric condition continue, the addictive cycle achieves a higher level of intensity when the addict inevitably experiences one of his triggers. Learning one's triggers or addiction-engaging events is important. The sex addict will want to learn how to recognize and deal with these events. For example, if the addict's trigger is a shaming encounter or interpersonal rejection, he will need to develop coping skills to introduce immediately after these events, such as calling a twelve-step sponsor or attending a twelve-step meeting.

If the sex addict was not able to deal effectively with the dysphoric condition nor able to intervene after a triggering event, he will find his addictive cycle in full swing. He will likely be engaged in sexual fantasizing and a ritualized preparation for the sexual behavior. While it is possible to intervene successfully at this stage, it is less likely to occur.

Once the relapse has occurred, the most dangerous thing the addict can do is to keep the relapse a secret. It is the secrecy of such lapses, and the addictions in general, that gives them their power. Bringing such behaviors into the open makes recovery possible. The sex addict needs to be ready for the possibility of a relapse. Recovery from a sex addiction is a process, and relapses, although regrettable, are expected. However, the counselor's goal should be to go over in detail the circumstances, feelings, and the behaviors so that they can understand what went awry. Rather than seeing such events as failures, they can be learning moments on the road toward a full recovery.

Concluding Remarks

The sex addict will likely first walk into the counselor's office in considerable denial and with a number of manipulative techniques that he has used for many years. While he may have some desire to be free of his sexual addiction, it is usually the case that he has come into counseling under pressure from family members or supervisors. He probably has much ambivalence about whether he can ever give up his addiction or whether he really wants to do so. The initial sessions may be filled with much rationalization, minimization, and projection of blame. He is likely to try to confuse or lie outright to the counselor about the extent and seriousness of his behavior.

Facing the sex addict requires supervision and training. Also, the counselor will need to have worked through many of her own issues as well as being honest with herself about how compassionately and objectively she can deal with sexual deviancy.

The stakes can be very high. Child sexual abuse is a crime that almost always must be reported. Rape, exhibitionism, and voyeurism are illegal and traumatizing to the victims. Many a public figure has had his or her career ruined and/or ended up in jail as a result of a police sting at a homosexual pickup place or the busting of a pornography or prostitution ring. Lesser deviant behavior, such as compulsive masturbation, may not be illegal but can debilitate one's emotional life and reinforce one's shame and negative self-worth.

Recovery is possible. The nay-sayers are often quoted in public, but there are thousands of people whose lives of sexual recovery witness to the contrary. There is hope for the sex addict. Recovery is possible.

The counselor's work with the sex addict is difficult. In some way, the social stigma that is fixed upon the sex addict is often experienced by the counselor who devotes his or her work to helping them get well. Self-care in such a profession carries a special urgency.

Nevertheless, the personal rewards of walking with sex addicts on the road to recovery are not insignificant, and, in the process, counselors might find that they, too, have experienced some of the same freedom and new life.

References

Carnes, Patrick J. *Contrary to Love: Helping the Sexual Addict.* Minneapolis: CompCare Publishers, 1989.

———. *Out of the Shadows: Understanding Sexual Addiction,* 2nd ed. Center City, MN: Hazelden, 1992.

Covington, Stephanie and Beckett, Liana. *Leaving the Enchanted Forest: The Path from Addiction to Intimacy.* San Francisco: Harper & Row, 1988.

Goldberg, Arnold. *The Problem of Perversion: The View from Self Psychology.* New Haven: Yale University Press, 1995.

Hollin, Clive R. and Howells, Kevin, eds. *Clinical Approaches to Sex Offenders and Their Victims.* New York: John Wiley & Sons, 1996.

Hope and Recovery: A Twelve Step Guide for Healing from Compulsive Sexual Behavior. Center City, MN: Hazelden, 1987.

Lew, Mike. *Victims No Longer: Men Recovering from Incest and Other Sexual Child Abuse.* New York: Perennial Library, 1990.

May, Gerald G. *Addiction and Grace.* San Francisco: Harper & Row, 1988.

Money, John. *Lovemaps: Clinical Concepts of Sexual/Erotic Health and Pathology, Paraphilia, and Gender Transposition in Childhood, Adolescence, and Maturity.* New York: Irvington, 1989.

Peele, Stanton. *Love and Addiction.* New York: Taplinger Pub. Co., 1975.

Rutler, Peter. *Sex in the Forbidden Zone: When Men in Power—Therapists, Doctors, Clergy, Teachers and Others—Betray Women's Trust.* New York: Fawcett Crest, 1991.

Sadock, Benjamin J., Kaplan, Harold I., Freedman, Alfred M., eds. *The Sexual Experience.* Baltimore: Williams & Wilkins, 1976.

Schaeffer, Brenda. *Is It Love or Is It Addiction: Falling into Healthy Love.* New York: Harper/Hazelden, 1987.

Sexaholics Anonymous. Alcoholics Anonymous World Services, Inc.: SA Literature, 1989.

Stoller, Robert J. *Perversion: The Erotic Form of Hatred.* Washington, DC: American Psychiatric Press, Inc., 1975.

Constance M. Mucha

11. Hospice, Pastoral Counseling, and Care in Response to Death and Dying

Nothing! No matter whether your grief seems too deep or too long-lasting or too shameful, you cannot make it go away any more than you can will a broken bone to knit overnight. And, like the shattered bone, a shattered heart needs two things before healing can happen: proper attention and sufficient time. In the meantime, it's going to hurt-a-lot. (Luebering, 1998)

Introduction

As we prepare to work with a dying client and with the family members and others who are bereaved, it is essential that we include proper attention to the client and sufficient grieving time in our treatment plan. I believe that the art of pastoral counseling is a special gift that is reflected through our skill. As with any skill, we must learn and practice to be effective. Honing our skill involves learning the theories of pastoral and grief counseling, integrating them with our gift (the art), and then applying them in our work with the client. Our art and skill together are necessary to ensure that each client receives proper attention. Our skill improves with time, practice, experience, continual updating of our knowledge base, and patience with our client's timeline.

The bereaved client does not have a strict timeline for grieving. However, the client does have a deep pain that will not go away on its own. It is important for us to understand the need for grief to evolve, and to work in partnership with the client according to his or her individual need for sufficient time. The dying client will have a sense of her own timing and what she wants to do with it. That could be one shortened session, which may be very challenging to us as pastoral counselors who may perceive a need for more time than does the client. The question for us is, Can we sit with helplessness and not feel a need to rescue the client from it or to fix it? "Truly, counselors have much to give, but in the end, they must be able to receive wisdom and insight from those they serve. Inevitably, the lives we touch also touch us in an incredible, not easily describable way." (Schweska, 1997)

The goal of this chapter is that we will gain a working knowledge of pastoral care and counseling with the dying and pastoral grief counseling with the bereaved. I begin the chapter with our personal preparation as counselors, which is critical, so that we can have an increased sense of balance for ourselves, and be ready to refine our art and skill in the specialty of care or counseling the dying and counseling with the bereaved. Next is a section on preparing the client for the journey. Following is a section on theories of grief counseling. The section on theory includes my own paradigm of pastoral grief counseling in which I have integrated counseling theory with theology. I end the chapter with case examples from personal experience to demonstrate the application of theory to practice.

The topic of grief as it relates to dying, death, and bereavement is too extensive to be covered in a single chapter. Also, working with children and teens in grief fill at least another chapter. The present chapter will focus on pastoral care and counseling within the hospice framework, where the family is the unit of care; children and teens are included within that context. My plan is to address the similarities and differences that I have encountered in working with both the dying and the bereaved as they move through the hospice experience.

Preparing the Counselor for the Journey

Since loss is a part of every person's life, it is necessary that we prepare ourselves for the journey. I refer to dealing with loss as a "journey" because grief work involves continuous movement through the pain. When a client gets stuck at some point in the pain, I refer to the experience as having hit some "ruts" in the road. There are times when the traveler must stop along the journey to rest from the weariness and pain. Timing is a key element in this type of counseling. We need to know just when to nudge the client to move forward or to stop and wait with him.

The metaphor of journey has been a significant part of hospice history. The word *hospice* means a house of shelter or rest for pilgrims. Our personal preparation will equip us, as co-pilgrims and grief counselors, for the sometimes rough terrain on the journey. A crucial aspect of this preparation will be to address our own issues as counselors.

> In order to remain in touch with our own unresolved conflicts and needs, and to see reality as clearly as possible, it is important to monitor our transferences on an ongoing basis. There must be

an effort to keep the interferences of the past to a minimum, while recognizing that it is impossible to screen them out altogether. The overall goal is to avoid superimposing personal needs and conflicts on the verbal and non-verbal messages we receive from others. This aim is particularly important when we function as pastoral counselor or pastoral psychotherapist. (Wicks, 1985)

Wicks makes the point that self-monitoring needs to be ongoing for our professional growth as pastoral counselors. As counselors we need to process our unresolved conflicts when they surface. I remember when my mother died and I was working as a pastoral grief counselor in a hospice. When I went back to work following her death, the first referral I got was a young man whose mother was dying. He wanted some help to manage the pain of his impending loss. My first thought was, "I don't know if I can do this. It has only been two weeks since my mother's death. The pain is still very intense. If my pain gets mixed up with his pain, how effective will I be?" Since I was working with my own therapist and managing my own pain, I was able to work with the client, helping him with coping strategies as he dealt with his mother's impending death. That experience increased my own sensitivity to one occupational hazard of grief counselors: our vulnerability in working with the dying and bereaved when we ourselves are newly bereaved.

This field of counseling touches our own story, in some way, with each new client. The client's story could trigger our own loss issues at any time during the counseling process. Burnout can be a very real problem for us as pastoral counselors, too, when we do not attend to our own mental health needs in an ongoing way. Remember that every client you see will either soon die or be left to mourn the loss of a loved one. Although the work is very rewarding, it can take a toll on the energy level of the unprepared and vulnerable pastoral counselor. We quickly learn that empathy alone is not sufficient. "It is necessary for Bereavement Counselors to be able to tolerate high levels of helplessness in order to be effective." (McKissock & McKissock, 1998)

If we decide that grief counseling will be our chosen specialty, we need to consider one very important recommendation from those who have worked in the field: The best way to monitor our own countertransferences is to see our own therapists. The saying that every counselor needs a counselor is not a myth to the pastoral grief counselor. In addition to having our own therapist, we can add to the balance in our life by having our own self-care plan. Balance will help us to integrate empathy with our art and skill. Another strategy for promoting balance is to balance grief counseling with something else—teaching, writing, and/or working with other clients who do not have grief as their presenting problem. Peterson and Nisenholtz have developed a self-care plan they call "BE NATURAL."

> The components of the plan include breathing, exercise, nutrition, attitude, time management, uniqueness, relaxation, associations, and laughter. All of these components are natural, inexpensive activities that when done systematically provide the nourishment, rest, and reenergizing necessary to maintain high-level wellness. (Peterson & Nisenholtz, 1995)

Peterson and Nisenholtz believe that the counselor who personally integrates and implements this plan will have a working model to offer clients. In addition, we would have adapted a healthy lifestyle for ourselves.

I have used this model personally and in my work with hospice families. It has increased my energy level and helped me to stay focused when I am with clients. Clients who have used it have told me that they feel more energized and able to concentrate for longer periods of time. Once they decide that they do have control over their attitudes they can improve most aspects of their lives. Although breathing is something we do without much thought, we need to know whether we are breathing for optimum health. For example, fear causes major changes in our breathing patterns. Therefore the fear needs to be identified and worked through to restore balance to breathing. Nutrition can get very unbalanced during grief, taking on either extreme—that of not eating or of overeating. Eating alone is difficult for many grievers, particularly widows and widowers. Proper nutrition is a part of grief assessment and grief education. Time management and accepting their own uniqueness are difficult for the grievers to implement. Time management because when grieving it is so difficult to concentrate and stay focused; uniqueness because their self-esteem is challenged as they attempt to redefine themselves in a world without the deceased. Associations are very important to the grieving person who is redefining who she is and where she fits in. Widows often talk of losing their couple friends. Support groups have been very effective for this time of transition. As with any self-care plan, the more we use it, the more it becomes a natural part of our daily routine. I encourage and give clients permission to laugh. Rabbi Earl Grollman says, "It's okay to laugh again. Humor acts as a safety valve offering a shift in perspective and energy that restores a sense of balance." (Grollman, 1999) Laughter can also improve our spiritual health. Proverbs (15:3) affirms this: "A merry heart doth good like medicine."

Preparing the Client for the Journey

How do we determine who needs grief counseling? The determination is made following an assessment of each referral. A comprehensive assessment provides the necessary information for treatment planning. Hospice referrals for pastoral counseling come from one of the health team professionals or through a self-referral. A physician may refer a patient whose grief is being expressed through physical symptoms that are impeding the person's functioning. The physician will have ruled out any physical cause for the symptoms prior to referral. Any self-referred client who comes to us experiencing physical symptoms is referred to the family physician, to be certain that there is not an underlying disease process related to or causing the physical symptoms. Often the physical symptoms relate to sleep deprivation, which is a common problem for people in grief. Referrals for grief counseling also come from friends, other family members, and the clergy. Self-referrals often come during what we call "the crazy time" of grief, when the client describes his life as completely out of control. It *is* a scary time, and the client comes in search of reassurance that he is not going crazy. The client needs to understand and make sense out of what is happening to her. She needs to know that this "crazy time" is not so unusual and will not go on indefinitely. Healing grief can be as predictable as healing a broken bone; both will heal, yet neither can heal unattended. The grieving person also requires proper nutrition, rest, spiritual and psychological support, and follow-up.

In our work with the dying and bereaved, we have found that the major difference in their care is the time allotted to each. The bereaved person has an indefinite amount of time to resolve "ruts" in the road, stumbling blocks in the grief experience. The dying person may have only a few hours.

Physical strength, mental status, and nearness to death all impact on the dying client's time frame, which more often than not may be only a single session of therapy. Focusing on and assessing a client's needs quickly in order to maximize the presence of the moment requires a therapist's art, skill, and sensitivity. (Read, 1995)

Brief therapy is the treatment of choice when the dying client is alert, oriented, and wants to work on some issues with a pastoral counselor. The dying and bereaved have similar types of issues to work on, such as unfinished business or current and past losses in their lives, while searching for meaning and purpose. One difference might be that the dying person may focus more on current than past losses. A significant similarity is that both the dying and bereaved are moving into a realm of the unknown. The dying person is leaving this life and entering a great unknown, taking with him only his faith. Everything else he must leave behind. The bereaved is ending the life she knew with the deceased and entering a new and changed life. However, the bereaved has a greater sense of what to expect and has more choices about what and who to include in her new life without the deceased.

Children and Teens

Grief issues of children and teens are managed by hospice social workers and pastoral counselors. Age-appropriate grief education is provided for parents and children. We encourage parents to learn about child and teen grief and help their children and teens. Most hospices have bereavement support groups for young people. The focus of these groups is education and support, normalizing the grief experience. We also have bereavement camps, usually a weekend experience for children and teens in grief. The camp normalizes grief by incorporating education and support with time for structured play and relaxation. These support programs help children and teens to understand, accept, and express their feelings in a safe environment. Children and teens with more complex issues in grief are referred to appropriate specialists for follow-up counseling.

Theories to Consider

Among the most helpful theories to consider in our work with the dying client are the works of Elizabeth Kübler-Ross, E. Mansel Pattison, Charles Corr, Kenneth Doka, and Ira Byock. Kübler-Ross (1969) was a pioneer in the death and dying movement of the late 1960s and early '70s. Her stages of dying—shock or denial, anger, bargaining, depression, and acceptance—were and continue to be used as a guide by counselors working with dying clients. Kübler-Ross found that her stages did not necessarily occur in order. She found that most dying patients go in and out of these stages until they are able to accept the finality of their lives. Her work has provided a solid base on which to add and/or redefine the experience of dying as we know it today. In *The Experience of Dying,* E. Mansell Pattison (1977) described the phases of dying, building on the work of Kübler-Ross. In the *acute* phase, the client experienced denial, anger, and bargaining. The *chronic* living/dying phase dealt with several fears. Pattison defined these fears as abandonment, loss of self-control, suffering and pain, loss of personal identity, fear of the unknown, and regression into self. The fears can be worked through with counseling. The counseling process facilitates entry into the *terminal* phase in peace. The terminal phase is the time of withdrawal, followed by physiological, biological, psychological, and social death. Kübler-Ross referred to the withdrawal as acceptance. She observed patients retreat into themselves, not as in a severe depression, but as a loss of interest in the things of this life, as the patients prepared quietly for death. Charles Corr (1992) presented his task-based model of dying, which described four needs—physical, psychological, social, and spiritual—to be met. The client's physical needs are nutrition, hydration, pain control, and sleep. The psychological needs are security, autonomy, ventilating feelings and fears. The social needs are relationships, unfinished business, advance directives, funeral arrangements, and wills. Corr described the spiritual needs as finding meaning in life, dying an appropriate death, and transcending death. Corr's tasks take Kübler-Ross's stages and Pattison's phases a step further by expanding on them. He believes that our role as pastoral counselors is to help the client identify her individual needs, work with those needs that can be resolved with counseling, and when appropriate, refer the client to the proper resource to facilitate completing her other tasks—funeral arrangements, wills, advanced directives—necessary to complete her preparation for dying. Kenneth Doka (1993) presents nine tasks for the terminal phase of a life-threatening illness:

1. Dealing with symptoms of discomfort, pain, and incapacitation
2. Managing health procedures and institutional stress
3. Managing stress, examining, coping
4. Dealing effectively with caregivers
5. Preparing for death and saying good-bye
6. Preserving self-concept
7. Preserving appropriate relationships with family and friends
8. Ventilating feelings and fears
9. Finding meaning in life and death.

Doka's tasks are comprehensive, including physical, emotional, psychological, and spiritual aspects of dying. They provide an integrated model for the pastoral counselor to follow and/or use as reference.

Dr. Ira Byock's thought-provoking question to the dying patient: "How are you feeling within yourself?" (Byock, 1997) is open ended, giving the dying patient permission to dialogue with loved ones, paving the way for the dying patient to accomplish some tasks in the dying process. Byock's tasks include:

- Experiencing love of self and others
- Completing relationships
- Accepting the finality of one's life
- Achieving a new sense of self despite one's impending demise.

There are many similarities in these theories, and each seems to build on another. They provide thoughts and information that we can incorporate in our work with the dying. Theories will continue to be fine tuned as we apply them in our own work with the dying. The dying client helps in the fine tuning to the degree that we are open to learning from each new experience. My paradigm for counseling the dying and for grief counseling is that the deepest pain of loss is located at our spiritual core, and it is there that the journey of complete healing begins. The journey of grief begins with the first awareness of an impending loss. I explain this to the client as a deep, open wound that needs to remain open so that it can heal from the inside out. In order to get to that deepest spiritual core, the grieving person has to move through several transitions, much like a birthing experience. The first transition is the physical pain, the client's physical symptoms. The physical symptoms can be managed with adequate nutrition, rest, and medical follow-up. The loss experience is physically and emotionally exhausting, draining the griever's energy. The physical body is often taxed to the limit. Grieving people have said that they didn't realize how completely exhausted they were until after the death of their loved one. They describe the experience as being on "automatic pilot," focusing their energy on their dying loved one. A client in physical pain will resist dealing with feelings until the physical pain has been managed.

The second transition is emotional, with wide mood swings and with feelings that seem out of control. A person experiencing intense emotional pain may have difficulty thinking clearly about present or future time. This transition seems to operate on an all-or-nothing principle. The grieving person often finds it difficult to keep feelings balanced. Either the feelings seem to be totally out of control, or so controlled that they are not expressed. This pain often becomes a very private part of the process because there are so few support people who cope well with the wide swings of emotion experienced by the grieving person. The grieving person is aware of the discomfort of others, and in response stops the tears rather than risk losing the support person.

The third transition is psychological, dealing with the client's thought patterns. By the time the pastoral counselor facilitates the griever through the first two transitions, the thought patterns seem to be more accessible to the client. Working within the realms of thought and feeling helps to prepare the client to go to the depths of pain, namely, her spiritual core. Integrating thought and feeling brings her heart and head together as she moves to the depths of her pain.

The fourth transition is the spiritual core, which incorporates her total pain and processes the healing through the client's faith roots and belief system. Meaning and purpose are major struggles at this deepest transition. The client also revisits faith roots and decides how these roots will facilitate forward movement into new life without her loved one. I believe that it is grace at this level that helps the griever to embrace her new self with a zest for life that she has not experienced in a long time. This new zest for life is like a birthing experience.

Working through the transitions is like working through the stages of labor and birth into this life and the stages of dying and birth into the next life. However, the transitions are not as clearly defined as I have stated. They often run together in the client's experience. Some bereaved clients go immediately to their spiritual core at the time of the loss. The dying person is at the cross-road between this life and the next. I experienced dying as a birthing experience with my first hospice patient. Immediately after his death, I realized that we had spent the last few hours of his life doing for him what I had done for mothers in the labor room. In my work in the labor room, I experienced birth into this life as a descending process, with the baby moving through the birth canal. In the hospice, I experienced birth into the next life as an ascending process, with the focus on the upper part of the body. We observe that breathing stops and eyes are fixed. The person has moved to the next life.

Questions that the dying often struggle with include: Is there really an afterlife? What will it be like? Do heaven and hell really exist in the next life? How much of this life will go with me? Will I have another body? Will I still be connected to this life? Where am I going? Will death be painful? Will I be aware of the moment of death? Will I meet those who have gone before me?

The bereaved is entering a new life without the deceased, and questions what that means to him. The bereaved has other questions, too, such as, Who is God? Where is God? Where was God when I needed God? Why didn't God answer our prayers for healing? Why didn't we experience a miracle? Why am I here? What is my purpose in this life? Why did God take my loved one now? This is the level of many unanswered questions. During this level of the journey, the counselor remains present to the client in the struggle, not searching for answers, just hearing the questions and reflecting them back to the client. It is through this process that the client begins to change the things he can and accept the things that cannot be changed. The grace at this level is that suddenly he possesses the wisdom to know the difference.

> Perhaps a deeper understanding of the mystery of God and God's ordering of the universe will come in time. Theological answers, though, are sometimes difficult to achieve. We inevitably do our reflecting within the context of some frame of reference provided by our time, place, intellectual acumen, and individual personality. And the frame may be too small to match the size of the mystery. (Parker, 1997)

That is why I believe that pastoral counseling and grief counseling are a natural combination to facilitate movement and healing for the dying and bereaved.

Grief theory is continually evolving and considering new possibilities for research and practice. It is being open to new ways of thinking as grief counselors listen to and learn from the bereaved. Grief theorists have learned that grief is a unique human experience. We now know that widowhood is more painful the second year than the first. We know that we have to expand the parameters of normal for parents who survive the death of a child. Sibling, particularly twin, grief also has its own parameters for healing. Neimeyer sees common elements in some of the newer models of grief theory:

- Skepticism about the universality of stages of grieving that lead from psychological disequilibrium to readjustment, coupled with an appreciation of more complex patterns of adaptation;
- A shift away from the presumption that successful mourning requires "letting go" of the one who has died, and toward a recognition of the symbolic bonds with the lost loved one;
- Attention to cognitive and active processes in mourning, extending the usual focuses on emotional consequences of loss;
- Greater awareness of the implications of major loss for the bereaved person's sense of identity, including the prospects of post-traumatic growth; and
- Broadening the focus to include not only the idiosyncratic experience of individual grievers, but also the reciprocal impact of loss on families and (sub) cultural groups. (Neimeyer, 1999)

In response to these trends, Neimeyer's new paradigm in grief theory argues that meaning reconstruction in response to a loss is the central process in mourning. His paradigm links to the work of Tom Attig, Dennis Klass, Phyllis Silverman, Terri Rando, and Janice Nadeau, who view human beings as meaning-makers, weavers of narratives that give significance to the stories of their lives. "One implication of this 'constructivist' view is that the narrative themes that people draw on are as variegated as their personal biographies, and as complex as the overlapping cultural belief systems that inform their attempts at meaning-making." (Neimeyer, 1999) With each death experience, the bereaved's life is forever changed. The secondary losses that follow shake the foundations of one's assumptive world. At the time of death, the griever begins a new life story in a new life with new relationships.

William Worden, in his book *Grief Counseling and Grief Therapy*, outlines four tasks for the grieving person to accomplish:

1. Accept the reality of the loss;
2. Work through the pain of the grief;
3. Adjust to an environment without the deceased; and
4. Emotionally relocate the loss and move on with life.

I explain Wordon's tasks to the bereaved, letting them know that accepting the reality of the loss has two parts, intellectually and in their heart. Grief work involves bringing the head and heart together, which takes time. Working through the pain is just as stated. There is no way around it, no shortcut, only to lean into it and go through it. The task of adjustment is multifaceted. The griever is adjusting to the physical, emotional, psychological, and spiritual environment without the deceased. This takes time and an environment of supportive people who do not try to hasten the process but are willing to be co-pilgrims with the griever. Reinvesting in other relationships and moving on doesn't mean letting go and forgetting the loved one. It does mean incorporating the loss in memory and being ready to make new memories with new relationships.

How would you, as a pastoral grief counselor, respond to the following question: What do you want to do with the rest of your life? I wonder if your answer would be different if you were dealing with the personal reality of six months or less to live. When preparing to work in hospice, a part of the hospice-training course is for each person to reflect on his or her response to that question. Every person who is admitted to hospice care is automatically in that reality. The reactions are as varied as the number of persons receiving hospice care. I am called upon to help a patient and/or family member cope with the immediate crisis of assimilating the information and what it means, not only to the dying person but to the family as well. After the crisis has resolved to a manageable level, the person can work on her unfinished business, which frees her to accept that this life is changing rapidly and coming to an end. Acceptance opens the door to a greater sense of peace when saying good-bye to loved ones. Grief counseling is usually short-term, unless complicated by the nature of the death, pre-existing psychological problems, multiple losses simultaneously, and/or many unresolved losses of the past. When the bereaved have had an opportunity to say good-bye to the dying person, they usually experience a greater sense of peace, and their feelings of unfinished business are reduced or less intense in their own grief work.

Pastoral Care and Counseling with the Dying

We use *pastoral care* and *counseling* interchangeably when working with the dying. We may have a scheduled counseling session that turns into pastoral care because of the client's energy level and/or mental state at the time of our session. The last session we have with the dying is more often than not a time for pastoral care as death is approaching. Our pastoral care visits include our presence, just sitting with and praying with and/or for the client.

I have chosen examples that demonstrate the application of pastoral care or counseling using a theoretical frame and the integration of care with counseling. My first example is a couple in mid-life, their family grown. My second example is a woman in mid-life. Though I worked only with the woman, she was part of a couple who were both coping with terminal illnesses. The husband had not requested any counseling; he was comfortable with the spiritual support of his church.

Case #1: Bret and Peggy

COUNSELOR PREPARATION: GATHERING DATA

Bret was referred to me by his wife, Peggy, who had been in therapy for a year prior to the diagnosis of Bret's brain tumor. Within the span of one week, they learned that his cancer had metastasized to his brain and that his prognosis had changed to fewer than six months to live. He had just been admitted to hospice care when he and his wife decided to undergo counseling together to help them manage the impact of this major change in their lives. Information about the new diagnosis and prognosis had left them feeling very overwhelmed.

Bret, who was sixty-seven, had retired at age sixty-five after thirty-eight years with the same company. At the time of his retirement, he had been diagnosed with bladder cancer.

The couple had already learned to make each day count. They were able to enjoy retirement and travel between Bret's chemo treatments, radiation therapy, and surgery. They had lived with the hope of cure until they received this new diagnosis.

They are active in the Episcopal Church. They are receiving pastoral care from their pastor and the Eucharistic ministers from their church.

The couple have four grown children and four grandchildren. They describe their family as open, loving, and caring.

Consider what your responses might be to the following questions:

- What is your initial impression of the couple?
- Does their story touch yours?
- What more information do you need to begin?
- What would be your goals with this couple?
- Do you like Peggy and Bret?

Now that we have gathered information and answered these questions for ourselves, it's time to respond to and set up a treatment plan for our clients.

CLIENT PREPARATION: DEFINING GOALS

Counselor (speaking to clients):

• How do you see me helping you through this experience?

Bret responds:

• I need help to understand what it means to be dying.
• I need help to manage my fears.
• I don't want to die alone.
• I need to know that my wife will be okay after I'm gone.
• I need to talk about the afterlife: What is it? What happens to the body in the afterlife?
• What if I can't forgive everyone who has harmed me in my life? Will I go to hell? What is hell?

Peggy responds:

• I need the strength and courage to help Bret live until he dies. I need not to let go too soon.
• I need the spiritual nurture of the sacraments.
• I need to have my thoughts and feelings heard, not just listened to.
• I want to be with Bret when he dies.
• I need to manage my fears.

Couple together asks the counselor:

• Do you think you can help us explore and meet our needs?
• How will you work with us?
• Can you help us to work through our individual issues as a couple? Remember, we have less than six months. We want to do the counseling as a couple.

Bret's Goals	Peggy's Goals
Understand the dying process	Strength and courage
Manage fear	Be present
Aftercare for my wife	Spiritual nurture
Understand afterlife	Be heard
Forgiveness	Manage fear
Fear of dying alone	Be with him when he dies

COUNSELOR'S PLAN

1. Work with Bret and Peggy as a couple;
2. Help them identify the commonalties of their expressed needs and wants;
3. Facilitate their process as a couple facing the death of one of them;
4. Use the modalities of talk therapy with the couple;
5. Life review, journaling, education on dying process.

OUTCOME

The couple worked with me for twenty-nine sessions. As it turned out, Bret lived for nine months after the diagnosis of his brain tumor. They were able to explore their individual and mutual fears together. Peggy was able to reassure Bret that she would be okay after he died. Peggy was able to meet Bret's last wishes to go to North Carolina, Rhode Island, and New Hampshire. They celebrated their last birthdays and wedding anniversary, Thanksgiving, and Christmas. They were able to tell one another what they admired and loved about one another, also regrets and irritations, asking forgiveness of one another. They shared their faiths and beliefs about death and the afterlife, heaven, forgiveness, and hell. Bret was able to tell Peggy that he wanted her to be holding him when he died. Peggy was able to share that she would hold him if she could. She shared that every time she went out the door she wondered if it would be the last time she'd see him alive. However, she had a sense that December 21 would be his last night on Earth. Before she got into bed with Bret, she placed the infant Jesus in the Christmas crib. She held Bret all night. At 6 A.M. she felt the life go out of him as he breathed his last.

The twenty-ninth counseling session was a pastoral care session for Bret, who could no longer speak, and a counseling session for Peggy, who needed additional support in letting go. He died four days later in his wife's arms, surrounded by family.

Case #2: Sally

COUNSELOR PREPARATION: GATHERING DATA

Sally was referred to me by the hospice social worker. She had requested a pastoral counselor. Sally had just been admitted to hospice care the day prior to my visit. She had metastatic lung cancer with a prognosis of less than six months to live. Sally's husband was also dealing with a metastatic cancer.

Sally was a sixty-three year old woman who had been a housewife and mother. She had three grown children; two were married, and she had one grandson. Her husband of forty-three years was also battling cancer. His cancer was in a bone in his left arm that had caused a pathological fracture, and he was physically ill from the chemotherapy treatments. He was not able to help with her physical care. The children were taking turns staying with their parents, and were managing the stress of the impending loss of both parents. The daughters seemed to draw on the strength of one another and their faith. The son was more withdrawn and didn't want to talk about it.

When I asked Sally what she wanted to do with the rest of her life, she said, "This house is really dirty and I need to clean it but I don't have the energy." At first, I was surprised by her response, as my initial thought was, "I would not spend the last days of my life cleaning my house." How can I use my countertransference in a positive way, by hearing what she was really saying? My interpretation of her statement was she had been a housewife all of her adult life, and she wanted her life back. She took pride in keeping a neat house and wished that she had the energy and health to have things the way they were prior to her illness.

The counseling sessions took place at the kitchen table while her husband was either napping in the bedroom or at his treatments. There were times when I wondered who would die first, because he seemed physically more ill. We had eight weekly sessions. Sally's goals for the counseling were

1. To tie up loose ends (unfinished business) with her family;
2. To manage the stress of her husband's decline and her inability to help him;
3. To prepare herself for her impending death psychologically and spiritually;
4. To do some life review with me and with her family;
5. To get help from a counselor so that she could complete her goals and help her children deal with the reality of losing both parents to cancer.

Sally had some personal possessions she wanted to give to family members. She wanted her grandson to have her engagement and wedding rings. She wanted to talk with him and say good-bye. She worried about her son and his grief. She felt that her daughters were doing okay, and that it was helping them to help her. At the end of the eight weeks, Sally was much weaker and closer to death. She was no longer able to sit at the kitchen table, and she was using her oxygen continuously. From the recliner in her living room, she smiled and reached for my hand. She whispered, "My house is now clean and I feel at peace. I don't think I will see you again. My goals are all finished. My pastor is coming to bring me and my family communion and have a family blessing. My family and I are at peace as we say good-bye to one another and the children and our grandchildren." Three days later, Sally died peacefully. Her husband died two months later.

I felt that her metaphor—"My house is now clean"—was twofold. Her house was cleaned by her daughters just the way she had taught them. Her internal house was cleaned because her unfinished business was resolved.

These two examples of working with dying clients had positive outcomes. I used these cases to illustrate a pastoral counseling model. Although any one of the theorists I have presented could have been used in our work with these clients, Dr. Ira Byock's theory best describes the work I did with Peggy, Bret, and Sally.

Pastoral Care and Counseling with the Bereaved

My next two work examples will be of bereaved clients. The pastoral care component is integrated with the counseling. We are present to our clients and pray with and/or for them as they request it. The models of grief counseling are integrated with theology as they address faith issues, belief systems, and meaning and purpose in life.

My first example is a grief therapist who lost her husband and very close friend and colleague within a two-week span of time. My second example is a young widow whose husband died within forty-eight hours of his hospice admission, leaving her with a three-month-old and a fourteen-month-old.

Case #3: Sonja

COUNSELOR PREPARATION: GATHERING DATA

Sonja is a fifty-eight year old widow who was referred to me by her pastor. Within the span of two weeks, Sonja's husband died and she lost a very close friend and professional colleague. Her husband died at home. He was a hospice patient. Her friend and colleague died at Shock Trauma.

Sonja is a psychotherapist who works as a grief counselor. She has closed her practice for six weeks and wants to work on her grief so that she will be able to return to work fully functioning. She believes that if she works through some of her intense pain over the next six weeks she will be able to re-open her practice on a part-time basis.

Sonja had anticipated her husband's death. However, her friend's death was totally unexpected. Her friend had been her primary support person during most of her husband's illness.

Sonja's grief is complex in that she is grieving two significant losses at the same time. While one was expected, the other is a shock. She does not want to be her own counselor, but she does want to follow her own advice, which is why she is seeking professional help for herself.

Sonja has four grown children, seven grandchildren, and one great-grandchild. She describes her children as very supportive in the midst of their own grief. Sonja's goals were

1. To accept the reality of both deaths;
2. To stay with the pain and work through it;
3. To improve and maintain her level of functioning;
4. To improve her coping skills;
5. To experience the support of her faith community.

Sonja was experiencing the following symptoms:

- Loss of appetite
- Inability to sleep through the night
- Inability to concentrate
- Uncontrollable tears most of the time
- Lack of energy

COUNSELOR'S PLAN

1. Work with Sonja on her goals;
2. Refer her to family physician for evaluation of physical symptoms;
3. Encourage journaling and life review;
4. Spend time focusing on each loss;
5. Provide additional pastoral support through the counseling service.

OUTCOME

Sonja had fifty weekly sessions followed by three months of biweekly, then three months of monthly sessions to termination. The counseling time for Sonja was long due to the close proximity of time of the deaths and to support her in returning to her work and functional level with other grieving clients.

She did practice what she taught others in grief. She began her grief journey with a four-day silent retreat followed by a long-overdue vacation in Florida with another close friend. She journaled every day and cried every day. She learned to space her time of tears so she could have that outlet and still function. For example, one day at work, her supervisor asked how she was doing. She replied, "If you want to hear my answer, you'll have to wait until the end of the day. If I respond now, I probably wouldn't be able to get through the day as my emotions are right at the surface." Her supervisor respected her request and spent some time with her at the end of the day.

Sonja did not really deal with her friend's death until close to the first anniversary of the death. She planned a memorial brunch for her friend and put a memory book together for her friend's family. In the planning of the brunch she began her active grief work. She was fully in touch with the pain at the end of the brunch. It was a very healing exercise for her. She continued journaling and working through the pain during the second year of her grief.

Sonja was able to return to her work within six weeks. She started back part-time and increased her caseload gradually over the next six months. She also continued with her own counseling.

Sonja was able to complete her counseling goals. At the time of termination she was re-investing in a new life without her husband and colleague. She was building a new life with a new support system. She had worked through Worden's tasks for the griever. According to my paradigm, she had come full circle. I say that because she started and ended at her spiritual core as she once again understood the meaning and purpose for her life.

Case #4: Naomi

COUNSELOR PREPARATION: GATHERING DATA

Naomi was referred for grief counseling by her mother. Naomi is a thirty-year-old woman recently widowed with a three-month-old daughter and a fourteen-month-old son. Her husband Tom had been diagnosed with leukemia and a systemic infection. He was considered terminal due to the overwhelming infection and a severely compromised immune system. He was admitted to hospice care and died within forty-eight hours.

Naomi's mother expressed concern about her daughter's ability to function and care for her two small children. Everything had happened so fast, and she was still in shock.

Naomi presented with sleep deprivation and anger. She was directing her anger at the doctors, her parents, God, and herself. She had a history of being treated for depression as an adolescent after a suicide gesture.

Naomi said that as a teenager, she rebelled against authority, particularly her parents. She was overweight and didn't feel accepted by her peer group.

Naomi denies any suicidal thoughts or feelings. However, she does feel overwhelmed by her current life situation. The baby is not sleeping through the night, and her son wakes early in the morning. She has been averaging three to four hours of sleep a night and feels exhausted. She asks her parents for help but they are not helping in a way that she perceives will meet her needs. She feels they don't understand what she is going through.

She is angry with her husband for leaving her and angry at her parents that she wasn't with him when he died. He had asked her to stay with him the night of his death, but her parents insisted she go home and get some rest. Neither she nor her parents realized just how close to death he really was. He was in a hospice inpatient facility because she couldn't manage his care at home with an infant and toddler to care for.

Naomi was experiencing guilt that she wasn't able to respond to her husband's last request, to stay with him that last night of his life.

NAOMI'S GOALS

1. Learn how to cope with her current life situation;
2. Resolve her guilt about leaving her husband alone the night of his death;
3. Work through her anger at her husband, parents, herself, and God;
4. Identify and use her support systems;
5. Learn some single parenting skills; and
6. Expand her support network to include young widows or widowers with young children.

COUNSELOR'S PLAN

1. Teach coping skills;
2. Facilitate working through guilt and anger;
3. Help her to utilize current support systems—family, friends, and faith community
4. Refer her to appropriate resources for single parenting skills, additional support systems, bereavement support group for young widows and widowers.

OUTCOME

I saw Naomi for fifty sessions at weekly intervals. We went to monthly sessions for four months, then terminated. During the therapy, we went through several firsts: Thanksgiving, Christmas, New Year's, anniversary, birthdays, Valentine's Day, Easter. The most traumatic times were Thanksgiving and going to her brother's wedding. She describes herself as having "lost it" on both occasions. Her brother's wedding was more traumatic than she expected. It emphasized that she was no longer part of a couple. It triggered the memories of her own wedding. Her parents were very concerned after the wedding and called me. It was then that Naomi realized they did love her and were a major support for her. She requested that we have a session with them and her brother. The session helped all concerned. Her parents were more aware of her needs, and she was more aware of what they could and could not do for her. She was also more aware that they did love her and wanted to be available yet not overinvolved. They were looking for some balance.

Naomi was able to resolve her guilt, forgiving herself and her parents. She worked through her anger in sessions and through journaling.

She participated in a widow and widower bereavement support group and went to a "surviving the holidays" bereavement seminar. With mutual consent, I was able to connect her with another young widow with young children. Naomi did expand her support network, which allowed her to be more realistic about what she could expect from her parents. Her parents agreed to help with child care so that she could return to school, taking one course a semester. Her parents also agreed to keep the children overnight an extra night a week so she could get two nights a week of uninterrupted sleep.

I gave her information on young children and grief. She started a memory book for the children with pictures and stories about their daddy.

Naomi terminated grief counseling with renewed self-esteem and hope for the future. She also resolved her anger with God as her faith community became a significant support system for her and her children.

Conclusion

Pastoral grief counseling and care in response to death and dying is a specialized ministry in hospice. Many hospices have their pastoral and bereavement care programs under one umbrella. The pastoral counselor who is introduced to the dying patient and family will have a good sense about the bereavement care and counseling needs of family members. I believe that I have grown more effective in my work as a grief counselor through the years. Having experienced multiple loss, personal, professional, and material, my awareness and sensitivity to the multifaceted issues that surround each loss has been an asset to my clients. I have been able to help them to move from their stuck places and tap into their own inner resources for healing. I also believe that knowledge is the key that opens the door to healing. When a person knows what is happening in grief and takes steps to ensure balance in self-care and reaching out to other grievers, both move toward healing. They know they hurt because they have loved.

When I am working with the dying and bereaved, I believe that I am on "holy ground." They have taught me that they can experience joy in the midst of pain and loss. They know that they hurt because they have loved. They also know that forgiveness can release them from the stuck places on the journey. As a pastoral grief counselor, I believe that our faith, our spirituality, our connectedness with God pave the way to our spiritual core, where complete healing takes shape and moves us forward.

References

Attig, Thomas. *How We Grieve: Relearning the World.* New York: Oxford University Press, 1996.

Byock, Ira. *Dying Well: The Prospect for Growth at the End of Life.* New York: Riverhead Books, 1997.

Corr, Charles. "A Task-Based Approach to Coping with Dying." *Omega: Journal on Death and Dying* 24, 2, (1992), 81–94.

Doka, Kenneth J. *Living with Threatening Illness.* New York: MacMillan Co., 1993.

Grollman, Rabbi Earl A. "Stressing Laughter" *Journeys.* Hospice Foundation of America, 1999.

Kübler-Ross, Elizabeth. *On Death and Dying.* New York: MacMillan Co., 1969.

Luebering. *Forum Newsletter* (1998).

McKissock, Dianne and McKissock, Mal. *Bereavement Counseling Guidelines for Practitioners.* Terrigal, Australia: Bereavement C.A.R.E. Bibliography, 1998.

Neimeyer, Robert A. "Meaning Reconstruction and the Experience of Loss." *Forum Newsletter* 25, 1 (1999), 1–13.

Parker, Harris H., "Untimely Death: A Challenge to Religious Faith." *Forum Newsletter* 23, 1 (1997), 9–10.

Pattison, E. Mansell. *The Experience of Dying 1977* Presentation by the American Academy of Bereavement. Tuscon, AZ, 1994.

Peterson and Nisenholtz. *Forum Newsletter* (1995).

Rando, Therese A. *Loss and Anticipatory Grief.* Lexington, MA: Lexington Books, 1986.

Read, Constance M. "Counseling the Dying." *Straight Forward* VI, 3 (Summer, 1995).

Schweska, John. "The Reflection." *Hospice Journal* (Winter 1997), 28–29.

Wicks, Robert J. "Countertransference and Burnout in Pastoral Counseling." *Clinical Handbook of Pastoral Counseling.* New York and Mahwah, NJ: Paulist Press, 1985.

Worden, William J. *Grief Counseling and Grief Therapy,* 2nd ed. Great Britain: Routledge, 1991.

Zucker, Rob. "You Do What for a Living? An Interview with Rabbi Earl Grollman," *Grief and Healing Newsletter,* Aquarius Publication, Fall 1999.

Richard D. Parsons

12. Suicide Survivors: Moving Beyond Intervention and Postvention

"One Suicide but Five Deaths"

Suicide is a horrifying and almost completely incomprehensible act. Over the last twenty-five years suicide has risen dramatically, and in some populations (for example, among adolescents) the increase has been astronomical, being recognized as the second major cause of death among persons aged ten to twenty-five.

Self-destructive acts are among the major mental health problems in almost every nation of the world. Suicide has risen from twelfth among causes of death in the United States during the 1950s to eighth in the early 1980s (Official statistic from the National Center for Health Statistics, annual volumes of Vital Statistics of the U.S.).

Most researchers agree that even such dramatic and alarming statistics may be underestimations. The lack of a standard definition of suicide, the reluctance to classify death as suicide, and the various means of suicide that afford the opportunity to misinterpret suicide as death by accident (such as autocide) lend support to this hypothesized underestimation.

The statistics on suicide point to the tragedy of a life stopped in process. These statistics may even hint at the pain and anguish endured by the suicide victim and from which he or she may have been seeking relief. However, the statistics fail to show the lives which continue to be destroyed by this one act of suicide.

As many have noted, and thousands have experienced, suicide is a singular act with plural effects. "There are always two parties to a death; the person who dies and the survivors who are bereaved," wrote historian Arnold Toynbee (1969, p. 267). He continues: "There are two parties to the suffering that death inflicts; and in the apportionment of this suffering, the survivor takes the brunt" (p. 271).

Spouses, children, siblings, parents, and even coworkers feel the impact of this devastating act. While the "bomb" of suicide impacts all, it is the victim's immediate family members who are at true ground zero. It is family members whose dreams have been shattered, whose roles and responsibilities have now come under scrutiny, and whose reason for living may even be suspect.

It has only been within the last fifteen years that rising concern has led researchers to widen their focus beyond the cause and even the prevention of suicide to include the effects on suicide survivors. In his 1967 outline for the Center for Studies of Suicide Prevention (CSSP), Edwin Shneidman, co-founder of the LASPC, wrote, "A comprehensive suicide-prevention program should attend to the psychological needs of the stigmatized survivors, especially children who survive a parent who has committed suicide" (Schneidman 1967, p. 6).

While termed *postvention,* the support, the counseling, the assistance afforded as interventions for the survivors of suicide function as preventive measures, reducing the stress and negative impact suicide has on the survivors—and thus reducing their potential for further damaging the survivor.

Harvey Resnik noted that "given the present state of our knowledge about suicide proper postvention seems the most promising avenue toward reducing the large number of suicides that occur annually" (Resnik 1972, p. 177).

The research on this intervention—this prevention—this postvention with suicide survivors, is far from definitive and much of what we know comes from anecdotal clinical reports. It is a beginning, however, a beginning of which we as counselors, ministers, and mental health specialist must become fully aware. It is this beginning which will be the focus of this chapter.

Pastoral Counselor as Preventionist

I have previously argued for pastoral counseling to move to a primary prevention model of service delivery (Parsons 1985). Nowhere else can the value and need of prevention be so clearly demonstrated as in the inevitable impact of suicide on the survivors. And perhaps there is nowhere else that the role of a pastoral counselor is so clearly suited to provide preventive service as in working with suicide survivors. As will be demonstrated later within this chapter, suicide survivors are not only in need of the "healing" presence of a therapeutic listener, but are also in need of the message of love conveyed by Paul:

> For I am certain of this: neither death nor life…nor any created thing whatever, will be able to come between us and the love of God, known to us in Christ Jesus our Lord (Rom 8:38–39).

This therapeutic, loving presence, for which the pastoral counselor can serve as vehicle, will facilitate the psycho-spiritual healing so needed by the survivors of suicide, and serve not only as an intervention, but a prevention, postvention, to deter the possible negative effects of the legacy of suicide.

Levels of Prevention

A number of authors have distinguished between the various levels of prevention (primary, secondary, and tertiary) and while I have argued elsewhere (see Parsons and Meyers 1984; Meyers and Parsons 1985) that primary prevention is the most desirable, each level of preventive service has a value for the pastoral counselor.

Primary prevention can be defined as efforts designed to prevent the occurrence of a disorder in a particular population by promoting the well-being of all of those in that particular group or community. It is generally agreed that primary prevention is designed essentially to prevent the development of mental health disorders. Secondary prevention, however, is focused on problems which have already begun to appear. The goal of secondary prevention is to shorten the duration, impact, and negative effects of the disorder; that is, to intervene in such a way so as to prevent the occurrence of the "typical" cycle of the illness and thus prevent it from reaching a point of severity. The third level of service, tertiary prevention, includes those techniques designed to reduce the consequence of severe dysfunction after it has occurred.

As we discuss the unique nature of the grief experienced as a result of a suicide, it will become evident that interventions prior to suicide (primary prevention) and early in the grief process (secondary prevention) will clearly assist the survivor in avoiding or reducing the extremely negative impact of suicide survival.

Whether we call our helping actions intervention, prevention, or postvention, they are clearly needed and most certainly pastoral.

A History of Shame and a Shameful History

In an article on the history of the suicide survivor George Howe Colt (1987) describes, in great detail, an eighteenth-century engraving called "The Desecration of the Corpse."

The engraving is of the naked body of a young man which has been pulled through the streets of Paris by a spirited white horse. Colt describes the man lying face down, "his ankles roped together, his arms outstretched behind him, his fingers clawing the cobblestones" (p. 3).

Apparently the horse has come to rest and a crowd surrounds the body. The horror of the scene is further evidenced by Colt's description of the onlookers. He notes that "one women shrinks from the scene in horror, covering her face with her hand. A curly-haired child on hands and knees watches in open-mouthed terror. A bearded man, his fingers in his mouth, cringes in disbelief and a dog gingerly sniffs the corpse" (p. 3).

While the scene is certainly one of a horrible event, the real horror rests in the reason for this treatment of this man. According to Colt the young man had been "convicted" of suicide.

Degradation of the suicide victim has a long and appalling history. While we are more "civilized" today in our treatment of the suicide victim, our "civilized treatment" may not always be extended to the other victims of a suicide—the survivors.

Perhaps on closer inspection of the engraving described by George Colt, we might find the face of anguish, the expression of shock and disbelief, or the lines of unbearable guilt etched on the face of this man's wife, parents, or children. Suicide is an act of violence not restricted to the official victim. Shneidman (1969) noted that each suicide intimately affects at least six other people (p. 22). It is a case of one buried, but many more dead or dying.

As for our "convicted victim," it is not clear from the engraving or from Colt's description why he took his life. However, a review of the history of societal response to suicide—and to the other victims of suicide, that is, the survivors—makes very clear the consequence of his action.

Suicide as Crime

Historically, suicide was treated as a crime with moral and civil outrage. As such, much effort was given to the total desecration and post mortem humiliation of the victim, and often his or her survivors. For example, in addition to dragging the body through the streets, the body would be taken to a public square and hung upside down. Similarly, the victim was denied a proper burial with the body often tossed in the town dump. If the victim was a man of property, his property (and thus the inheritance of the survivors) was most often forfeited. In addition to destroying the physical remnants (body and possessions) of the offender, the practice typically included destroying the memory and the good name of the person. The practice was to defame the person's memory *ad perpetuam rei memoriam,* "to the end of memory" (Colt 1987, p. 3).

Suicide as Sin

These civil actions, as barbaric as they may sound, found support in the attitudes and practices of the early church. By the seventeenth century the church generally viewed suicide as a sin, which had to be punished.

While neither Hebrew nor Christian scriptures specifically prohibits or condemns suicide, incidents of suicide are described in each. In the Old Testament some descriptions almost present suicide as an honorable act: Samson's suicide as revenge against the Philistines (Jgs 16:23–31), or Saul's suicide as an act of honor (1 Sm 31:1–6). It is only in the New Testament's description of Judas's suicide that we begin to see the action as one of self-destruction, self-punishment, and a result of shame and lack of hope (Mt 27:5).

The sinfulness of suicide as viewed from the Judeo-Christian orientation appeared to rest on three foundations as explicated by St. Augustine and later expanded upon by St. Thomas Aquinas. The basic position was that life belongs to God and only God can terminate it (Gn 2:7). Further, suicide was viewed as a transgression against the fifth commandment, "Thou shalt not kill" (Ex 20:13). And finally, as Paul noted, individuals are the dwelling place of God; as such, suicide not only defiles the individual but also defiles God who dwells within (1 Cor 3:9–17).

The dilemma for early Christians and society's overseers was that the sinner—the criminal—was no longer available to amend for his or her wrongdoing. Thus the church and society imposed severe penalties not only on the victim's dead body and memory, but also on his or her family. The survivors were treated as an accessory to what was now a crime, and therefore needed to suffer the civil and moral consequences. The survivors not only had to endure the pain associated with such a tragic loss, but were also treated as hostages, held as "payment" for the victim's crime, an atonement for his or her sin.

Perhaps such ghastly treatment was an attempt to demonstrate by example what happens when one perpetuates such as "crime." It may be argued that this was but a primitive attempt at primary prevention, a warning and a deterrent to all those who considered suicide. A deterrent to future suicide victims aside, what was not considered was the potential devastation and destruction such a societal and church response had on the other victims of suicide, the survivors.

Suicide as Insanity

By the nineteenth century suicide was no longer considered a moral problem but rather an emotional or mental problem. The act of suicide became its own evidence of insanity. Viewed as an illness rather than a sin or a crime, the stigma associated with suicide, while not removed, changed.

With the perspective that the individual did not know what he or she was doing, most churches became sensitive to the pastoral needs of the family. Rather that desecrating or defaming the victim and his or her survivors, churches began to provide meaningful religious rituals that offered survivors the caring of a faith community. Suicide victims were permitted burial in consecrated ground and their property and possessions were no longer confiscated.

While certainly a more caring and pastoral position, survivors still experienced other forms of rejection, punishment, and stigmatization. Survivors traded the stigmas associated with criminal and sinful behavior for the stigmas and superstitions associated with insanity. Many believed that they themselves were doomed, if not to suicide, to insanity. And society's reaction to suicide as a social disgrace, while not as blatant as that of the seventeenth century, continued in subtle yet very destructive ways to place the survivors physical and mental well-being at risk.

Survivors of suicide were and continue to be denied free and honest access to the grieving process, a process which is essential if healing is to take place. Pastoral counselors, working from a preventive mode, need both to assist the bereaved overcome their self-admonitions against grieving and also to remove the subtle forces within the church community that repress the open, therapeutic expression of grief following a death by suicide. For pastoral counselors to assist in this healing process, they must first understand the nature of "normal" grief work and then the pathogenic impact suicide has on the grieving process.

Bereavement—The Potential for Healing

The death of a loved one is a great stressor; it evokes complex physical, psychological, and social reactions. These reactions taken together comprise what is known as the bereavement process. According to Hauser (1987) bereavement is a homeostatic process; it enables the bereaved to recoil, react, adjust to the loss, and then continue on with life. The emphasis is on continuing on with life, but quite often circumstances surrounding the grieving block the individual's movements through the stages of healing in order to accomplish this.

Stages of Bereavement

Bowlby and Parkes (1970) have investigated this homeostatic process in non-suicidal mourning and identified a number of predictable stages survivors go through in the process of reestablishing balance in their life. While depicted as a set of sequential steps or stages, bereavement and grief work do not proceed in a nice, neat, straight line. Rather, they resemble more a roller coaster with many twists, turns, and ups and downs. As care-givers to those in grief, it is important to understand the generalized schema in order not only to predict certain reactions but to prepare better for the type and form of intervention and support required. Regardless of the general framework from which we view grief work, we must remember that grieving is a highly individualized experience.

1. SHOCK

Following the death of a loved one, the individual absorbs the shock of the loss. Quite often denial along with a general numbness and sense of being overwhelmed are characteristic of this stage. This denial appears to function as a buffer, a shield to the ego, that protects the survivor from the full impact of the loss.

One of my clients, a forty-seven-year-old widow whose husband had died suddenly from a heart attack, described this experience vividly.

> The doctor approached us, and I know he said, "I'm sorry, but but.....," I really can't remember what else he said. I don't know where the next three days went. It didn't seem real. I know I went to the funeral home and out to the cemetery, but even now it doesn't seem real. It really was like I was watching a play and I was one of the actors. I kept thinking, he'll get up and take his bow, but I know he won't![1]

With time, this shield slowly gives way to increased intrusion from reality. The various demands and processes which need attention (such as the need to make funeral arrangements, attend the funeral, and so on), chip away at this denial until slowly and manageably the impact of the loss can be accepted.

2. YEARNING AND PROTEST

As shock and denial diminish, the active, open expression of sorrow begins to be manifested. The bereaved experiences a variety of emotional outbursts—tearfulness, anger, restlessness, tension, irritability, intense yearning, and panic. The variations and intensity of the feelings give evidence to what has been called the *separation pain*. This is an extremely stressful time of anguish and disorganization in terms of living.

The bereaved may obsessively review the circumstances of the deceased's death and literally long for the person's presence. For example, a sixty-three-year-old retired man whom I counseled noted that be would find himself crying almost uncontrollably at unexpected times and places. He reported that he would just start to sob while grocery shopping or watching television. He also noted that he found himself sitting for what seemed like hours "day dreaming" and almost dazed, thinking about his wife of forty years.

3. DISORGANIZATION

The sense of yearning and loss eventually give way to a general malaise, a feeling of apathy and aimlessness. The emptiness experienced leads bereaved people to wonder and worry about the future and their redefinition of life. They may be overwhelmed by a sense of "What now?" The stress associated with letting go of the past life with the deceased and planning for a life without the person often results in the appearance of physical symptoms associated with stress (headaches, gastrointestinal distress, sleep disturbance, and others). The bereaved may also become preoccupied with the deceased and find that they are unable to concentrate or take the initiative in social situations. Rather than returning to their previous activities, hobbies, and friends, bereaved individuals may start to withdraw, remain in the house, and manifest what might be called a psychological living death.

Along with the depression, despair, and general dread about the future, the bereaved may experience feelings of hostility toward the deceased (for doing this to them) and subsequently intense guilt. Progress through this stage is often slow and may span years.

4. REORGANIZATION

The final phase of the grieving process requires that bereaved individuals relinquish the past and rebuild a life without their loved one. Such a rebuilding requires an alteration of their self-image, the development of new roles and behaviors, and even the establishment of new social networks. As one woman trying to start anew said:

> For thirty years of my life, over half of my life, I was Mrs. _____ , and now I'm supposed to simply get on with it! OK, so I'm forty eight years old. People say I'm bright, attractive, but I haven't worked outside the home or dated for more than twenty years, I don't know how or where to go to meet people. For God's sake, I am not sure I can balance the checkbook much less get a job. I have so much to do, so much to learn, it's scary.

Such a reworking of self, is neither easy nor guaranteed. It is a process that even when successful may require a lot of time and support.

Grieving a Suicide

The normal grieving process is fraught with challenges and stumbling blocks. All mourners could use some psycho-spiritual support, some pastoral care. This need for support is significantly magnified when one considers the special experience of grieving following death by suicide.

While there is no quick and easy formula for assisting one with the grieving process—or any guarantee that any one individual will or will not have pathogenic reactions to the experience of a loss—the research (Cain and Fast 1972a; Hauser 1983) suggests that a number of factors have been associated with "successful" resolution of grief. These facilitative factors are almost always absent in the grieving process of a suicide survivor. With the absence of facilitating factors and the presence of increased stressors, it is not difficult to understand why suicide survivors have an increased risk of pathogenic grief response.

Cain and Fast (1972a) noted that a careful analysis of the inherent nature, context, and almost inevitable consequences of suicide gives strong indication of why the impact of a suicide may have pathogenic potential distinct from and well beyond the disruptive factors generally surrounding and following a death.

Hauser (1983) noted that the bereavement process appears more difficult when the death is sudden or unexpected. By definition, suicide is almost always unexpected and sudden. Because survivors were unable to prepare for the possible death, they were left without time nor opportunity to work on any unfinished business in the relationship. The suicidal act denied them any opportunity for closure with the deceased, and thus the suddenness and unexpected nature of the act of suicide accentuates the shock and disbelief. This alters the initial stage of grieving.

Hauser (1983) further noted that the grieving process is made more difficult when the death is violent or traumatic. The act of suicide, regardless of whether the means or mode was one of dramatic violence, is in itself both violent and traumatic. This trauma is accentuated for the survivor who discovers the victim. One can only imagine the pain and trauma for Mr. J, who arrived home from work one Friday evening expecting to leave early Saturday morning for a fishing trip with his three sons, when he opened the garage door and found his middle son, age nineteen, hanging from the rafters. The shock, the trauma, the haunting images make it more difficult to accept the death in order to move on through the grieving process.

In addition to the unexpected, traumatic nature of suicide other factors which Hauser (1983) has linked to unsuccessful or inhibited bereavement are clearly evidenced in many, if not most, deaths by suicide. Elements such as feeling responsible for the death; having a death accompanied by additional stressors; limiting permission to express one's grief and reducing social support for the bereaved; all these inhibit movement through the grief process. With these factors as a backdrop, it is not difficult to understand the added stress and trauma experienced by the bereaved of a suicide and the resultant increase in pathogenic response.

1. SHOCK FOLLOWING SUICIDE

The difficulty with surviving and "successfully" grieving a suicide is that one must accept two very traumatizing realities. First, suicide survivors must accept the death of their loved one, as do all who are in mourning. Second, and perhaps much more difficult, they must accept that the death was one of suicide (Seiden 1969). Without acceptance of both of these realities, movement through the grieving process will not be possible.

Denial is often the ego defense first noted in the initial stage of bereavement. For one to work successfully through grief, denial must give way to acceptance of the reality.

Suicide dramatically alters the life of the survivors. Plans and dreams fall apart; the life story is interrupted. The stress existing within the family prior to the suicide, along with the stress that results from the death, is only aggravated by the isolation and social stigmatization which often accompanies death by suicide.

Because of feelings of unacceptability and shame, survivors quite often attempt to conceal suicides. Denial, concealment, and refusal or inability to talk about the suicide tend to halt the mourning process. The conspiracy of silence which tends to surround a suicide sharply limits opportunities for catharsis. Family members consciously and unconsciously develop elaborate family myths regarding the nature of the death: "It was an accident," or "He had a long illness." These schemes emphasize the importance of denial and repression rather than acceptance of the grief. With such strong denial, movement through the healing process of grieving is all but eliminated.

In addition to the stress accompanying the death of a loved one, survivors of suicide often experience added stressors not typically experienced by mourners of non-suicide deaths. For example, consider the unpleasant meetings with police, who overtly or implicitly consider the alternative possibility of murder rather than suicide, or the contacts with sometimes hostile insurance representatives focusing on ways out of their policy payments.

These additional intrusions and additional demands tend to highlight the stigma associated with suicide. This stigma not only adds to the stress experienced by the survivors but often makes them unable to depend upon usual avenues of support to work through grief. Funerals are hurried and hushed, even to the point of not informing friends and relatives. "John didn't want to inconvenience anyone, even to the end!" Even church representatives may impede the opportunity to grieve by refusing to conduct burial services, or to do so only with much modification and compromise.

These added stressors and pressures encourage escape through denial and inhibit the healing movement toward acceptance.

2. YEARNING AND PROTEST/SUICIDE

In order for the next phase of the grief work to begin, survivors must freely experience their sorrow and the variations and intensity of feelings which accompany it. As noted above, such expression is often denied the bereaved of a suicide because their emotions are often repressed. The expression of even normal grieving has been confounded by the fact that they suffer under cultural confusion and stigmas surrounding suicide. They are encouraged to continue to deny and repress, not express.

Whereas it is most understandable and acceptable to feel intense sorrow at the loss, of the loved one, all too often it is anger, not sorrow, which is first experienced by the survivor of a suicide. Intense anger is often directed at the victim for "giving up." Or the anger may be a direct result of the personal rejection implied by the suicidal act. Often, however, the pain of such rejection is too great to bear, and thus it is denied and only unconsciously expressed, again in the form of projected blaming. Under these conditions, the survivors' anger at the victim may be directed toward elements in the system which the survivors believe may have caused or contributed to the suicide. And finally, the expressed anger may be a manifestation of the survivors' unconscious transformation of guilt over not having prevented the suicide, with the guilt being projected in the form of anger onto a scapegoat.

In a culture that allows only sorrow, anger following a death is not only not understood but is often viewed unsympathetically and even punitively. This point is depicted in the self-accusation of one widow: "I looked at him—so peaceful—and I wanted to strangle him, to hurt him. I know it's stupid. For God's sake, he's dead. But I feel so angry, so furious. I am so ashamed for feeling like this. How can you be angry at someone you say you loved, someone who is dead? I must be horrible, God forgive me!"

The feelings experienced during this second phase of grieving are many and varied. In addition to anger many survivors of suicide experience a sense of relief. Because such a feeling following upon the death of a loved one is not socially accepted, the survivors often suppress the feeling and or again feel intense guilt about having it. The reality is that for most the sense of relief is not evidence of lack of love, but rather of the tension, the conflict that preceded this act. The suicidal death of an extremely troublesome child, or of an alcoholic and abusive parent or spouse will most likely be followed by a sense of relief The danger is that many soften their memory of the abuse or the conflict and thus feel guilty over this "unacceptable" sense of relief that they experience.

Survivors of suicide most often share intense guilt as a common emotional reference point. As noted, they are guilty over feeling angry or experiencing relief, or because they failed to prevent the death. Survivors are often absorbed in obsessive thoughts regarding their own role in the precipitating events or the fact that in retrospect they see that they missed significant clues and should have acted differently.

The role of irrational guilt following bereavement has been amply recognized, but the ferocity of guilt in the survivors of a suicide is particularly striking. This guilt and the accompanying sense of blame redirects the grieving from a process of healing to a process of self-reprisal and even destruction.

The healing process is further inhibited by the lack of social support and the felt injunction not to discuss the suicide. Survivors of suicide often fail to share their experience, their thoughts, and their feelings. Such failure to share and openly experience the many, varied feelings denies suicide survivors the opportunity to check distorted fantasies against the realities of the suicidal act. Without such reality checks on the variety of gross misconceptions often experienced, suicide survivors have little hope of successfully resolving the irrational guilt or the angry reproaches they feel toward themselves or the person who committed the suicide. Thus they are unable to move from this stage of grief.

3. DISORGANIZATION/SUICIDE

In addition to the general apathy and aimlessness typically experienced in grief, bereaved suicide survivors often experiences self-pity and long-lasting depression. You will often hear this expressed in terms such as, "He killed himself, now he is killing me," or "I'll never get over it."

As with the previous feelings and experiences, this sense of hopelessness and depression is compounded by the general lack of support available to the bereaved of a suicide. Unlike more "typical" grievers, whose social support systems assist them to find meaning and direction in their lives, the bereaved of a suicide are often unable to depend upon the usual avenues for support in working through their grief.

The stigma still associated with suicide often results in survivors failing to find support from their social network. Quite often they experience network avoidance, gossip, and even finger pointing (Cain and Fast 1972b), which in term reinforces and perpetuates their sense of isolation, shame, and disequilibrium.

It appears that this massive avoidance, this lack of communication, this lack of free acceptance of the experience of grief with all of its various manifestations, virtually prevents the working through of mourning and therefore serves as the primary cause for dysfunctional, pathogenic responses to grief. Suicide survivors not only struggle through their grief work, but they often completely block successful grief work. The end result is the development of potentially self-destructive response patterns.

Pathogenic Grief Response

One set of pathogenic responses to grief involves attempts at completing avoiding the entire grieving process. Such survivors are pathogenic in that they inhibit free, open, and healing expressions of grief and thus stimulate grief manifestation through less than productive ways. Wolfet (1987) noted five forms of such grief avoidance.

Postponing occurs when the individual believes that if you delay your grief it will go away. However, the truth is that rather than dissipating, the grief builds up and comes out in other ways (depression, insomnia, destructive personal patterns, and so on).

Displacing occurs when the individual attempts to move his or her grief in other directions. For example, the displacer may begin chronically to complain about difficulty at work or in another relationship. He or she may appear agitated and upset at minor events, in general bitter toward life.

Replacing is the process by which the bereaved takes the emotions that were invested in the relationship and reinvests those emotions prematurely in another relationship. When another relationship is not available, the replacer may invest excessive energies into work, becoming a compulsive overworker, when there was no prior history of such behavior.

This was true of Mary, an elementary school teacher of eleven years. Following the suicidal death of her daughter, Mary began to "live at work." She would stay within her classroom until late into the evening, "preparing for *her* children and the next day." Mary began inviting some of the children in her class to stay and help her, even offering to take them to dinner with her as thanks for their assistance. Through counseling it became clear that Mary, who by her own description handled the death and funeral like a "little soldier," was now avoiding any possible reminders of the loss and attempting to find substitutes for her daughter in the work, and "her" children at work. Such replacement compounds the pain, confusion, and disequilibrium in one's life and needs to be confronted.

The fourth form of avoidance described by Wolfet (1987) is *minimizing*. Minimizing is the process by which the survivors take their feelings and through extensive rationalization attempt to reduce the significance and impact of these feelings. On the surface the minimizer looks good and appears to have rational answers to all that has happened. "He's with God, now," "At least she is no longer in pain," "But we had eighteen wonderful years together—these could all reflect an attempt at avoidance through minimizing. Even though the surface looks and sounds good, feelings are building up and emotional strain will inevitably result.

Somatizing is the final form of grief avoidance. This is the process by which individuals convert their feelings into physical symptoms. The pattern may take the form of rather benign complaints, or it can take the form of a chronic pattern of multiple vague somatic complaints with no organic findings (somatization disorder). It is as if the survivors sense that such somatization legitimizes their need to be comforted, whereas their direct expression of grief following a suicide may chase people away.

While Wolfet's listing is certainly non-exhaustive, it is clear that such patterns of grief avoidance result in deterioration of relationships with friends and family; symptoms of chronic physical illness either real or imagined; and symptoms of chronic depression, low self-esteem, and chronic anxiety, agitation, restlessness, and difficulty in concentrating. While attempting to avoid the pain of grief, these attempts only serve to compound and extend the pain experienced.

In addition to such delay or avoidance patterns, suicide survivors appear to be particularly susceptible to a number of additional pathogenic grief responses (Cain and Fast 1972a, 1972b).

Pattern 1: In their study Cain and Fast (1972a) noted that many survivors attempted to resolve their unconscious conflicts and anguish over the loss of their loved one by re-engaging in a relationship as quickly as possible. Quite often these relationships were marked for failure, apparently neurotically determined.

Survivors would often remarry individuals who had evidence of chronic illness or gross physical handicaps. It is as if they were selecting individuals who needed nurturance as a way to redefine themself and their value in the face of the post-suicide guilt.

This was clearly the case with Tina, a thirty-nine-year-old widow with whom I worked. Following therapy Tina was able to explain the value of her remarriage following the suicidal death of her first husband; "Marrying Jack proved to me (and everyone else) that I was lovable. After all, he wouldn't have married me if I was the terrible person who would make somebody want to kill himself." Fortunately for Tina, the marriage to Jack did work out, but this is not always the case. In situations where the remarriage fails, survivors have additional "data" to support their guilt and feelings of unacceptability. This compounds the dysfunctionality of their grieving.

Pattern 2: The second pattern noted by Cain and Fast (1972a) was characterized as a plan for world rescue. These individuals identified with special interests and causes (cancer cures, grand economic designs, and so on), taking to these causes with unusual fervor. In the Cain and Fast research, the degree of their involvement proved pathogenic in that it deterred them from their normal functioning, interests, and responsibilities.

Pattern 3: The third form of dysfunctionality is much more direct in its form of self-destructive. Often survivors manifested openly self-destructive impulses and behavior, including suicidal ideation, attempts, and even "successful" acts.

Jack, age thirty-one, was a mechanical engineer. Within the last two years, he had three near-fatal car accidents. Through the course of therapy it was revealed that Jack often fantasized about his death. His imaging typically involved death at the hands of some dramatic and daring stunt, such as sky diving, car racing, or bungie jumping. In therapy Jack disclosed his thoughts about taking his own life, but felt that he was "too chicken" to ever do it. With time, Jack told his story. Jack was the youngest of three sons. His brother Al had a fatal car accident at the age of thirty, but Jack knew it wasn't an accident. On more than one occasion Al had shared with his younger brother the fact that he wished he was dead. Jack admitted that he never openly grieved for his brother; in fact, he had refused to go to his brother's funeral.

It appeared that the occasion of Jack's own thirtieth birthday, resurfaced the guilt and remorse he felt at not telling anyone about his brother's "death wish." Further, it appeared that his own dangerous actions were a dysfunctional attempt at self-reproach.

Pattern 4: Cain and Fast (1972a) found that for some of the survivors, reparation and undoing were not the choice of resolution. Rather, they used their new marital partner to assuage their guilt by playing out in the new relationship the complaints, grievances, and accusations previously held and belonging to the relationship with the suicidal partner. It appeared almost as if they were attempting to externalize and then master their own superego accusations.

Such a pattern was evidenced by Toni, a fifty-three-year-old widow. Toni remarried one year after the suicidal death of her husband. She and her new husband, Peter, entered therapy because of their almost constant fighting about his "always being out." Through the early sessions it became clear that Toni was distorting the reality of Peter's nights out. In fact, his evenings out were restricted to a once a week bowling league and once a month card club, to which she was invited. Through the sessions Toni consistently made reference to her first husband—how he, like Peter, never stayed home. On closer inspection it became clear that Toni was furious with her first husband, and that her first marriage had been characterized by continuous arguments over his tendency to go "out with the boys, and never take me anywhere." During the year following his death, Toni romanticized the relationship, having nothing but praise and warm feelings for how close they had been. She did not allow herself to accept or embrace her anger following his death and, as a result, looked for a "more acceptable" way to vent her feelings. The current marriage to Peter provided her with the opportunity to continue to play out that anger.

Pattern 5: The final pattern noted by Cain and Fast (1972a) appeared to involve the unconscious attraction to suicidal persons. One could speculate that such an attraction is an attempt at continued punishment and rapprochement or that it is a symbolic attempt to prevent the first event from having occurred. It is as if one is given another chance to stop the suicide.

Regardless of the hope or motivation, the reality is that connecting in such a relationship is not only a dysfunctional way to cope with the original guilt and remorse, but also exponentially compounds the survivor's stress, pain, and dysfunctionality, should this second relationship end in suicide.

A Model for Ministering to Survivors

The clinical data and an analysis of the pathogenic factors inherent in the consequences of suicide strongly suggest the need for postsuicide interventions with the bereaved. Conceptualizing grief work as occurring within a community context, a context which can exacerbate or facilitate healthy movement through grief—and which is also affected (positively or negatively) by the experience of the suicide and the grieving of the survivors-highlights the need for a prevention focus to our ministering. Whether we term it intervention, prevention, or postvention, facilitating movement through the grief process is essential.

While it is important to note that the grieving process is highly idiosyncratic and thus to avoid generalizations, there are still some common issues most suicide survivors need to address. As such, a general goal or aim for postvention is to help the survivors work through their feelings of grief, which invariably accompany a death. This includes the issues typically addressed within non-suicidal mourning, along with the special concerns so often aroused by suicide.

Tertiary Level Prevention

Quite often it is only after survivors have struggled with the grieving process and have experienced a degree of dysfunctionality that they seek the support of a pastoral counselor. With the focus on not only providing remediation but also assisting survivors to develop a more adaptive (preventive) coping style in the future, the pastoral intervention serves as a tertiary level of prevention.

Survivors of suicide may come to counseling through a variety of routes. Quite often they come for immediate assistance, a form of psychological first aid or crisis intervention. Others come only after exhausting all other means of coping and still finding the months or years since the suicide unbearable.

While both of these groups are clear as to the source of their life difficulty, some survivors may present themself as having difficulty with some other area of their life (a problem with a relationship, a child management problem, a work-related difficulty). On closer inspection it becomes clear that the unfinished nature of their grief is the issue which needs to be addressed.

Treatment with survivors of suicide is complicated by the tortured and erratic course of suicide grief. Some theorists have even suggested that it is better to wait up to a year before beginning an intervention since the shock, disorganization, and denial are so strong.

It has been my experience, and one supported by others within the literature (e.g., E. J. Dunne and Dunne-Maxim 1987) that suicide survivors who seek therapy after years of struggling with unresolved grief often present a number of recurring thematic issues. Quite often they will present as individuals who are "stuck" in a perpetual need to search (often physically as well as psychologically) for the reasons for the suicide. While understanding can be an element which facilitates their own closure, obsessional rumination often reflects their own denial and an attempt to defend via intellectualization. When such is the case, they must be confronted and encouraged to let go and move on.

A second theme often presented is that of being socially stigmatized. For example, consider the following case illustration. Albert was only thirty-one years old when his wife of five years committed suicide. Albert was seen in therapy three years after his wife's death. Initially he presented as someone who was depressed about his inability to make and keep friends. As the therapy developed, it became obvious that Albert's social isolation was self-induced and motivated by his own internalized negative attitudes toward himself. Albert felt that all of his old friends were avoiding him and that anyone he would meet would soon find out about the suicide and similarly move away from him. Through a number of cognitive debating exercises as well as in-vivo desensitizations these faulty beliefs were tested and reformulated (see Parsons and Wicks 1986). Albert was encouraged to begin to associate with old and new associates, and he soon found that his projected rejections never came to fruition.

Perhaps the most common theme reported in the literature is that of inexorable guilt. Survivors may express such guilt as self-reproach for not having done all that they could to prevent the suicide, or they may even project this guilt on to others in the form of anger. In working with a number of clients with intense non-suicide related guilt and anger, I have found the cognitive restructuring techniques effective and efficient strategy (see Parsons 1989).[2]

Secondary Prevention

Rather than waiting for the dysfunctionality to become fully manifested, the pastoral counselor may be able to intervene early in the grieving process in order to reduce the potentially negative impact of a pathogenic response at each stage of the grieving. Interventions occurring prior to full manifestation of a disorder and aimed at shortening the duration, impact, and negative effects of such pathogenic responses could be viewed as secondary prevention.

THE INITIAL STAGE OF SHOCK

It is clear that the most valuable thing the pastoral counselor can do at this stage of the grieving process is to be available to the survivor. The presence of a mental health professional, a counselor, or a minister immediately after the death can facilitate the family's expression of confusion and thus minimize subsequent unwillingness to communicate. As Herzog and Resnik (1969) reported, such early contact can serve as a needed and valued cathartic experience.

What is called for at this point is not so much directive interventions but crisis and supportive counseling. It is important to establish a compassionate tone for the grief process. During the initial shock stage it is especially important to present an atmosphere of both gentleness and understanding. Relationship skills (see Carkhuff 1969; Egan 1973) such as genuineness, warmth, unconditional prizing of the bereaved, and empathic understanding are essential during this particular phase of the grief process. It is not so important to "do for" or "do to" as it is to "be with" the bereaved.

Chilstrom (1989) noted that pastoral care is the vehicle by which God sends "listeners for the grief story," where the "telling and the retelling of details" will gradually help to ease the pain. The survivor needs emotional support and a large measure of reality testing. The presence of the counselor can assist the family to move from denial to acceptance of this death by suicide.

MOVEMENT THROUGH ANGER...GUILT...SHAME

As the survivors continue through the grieving they will be barraged by a variety of emotions, many of which they will find unacceptable, clearly not something one can admit. At this stage the helper needs to encourage expression of *all* feelings.

It is essential to convey a real sense of unconditional valuing or prizing for the bereaved and to offer a style of non-judgmental responding in order to allow them to express all their feelings, including their hostilities toward the deceased and even their own self-recriminations.

It may also be necessary to provide survivors' permission to express anger at God. Quite often the bereaved feel that such anger is sinful and its expression blasphemous. However, their anger is understandable given their perceptions of the "unfairness" of all that they are experiencing. The pastoral counselor can assist the bereaved to accept these feelings and to place their anger, their difficulty in forgiving God, in contrast to God's ability to always forgive.

Throughout the early stages of the grieving it is important to address the fact of suicide openly. This is not meant to imply that the suicide should be the focal point, but that the counselor must present a frank and undistorted view of reality. However, it is of very little therapeutic value to be argumentative or confrontational at this time. It is not so essential to point out minor omissions or commissions, which in our minds may appear to be of monumental importance. More than such intense reality checking, the bereaved need permission to embrace and accept all of their feelings along with the freedom to express these feelings as they wish.

SELF-PITY AND DEPRESSION

As the grief progresses survivors may become filled with self-pity. Quite often this stage manifests in severe depression with extreme anxiety and/or somatic involvement. The focus of the therapeutic intervention is to address the depression in such a way as to assimilate the grief and facilitate the survivors' growth through it.

One issue which needs to be confronted is survivors' irrational distortions of the reality surrounding the events leading up to the suicide as well as the import and impact of the suicide. Irrational beliefs and self-talk which defines their life condition as "hopeless," or "unbearable," and their self as "worthless" and "damnable" need to be confronted actively and debated (see Parsons and Wicks 1986; Parsons 1989).

The healing which results from successful navigation through the mourning process requires that the bereaved develop an honest, realistic regard for the circumstance of the death—and an honest, realistic appraisal of themselves.

SPECIFIC PASTORAL ISSUES

In addition to concerns and questions such as "Why did he (she) have to do it?" "What could we have done?" "What will I do now?" the bereaved may have anxiety and confusion around the issues of salvation and damnation for the victim.

Questions regarding the forgiveness of God, God's sense of justice, and the sinfulness of the act of suicide are questions to which the pastoral counselor needs to be prepared to respond. In order to deal adequately and therapeutically with these concerns the pastoral counselor needs to be able to identify his or her own feelings about, and theology of, suicide, death, forgiveness, and resurrection *before* entering the counseling relationship. It is hoped that the pastoral counselor will be able to give witness to the mercy, forgiveness, and love of God.

This author has found it helpful to assist the bereaved to understand the various factors which often cloud the judgment of a person committing suicide. Perhaps there was evidence of extreme pain, despair, depression, or dysfunctionality. From that perspective we might assume that it is unlikely that God would judge a desperate or ill action as immoral. It is also helpful if survivors can understand that we should not assume God's judgment is based on behavior performed under the influence of severe and debilitating illness rather than a person's life-time ledger of moral and immoral actions.

Hope is the cornerstone of all major religions, and forgiveness and mercy the message of a crucified and risen Christ. Hope—for themselves and for their loved one—is the therapy most needed for the bereaved of a suicidal death.

For all those wondering whether their loved one is happy or suffering, Jesus' prayer from the cross—"Father forgive them, they do not know what they are doing" (Lk 23:34)—is an invitation to trust in the Lord. It is this hope, this message of the risen Christ, which we need to reflect and affirm for the survivors.

There are a number of "non-counseling" activities which can prove therapeutic and have secondary preventive value. For example, it is helpful to involve survivors in planning the church services. Not everyone has to be involved or even attend, but, the more involvement and participation the more readily they will accept the reality they are facing and the more readily the healing will begin. Making a ceremony out of the tasks of buying markers or developing plans for remembrances and perpetuation assists the family in both accepting and letting go, knowing that their loved one will be remembered.

Finally, as pastoral counselors we must accept that the grieving process does not end with the burial; it really only begins. Therefore it is important to maintain regular follow-up contact with bereaved. The roller coaster nature of the grieving process, especially when it is the result of suicide, requires that ministry to the bereaved become a long-term commitment.

Primary Prevention

Any steps which reduce the stress of the entire church community increase the competency and ability of the community members to handle stress. To develop a sense of church as a supportive, caring environment may actually function to prevent not only dysfunctional grieving, but even the act of suicide itself. All such efforts designed to prevent the occurrence of a disorder or dysfunctionality by promoting emotional well-being have been termed primary prevention.

The pastoral counselor should use the occasion of this tragedy as an opportunity to involve and educate the entire congregation on the phenomenon of suicide and the impact of suicide on survivors. (Be sure that any homily, lecture, or presentation be done with the permission of the bereaved and without specific reference to this incident.) Congregational growth and health can be stimulated by sharing the feelings commonly experienced by survivors (guilt, shame, embarrassment, stigma, anger, rage, shock, confusion, fear, anxiety, and social isolation) and encouraging the congregation to reach out and offer support to the survivors. Efforts to provide such community support provides secondary prevention to the survivors and may serve to reduce stress and a sense of isolation for others, which if unattended may evolve into a destructive, suicidal force. Thus such education and church community development has a high degree of primary prevention potential.

Conclusions

Clearly much has changed in the years since English law provided for the confiscation of the property of suicide victims and the disinheriting and stigmatizing of the surviving family members. However, societal attitudes toward survivors of suicide, if not overtly destructive, are still not uniformly supportive and helpful.

The potential pathogenic impact suicide has on the "other victims," the survivors, has only begun to receive the serious attention it and they deserve. The research describing the extent of the impact, its specific manifestations, and the recommendations for instituting programs of remediation and prevention has only begun. Much more empirical research is needed.

However, the bereaved, the survivors of suicide, cannot wait for the definitive research. They are in pain now. All too many are isolated from family, from society, and from their church at a time when they need the support and love which should be the hallmark of a Christian community. The various social-psychological forces that exist and encourage denial, repression, and isolation need to be reduced, and survivors need to find the caring support they require to openly and honestly grieve.

The pastoral counselor who can walk with the bereaved—and encourage the local community to serve as a constant reminder of the living reality of Christ's love and forgiveness—intervenes, prevents, postvents, but most important, helps to heal all who are touched by the tragedy of suicide.

Notes

1. All case material has been modified to ensure anonymity.
2. The nature of this chapter doesn't allow for a full exploration of these techniques. Interested readers are referred to this article or the works of A. Beck or A. Ellis.

References

Bowlby, J., and Parkes, C. M. 1970. "Separation and Loss Within the Family." In *The Child in His Family,* vol. 1, edited by E. J. Anthony and C. Koupernik, pp. 197–216. New York: Wiley Interscience.

Cain, A. C., and Fast, I. 1972a. "The Legacy of Suicide: Observations on the Pathogenic Impact of Suicide Upon Marital Partners." In Cain, *Survivors of Suicide,* pp. 145–54.

———, and Fast, I. 1972b. "Children's Disturbed Reactions to Parent Suicide: Distortions of Guilt, Communication, and Identification." In Cain, *Survivors of Suicide,* pp. 93–111.

Carkhuff, R. R. 1969. *Helping and Human Relations.* 2 vols. New York: Holt, Rinehart and Winston.

Chilstrom, Corrine. 1989. "Suicide and Pastoral Care." *The Journal of Pastoral Care* 43, 3: 199–208.

Colt, G. H. 1987. "The History of the Suicide Survivor: The Mark of Cain." In Dunne, et al., *Suicide and Its Aftermath,* pp. 3–18.

Dunne, E. J., McIntosh, J. L., and Dunne-Maxim, K., eds. 1987 *Suicide and Its Aftermath: Understanding and Counseling the Survivors.* New York: W. W. Norton.

Egan, G. 1973. *You and Me.* Monterey, Cal.: Brooks/Cole.

Hauser, M. J. 1983. "Bereavement Outcome for Widows." *Journal of Psychosocial Nursing and Mental Health Services* 21, 9: 22–31.

————. 1987. "Special Aspects of Grief After a Suicide." In Dunne, et al., *Suicide and Its Aftermath,* pp. 57–70.

Herzog, A., and Resnik, H. L. P. 1969. "A Clinical Study of Parental Response to Adolescent Death by Suicide With Recommendations for Approaching the Survivors." *British Journal of Social Psychiatry* 2, 3: 144–52.

Meyers, J., and Parsons, R. D. 1985. "Prevention Planning in the School System." In *Prevention Planning for Mental Health,* edited by J. Hermalin and J. Morall. Beverly Hills, Cal.: Sage Publications.

Parsons, R. D. 1989. "Forgiving-not-Forgetting." In *Psychotherapy and the Remorseful Patient,* edited by E. Mark Stern, pp. 259–72. New York: The Haworth Press.

————. 1985. "Prevention: A Duty, Responsibility, and Guiding Value for Pastoral Counseling." *Journal of Pastoral Counseling* 20: 37–46.

————, and Meyers, J. 1984. *Developing Consultation Skills.* San Francisco: Jossey-Bass.

————, and Wicks, R. 1986. "Cognitive Pastoral Psychotherapy With Religious Persons Experiencing Loneliness." In *Psychotherapy and the Lonely Patient,* edited by S. Natale, pp. 47–59. New York: The Haworth Press.

Resnik, H. L. P. 1972. "Psychological Resynthesis: A Clinical Appeal to Survivors of a Death by Suicide." In *Survivors of Suicide,* edited by A. C. Cain, pp. 167–77. Springfield, Ill: Charles C. Thomas.

Seiden, R. H. 1969. "Suicide Among Youth: A Review of the Literature." *Bulletin of Suicidology,* pub. #1971, pp. 1–51.

Shneidman, E. S. 1967. "The NIMH Center for Studies of Suicide Prevention." *Bulletin of Suicidology* 1: 2–7.

————. 1969. "Prologue: Fifty-Eight Years." In *On the Nature of Suicide,* edited by E. S. Shneidman, pp. 1–30. San Francisco: Jossey-Bass.

Toynbee, A. 1969. *Man's Concern With Death.* New York: McGraw Hill.

Wolfet, A. D. 1987. "Understanding Common Patterns of Avoiding Grief." *Thanatos* (Summer): 2–5.

For Further Reading

Cain, A. C., ed. 1972. *Survivors of Suicide,* introduction, pp. 5–33. Springfield, Ill. Charles C. Thomas.

Davis, J. M., Sandoval, J., and Wilson, M. P. 1988. "Strategies for the Primary Prevention of Adolescent Suicide." *School Psychology Review* 17, 4: 559–69.

————, Bates, C., and Velasquez, R. J. 1990. "Faculty Suicide: Guidelines for Effective Coping With a Suicide in a Counselor-Training Program." *Counselor Education and Supervision* 20: 197–204.

Hajal, F. 1977. "Post-Suicide Grief Work in Family Therapy." *Journal of Marriage and Family Counseling* 3, 2: 35–42.

Hill, W. C. 1984. "Intervention and Postvention in Schools." In *Suicide in the Young,* edited by H. S. Sudak, A. B. Ford, and N. B. Rushford, pp. 407–16. Boston: John Wright/P. G. S. Inc.

Lamb, F., and Dunne-Maxim, K. 1987. "Postvention in Schools: Policy and Process." In Dunne, et al., *Suicide and Its Aftermath,* pp. 245–60.

Resnik, H. L. P. 1970. "Center Comments." *Bulletin of Suicidology* 6: 2–4.

Rosenfeld, L., and Prupas, M. 1984. *Left Alive: After a Suicide Death in the Family.* Springfield, Ill.: Charles C. Thomas.

Rudestam, Kjell E. 1987. "Public Perceptions of Suicide Survivors." In Dunne, et al., *Suicide and Its Aftermath,* pp. 31–44.

Ruof, S. R., and Harris, J. M. 1988. "Decisive and Prepared Response After Suicide or Attempt Crucial." *NASP Communique* 16 (September): 12.

David W. Foy
Kent D. Drescher
Allan G. Fitz
Kevin R. Kennedy

13. Post-Traumatic Stress Disorder

Catastrophic experiences within the church family present pastors critical opportunities to minister to people made vulnerable by extreme adversity. Indeed, victims' feelings about how pastors and the church family respond to their needs in times of crisis often color their relationships with the church from that time on. Not only are trauma survivors' relations with the church affected by their experiences, their physical and psychological well-being is also challenged, placing them temporarily "at risk" for stress-related disorders. On a more positive note, evidence is accumulating which demonstrates that supportive behavior by caring members within victims' social circles can be important in reducing risk for stress-related disorders. Thus, pastors and others in the church family may serve vital roles in helping to prevent post-traumatic stress disorders (PTSD) in vulnerable members.

The purpose of this chapter is to acquaint pastors with current information about PTSD, including its primary symptoms and related traumatic experiences. Additionally, we will provide distinctions between "normal" traumatic crisis reactions and pathological adjustment to assist clergy in making screening assessments regarding the need for professional referral. Several theological implications of traumatic experiences will be presented, along with pastoral responses which may help trauma survivors to work through their experiences. Finally, an "anti-burnout survival kit" is offered for pastors who are heavily engaged in ongoing ministry to trauma survivors.

Definition of PTSD

Surviving a life-threatening personal experience often produces intense psychological reactions in the forms of intrusive thoughts about the experience and fear-related avoidance of reminders. in the first few weeks following a traumatic experience these patterns are found in most individuals and thus seem to represent a natural response mechanism for psychological adaptation to a life-changing event. Persistence of this reaction pattern at troublesome levels beyond a three month period, however, indicates that the natural psychological adjustment process, like mourning in the bereaved, has been derailed. At that point the psychological reactions natural in the first few weeks become symptoms of PTSD. In other words, PTSD may be seen as the persistence of a natural process beyond its natural time frame for resolution.

The cardinal features of PTSD are trauma-specific symptoms of intrusion, avoidance, and physical arousal. The primary requirement (Category A) is the presence of "an event that is outside the range of usual human experience and would be markedly distressing to almost anyone" (American Psychiatric Association 1987, p. 250). A life-threatening event, such as serious injury in a traffic accident, would satisfy this criterion, while the expected death of a loved one from natural causes would not. The current diagnostic system then groups PTSD symptoms into three additional categories. Category B includes the presence in some form of persistent intrusive thoughts and feelings. Recurrent distressing dreams or flashbacks while awake about the traumatic experience are examples. Category C represents the presence of avoidance symptoms associated with the trauma, such as avoiding driving following a severe traffic accident or fear of sexual relations following sexual assault. More subtle forms of avoidance would be general numbing of responsiveness or the absence of strong feelings about the trauma. Category D reflects the presence of symptoms of increased physical arousal and hypervigilance. Feelings of panic may be experienced in situations similar to the trauma; for example, combat veterans with PTSD may show powerful startle reactions to loud noises that resemble gunshots or explosions.

The medical history of PTSD can be traced back to studies of human reactions to trauma in the nineteenth century by German psychiatrists who discovered the similarities in the clinical courses of survivors of mining accidents and accidents which involved toxic exposure (Kolb 1988). Two major developments at that time stimulated investigations into what was then called post-traumatic neurosis. The initial spark of medical interest in the subject was ignited by a series of wars, including the Civil War in America and the two World Wars in Europe. Early conceptions of combat-related PTSD by physicians working with veterans of World War I presented it as "shell shock," a consequence of organic dysfunction rather than a psychological process. This formulation arose from use in World War I of both chemical agents and explosives of a power that previously had been unimaginable.

The second impetus was the emergence of social programs in several countries which began to provide compensation for work-related or military service-related disabilities. The early description of traumatic reactions as "compensation reactions" referred to a perceived rise in numbers of victims seeking restitution after the first compensations laws were introduced in Europe (Trimble 1985). This phenomenon presented an example of the tendency to relate symptoms of a trauma reaction to some process other than exposure to intense trauma itself.

While early views of post-traumatic reactions reflected the assumption that various types of trauma produced similar reactions, studies in the past twenty years have tended to be trauma-specific in their focus. Thus, labels for PTSD such as battle fatigue, rape trauma syndrome, and disaster survivor syndrome have developed in the literature (Foa, Steketee, and Olasov Rothbaum 1989). However, most recently, studies have shown similarities among several survivor groups, including combat (Foy, Sipprelle, Rueger, and Carroll 1984; Keane, Fairbank, Caddell, and Zimering 1989), rape (Neumann, Gallers, and Foy 1989), domestic violence (Houskamp and Foy, n.d.), childhood sexual abuse (Briere 1989; Lindberg and Distad 1985), childhood physical abuse (Ammerman, Cassisi, Hersen, and Van-Hasselt 1986), transportation accidents (McCaffrey and Fairbank 1985), and natural disasters (Green, Grace, and Gleser 1985). Since 9/11, terrorism has been added to the list.

Common elements of traumatic experience include being physically and psychologically overwhelmed by a life-threatening event which is beyond the victim's prediction and control. To understand such complex reaction patterns requires the integration of findings from bouth biology and psychology. Thus, current perspectives on the nature of PTSD include contributions from several approaches, including biological (Pitman 1989), behavioral (Keane, Fairbank, Caddell, Zimering, and Bender 1985), cognitive (Foa, Stekelee, and Olasov Rothbaum 1989), and integrative (Foy, Osato, Houskamp, and Neumann, n.d.).

From a biological perspective a number of studies in the past ten years have been conducted with Vietnam combat veterans with PTSD to examine their physiological reactions to combat trauma reminders or cues. Results from these studies have been consistent in showing large heart rate increases in most combat veterans with PTSD when they were exposed to combat cues. Other biological studies have also shown that combat veterans with PTSD have experienced changes in their central nervous systems so that they are overly sensitive to startle-producing noises. Studies are currently being conducted to determine whether these biological features are also applicable to PTSD associated with other types of trauma. Since these physical features of PTSD are almost universally described as painfully distressing in nature, this biological reactivity may be a critical element in the onset of social irritability and withdrawal in PTSD victims.

Contributions from behavioral psychology help in understanding how PTSD symptoms develop. Pavlovian conditioning occurs at the time of the trauma so that the overpowering feelings of life-threat and helplessness are paired with other cues present (which are not life-threatening). By this learning process these cues acquire the potential for evoking extreme fear when they are encountered later. The survivor also learns that escaping from these cues terminates the distressing fear. Planning life activities to avoid painful reminders, an example of instrumental learning, may become a preferred coping strategy since it reduces the painful exposure to trauma reminders.

From a cognitive psychology perspective, the meaning which the survivor attaches to the traumatic experience may play an important role in PTSD. Perceptions of helplessness associated with the traumatic experience may serve to immobilize survivors' more active coping efforts, thereby serving to maintain PTSD symptoms.

While these approaches are helpful in explaining possible mechanisms for the development of PTSD, they do not explain why some individuals exposed to intense trauma do not develop enduring PTSD symptoms. In order to address this issue an integrative approach is necessary which includes additional factors beyond biological reactivity, Pavlovian and instrumental learning, and symbolic meaning. In our integrative model of PTSD the experience of an overwhelming biological reaction during a life-threatening traumatic event lays the necessary foundation for the development of PTSD through behavioral and cognitive mechanisms of learning. However, other factors serve to mediate between exposure to trauma and the development of PTSD symptoms. Thus, an integrative approach to understanding PTSD includes the interaction between traumatic experiences and other non-trauma factors to account for the development or non-development of PTSD.

Non-Traumatic Factors Influencing PTSD Development

Much research has already established that the severity of exposure to traumatic events plays a primary role in the development of symptoms of PTSD (Foy, Sipprelle, Rueger, and Carroll 1984). For example, combat veterans who are wounded are at greater risk for PTSD than soldiers who saw limited combat without personal injury. However, other factors also serve to increase the risk or provide protection from the development of symptoms. Attributions or meanings that individuals assign to traumatic events may also influence the development of PTSD. Janoff-Bulman (1985) has shown that three basic life assumptions are often shattered by trauma. These are:

1) "I am safe," that is, self-invulnerability or, "It won't happen to me"; 2) "life is fair and equitable"; and 3) "I am a good person," that is, self-esteem from positive life experiences. A traumatic experience may cause shifts in these life assumptions toward extreme defensiveness. Inability to moderate "shattered" assumptions toward a more balanced view may worsen symptoms of PTSD in some victims (Foy, Resnick, Carroll, and Osato 1990).

Another influence involves previous life experiences, which may contribute positively or negatively to the development of PTSD symptoms. Events such as previous child physical or sexual abuse, severe marital or family dysfunction, and the presence of other life stresses at the time of trauma have been implicated in increasing risk for the development of PTSD. Conversely, protective factors such as strong social support before and after the trauma may act to prevent or diminish the severity of PTSD symptoms. In a related context it is interesting to note that there is some recent evidence that intrinsic religiosity, that is, religion as a central focus of life, may serve as a protective factor in reducing risk for developing PTSD or in moderating the severity of symptoms (Astin, Lawrence, Pincus, and Foy 1990).

Spiritual Challenges of Traumatic Experiences

The experience of trauma evokes intense emotions including rejection, betrayal, futility, alienation, estrangement, grief, guilt, shame, isolation, and withdrawal. While these emotional expressions are normal and expected, they may render the survivor temporarily more vulnerable in other areas. In particular, the experience of trauma may challenge the survivor's spirituality.

What are some of the most troublesome theological issues for those with PTSD? Perhaps the most common one concerns the problem of evil. The aftermath of trauma often produces reflection by both victim and helper on how and why the events occurred. Questions such as, "Why did this have to happen?" or, "How could a loving God allow such suffering?" are difficult to answer even for the best-trained theologian. Traumatic events have the power to shatter the most basic assumptions upon which people base their lives. The assumptions that life is basically fair and safe may be called into question permanently when traumatic events occur. Theologically, the idea that God cares for and protects individuals can be radically shaken by catastrophic events. Most victims are forced to reshape their thinking in some way to accommodate life-changing experiences.

Surprisingly, guilt and shame are also common emotional expressions by victims of severe trauma. If life is assumed to be ultimately fair, there may be a tendency to assign or assume unwarranted blame. Victims may blame themselves, especially if there is no readily available way to understand why the traumatic event occurred. "Survivor guilt" is a common emotional reaction in many types of traumas, exemplified when survivors ask themselves, "Why was I spared while others died?" Additionally, trauma victims often believe they should have done something to prevent the trauma from occurring, thereby blaming themselves for their actions or lack thereof. Self-blame may further be compounded through "secondary victimization," in which others hold victims responsible in some way for the events they have experienced. For example, in traumas like rape, incest, or physical abuse, some people assume that victims must have played a part in their own traumatization. Unable to comprehend or accept that anyone would perpetrate such terrible acts, these individuals may suggest that victims must have been overly seductive or provoked the abuse in some unknown manner. These assumptions may cause victims to be further traumatized, which in turn may increase their hesitancy to disclose to others.

Anger is another common response to trauma. Intense rage may be directed toward the event itself, the perpetrator of the event, and at others who do not seem to understand. Anger can also be self-directed when recovery is slow. Victims may commonly feel that "I should be able to get over this faster." This anger may further contribute to a sense of isolation and estrangement from others.

The Bible directly informs the religious community as to the kinds of responses it needs to make toward those who have been victimized by traumatic events. One scriptural theme emphasizes special concern for the weakest, most vulnerable members of society, often categorized as widows, orphans, and strangers. This directive seems no less relevant now since there is growing evidence that these individuals are most vulnerable to repeated victimization by human-induced traumas.

In the New Testament the church was assigned the task of caring for those in need: feeding the hungry, healing the sick, clothing the naked, and protecting the oppressed. The church is described as a community of mutual support, where individuals weep with those who weep and who bear one another's burdens. Thus, the religious community has a special responsibility by biblical mandate to care for the needs of those who have been oppressed by natural or human-made circumstances.

The Role of the Pastoral Counselor

Since the clergy represent the front lines of the mental health delivery system for many individuals, pastors are often the first contacts for parishioners in crisis. Pastoral counseling may serve as the sole professional resource for many who may never seek treatment from other mental health professions. Because of this key role, it is important that pastoral counselors be aware of the types of traumatic events which produce symptoms of PTSD. By recognizing risk in parishioners who have experienced these traumas, the clergy can take active steps to help in the crisis and thus reduce the risk for PTSD.

Though much research and public attention has been devoted to the difficulties many Vietnam combat veterans have had following the war, increasing evidence shows that many different types of traumatic events can produce PTSD. The most commonly known types of events are criminal assault, rape, transportation or industrial accidents, and natural disasters. Not only are the victims of such traumas at risk for developing PTSD, their family members, observers, police, and other help-providers may also be at risk for the disorder.

It has become increasingly clear that family violence presents the most frequent source of trauma through experiences such as childhood physical and sexual abuse, incest, and woman-battering. Because of cultural and family tabus against disclosing these experiences, many individuals suffer alone for years with symptoms of PTSD. Victims of such traumas are found in all segments of society, and among all socioeconomic groups, genders, ages, and races. Each of these individuals needs a place where there is no risk of being retraumatized, a place where to experience acceptance and nurturance. Since each church community includes individuals who, at some point, have been victims of traumatic experiences, pastoral counselors need to prepare themselves to assist these victims. Additionally, clergy need to also be aware of ways in which they could be affected by the traumatic experiences of others.

The Church's Response

When victims of personal assault, devastation, or loss seek comfort and support from people who share their faith, pastors can use their unique relationships to facilitate healing. By being knowledgeable about the ways in which traumatic events affect individuals psychologically, ministers can be prepared to give timely and meaningful help to individuals throughout the recovery process. One of the most significant contributions that clergy and the church can make to the recovery of persons, including those suffering from PTSD, is to provide a strong social support system to these individuals. Whether support is found among family, friends, or a formal support group, victims need others with whom they can disclose the events which have occurred without fear of misunderstanding, ridicule, or blame. A counselor should assess the physical and psychological resources which the victim has and be prepared to help find other needed supports as necessary within the community. Informal opportunities for the survivor to recount the story to others in a safe environment are often major parts of the healing process. Victims need to be able to process their experiences by talking about their feelings and by having the freedom to express a wide range of strong emotions about the events including rage, sorrow, hurt, and grief.

Recent research on the influence of social support on recovery from sexual assault shows that women with supportive networks cope much better with the assault and its aftermath than women without available support (Ruch and Hennessey 1982; Ruch and Chandler 1983). It is a cruel paradox that while persons suffering from emotional distress benefit from social support, this support frequently disintegrates or becomes severely strained following a severe trauma (Ellis 1983). This may be related to the fact that individuals with PTSD are unable to relate effectively to others in their support system because of fear of disclosing the details of the trauma. Schwartz (1990) commented:

> Often the patient is fearful of expressing to others the nature of the trauma, not knowing what reactions to expect. This tends to increase the person's sense of isolation. In addition, patients who have flashbacks in association with loss of control, are frightening to others and are avoided by others. Last, many of these patients...have associated substance dependence and abuse problems....Ultimately, through this type of behavior, the patient brings about from other people the rejection the patient had already expected to occur (p. 233).

Victims may find it difficult to talk about their traumatic events because when they "relive" them the experience comes flooding painfully back into memory. Avoiding people, objects, or events which serve as reminders of the trauma is, of course, one of the classic symptoms of PTSD. However, victims' experiences of isolation and feelings of estrangement may be due, in part, to accurate perceptions that other people are uncomfortable with their experiences and shy away accordingly. Often the support group itself resists the experiences of the traumatized person, particularly when the trauma is directly caused by human behavior. Thompson (1989), for example, noted that church settings may not be safe environments to initiate discussions about victimization through domestic violence and sexual assault since congregations may be unprepared or unwilling to acknowledge that the problem exists within the church community. Some church members may naively assume that spiritual maturity ensures universal psychological health. Such contentious attitudes may isolate trauma victims who have psychological difficulty in dealing with a traumatic event. Distressed individuals may leave the church or learn to hide their true feelings because of the implicit message that "true" Christians should be able to withstand trauma without distress. To better serve the needs of victims of traumatic events, the church needs to initiate and sustain support in a consistent, non-judgmental manner for members who have been victimized.

Pastoral counselors need to begin the helping process by normalizing, the strong feelings survivors have about their traumatic experiences. Victims need to understand that it is common for ordinary events in daily life to serve as powerful reminders of their trauma and, consequently, to elicit strong feelings at seemingly inappropriate times and places. Flashbacks, fears, nightmares, and physical responses such as a pounding heart, sweating, and nausea can all be normal responses to everyday cues which serve as reminders of the trauma. The pastoral counselor can help survivors identify the types of reminders which produce trauma-related distress, thus helping prepare for future coping efforts.

Pastors and other church friends can particularly support survivors and traumatized individuals by recognizing that pain is often associated with "anniversary reactions," which many survivors experience each year. For example, the loss of a child in an auto accident may be especially painful to the surviving parents each year on the actual date of its occurrence because it is an inescapable reminder which may temporarily "re-traumatize" them. Accordingly, pastors can help by showing sensitivity to the emotional stress of trauma anniversary dates and by attempting to offer additional support during these times. Something as simple as a timely phone call or an encouraging note can be meaningful to a parishioner who is reexperiencing painful memories.

There are additional ways in which prepared pastors and lay counselors can help parishioners cope with the emotional pain of trauma. Several principles or guidelines are offered in Table 1 to assist clergy when dealing with trauma survivors (Bailey 1981; Dutton, n.d.).

Table 1 also represents a "bill of rights" for victims during the counseling process. The first principle, *non-judgmentality,* is the sine qua non of relationship building with traumatized persons. Hints of non-acceptance or blame in work or deed by the counselor may evoke strong feelings of helplessness or "re-traumatization" in the survivor. *Validation* refers to counselor acceptance of whatever emotional expressions the survivor experiences as normal and expectable, thus facilitating the necessary self-disclosure for trauma processing or working through to occur.

Pastoral involvement may range from minimal, as in providing temporary support during the crisis phase, to extensive, as in provision of counseling services to help resolve PTSD symptoms. An intermediate level of involvement would be represented by advocacy assistance with the legal or mental health system or providing a list of qualified therapists for psychotherapy referral.

Table 1
Principles for Pastoral Counselors Working with Trauma Victims

1. Non-judgmental acceptance and validation of the survivor set the psychological tone for helping.
2. Support, alliance, and advocacy are appropriate role expectations for the helper.
3. It is assumed that post-traumatic distress is primarily related to the traumatic experience(s), not personality or spiritual "weakness."
4. Willingness and ability to be exposed to the survivor's recounting of the traumatic experience(s) and consequences.
5. It is recognized that trauma transformation is a lifelong process.
6. Losses from traumatic experiences may not be compensable, but they can be grieved.
7. The right to self-determination is retained by the survivor.
8. Pastoral self-care is assured.

Regardless of the particular role appropriate in each situation, pastors' attitudes and behavior toward survivors need to show a willingness to share in survivors I experiences of their trauma. This is actively promoted by application, both implicitly and explicitly, of the principle that assumes the "business" of trauma processing is the traumatic experience(s) and the consequences the survivor experiences. Further, since trauma represents a life-changing experience, the influence is expected to be profound and enduring. There is no time limit for trauma processing after which reminders are no longer potent. It is neither possible nor desirable for traumatic experiences to be forgotten.

In a similar vein personal losses suffered through trauma may be grieved, but they cannot be compensated or restored. Thus, the focus of trauma-related counseling is on facilitating the natural grieving process. In so doing counselors are mindful that survivors must retain the right to self-determination in order to regain control over their lives. Urges to preempt decision-making through the use of "shoulds" and "should nots" must be resisted.

Finally, pastoral counselors must be responsible for maintaining their own psychological well-being while ensuring that survivors' needs are uppermost in counseling relationships. Personal beliefs and attitudes toward the different forms of human-induced trauma—such as, e.g., the Vietnam war, incest, domestic violence in wife-abuse and child physical abuse, and rape—must be explicitly acknowledged. Self-examination and possible modification of prejudicial attitudes will equip pastors to deal with powerful countertransference feelings, which may often be evoked in the course of trauma work.

If a trauma victim's symptoms seem to continue unabated despite good social support and the opportunity frequently to verbalize and express feelings concerning the event, it is appropriate to refer the individual to a trained professional who specializes in work with trauma. Relatively brief therapeutic interventions focused specifically on the traumatic experience can often provide relief from the painful physical and emotional reactivity that is a characteristic of PTSD, facilitating the natural healing process.

Helping the Helper: Avoiding Burnout

In addition to understanding ways in which the church can help trauma victims, clergy must also be aware of how they may be adversely affected by the traumatic experiences of those they seek to help. Vicarious victimization refers to signs and symptoms of traumatization which persons close to traumatized victims may experience. Specifically, persons who are exposed to the traumatic experiences of victims may experience the same numbing of feelings, avoidance patterns, intrusive thoughts and images, estrangement, and physiological reactions as those experienced by the trauma victims (Lindy 1988).

McCann and Pearlman (1990) expand on the concept of vicarious victimization by emphasizing the changes in thinking and feeling that occur as a result of both the external stress of dealing with trauma survivors and the unique psychological needs and cognitive patterns of the counselor. Disruptive and painful psychological effects may be experienced by persons who work with traumatized persons when helpers' cognitive schema are challenged by survivors' experiences. These schema include beliefs, assumptions, and expectations about the self and the world by which meaning is ascribed to experiences. Trauma disrupts basic assumptions in both survivors and helpers, such as beliefs in a meaningful, orderly world; that the self is safe and worthy; and that other people are trustworthy.

First, those who work with victims are often exposed to the many cruel ways that people deceive and betray each other. This may then, in turn, disrupt helpers' assumptions about trust, causing them to become cynical, distrustful, or suspicious of other people's motives. Second, helpers who work with trauma victims, particularly where threats or harm to innocent people have occurred, may have their assumptions about safety challenged and may experience a fear-related need to take precautions against such violations. In particular, individuals who work with victims of random violence or accidents may experience a heightened sense of vulnerability and an enhanced awareness of the fragility of life, especially if there are strong needs for security. Third, exposure to traumatic situations through survivors' memories may evoke concerns about pastors' own sense of power or efficacy in the world. In particular, those with high needs for power may be more adversely affected by the powerlessness reported by their parishioners. They may personally experience intense feelings of helplessness or despair about seemingly uncontrollable forces of nature or human violence (McCann and Pearlman 1990).

Pastors repeatedly exposed to the traumatic experiences of others may have their assumptions about causality or "why things occur" challenged. This may be particularly applicable for clergy who hold specific beliefs about the way in which God controls and orders the affairs of the world. Traumatized individuals may present direct challenges to religious assumptions about God's control of events through questions such as, "Why did this happen to me?" In order to deflect challenge to their own assumptions and to maintain their sense of order, religious helpers may try to redirect blame to the victim in order to "defend" God as the ultimate originator of the tragedy. Clergy may also experience an overall sense of disillusionment and confusion ("loss of faith") if their assumptions and beliefs are continually challenged by reports of traumatic experiences.

Pastoral counselors can reduce personal vulnerability for experiencing long-term negative emotional symptoms as a result of working with trauma victims. Above all, pastors need ongoing consultative relationships in which they can recognize, communicate, and work through their painful experiences in a supportive, confidential environment. This professional network of support is essential and must be readily available. Isolation from contact with other professionals who work with victims constitutes a major personal risk.

Pastoral counselors must understand how their assumptions and beliefs are disrupted or threatened through the course of their work and how their reactions to survivors may be influenced. As helpers discover their own salient need areas, they will be better able to understand their reactions to the experiences of their counselees. For example, pastors who have considerable concerns about safety may find it very stressful to work with victims of crime or rape; they might appropriately consider referring these cases.

Finally, pastors need to use positive coping methods to reduce some of the potential hazards of working with trauma victims. Some of the strategies which may be helpful include striving for balance between personal and professional activities; developing realistic outcome expectations; maintaining personal boundaries with trauma victims; giving themselves permission to experience fully any emotional reactions; and maintaining optimism and hopefulness in the face of tragedy (McCann and Pearlman 1990). Transcending the tragedy and pain of trauma to find positive meaning in the sharing of life experiences with "other strugglers" is the ultimate task of each trauma counselor.

Summary

Catastrophic experiences that provoke crisis reactions in survivors include combat, sexual and physical assault, natural disasters, transportation accidents, and catastrophic illnesses. Immediate reactions in survivors consistently include intrusive thoughts about the trauma, fear and avoidance of related memories and situations, and panic-like reactions to reminders of the experience. While almost everyone exposed to a traumatic experience will show temporary symptoms of a crisis reaction, not all survivors continue to be affected negatively by their experience. Within three months of the experience many survivors have shown positive signs of relief from intrusive thoughts and fears related to it. However, for some survivors these symptoms persist in the form of PTSD.

A primary factor for determining risk for PTSD is the severity of the trauma experience. Other factors which also influence disorder rates can be divided into "risk" or "protective" categories. Those individuals who have had previous traumatic experiences or who are under high stress from other sources may be more vulnerable for developing PTSD. Conversely, individuals who come from stable family backgrounds or who are well-supported throughout their traumatic experience by those in their social network may be resilient.

Pastors and other members of the church family may serve as important elements within survivors' social networks. Shame, rage, survivor guilt, and self-blame are common emotional reactions in trauma survivors which may present spiritual challenges. The pastor may be uniquely positioned to help survivors resolve those negative trauma reactions and their related theological issues.

Clergy who minister regularly to trauma survivors are especially vulnerable to "helper burnout." Risk for vicarious victimization in pastors serving trauma survivors can be reduced by regular use of collegial consultation whereby pastors' feelings and attitudes about the victims and their perpetrators can be processed.

References

American Psychiatric Association. 1987. *Diagnostic and Statistical Manual of Mental Disorders*. 3d ed. rev. Washington, D.C. Referred to in text as *DSM III-R*.

Ammerman, R. T., Cassisi, J. E., Hersen, M., Van-Hasselt, V. B. 1986. "Consequences of Physical Abuse and Neglect in Children." *Clinical Psychology Review* 6:291–310.

Astin, M., Lawrence, K., Pincus, G., and Foy, D. W. 1990. *Moderating Variables in the Development of PTSD in Battered Women.* Paper presented at the Society for Traumatic Stress Studies, New Orleans, La.

Bailey, L. 1981. "Women and Rape." *Pastoral Psychology* 29:169–77.

Briere, J. 1989. *Therapy for Adults Molested as Children: Beyond Survival.* New York: Springer.

Dutton, M. A. N.d. *Psychological Trauma of Woman Battering: Assessment and Treatment.* New York: Springer. In press.

Ellis, E. M. 1983. "A Review of Empirical Rape Research: Victim Reactions and Response to Treatment." *Clinical Psychology Review* 3:473–90.

Foa, E. B., Steketee, G., and Olasov Rothbaum, B. 1989. "Behavioral/Cognitive Conceptualizations of Post-traumatic Stress Disorder. *Behavior Therapy* 20:155–76.

Foy, D. W., Osato, S., Houskamp, B., and Neumann, D. N.d. "Etiology Factors in Posttraumatic Stress Disorder." In *Posttraumatic Stress Disorder: A Behavioral Approach to Assessment and Treatment.* Oxford, edited by P. Saigh. Pergamon Press. In press.

———, Resnick, H. S., Carroll, E. M., and Osato, S. S. 1990. "Behavior Therapy in Posttraumatic Stress Disorder." In *Handbook of Comparative Adult Treatments,* edited by M. Hersen and A. Bellock, pp. 302–15. New York: John Wiley and Sons.

———, Sipprelle, R. C., Rueger, D. B., and Carroll, E. M. 1984. "Etiology of Posttraumatic Stress Disorder in Vietnam Veterans: Analysis of Premilitary, Military, and Combat Exposure Influences." *Journal of Consulting and Clinical Psychology* 52:79–87.

Green, B. L., Grace, M. C., and Gleser, G. C. 1985. "Identifying Survivors at Risk: Long-term Impairment Following the Beverly Hills Supper Club Fire." *Journal of Consulting & Clinical Psychology* 53, 5:672–78.

Houskamp, B., and Foy, D. W. N.d. "The Assessment of PTSD in Battered Women." *Journal of Interpersonal Violence.* In press.

Janoff-Bulman, R. 1985. "The Aftermath of Victimization: Rebuilding Shattered Assumptions." In *Trauma and Its Wake,* edited by C. R. Figley. New York: Brunner/Mazel.

Keane, T. M., Fairbank, J. A., Caddell, J. M., Zimering, R. T., Bender, M. E. 1985. "A Behavioral Approach to Assessing and Treating Post-traumatic Stress Disorder in Vietnam Veterans." In Figley, *Trauma and Its Wake,* pp. 257–94.

——, Fairbank, J. A., Caddell, J. M., and Zimering, R. T. 1989. "Implosive (Flooding) Therapy Reduces Symptoms of PTSD in Vietnam Combat Veterans." *Behavior Therapy,* 20:245–60.

Kolb, L. C. 1988. "A Critical Survey of Hypotheses Regarding Posttraumatic Stress Disorders in Light of Recent Research Findings." *Journal of Traumatic Stress* 1:291–304.

Lindberg, F. H., and Distad, L. J. 1985. Post-traumatic Stress Disorders in Women Who Experienced Childhood Incest. *Child Abuse & Neglect* 9:329–34.

Lindy, J. D. 1988. *Vietnam: A Casebook.* New York: Brunner/Mazel.

McCaffrey, R. J., and Fairbank, J. A. 1985. "Behavioral Assessment and Treatment of Accident-Related Posttraumatic Stress Disorder: Two Case Studies." *Behavior Therapy* 16:406–16.

McCann, I. L., and Pearlman, L. A. 1990. "Vicarious Traumatization: A Framework for Understanding the Psychological Effects of Working with Victims." *Journal of Traumatic Stress* 3:131–49.

Moss, D. M. 1979. "Near-Fatal Experience, Crisis Intervention and the Anniversary Reaction." *Pastoral Psychology* 28:75–96.

Ruch, L. O., and Chandler, S. M. 1983. "Sexual Assault Trauma During the Acute Phase: An Exploratory Model and Multivariate Analysis." *Journal of Health and Social Behavior* 24:174–85.

——, and Hennessey, M. 1982. "Sexual Assault: Victim and Attack Dimensions." *Victimol. International Journal* 7:94–105.

Schwartz, L. S. 1990. "A Biopsychosocial Treatment Approach to Post-Traumatic Stress Disorder." *Journal of Traumatic Stress* 3:221–38.

Silverman, D. 1977. "First Do No More Harm: Female Rape Victims and the Male Counselor." *American Journal of Orthopsychiatry* 47:91–96.

Thompson, C. 1989. "Breaking Through Walls of Isolation: A Model for Churches in Helping Victims of Violence." *Pastoral Psychology* 38:35–38.

Walter J. Smith

14. Embracing Pastoral Ministry in the Age of AIDS

The Human Immunodeficiency Virus (HIV) has characteristics that make it terrifying: it seems uncontrollable, can infect anyone at any age, and is often fatal. Ignorance, prejudice, and uncertainty about the future course of this pandemic compound the challenges facing the entire corps of care providers, including pastoral counselors. In addition to awareness of the psycho-social issues affecting care, effective pastoral ministry to any person with HIV infection requires that the provider have a basic yet competent understanding of the underlying infection and of the diseases afflicting the person, their course and treatment.[1]

Persons living with HIV infection develop a specialized understanding of the various illnesses that comprise this syndrome. Many struggle to learn ways to live with an infection for which there is, at present, no permanent, definitive, curative treatment. It is not uncommon that the experiences of a life-threatening illness dominate their conscious thoughts and conversation. A pastoral counselor needs basic factual knowledge about HIV if he or she is to interact effectively with infected persons who either have become sick or who fear they will get sick.

Throughout our discussion, we refer to HIV infection and its related diseases rather than to the more common designation of Acquired Immunodeficiency Syndrome (AIDS). When reference is made to AIDS, it means the terminal result of HIV infection. This distinction has as much relevance for pastoral counselors as it does for physicians. Persons with HIV infection put a high premium on the terms used to describe their disease. Some associate the word AIDS with a hopeless, terminal condition. The same individual may view a diagnosis of HIV infection with fear, but also with a sense of hope. For this reason, sensitivity to language in speaking about HIV and the syndrome of illnesses related to this virus is important (AIDS Education Project of the American Psychiatric Association 1989).

In this chapter on pastoral ministry to persons with HIV infection and disease we shall review some basic data on Acquired Immunodeficiency

Syndrome. To accomplish this, we shall reflect upon the three principal words that define this medical condition. Subsequently, we shall consider some psycbo-social aspects of HIV that have bearing on pastoral counseling and comment upon opportunities for pastoral care of persons with HIV and their families. Finally, we shall suggest some ways to minister effectively in an age of AIDS.

Acquired Immunodeficiency Syndrome: Some Perspectives

Acquiring HIV Infection

AIDS is acquired through infection with the Human Immunodeficiency Virus (HIV). The virus is transmitted when HIV particles or infected cells gain access to another person's bloodstream. This transfer can occur in a variety of ways. Five principal routes of transmission have been identified. The first results from engaging in high-risk sexual behaviors, including vaginal, anal, or oral genital intercourse. A second route of infection comes from sharing improperly sterilized needles in intravenous drug use. A third source of infection is from an infected mother to her developing fetus, *in utero*. A fourth risk of infection to a breast-feeding infant comes from an infected mother's milk. The fifth route of HIV infection is from transfusion of contaminated blood or blood products. Since mid-1985 all donated blood is carefully screened for antibodies to the virus. It is important to note that the disease is *acquired*. For adults, this means that one is often responsible for getting it. Unfortunately, numbers of sexually active individuals, particularly adolescents, and persons using drugs continue to be infected with HIV even though much is known about the virus and how it is transmitted.

From the point of infection there is ordinarily an incubation period before a person develops an HIV-related disease and is diagnosed. Infected infants frequently become sick in their first or second year of life. Those over the age of fifty also have shorter incubation periods, between five and seven years. The majority of infected adults can remain ostensibly well for ten years. Apart from age, the length of the incubation period may be linked to the amount and virulence of the strain of HIV transmitted. Some individuals may be genetically more resistant to the virus than some others whose general health or body immunity may be compromised. The relatively long incubation period is a primary source of anxiety for many persons who know that they have been exposed to HIV.

Investigators are trying to understand the relationships between cofactors that may influence infection, incubation, and the clinical manifestation of disease. Issues such as general health, previous medical history, nutrition, exercise, environmental and economic variables, and a host of other related issues may have some significant role to play in explaining the wide variability among long-term survivors (see Callen 1990).

Pastoral care is not ordinarily focused on the issue of how or why a person has acquired the disease. However, the person with HIV may need to identify and discuss these issues. Non-judgmental dialogue with the pastoral counselor can help a person to process effectively these feelings and concerns related to incubation and survival.

The Basic Meaning of Immunodeficiency

AIDS is principally a disease of the body's immune system. The immune system relies on effective physical, chemical, and biochemical interactive barriers and is made up of a variety of cells whose function is to identify, isolate, and eliminate viruses, bacteria, and other foreign substances (antigens) from the body. The human body's immune system is designed in such a way that it is virtually impenetrable by threatening organisms. When the immune system recognizes a "foreigner," a number of specialized cells move into action.

Phagocytes are one of these defensive weapons. As its Greek name suggests, phagocytes have the ability to "eat" invading viruses, bacteria, fungi, protozoa, or worms, as well as any other debris that washes into the bloodstream. These cells are largely scavengers, whose purpose is to rid the body of any foreign material as well as dead tissue and degenerated cells. They play an indispensable role in immune system functioning. However, some of these foreign microorganisms, like HIV, have physical or chemical properties that make detection and destruction exceedingly difficult.

Lymphocytes, a specific subset of cells involved in these defensive immune functions are white blood cells that also patrol the body, alert to foreign invaders. These circulating lymphocytes routinely attack infected cells and prevent the invading microorganisms from reproducing themselves and migrating to other sites.

A class of lymphocytes are the T-cells, the "helper cells." Their specific function is to coordinate and manage the activities of the immune system. The T-cells stimulate the B-cells, which produce specific antibodies that attack, neutralize, or eliminate the invading virus or bacteria. Some have described T-cells as the watchdogs of the immune system. When the infection is under control, the CD8, or suppressor cells, call off the attack and the body returns to normal functioning.

Unfortunately, some of these foreign microorganisms, like HIV, have physical or chemical properties that make detection and destruction exceedingly difficult.

Viruses are incapable of independent life. A virus is nothing more than inert, organic material looking for a living cell in which it might reside. Only by invading a fully metabolized "host" cell can a virus become active, capable of reproducing its genetic material. A virus exploits the living cell it invades. It uses the host cell's metabolic machinery to make many more virus particles, which in time seek out other host cells in order to perpetuate the process.

HIV directly attacks the T-cells by invading the cells' structure, neutralizing their defenses, and rendering them ineffective. These helper cells are prevented from performing their infection-fighting functions. HIV can migrate freely within the body, proliferating within the T-cells it invades. These cells become effective partners with the enemy, HIV.

When the HIV invades the T-cells, it becomes part of the cell's DNA, the molecular chain containing the genetic information enabling cells to reproduce. We noted previously that during an incubation period the virus can remain dormant for a variable period of time. The only clear effect is that the T-cells are prevented from performing their normal defensive functions.

When the HIV is activated, stimulated perhaps by some specific triggers, which may include gender, genetic predisposition, physical and emotional health, and IV drug use, the virus does not waste any time reproducing itself and infecting other cells. The genetic components of HIV allow it to replicate itself a thousand times faster than many other kinds of viruses. The T-cells in which HIV has made its home become "factories" in which the virus is released into the circulating blood it seeks out other T-cells, thus further debilitating the immune system and interrupting its important functions. The depletion of helper cells appears to precipitate immunological breakdown, and the symptoms of HIV disease probably result from this event.

The immune system of a person infected with HIV attempts to fight the presence of the virus and produces antibodies. However, these antibodies appear to be ineffective in neutralizing and destroying the virus. With a decrease in the number of T-cells, the immune system is unable to discharge its important defensive and regulatory functions. The person who is immunocompromised is thus unable to mount effective antibody reactions to new antigens and becomes vulnerable to a host of recurrent or new infections.

This description of the immunodeficiency resulting from exposure to HIV has symbolic relevance to pastoral care. An immunocompromised individual becomes defenseless. Immunodeficiency leaves a person feeling vulnerable, unprotected, under siege. The psychological and spiritual states of a person with AIDS frequently mirror the biological portrait of immunodeficiency. The biochemical characteristics of this disease can precipitate a number of related negative psychological and spiritual reactions. A person who feels defenseless looks for someone who will be supportive. Pastoral care has the potential to be this much needed source of support.

A person with HIV is vulnerable to subtle forms of rejection, real or perceived. An individual in a weakened physical state is prone to become disengaged, hopeless, and depressed, sometimes surrendering the will to fight, the will to live. While this is not a universal experience of persons with AIDS, the drama of human immunodeficiency can interpret the psychological and spiritual defenselessness some individuals feel.

A Syndrome of Diseases

In contemporary medical usage, a syndrome describes an aggregate of symptoms associated with any disease. When all of these symptoms are put together, they form the clinical picture of the disease. With a weakened immune system, an individual is prone to develop a variety of opportunistic infections which contribute to the clinical picture of this syndrome.[2] The term *opportunistic* is used to describe a wide range of illnesses. These illnesses are attributable to organisms commonly present in the environment, but threatening only to persons whose immune systems have been weakened. These organisms use the opportunity provided by the body's compromised defenses to gain a firm foothold.

A unique characteristic of HIV disease is the tendency for an infected person to develop many problems with the common denominator being the suppression of normal immune functions. Immunosuppression makes medical management difficult since the body is not effective in dealing with infections and cancers. Not only do the body's natural helper cells fail to fight off the HIV invader, but other viruses ordinarily living in check within the human body can express themselves as new, hostile forms of disease. Although the immune system is seriously impaired as a result of HIV infection, this does not mean that the individual is vulnerable to every infection.

One of the characteristics of this syndrome is that the HIV-infected individual appears to be particularly vulnerable to certain diseases. It will be helpful to discuss those life-threatening HIV-related diseases that pastoral counselors will most commonly encounter in practice.

Pneumocystis Carinii Pneumonia (PCP)

Among life-threatening opportunistic infections associated with immunodeficiency, Pneumocystis carinii pneumonia (PCP) is among the most common. Pneumocystis carinii pneumonia is caused by a yeast infection of the lungs by a single-celled parasite (protozoan). The parasite, *Pneumocystis carinii*, has been found in the lungs of animals and healthy humans. Although present, it does not flourish unless the immune system is significantly weakened. If the parasite is activated, it multiplies and consolidates the air spaces in the lungs in a honeycomb-like fashion. The initial manifestations of this disease are similar to other forms of pneumonia: dry cough, fever, and breathing problems. PCP occurs at least once in 60 to 80 percent of persons with AIDS.

Improved treatment and maintenance programs have increased survival rates for those who develop PCP. The pneumonia is responsive to a variety of antibiotic and other drug treatments, although none of these treatments eradicates the *Pneumocystis* organism. The possibility of recurrent infection is high because the immune system does not appear to recover. If the immunosuppression reversed, the infection would be checked in its progress.

With each successive bout of PCP an individual's chances for survival are decreased. Overall mortality rates for this infection have remained relatively constant with a 15 to 25 percent mortality for each episode. PCP continues to be the major cause of death in persons with AIDS.

Kaposi's Sarcoma (KS)

Kaposi's sarcoma is a cancerous tumor of the cells lining blood and lymphatic vessels. Apart from its association with AIDS, the cancer is not life-threatening. The cancer produces slowly developing lesions, disseminating on many body surfaces, most commonly appearing on the skin of the feet, the trunk of the body, on the head, neck, face, eyes, mouth, and throat. Lesions can also appear in the internal organs, such as in the gastrointestinal tract as well as on the lymph nodes.

The cancer is first visible when painless purple to brown colored, flat or raised, irregularly shaped blotches appear on or under the skin. Initially they look like ordinary bruise marks, but they do not disappear after a week or so. The lesions frequently are raised above the level of the surrounding skin and are hard to the touch.

Kaposi's sarcoma is rarely the primary cause of death for a person with AIDS. If the cancer appears in the throat or other internal organs, the threat to life increases. The treatments for these lesions with radiation and chemotherapies can be effective, but they can further suppress the immune system to such a degree that the treatments for KS may pave the way for other opportunistic infections.

From a pastoral counseling perspective, the disfigurement associated with this cancer, particularly on exposed skin surfaces like the face, neck, upper torso, and limbs can cause psychological distress for the person. The proliferation of lesions can disturb individuals who interact with KS patients and may become an obstacle to effective pastoral care.

Cytomegalovirus (CMV)

There are also a number of other viruses that can cause opportunistic infections in a person with HIV. Cytomegalovirus (CMV) is frequently encountered in persons with AIDS. The infection contributes to inflammation and destruction of the retina resulting in partial or total blindness. CMV also triggers seizures and dementia, and is associated with pneumonia, inflammation of the esophagus, and pernicious diarrhea.

Toxoplasmosis and Cryptosporidiosis

Another source of opportunistic infections is found in the family of protozoa. *Toxoplasma gondii* is one species of these protozoa associated with HIV-related disease. The *Toxoplasma gondii* parasite invades the central nervous system, triggering brain seizures, high fevers, and delirium, resulting in decreased levels of consciousness. Personality and behavior changes associated with this brain infection are often the most disturbing aspects of this disease. Some persons infected with this parasite become unable to speak.

Family members and those caring for an individual with HIV-related toxoplasmosis report difficulty in coping with the alterations in personality associated with this disease. The infection is one of the most treatable, but the treatments must be maintained for the life of the infected persons. The long-term use of drugs can have many undesirable side effects and can do additional damage to the immune system.

Cryptosporidiosis is another parasitic infection, virtually unknown in humans prior to the advent of AIDS in the early 1980s. The parasite, *Cryptosporidium difficile*, had been found in a number of animals and reptiles, but rarely in human beings. In the few human cases in which the parasite had been documented, the diarrhea resulting from infection was self-limiting. This is not the case when the parasite attacks a person with HIV. The diarrhea is sustained, high-volume, and life-threatening. This pernicious diarrhea results in a person being unable to absorb nutrients from food, contributing to severe loss of weight, dehydration, and malnutrition. Although there have been several drugs used to treat the cryptosporidium parasitic infection, none has proven to be effective in controlled human trials. The best that medications have been able to achieve is a reduction in discomfort associated with persistent diarrhea.

Mycobacterium Avium-Intracellulare (MAI)

Bacterial diseases are also related to HIV. One of this group of opportunistic infections is *Mycobacterium avium intracellulare*. The bacterium, MAI, is commonly found in the environment, for example, in dust, soil, water. Despite its ubiquity, it rarely causes disease in humans, except in those who are immunocompromised. The associated symptoms of MAI are similar to other HIV-related diseases: fever, weight loss, cough, respiratory distress, swollen lymph glands, abdominal cramping, and diarrhea. The lungs are usually affected, and the infection will frequently spread to the liver, spleen, lymph nodes, gastrointestinal tract, bone marrow, and brain. MAI is resistant to standard antituberculosis drugs, although some new experimental treatments are promising.

Summary of HIV-Related Diseases

We have described briefly a few of the more than, eighteen fungal, viral, protozoal, and bacterial agents associated with opportunistic infections seen in persons with HIV disease. In addition, we spoke about a rare cancer commonly diagnosed in persons with AIDS. Many of these diseases cause neurologic impairments in addition to physical symptoms. These related neurological problems are often the most difficult for patient and care-giver alike. Higher cortical functions, such as thinking and remembering, are frequently disrupted. Emotional and behavioral changes, including disengagement from affectional bonds, lifelong personal and professional interests, and spiritual practices, as well as disturbances in gait and motor coordination are frequently noted. The person may also lose control over bowel and bladder functions, creating situations of added embarrassment and distress.

Pastoral Implications

We have begun our discussion of Acquired Immunodeficiency Syndrome with a survey of some of the basic clinical facts related to HIV. These basic issues help us to understand better the physical, emotional, and spiritual experiences of persons living with HIV. Pastoral counselors may debate the necessity and usefulness of knowing these clinical details. It is our contention that the pastoral care of persons with AIDS is enhanced when the pastoral counselor appreciates the physical, psychological, spiritual, and social concerns they share. For these reasons, it is important that pastoral counselors stay current as new knowledge about AIDS and its treatment are published.

We may conceptualize pastoral care as an essentially spiritual ministry. However, our efforts are enhanced to the degree we understand the ancillary concerns of the persons to whom we minister. As pastoral counselors we need to think about AIDS holistically. Our strategies for pastoral care hinge on how able we are to integrate effectively our knowledge about this new disease with our other experiences in ministering to persons with life-threatening illnesses.

Engaging in Pastoral Care with Persons with AIDS

AIDS has been experienced as a frontal attack on the death-denying character of our American culture. We are confronted continually with statistics and projections about this epidemic. The World Health Organization estimates there were 42 million people living with HIV/AIDS worldwide in 2002, with just under a million in the U.S. A total of 3.1 million people died of HIV/AIDS in 2002 alone.

The proportion of gay or bisexual men is gradually representing a smaller proportion of the whole. Heterosexual IV drug users, their sexual partners, and the offspring of infected women account for an increasing proportion of the whole. The numbers of African Americans is increasing dramatically. While African Americans represent approximately one-eighth of the population of the United States, they accounted for over one half of the HIV infections in 2000. Similarly rates for Latinos are also disproportionately high.

Alarming increases of HIV infections among minorities are related to IV drug use. Since IV drug use is the direct or indirect route by which many pregnant mothers are being infected with HIV, as many as 85 percent of all pediatric cases are seen among infants of color. In the first decade of this pandemic the proportion of women infected with HIV was relatively small, accounting for 7 percent of all cases reported in the 1987. By 2000 this percentage increased to 33 percent. It is expected that these percentages will continue to rise. Finally, the documented sexual activity among adolescents and the high incidence of cases of teen pregnancies and of sexually transmitted diseases, among which HIV is numbered, coupled with an average incubation period of ten years before the presentation of HIV-related symptoms, is a cause of grave concern to epidemiologists who are tracking the transmission of this virus. In short, we can look forward to a significant increase in the number of cases of persons in their late teen and early adult years unknowingly transmitting the HIV infection and developing AIDS in the next decade.

Thus, in this third millennium America will have to face the reality that deaths resulting from HIV infections will continue to rise. It is with this escalating medical and psychological crisis in mind that health care is preparing itself in order to meet effectively new challenges to provide counsel and care. It is within this same context that those involved in pastoral ministries within the churches and synagogues must prepare for the new demands they will inevitably encounter in increasing numbers.

In the natural history of medicine, AIDS is without parallel. It is a disease that has exposed many flaws in our social fabric. Because it is a severely stigmatizing disease, persons with HIV fear discovery, discrimination, rejection, and abandonment. The social and psychological stresses that compound the physical characteristics of HIV are significant, and effective management of these problems challenges all providers of care. We shall consider some of the specific problems pastors encounter in ministering to persons with AIDS and the significant others (spouse, parent, child, sibling, lover, friend) who are their primary care-givers.

In pastoral practice we are continually confronted with human struggles that demand a fresh examination of our thoughts, feelings, biases, prejudices, and fears. Pastoral care requires continual reengagement with personal values, religious beliefs, and theologies.

Involvement in the pastoral care of persons with HIV raises its own particular set of questions. To work effectively with persons with HIV disease, pastoral counselors must be open to understand the world of the gay community and the communities of drug users and prostitutes, as well as the unique sociocultural features of the Black, Hispanic, and Native American communities. In addition, pastoral counselors must have special sensitivities to the mores of sexually active adolescents.

Unlike other life-threatening illnesses, persons infected with HIV or who develop symptoms related to the syndrome, experience stigma. Persons with HIV are not the only ones affected by social response to the disease; those individuals who become involved in providing care likewise are vulnerable to the negative reactions of others. It is important to acknowledge this social reality before embarking on a decision to assume a pastoral role in the care of a person with AIDS. Some counselors have reported the objections of their spouses, colleagues, and congregants to their pastoral involvement with persons with HIV. Despite strong evidence about how the virus is and is not transmitted, fear of infection can still exist among individuals exposed to persons with HIV. These fears and concerns about contagion and infection continue to be expressed, even in the second decade of this pandemic. A counselor must confront and reconcile any fears about becoming infected through contacts in ordinary pastoral care and must be ready to help others to allay their concerns.

In any helping relationship, it is important for the helper to pay attention to feelings he or she experiences toward the person seeking assistance. It is difficult to be effective in a helping relationship if one has strong negative feelings and judgments toward the individual seeking help. To attempt to provide care without attending to and resolving personal issues related to the individual is irresponsible. Sometimes helpers create more problems for the helpee than they solve. In medicine, these problems are termed *iatrogenic*, meaning they have their origin in the attitudes and behaviors of physicians toward their patients. The same phenomenon can exist in pastoral care, when a pastor's overt or covert hostility or negative attitudes can intensify a person's suffering.

Pastors and physicians share parallel responsibilities in relation to the provision of care for persons with HIV. Society presumes that doctors and religious professionals will provide care for all persons. In return for the special status that society accords physical and spiritual healers, it expects its physicians and pastors to be self-sacrificing. Acknowledging medicine's tradition of providing care to infectious persons, the American Medical Association says: "Not everyone is emotionally able to care for patients with AIDS" (AMA 1986). Not every pastoral counselor is emotionally able to care for a person with HIV. It is important to recognize this fact and make other provisions for the person's care. We rarely encounter a situation where a pastor overtly refuses ministerial assistance to a person with HIV. To do so would be scandalous and unacceptable behavior, not in keeping with one's public profession. What is more disturbing, however, is covert refusal.

The majority of persons with HIV for whom we care as pastors are young men and women. Many of these afflicted persons profess a valiant commitment to live despite the disabling aspects of HIV. Yet for the majority of these individuals, the disease proves to be a terminal illness. Their trajectories to death may be either slow or accelerated, but eventually most die. People in the health care professions who provide care for persons with HIV speak about their frustration in seeing so many promising young people become ill, struggle with a variety of recurring illnesses, progressively deteriorate, and ultimately die. These physicians, nurses, and other care providers become very involved with persons with HIV and with their families and friends. Inevitably bonding takes place. Where there is attachment, there will be experiences of loss and grief when the person dies. The deaths of persons with AIDS have a way of eroding a thin protective barrier and forcing us to come to terms with our personal mortality.

Health care providers not only describe their subjective experiences of burnout from working so hard to manage the multiple physical and emotional problems of persons with AIDS, but they also acknowledge the cumulative effect of working with so many people who die. Although they are dedicated to this work, a number of individuals find that they have to leave work with persons with AIDS because the confrontation with death proves to be too strong.

Dealing with the Experiences of Persons with HIV

Healthy psychological functioning depends upon the effective use of defense mechanisms. The principal purpose of psychological defenses is to assist a person to meet the challenges presented by a specific crisis. Denial is one of the more common of these defenses. It takes time to assimilate the facts and consequences about one's condition, especially when the information is that one has HIV or a disease that defines AIDS. It is understandable that a person may resist the medical facts, may plead diagnostic error, or may dispute the prognosis offered. After a while, denial often gives way to acceptance.

In healthy individuals denial is a temporary solution, not a permanent one. It is a transitional state, a bridge between the world as it is and the world as we would like it to be. The majority of people utilize denial as a temporary retreat while they better prepare themselves for engagement with the facts and consequences of their illness. Some pastoral counselors experience difficulty in dealing with persons who deny the reality of their situation. However, it is important to underscore the appropriateness, normality, and for a number of people, the necessity of denial. Denial may resurface a number of times in the course of ministering to a person with HIV, and to those who are their loved ones and care providers.

Denial operates in other ways as well, such as rejecting treatments and dispensing with taking prescribed medications. Because such individuals do not accept the seriousness of their illness, they can engage in injurious behaviors, including excessive drinking and other forms of substance abuse. They may not monitor diet and sleep habits, adding further stress to the body's ability to fight infection. If they are sexually active, they may continue to expose others to infection through unsafe practices.

Denial can be employed by family or friends as well. Admittedly, it is difficult to acknowledge that someone you love is seriously ill and may die. It is a fine line to walk between continuing to treat a person with AIDS as alive, while also recognizing and adjusting to the reality that the person may not survive as a result of this disease. There are situations in which a person with HIV, who is aware and accepting of the reality of his or her diagnosis, is faced with family, lover, or friends who are unwilling to accept the same reality. In essence, denial functions as a psychological block preventing open awareness of the life-threatening diagnosis and acceptance of the fact of death. By their words and behavior, others pretend that the evidence of the disease is not compelling and that the person with HIV will be able to conquer the illness. This pretense is different from a realistic attitude of hope and the desire to live, which will be discussed later in this chapter.

Living with a life-threatening illness requires that the person with HIV and those who are important members of his or her support network be able to experience the feelings which are catalyzed by the illness. Together they need to experience the losses that are a natural part of this process and be able to talk freely as the time of death draws closer. If a person with HIV is to engage positively in this process, he or she must feel support and acceptance from those who share this experience. If that support and acceptance is not perceived, then the person with HIV may feel isolated and vulnerable to fears of being abandoned.

Some pastors, in efforts to express positive support and to help maintain hope, become confederates in denial. They pretend either that the person is not as sick as he or she truly is, or they become allies with the denial of some important members of the family.

Anger is also a common, normal, and legitimate psychological defense of a person living with HIV. There are countless reasons which explain his or her anger. It is not necessary to chronicle these multiple sources of anger. Any person facing potential or certain death may feel anger. Such individuals see other people, comparable in age and life experience, who are well and alive. They may resent the perceived "wellness" in others, while hating the "illness" in themselves. For example, a gay man with HIV may become angry with a lover who is not sick.

In its Scandinavian and Icelandic origins, the word *anger* means "grief" and "sorrow." In pastoral and psychological practice it is not uncommon to discover underneath expressions of anger an individual's more painful experiences of loss, sorrow, and grief. In order to gain access to these more important feelings, it is essential that the counselor not react negatively to angry outbursts or attacks. Family members and caring friends acknowledge that one of the most difficult things with which they contend in assisting a person with HIV is dealing with individuals who are most accessible and who are the closest supports to the sick person.

Caring for a person with HIV is demanding, both physically and emotionally. The task is compounded when the person whom you are assisting makes you the focused object of anger. The most natural response is to retaliate, to express anger in return.[3] Walking away from a person with HIV is one strategy. It helps to dissipate or diffuse negative feelings, provides perspective, and gives recovery time. However, it is important to interpret the walking away, since the person with HIV may read this behavior as abandonment. Perceived rejection or abandonment can intensify anger. When a person in need perceives being abandoned, he or she may also experience a weakening or loss of control, heightened anxiety, and real fears. Anger is one of the exterior masks behind which many frightened feelings play.

Pastoral counselors will encounter expressions of anger in caring for persons with HIV. Effective care is contingent upon a clear understanding of the genesis of the person's anger and what it means in the context of life-threatening illness. Pastoral care may be able to help the person to focus anger better. A pastoral counselor needs to find appropriate ways to respond to projections of anger directed either to the church or to his or her own person.

Persons with HIV display multiple levels of anger. Anger may be focused on the HIV itself, which surreptitiously has gained access to their bodies and silently and successfully begun to overwhelm the body's defenses. For example, they may make the virus the enemy, the focus of visualization exercises, using anger constructively in this way.

Persons with HIV may be angry at those individuals whom they suspect have been involved in transmitting the virus to them. They may be angry at medicine's inability to check the virus or cure the diseases that threaten their survival. They may be angry at the government bureaucracy for not making an adequate response to the AIDS pandemic by increasing the amount spent on research on HIV and its related diseases. Some persons perceive the government as an all-protective parent and are angry that the problem reached the magnitude it did before the government became seriously involved in the fight.[4]

Persons with HIV may be angry at pharmaceutical companies, which appear to be profiting unreasonably with drugs that have shown promising results in the management of HIV and its related diseases. Or anger may be focused on agencies like the FDA, which may delay approval and availability of promising new drugs.

Anger is often directed at God or the church. Or a person with HIV may be angry at himself or herself for becoming infected with the virus.

Clearly, it is not uncommon to find several sources of anger in a single individual with HIV.

It is never easy to encounter anger in the context of pastoral care or pastoral counseling. Pastors may be exposed to verbal abusiveness, aggressive and hostile accusations, sarcasm, and insult. It is difficult ministering to a person who is negative, withholding, or withdrawn. It is helpful to recall that a person with HIV has reason to be angry, and that anger may be one strategy the person utilizes in his or her attempt to cope with an HIV diagnosis. Anger is a common camouflage for the deeper pains of anxiety, fear, guilt, and grief. If a pastoral worker can patiently endure the vitriol of a person's anger, he or she may be in a strategic position to assist the person to deal with the more substantive needs which the anger is masking.

Ministering to the Psychosocial and Spiritual Needs of Persons with HIV

The physical aspects of an illness and the treatment programs used to manage it can overtax a person's energy reserves. Serious illness is also an emotional strain. It is important to be able to assess how the experience of illness is affecting a person's basic functioning, particularly psychological activities. At the bedrock of healthy psychological functioning are issues of safety, trust, and security.

Illness, by definition, upsets the balance of safety, trust, and security. Illness exposes an individual to potential dangers, doubts, and risks. It is important to assess how much an illness threatens these basic needs in order to determine how effective any form of interpersonal assistance will be.

HIV is perceived by many infected persons to be a very threatening enemy. Not only does the virus destabilize the functioning of the body's immune system, but its associated diseases can negatively affect basic psychological functioning. What relevance does this have for pastoral counseling? For an interpersonal relationship to be helpful, the person being assisted needs to experience the helper and the environment as trustworthy, safe, and secure. As noted before, it takes time, skill, and patience to establish these foundational experiences.

In working with a person with HIV the pastor will frequently encounter a weakening of the person's self-esteem. There are many things that affect self-esteem. A person's perceived inabilities to supply for his or her own basic physical and psychological needs can weaken self-esteem. In a culture where a person's worth is defined as a function of what he or she is able to do, disability related to disease can have profound effects on self-esteem.

Changes in self-esteem may be dramatic, but more often they are gradual, and sometimes imperceptible to others. Mental health practitioners are alert to issues that weaken self-esteem and work to help individuals maintain and improve their self-esteem. Since mental outlook has a significant role either in improvement in health and functioning or in the progression of illness, this is something that demands attention in the pastoral care of persons with HIV.

The physical care of a person with HIV can be so demanding and time-consuming that there may be less time available to identify and respond to psychosocial and spiritual issues. Competent pastoral care can respond effectively to these needs. In order to do this, the pastoral worker needs to understand how the diagnosis of HIV is affecting the individual's self-esteem. A few quick words of encouragement or some trivial cliche is rarely an adequate antidote to the HIV-related problems of self-esteem.

Providing pastoral counsel and care to a person with HIV is comparable to Jesus' ministry to the leper as recorded in the opening chapter of Mark's gospel (Mk 1:40–45). In the Jewish society of Jesus' day leprosy was the ultimate form of uncleanness. Lepers were excluded from participation in the community. They were thought to be a source of defilement for others. In the Marcan story the leper approached Jesus and begged, "If you will, you can make me clean." The evangelist focuses on the reaction of Jesus. Many texts translate Jesus' emotional response as "moved with pity." However, some commentators note that a more accurate rendition of Jesus' reaction is, "moved with anger." It is reasonable that when Jesus was confronted with a person whose illness had excommunicated him from others, he felt anger and indignation. The leper brought Jesus face to face with the powers of evil. The emotional response of Jesus, the sense of injustice he felt at the leper's social isolation, interpret his subsequent actions. The gospel writer tells us that Jesus touched him, a most unlikely thing since it meant Jesus himself was defiled by that physical contact. It was—and is—a gesture of acceptance, support, of solidarity with the afflicted. By that gesture, the text observes, the leprosy "left" him, as if the power of evil departed from him. Jesus' physical gesture of touch and his words helped restore the man to a rightful place in the community. Emphasis is not placed on the healing act itself, but on the indignation, understanding, compassion, and reconciliation of Jesus.

Some have referred to HIV and its associated diseases as a new form of leprosy. To be able to minister effectively to this new group of lepers requires a variety of helping skills. One of these skills involves making a competent assessment of the psychosocial and spiritual strengths and weaknesses of the person being helped. While it is clear that persons with HIV have physical stresses related to weakened body immunity, one should not assume that there is a parallel weakness in psychological or spiritual functioning. We shall consider some of the issues to which pastoral counselors should be sensitive in offering assistance to persons with HIV.

Initial contact with a person with HIV is important, both for the individual and for the pastoral counselor. For the person with HIV, it represents the establishment, reconnection, or continuation of relationship with a community of faith. For the pastoral care provider it provides an occasion in which to reach out, to *touch* a person. This mean to establish rapport, trust, and confidence, as well as to begin to assess what will be required further in pastoral care. Some pastors prematurely select resources they judge might be helpful, only to discover that the individual is indifferent, nonresponsive, or rejecting of such ministries. In some cases, the resources the pastor selects are disturbing, counterproductive, or damaging to the person in need. It is important that the proper resources be selected and utilized.

Some pastoral providers are inclined to begin a relationship by "doing" something, rather than by taking the essential time to establish a relationship, make a competent assessment of the person's needs and assets, and then beginning to help the individual choose the appropriate resources in order to respond to these needs. Taking the time to attend to the establishment of a relationship with the person with HIV is an indispensable prerequisite to any effective pastoral care ministry. The Who are you?, What do you have?, and What do you need? questions are indispensable. The establishment of an accepting and understanding relationship makes it possible for a pastor to begin assessing the person's inner resources.

It might be helpful to consider some specific areas a pastor may wish to explore with a person with HIV. A person with HIV may have had experience with the disease predating his or her diagnosis. Because AIDS is now well into its second decade, many people have firsthand knowledge and experience about the syndrome. Knowledge, however, is variable, and a person's perceptions of the disease will also vary. It is essential to know how the individual understands HIV, and how he or she is prepared to respond. A pastor needs a basic understanding of the person's perception of his or her illness.

Concerned about providing complex medical services, the psychosocial and spiritual needs of a patient may be neglected by some health care providers. A skilled pastor can respond to this deficit in care. In practice, most persons with HIV adjust to their diagnoses and life-threatening diseases; they do not develop extraordinary psychosocial problems. As noted earlier, many persons with HIV are positively committed to living a quality life. Persons with HIV make decisions in light of this goal of *living*. However, they do need understanding and support to realize this objective.

Stress

Coping with any life-threatening illness is inherently stressful. Stress may be evident on various levels of care: medical, physical, psychological, spiritual. *Stress* is defined as a person's emotional and bodily responses to demands that either approach or exceed the limits of his or her coping abilities. Because of the nature of opportunistic infections and immunodeficiency, a person with HIV lives with the ever-present possibility of a new threat or a new medical crisis, often occurring before the body has been able to recuperate or detoxify from earlier physical battles. This is a major source of stress for persons with HIV illness.

Stress also is evident on many levels of psychological functioning. How a person perceives, interprets, and understands the environment in which he or she is situated determines to a great extent the degree of stress and anxiety he or she will experience. It will influence how he or she reacts to it emotionally and physiologically. Life situations present a person with information and provide the necessary feedback for forming an understanding of the world. A person with HIV relies heavily on these sources of data. Behavioral responses are understood in relation to these situational conditions. Behavior does not exist in isolation from real life situations. Some persons with HIV are more vulnerable than others to the physical and psychological stressors associated with this diagnosis.

Stress and anxiety are not synonymous. Anxiety always involves stress, but the reverse is not necessarily true. An HIV diagnosis, for example, may lead to stress, but not necessarily to anxiety. Which stressors lead to stress depend upon the person's assessment of them as threatening. Although many clinicians like to separate the physical and psychological dimensions of stress, they are related.

Pastoral counseling may be one vehicle for assisting a person with HIV to manage some sources of stress. To do so, a pastoral worker must have a clear understanding of what these issues are, and how much and how disposed an individual is to explore these concerns. Knowing these things, the pastor can determine which issues might be addressed and on what timetable.

Pastors can do some practical things to help a person manage stress. The first is the simple recognition, acknowledgment, and acceptance that the person's situation is stressful. Recognition and rehearsal of these *facts* may assist a person to plan ways of dealing with subsequent crises. The second thing a pastor can do is to begin to work with feelings of helplessness, hopelessness, and demoralization by emphasizing the individual's personal and social coping resources. A person can be assisted to feel reasonably confident that he or she has the resources to face the current situation and manage well.

Persons with HIV can manage to live in spite of the serious physical, psychological, and spiritual threats they may perceive. A pastor can also assist an individual to work out plans for protecting himself or herself from sources of personal stress. A pastoral worker can help a person with HIV disease to maintain or regain independence so that he or she does not rely exclusively on others for protection from the sufferings and losses associated with HIV. In helping a person with HIV to manage stress, a pastoral counselor needs to strike a balance between the arousal of anticipatory grief and fear on the one hand, and realistic hope and genuine reassurance on the other. Some people can deal well with the facing reality, others cannot. A pastor needs to be able to recognize the difference.

Stigma

A person with HIV can feel stigmatized. When we speak about stigma, we refer to the ways in which society deals with undesirable differentness. In America today a person who is stigmatized is perceived as abnormal, deviant, and in some instances, is, dehumanized. A person in our society who is stigmatized is set apart from others. People treat the individual as dangerous, untrustworthy, objectionable. The person is not considered a fit member of society. The impact of stigma extends beyond the people so marked to affect the person's family, friends, and business associates, as well as those professionals who are involved with the stigmatized individual.

Many persons whose behaviors place them at high-risk for becoming infected with HIV bear stigma labels apart from their HIV status. Pejorative terms such as *junkies, druggies, whores, niggers, faggots,* and *queers* translate society's stigmatization of members of these groups. Although AIDS is a syndrome of diseases, the acronym has become a new stigma label.[5] Persons with HIV are legitimately afraid that others will learn of their diagnosis, realizing that they will be stigmatized if such knowledge is communicated further.

For the pastoral worker initiating ministry to a person with HIV, these issues have immediate relevance. A pastor will recognize the emotional effects of stigma. A person with HIV may feel unclean, despicable, unworthy. Although HIV is not easily transmitted, certainly not in ordinary non-sexual contact, some persons with HIV feel that others think they are contagious and thus to be avoided. Some are surprised when they are touched or embraced. A person with HIV may be embarrassed to face the pastor, fearing that he or she will be judged as deserving of this fate.

Stigmatization is emotionally scarring; it victimizes the person so branded. It is very important that a pastor recognize, acknowledge, and respond to the personal apprehension, frustrations, and tensions associated with the stigma of an HIV diagnosis. Pastoral care must encompass the family and friends, whose lives are also affected by the stigma of AIDS. As health care workers have experienced stigma because of their work with persons with HIV, so pastors must be prepared for the negative affect associated with our AIDS-related ministries.

Stigma can be reduced by effective education and modeling. As pastors we can do much to confront the attitudes, misinformation, and prejudices associated with this disease and the individuals who have become infected. The quality of our interpersonal relationships with persons with HIV will help to neutralize the negative effects of the stigma associated with this disease. As trusted leaders within our local communities, parishes, and congregations, pastors can do much to confront the injustices associated with the growing stigmatization of persons with HIV and the alienation of their families.

Communication

Whenever human beings interact, communication operates on a variety of levels. The most obvious level is when plain, direct words are exchanged. Another level involves non-verbal language or cues, posture, gestures, and facial movements. And finally, there is symbolic, verbal language. The images we select, the poetry we cite, and the jokes we tell all carry important messages. Too many of us limit what we receive in communication from another to the first level: plain language. Even then, we may not listen effectively to that message. There are many non-verbal cues that provide useful information about an individual's psychological, and spiritual adjustment. An individual may not be able to express emotions or feelings in words, but they are being communicated nonetheless, even though the person may be unaware that they are being transmitted. How to interpret accurately the meaning of non-verbal cues—physical behaviors, facial expressions, gestures, postures—is an important and demanding task of the pastor in ministering to a person with HIV.

The sensitive pastor must be aware of all the ways in which the person with HIV is attempting to communicate. Non-verbalized feelings are an important component of human communication. They are the only reasonable alternative to spoken communication. Many people in life-threatening situations rely heavily on this latter form of communication. A comprehensive understanding of a person's needs and behavior is often contingent upon a correct assessment of the non-verbal cues and feelings. Correctly interpreting these various strata of communication will assist greatly in deciding how best to respond to the messages being sent and received.

Our discussion has identified areas of deficit that are related to HIV illness. This underscores the importance of accurate assessment of these issues prior to providing specific pastoral care to a person with HIV. It is equally important to assess the person's strengths. These are important resources upon which to build. In the face of the many disabling aspects of

HIV, we may sometimes overlook the fact that a person has resources which are not necessarily weakened by the disease.

A Ministry of Hope to Persons with HIV

There are many ways to describe the role of a pastor in the care of persons with HIV. The enabling role, a ministry of hope, is certainly among the most important. Among HIV+ persons living in places where there is a high prevalence of HIV-related disease, there can be the perception that the whole world is dying of AIDS (Weiss 1989; Helquist 1989). This perception can contribute in great measure to feelings of hopelessness, depression, and despair. At a time when people most need encouragement and support, family, friends, health care professionals, and pastoral care professionals may directly or indirectly withdraw from them. Physical and emotional distancing is experienced by persons with HIV as abandonment and rejection. It is understandable why some individuals speak of feeling miserable, not only as a result of the effects of their illness, but because they feel they have no one on whom they can depend.

Effective and consistent support helps maintain hope. We know that persons with HIV adamantly resist being labeled as victims. In ancient religious usage the term *victim* referred to a living creature that was sacrificed. By definition, a victim has little hope. Victim implies passivity. Persons with HIV, by rejecting the label victim, assert their prerogative to be treated as persons. They retain full possession of their human rights and dignity, and maintain control over their lives as long as they are alive.

The human psyche is complex. How a person thinks significantly affects how he or she feels. If a person believes that life is controllable, then he or she will work to exercise control. From research with both animal and human subjects, psychologists have concluded that there is a demonstrable relationship between psychological surrender and physical death. If the judgment is made that there is no basis for hope of living a dignified life, then a person surrenders the will to live. That decision may act as a trigger that accelerates the process of dying.

Two issues of general significance to helping persons with HIV to maintain hope are worthy of mention. The first is the issue of support. It is difficult to sustain hope in the face of uncertainty unless there is real and perceived support. Although sources of support are available, some people may be unable to use them. A second issue has to do with control and pastoral intervention. Pastors must diligently avoid exercising control by projecting their own values onto a person with HIV. Bernie S. Siegal continually confronts the value questions related to life-threatening illnesses—"It's not for us to evaluate the worth of continued life for another person; as long as my patients are living in a way that has value for them, I'm there to help them continue" (Siegal 1986). A pastoral counselor might benefit from reflecting on this principle of care [6]

For some individuals AIDS means death, and they may find little meaning in attempting to live with HIV. However, for the majority of persons with living with HIV and its related diseases, AIDS presents a formidable challenge to live, one many are ready to embrace. There are many variables that contribute to the determination of a person with HIV to live. It will be helpful to identify and comment upon some of these resources.

Principal Relationships

Whether it is a parent, sibling, lover, friend, or counselor, a person with HIV needs a deeper relationship with someone. The needs in terms of physical care are evident and should not be minimized in any discussion. However, the emotional and spiritual dimensions of a deeper interpersonal relationship deserve further discussion. A decision to attempt to live with HIV disease exposes some profound human feelings. They run the spectrum from moments of exhilaration to moments of despair; from great optimism about a new treatment or drug to profound disappointment when it does not prove to be the hoped for remedy. There are moments of almost symbiotic closeness and times of frightening distance; of tenderness and warmth, of hardness and stoic disregard.

These are but some of the multiple and changing faces of relationship with a person with HIV. Constancy weaves together the threads of these transformations. The sense that "we'll see this through together" forms the *cantus firmus* of all successful relationships with persons with HIV. The importance of a deep human relationship for maintaining a commitment to live is evident. In some cases the relationship involves primary responsibilities for providing physical care. In other cases those responsibilities may be discharged by a number of persons, while the principal emotional needs of the person with HIV are addressed by one individual.

Pastors frequently find themselves in the latter category. A pastor may find himself or herself moving out of traditional ministerial roles and assuming other nontraditional roles in caring for a person with HIV. For example, the pastor may be the one with whom the individual wishes to share an evening at the theater or a picnic on a warm summer day. Regardless of the way in which the pastoral role is exercised, all pastoral care tries to enkindle and sustain hope in the face of the serious challenges which HIV presents. The ability of the pastor to forge a deeper relationship with the individual with HIV and his or her family can influence significantly not only the effectiveness of spiritual ministrations, but the person's very will to live.

Changing One's Mental Outlook

For centuries people have debated the intrinsic relationship between mind and body. Persons involved in the practice of dynamic psychotherapy know experientially that if one is successful in helping persons alter the ways in which they think about themselves or about a particularly distressing issue, that change in thinking will affect both bodily functions and behavior. Pastoral care implicitly engages in helping people change the ways in which they think about many aspects of their lives. In Judeo-Christian traditions the scriptures have been read and explained to help people modify the ways in which they understand their relationship to God and to each other. The work of conversion is essentially the work of changing one's thinking in order to change one's behavior. The work of reconciliation helps people see what is disordered in their approach to life and relationships, and to commit themselves to act upon what they see.

The traditional religious notion of inspiration appeals to a divine influence directly and immediately exerted on the mind or soul of a person. The theological significance of such inspiration is apparent: a person is animated, influenced, affected to such a degree that the body actively responds and behavior is changed. The consoling ministries of the church strive to help people rid themselves of unhealthy thoughts and to discover inner peacefulness. Peacefulness is more than a static state of harmony, serenity, or tranquility. Achieving peace of mind involves active engagement in the tasks of confronting and challenging the mental outlooks that threaten the very foundations of bodily health.

If the work of pastoral counseling is successful, a person will be involved in changing the mental outlooks that compromise bodily health and integrity. From a holistic perspective, the relationship between effective pastoral care and physical health is assumed.

Some Practical Ways to Support a Person's Hopes

Let us look at some of the ways in which pastoral care to persons with HIV can influence bodily health. Few persons with HIV want to think about the disease as a terminal illness. As we stated in the introduction, language colors how a person thinks about a disease. In order to maintain hope and engagement with life, a person needs to believe there is some possibility of survival. As pastors, we need to be sensitive to the ways in which we talk about

HIV. just as health care providers can use words like *lethal* and *terminal* in conversation with persons with HIV, a pastor can inadvertently use the same language. Unconsciously, language can destroy a person's hope, take away the will to survive, and force an individual to surrender the remaining controls he or she has over life. In the words of Peter Vom Lehn, an AIDS patient:

> I think that terminal is insulting, offensive to the patient, because it takes away all his hope and can discourage him immediately. And hope is a very important part of the patient's mental and physical health, and essential if he's going to get any better and not give in. It's not fair to take away someone's chances for survival by taking away his hope, and if he's told that he has a terminal disease, that's just what you do, right at the start (Peabody 1986, p. 192).

In the practice of pastoral counseling with persons with HIV there are some specific ways to assist a person to maintain a positive and engaged approach to life. It is imperative that the pastoral worker understand what the person with HIV holds as life values. It may take some time to create the appropriate emotional climate in which a person is willing to share these important values. Beyond understanding, the pastor needs to communicate acceptance of these values. Acceptance does not imply agreement or approval. Some pastors find it difficult to make this distinction. In working with persons with HIV it is to be anticipated that some of their expressed values will not be held by some religious faiths. Pastoral counselors must learn to be non-judgmental in dealing with clients' values that differ from their own or those of the religious tradition they represent.

A person with HIV needs to feel that a prospective helper understands his or her inner struggles. The person with HIV is helped when the pastor is effective in communicating that he or she also understands and shares the individual's feelings.

Because of the nature and course of the disease, there is a problem in finding anything positive to say. In working with persons with HIV there is a danger that the orientation in conversation often may be negatively skewed. In order to maintain a person's realistic hopes in the face of this disease, efforts must be focused on reinforcing small, positive gains. This might involve helping a person to communicate directly with parents or friends. It could involve the person's resumption of work on a limited schedule. Gaining two pounds might be an important milestone. Having a day without a debilitating reaction to a therapeutic drug can be a small victory. Pastors should be alert to identify and respond to these cues. Those with HIV need to find encouragement in efforts they may be making to survive. They need others to recognize and celebrate with them the small gains they may be achieving.

It is easy to think and treat persons with HIV disease as handicapped persons. At some stages of the illness, and when HIV infection expresses itself in certain ways, a person may need special forms of physical and emotional support. However, it is imperative that we not generally think of the person with HIV as handicapped. Rather, it is important to help the person with HIV to maintain autonomy and to retain control over his or her decisions and behaviors.

It is not uncommon to note among the behaviors of sick persons a certain amount of regression. This is evident in their passivity, their abrogation of decision-making, their expectations that others should take care of all their basic needs. These are normal reactions to illness, and such behaviors are sanctioned by our social mores. However, if these regressive tendencies are not challenged appropriately, a person can lose the motivation to recover.

Some people adopt the "sick role" as a habitual mode of being and resist getting better. Some of these psychological dynamics, common to many individuals with acute illnesses, are observable in some people with HIV. Care providers must be able to strike a balance between providing necessary services and creating a situation of over-dependency.

Pastoral care of persons with HIV always should be enabling, encouraging, and supportive. It should foster independence of thinking and choosing. It should create a feeling of partnership rather than of paternalism. In pastoral care the pastor needs to be aware of the potentially counterproductive effects of an overly paternalistic approach. Paternalism is expressed not only in behaviors but also in language. While words and gestures might appear to be accepted by the sick individual and ostensibly be comforting, at the same time they can contribute to passivity and dependence.

Pastoral care should strive to create an environment where the individual feels encouraged to do more for himself or herself, knowing that he or she has support. Interventions should aim to help the person seek personal solutions to problems rather than to solve problems for the person. Depression results when others take control and solve problems. A person needs to determine goals and decide ways to achieve those goals. An effective model of this strategy of pastoral care is found in the ministry to the paralyzed person who is cured by Jesus (Lk 5:18–25). In this passage some people carried a paralyzed man on a pallet and placed him before Jesus, hoping that he would cure him. In this situation the paralyzed person needed physical assistance. This was an appropriate use of other people's assistance. There were enormous crowds around the house in which Jesus was staying, so they had to climb up and lower the man through the roof. Recognizing their determination and faith, Jesus expressed forgiveness and healed the man. His dismissal to the formerly paralyzed man was: "Arise, take up your bed and go home."

Luke notes that the man immediately arose, took up the stretcher upon which he had been lying, and went away to his house, glorifying God. Jesus placed direct responsibility for the future on the formerly paralyzed individual. He didn't say to the others, "Take his bed home for him." Healing is linked with belief and personal action. Faith and personal, responsible action are underscored in Jesus' statement to this individual. Pastoral care should attempt to facilitate both faith and the exercise of personal responsibility.

In his classic book *On Dying and Denying*, Avery Weisman talks about hope as it relates to perceived self-worth and self-acceptance:

> Hope is not dependent upon survival alone. Hope means that we have confidence in the desirability of survival. It arises from a desirable self-image, healthy self-esteem, and belief in our ability to exert a degree of influence on the world surrounding us....Hope is decided more by self-acceptance than by objects sought and by impractical aspirations....Foreshortened life does not in itself create hopelessness....More important is our belief that we do something worth doing, and that others think so, too. Thus, people lose hope when they are unable to act on their own behalf and must also relinquish their claims upon others (Weisman 1972, pp. 20–21).

Or, as Bernie Siegal puts it: "Hoping means seeing that the outcome you want is possible, and then working for it" (Siegal 1986, p. 178). The purpose of any form of assistance to persons with HIV should be to help the individual to achieve personal goals. Integrity, self-acceptance, and love are necessary, common, and realizable goals (see Kirkpatrick 1990). They presuppose emotional honesty. For some individuals infection with HIV may exposes areas of personal life that have been hidden or inadequately addressed. The nineteenth-century German philosopher Friedrich Nietzsche emphasized the importance of the will to power as the chief motivating force of both the individual and society. He asserted that the person who has the *why* to live can endure almost any *how*. Pastoral counsel can be effective in maintaining a spark of hope in the darkness of the world of a person with HIV. As many persons living with HIV acknowledge, they depend upon these caring partnerships to keep their hopes alive.

Epilogue

By way of conclusion, the following case may bring together many of the issues discussed in this chapter on ministry to persons with HIV.

Matthew was twenty-nine years old when he was referred by his physician for pastoral counseling.

Matthew was the youngest in a family of twelve children. Both of his parents were alcoholics with erratic histories of sobriety. Matt had left home when he was fourteen; he survived through prostitution, selling drugs, and other criminal activities. In his late adolescence he met an older man with whom he lived for almost six years in return for sexual favors. After almost fifteen years living away from his family of origin, Matt found his way back to his place of birth. Soon after his return he developed symptoms related to an underlying immunodeficiency, was tested for HIV, and was found to be positive.

At the time of his referral for pastoral counseling to address his anxiety and related concerns, he had been drug-free for eleven months, and was asymptomatic. He had been seen previously in individual and group counseling settings by a hospital social worker experienced in working with HIV clients. These interventions did not appear to help alleviate his anxieties, fears, and night tremors. As part of his recovery he experienced a religious reawakening. His medical team thought that pastoral counseling might be able to do what more traditional psychotherapeutic interventions could not achieve.

Matthew came willingly for weekly conversations. Four months into his pastoral counseling he developed Kaposi lesions on his leg, a definitive diagnosis of AIDS. He maintained regular counseling contact throughout the final fifteen months of his battle with several HIV-related illnesses, four of which required hospitalizations. During his treatment he reviewed his family history, his adolescent and young adult experiences, and his struggles with HIV disease. He set some definite and realizable goals, and he solicited help in achieving these objectives. The most significant goal was to establish an independent residence for himself. With the help of a local AIDS Action Committee, he was able to rent and furnish a small apartment in a low-income housing complex.

Matt also needed to address his religious needs. As a child he had been baptized in the Roman Catholic faith, but be never benefitted from religious education and never received the sacraments of penance or eucharist. One of the ways in which pastoral counseling helped him in his "living with HIV" was by supplying basic religious education and preparing and celebrating sacraments with him.

A year before his death Matt received the sacraments of penance and the anointing of the sick, and shared holy communion at a eucharistic celebration attended by many members of his family, including both of his parents. The family organized itself sufficiently well for this milestone occasion to prepare and host a party following the small, private celebration of Matthew's first communion.

His several serious illnesses disposed Matt to direct and comfortable discussions about death. These conversations were thoughtful and uncovered a primitive but strong faith. He drew enormous comfort in the notion of "communion of saints." When he thought about his own death, he viewed it in terms of reunion with Jesus and Mary and many of the saints whom he was discovering through reading brief accounts of their lives.

Although Matt did not have the ordinary benefits of formal secondary education, he was naturally intelligent and articulate. He actively investigated how he might earn a high school equivalency diploma, although he never realized this goal. His life experiences had taught him many things, and he was instinctively a reflective person. He wanted to learn how to pray and responded well to traditional devotional practices. He used a small book of prayers that he received on the occasion of his first communion, and these brought him much consolation.

During his final years of life he met another person with HIV who was fifteen years his senior. They became close friends, and Matthew assumed the role of primary care provider for this other person, who, at the time they met, was considerably more advanced with AIDS. Matthew used pastoral counseling as a way to monitor this relationship, develop strategies to resolve conflicts that arose, and as a primary support to his need for independence and autonomy.

Before Matthew died in June of 1990, he received anointing and communion one final time. In his last conversation with his pastoral counselor before his death, he summarized what this relationship had meant to him. He noted that in his whole life he had never known a relationship with another man where there was not a sexual, exploitive, or manipulative agenda. He confessed that for a long time he wondered why anyone would do so much for him without expecting something in return. He said it occurred to him after about five months into the counseling relationship that there are some people in the world who do care and really don't look for anything in return.

In his mind this was the pivotal turning point, the time when he began to trust confidently, to hope enthusiastically, to accept being loved without the fear of abandonment. His final words to his counselor were these:

> Looking back on my life, I many times asked myself why God would send someone like you into my life at this time. Now I know the answer. God does love me, and sent me an angel to bring me home. You've been that angel, and I want you to know how much this has meant to me. When the days were the darkest, you were always there. You helped me through some rough times, You said you would stay with me, and you have. Thank you, my friend. I love you.

Notes

1. For an expanded treatment of many of the topics discussed in this chapter, with case studies that interpret key issues in pastoral care, see Smith (1988). The reader might also wish to consult Shelp, et al. (1986); Dilley, et al. (1989); and Kirkpatrick (1990).

2. The Centers for Disease Control (CDC) have classified persons with HIV disease in four groups: (1) Group I have acute HIV syndrome; (2) Group II are without symptoms (asymptotic); (3) Group III have persistent swelling of the lymph nodes (generalized lymphadenopathy); and (4) Group IV have specific manifestations of HIV disease, further delineated as constitutional symptoms (IVa), neurologic disease (M), infections (IVc), cancers (IVd), and others (IVe).

3. It may be helpful to read Barbara Peabody's account of her care of her son, Peter, who died from complications of AIDS (Peabody 1986). Reading Barbara Peabody's sensitive account of her relationship with her son during his final year of struggle with AIDS, one is aware that she tolerated a good deal of his anger, yet there were limits to how effective she was in the management of anger.

4. There have been several interesting chronicles of the government's response during the first decade of the pandemic, for example, see *And the Band Played On* (Shilts 1987).

5. For an insightful reflection on this issue, see *AIDS and Its Metaphors* (Sontag 1989). The reader may also wish to read her earlier work, *Illness as Metaphor* (Sontag 1979).

6. Readers may also wish to consult *Head First: The Biology of Hope* (Cousins 1989). An adjunct professor in the School of Medicine at UCLA, Cousins presents a lay person's perspective on scientific evidence that supports the place of faith, love, will to live, purpose, and humor in managing serious disease.

References

AIDS Education Project of the American Psychiatric Association. 1989. *A Psychiatrist's Guide to AIDS and HIV Diseases: A Primer.* Washington, D.C.

AMA (American Medical Association). 1986. Statement on AIDS reported by the Council of Ethical and Judicial Affairs of the American Medical Association (December).

Callen, Michael. 1990. *Surviving AIDS.* New York: HarperCollins.

Cousins, N. 1989. *Head First: The Biology of Hope.* New York: Dutton.

Dilley, J. W., Pies, C., and Helquist, M., eds. 1989. *Face to Face: A Guide to AIDS Counseling*. San Francisco: AIDS Health Project UCSF.

Helquist, M. 1989. "Too Many Casualites: HIV Disease in Gay Men." In Dilley, et al., *Face to Face*.

Kirkpatrick, B. 1990. *AIDS: Sharing the Pain: A Guide for Caregivers*. New York: Pilgrim Press.

Peabody, Barbara. 1986. *A Screaming Room*. San Diego: Oak Tree.

Shelp, E. E., Sunderland, R. H., and Mansell, P. W. A. 1986. *AIDS: Personal Stories in Pastoral Perspective*. New York: Pilgrim Press.

Shilts, Randy. 1987. *And the Band Played On: Politics, People, and the AIDS Epidemic*. New York: St. Martin's Press.

Siegal, Bernie S. 1986. *Love, Medicine, and Miracles*. New York: Harper & Row.

Smith, Walter J. 1988. *AIDS: Living and Dying With Hope*. New Jersey: Paulist Press.

Sontag, Susan. 1979. *Illness as Metaphor*. New York: Vintage Books.

———. 1989. *AIDS and Its Metaphors*. New York: Farrar, Straus, Giroux.

Weisman, A. 1972. *On Dying and Denying: A Psychiatric Study of Terminality*. New York: New York Behavioral Publications.

Weiss, A. 1989. "The Aids Bereaved: Counseling Strategies." In Dilley, et al., *Face to Face*.

SECTION III
SPECIAL CHALLENGES AND
RESPONSIBILITIES OF THE
PASTORAL COUNSELOR

Care of others is a driving force for those in pastoral counseling. However, pastoral counselors too often ignore the responsibility to care for themselves as caretakers. The essays within section III challenge all pastoral counselors to employ steps to maintain not only their professional competence but their personal health and well-being. These are not just good ideas; they are professional and ethical responsibilities for each pastoral counselor.*

The first chapter in this section, chapter 15, "Countertransference and Burnout in Pastoral Counseling," is written by Robert J. Wicks. Through a blending of the research and case illustrations, Wicks provides the reader with insight into the cause and course of the development of both countertransference and burnout. In his article Wicks enumerates the ways that both of these conditions can be detected and cautions that counselors need to care for themselves, resisting the development of a "savior complex" and modeling "healthy limit-setting for patients." In light of this directive to care for self, Wicks provides a number of interventions to be considered when faced with loss of professional objectivity at the hands of either countertransference or burnout.

Sadly, the inclusion of the next chapter (chapter 16), "Sexual Exploitation and Other Boundary Violations in Pastoral Ministries" by Pamela Cooper-White, reflects a reality that has proven damaging to clergy and devastating to many parishioners and clients. As noted in the chapter, sexual behavior with clients, patients, and students or supervisees is clearly prohibited by the codes of ethics of the American Association of Pastoral Counselors and the Association of Clinical Pastoral Education. However, the

---

* The reader should be aware that, while an editorial effort has been made to update statistics in places, some outdated statistics have been kept in order to respect the theses of the original articles. In each case, it was determined that the pastoral content of the article is still valuable and relevant for contemporary pastoral counseling.

intensity found within the dynamics of a helping relationship and the power imbalance experienced can prove seductive to clergy who are neither in touch with or in control of their professional boundaries. The author identifies a number of the factors and dynamic elements that may underlay clergy boundary violation. In addition, she challenges pastoral counselors to attend to our own ethical and theological mandates, maintaining the highest standards of sexual professional ethics, and refraining from "colluding or 'turning a blind eye' toward colleagues" who violate boundaries with clients, patients, or congregation members. To this end she offers a number of concrete steps pastoral counselors can take to contribute to the prevention and healing of clergy sexual misconduct.

One step, targeted to maintain professional, ethical practice, that each pastoral counselor should consider is to engage in a supervisory relationship. In chapter 17, "Supervising Pastoral Counseling," David A. Steere presents supervision as an effective tool for continuing one's development as a competent caregiver. Steere suggests that "the conceptual tools and the specific techniques needed to work effectively with others can be mastered only through ordered reflection....And that is what supervision is designed to accomplish...." Steere provides an excellent review of four supervisory traditions—Clinical Pastoral Education, the psychodynamic tradition, the humanistic tradition, and the systemic tradition—and concludes the chapter by providing a model of supervision that is broad enough to encompass diverse contemporary approaches yet focused enough to provide clarity and integrity to the task of supervision.

The last chapter in this section, and in this text (chapter 18) is "Research in Pastoral Counseling: A Responsibility and an Opportunity" by Joanne Marie G. Greer. While many pastoral counselors perceive themselves as "doers," not researchers, the truth is that being a competent, ethical professional demands a knowledge of the current research and the ability to discern good research from that of questionable validity. In her chapter, Greer provides an excellent depiction of pastoral counseling as both "pastoral" and "scientific." From this framework, the author provides the reader with a fundamental review of the characteristics and elements of research methodology and hypothesis testing, along with the value of this method of searching for "truth." Greer ends the chapter by calling on pastoral counselors to "begin to systematize their theories and chip away at validating them."

Robert J. Wicks

15. Countertransference and Burnout in Pastoral Counseling

Christians encounter many problems and pitfalls when in their pastoral counseling they employ a system of psychology in which the study of unconscious mental processes plays a major role. One way of handling these difficulties is by attempting to learn more about their own personalities in general and how to understand and deal with "countertransference" and "burnout" in particular (Wicks, 1983).

Countertransference

Our personality is responsible for the way we view ourselves and the world. No matter how well people know, love, or care for us, they will never view us or the world in quite the same way we do. No one can have the same personality as someone else because personality is a special singular product of heredity, pre-natal environment, and the formative relations we have had with significant others early in life.

These early important interpersonal encounters with the key figures in our life help us form a blueprint for dealing with the world. Naturally the blueprint needs constant revision. People we encounter now are not the same as those we interacted with early in life, nor are they in a position to meet our childhood needs. When we act as if they are, we are demonstrating "transference."

Transference is common because we all have ingrained learned patterns of dealing with the world. Likewise, everyone has at least some unresolved childhood conflicts which are beyond awareness. There is no such thing as the *totally* analyzed, personally aware individual. Anytime people interact there is some aspect of distortion in the way one person views the other.

In order to remain in touch with our own unresolved conflicts and needs, and to see reality as clearly as possible, it is important to monitor our transferences on an ongoing basis. There must be an effort to keep the interferences of the past to a minimum, while recognizing that it is impossible to screen them out altogether. The overall goal is to avoid superimposing personal needs and conflicts on the verbal and non-verbal messages we receive from others. This aim is particularly important when we function as pastoral counselor or pastoral psychotherapist.

Transference in the counselor is referred to as *countertransference*. It is the counselor's transferential reaction to the patient or client. It is an unrealistic response to the patient's realistic behavior, transferences, and general relationship with us and the world. Langs (1974, p. 298) in his two volume treatment of psychoanalytic psychotherapy views countertransference in the following way: "We may briefly define countertransferences as one aspect of those responses to the patient which, while prompted by some event within the therapy or in the therapist's real life, are primarily based on his past significant relationships; basically, they gratify his needs rather than the patient's therapeutic endeavors."

Not everyone in the field of mental health views countertransference as Langs does. Countertransference has been portrayed in a number of ways over the years since Freud introduced the concept. For example, it has been seen negatively and narrowly as being solely a block to effective counselor-patient communication. In this light it was considered as something to be discovered and analyzed out of existence (Fenichel, 1945; Ruesh, 1961; Tarachow, 1963). Its presence was seen as evidence of weakness in the counselor. Those who followed this line of thought sometimes found it difficult to be natural and genuine in the counseling session. They feared that by relaxing or letting their guard down, they might accidentally show some of their countertransference. Needless to say, this resulted in quite stilted and unrealistic counseling sessions.

When this happens in a pastoral counseling setting, those who come for help are unpleasantly surprised. They are seeking a warm caring religious leader and instead find a distant, "professional," aloof person filling the role of "helper."

This is the result of a misunderstanding of how one works as a counselor. It is attributable to a failure to appreciate that therapeutic techniques are presented to help the pastoral counselors project their own personality in a healthy way, not bury or disguise it out of fear of demonstrating countertransference. In not allowing personal needs, conflicts, and personality style to interfere with the patient-counselor relationship, the pastoral helper must not become a robot in the process.

On the other end of the continuum with respect to countertransference, some in the field have elevated its importance to the point where it is seen as practically the cornerstone of treatment (Fromm-Reichmann, 1950) or as a source of prelogical communication which the helper must tap into if he is to appreciate the deep messages the patient is unconsciously trying to send out (Tauber, 1954). Such positions with regard to countertransference are still being looked at today. However, most theorists and practitioners now take more of a middle ground.

They accept the reality of countertranference. No matter how well analyzed a counselor may be, the occurrence of countertransference is seen as being a natural part of life, albeit to a lesser extent than in the unanalyzed person. With this position in place, most counselors or therapists don't adhere dogmatically to the principle that it must be feared and eliminated at all cost. Rather, they believe they should take all steps possible to reduce unruly countertransference. Along with this they recognize that the counselor's own transference will occur to some extent and that utilization of the knowledge it brings should take place as a means of furthering the patient's treatment.

The premise is that by monitoring the personal feelings patients elicit—initially and throughout the treatment—it is possible to learn about the patient's problems in living as well as about oneself. Consequently, in this light, countertransference is not something to be feared. Instead it is an inevitable process which needs to be recognized, uncovered, and dealt with in a useful direct fashion each time it appears.

Recognizing and Uncovering Countertransference. Self-awareness and use of a consistent therapeutic style are the best measures to prevent countertransference from developing and remaining hidden. Counselors who monitor personal feelings and thoughts on a regular basis while with clients can readily appreciate how they are responding to them. By using a consistent style in dealing with patients, counselors can become sensitive to those times that they for some reason (i.e., possibly countertransference) veer from their normal approach. Such variance would be a clue that something the patient is doing might somehow be eliciting an unwarranted response. This allows one to get a quick grasp on the situation before it goes on unnoticed and unchecked for a long—and possibly destructive—period of time.

Chessick (1974) says that helping agents should treat those who come for help in a courteous fashion, but one that has normal reserve. He suggests to secular therapists that they behave toward their patients as if they were guests in their home and their spouse were present. In another attempt to bring the point across he also suggests preventing countertransference from being acted upon by doing only those things in therapy that can easily be shared with one's colleagues without hesitation or embarrassment.

One of the most succinct listings of ways to recognize and quickly uncover potential countertransferences is presented by Karl Menninger in his book *Theory of Psychoanalytic Technique* (1962, p. 88):

The following are some (countertransferences) I have jotted down at various times during seminars and control sessions in which they appeared: I think that I have myself been guilty of practically all of them.

Inability to understand certain kinds of material which touch on the analyst's own personal problems.

Depressed or uneasy feelings during or after analytic hours with certain patients.

Carelessness in regard to arrangements—forgetting the patient's appointment, being late for it, letting the patient's hour run overtime for no special reason.

Persistent drowsiness (of the analyst) during the analytic hour.

Over- or under-assiduousness in financial arrangements with the patient, for example, letting him become considerably indebted without analyzing it, or trying to "help" him to get a loan.

Repeatedly experiencing erotic or affectionate feelings toward a patient.

Permitting and even encouraging resistance in the form of acting-out.

Security seeking, narcissistic devices such as trying to impress the patient in various ways, or to impress colleagues with the importance of one's patient.

Cultivating the patient's continued dependence in various ways, especially by unnecessary reassurances.

The urge to engage in professional gossip concerning a patient.

Sadistic, unnecessary sharpness in formulation of comments and interpretations, and the reverse.

Feeling that the patient must get well for the sake of the doctor's reputation and prestige.

"Hugging the case to one's bosom," i.e., being too afraid of losing the patient.

Getting conscious satisfaction from the patient's praise, appreciation, and evidences of affection, and so forth.

Becoming disturbed by the patient's persistent reproaches and accusations.

Arguing with the patient.

Premature reassurances against the development of anxiety in the patient or, more accurately, finding oneself unable to gauge the point of optimum frustration tension.

Trying to help the patient in extra-analytic ways, for example, in making financial arrangements, or housing arrangements.

A compulsive tendency to "hammer away" at certain points. Recurrent impulses to ask favors of the patient.

Sudden increase or decrease of interest in a certain case.

Dreaming about the patient.

Though Menninger is directing his comments to those involved in doing analysis, they can also help pastoral counselors or psychotherapists to appreciate when they are responding or acting in an unusual fashion during the session. Some religious counselors though may feel that the comments don't apply to them. For instance, some may say, "Well as part of my work I have to help persons with their finances, so his comments with respect to that area and similar ones just don't apply to me."

When pastoral workers are helping in this way they are involved in the process of social work. This certainly is an important part of ministerial work but at the same time such efforts may hinder the psychotherapeutic process. Active social work is difficult to undertake at the same time as counseling. So, at the very least, Menninger's comments can provide guidelines to help determine which role we are assuming with the person coming for help. Many roles are therapeutic in nature; social work is certainly one of them. However, one can't be everything to everyone, and counseling, of its very nature, has certain limits and structures built into it. Not seeing this may result in frustration for both the counselor and the patient.

Another reason this list is important for pastoral counselors is that it helps them to keep in mind the old maxim: "Give a person a fish, feed him for a day; teach him to fish, feed him for life." Training in the ministry may encourage *doing* in the sense of active intervention even when it isn't the best course of action.

In many cases direct intervention may be warranted, but reaching out to others in a social work fashion is not always called for and sometimes has negative results. Rather than helping the person to become independent our active efforts to intervene in their lives result in encouraging infantile dependence. Instead of learning how they may help themselves put their lives and situation in perspective on their own, their own coping abilities are undercut.

Some pastoral counselors would also vehemently and quickly dismiss the Menninger guidelines as being inappropriate for them on other grounds. They would argue that their pastoral role supersedes their purely therapeutic one and that such limits are only for secular therapists. For instance, Natale (1977) says, "When at the end of a long and tiresome day the pastoral counselor agrees to see yet another patient, the counselor is expressing a Christian acceptance which surpasses psychological theory" (p. 20).

This distinction would seem to be a questionable one. A good counselor or psychotherapist would see another patient at the end of the day *if it were an emergency.* if not, there is a questionable advantage in seeing yet another person. Counselors model healthy limit-setting for patients and help them learn to fulfill their needs within the givens of reality whenever possible. In addition, when a pattern of expending energies without an appreciation of personal limits exists, it may lead to burnout. Moreover, in falling into the trap of trying to meet every need that people bring to him no matter how great it is, the counselor is demonstrating the pattern referred to as the "savior complex."

This pattern results when individuals unconsciously accept the role of savior and believe they can produce results in all cases without the process taking a personal toll. From the Christian perspective it is a distortion of the belief that with Christ anything is possible.

Part of the reason why this is especially a problem for pastoral counselors is due to their obvious connection with the church. In being seen as aligned with religion, persons may transfer the feelings they have toward God onto the religious who is a counselor. The same problems pastors have with their parishioners, persons who are pastoral counselors can expect to have. In terms of the "savior complex," this may especially be so with very dependent types of individuals, as can be seen in the following comments by Pattison (1965, p. 197): "Infantile images ultimately affect the pastoral role....The person who sees God as a protective, all-giving, warm mother may expect the pastor to be all-giving and ever-protective, and react with anger if the pastor does not fulfill these expectations. Those who react to authority with a passive-submissive stance may acquiesce to all suggestions as if they were commands. Or, they may react angrily if the pastor does not give them explicit guidance or commands to follow; they demand to be told what to do." It isn't any wonder then that many pastoral counselors give in to strong transferences and try to fulfill the unresolved needs of others by being God-like; the "advantage" is to avoid the immediate wrath and disappointment of those whose view of God and life is immature.

Menninger's guidelines, and the limits and norms of the therapeutic situation discussed here and later in the book, need to be modified in certain situations by the pastoral counselor; this much is true. However, too often these modifications of the therapeutic guidelines are indicative of countertransference on the part of the pastoral counselor, rather than as an example of a necessary exception which is an outgrowth of the fact that the therapist is answering a higher call to God. Therefore, whenever possible, counselors need to work hard to be aware of themselves and their normal style of helping others and think through any exception to the therapeutic rules they have set down. In this way, when a decision is made to make an exception and go the extra mile with the person, it will be to benefit the patient and not to satisfy the counselor's anxiety or unconscious needs in some way.

Dealing with Countertransference. Countertransterence exists; though there are differing opinions, many now feel it can play an important facilitative role in therapy if dealt with properly. The following then is a logical question: How should countertransference be handled so it can be beneficial rather than counterproductive in the treatment?

Some of the primary methods for dealing with countertransference include:

1. Personal analysis/intensive psychotherapy and/or systematic self-analysis
2. Supervision
3. Case-by-case countertransference review
4. Consultation with a colleague
5. Reanalysis

All of these approaches except the last two are primarily preventive in nature. That is, they are designed to keep the countertransference from getting unruly to the point where it becomes destructive and resistant to use in the service of the patient. The final two approaches are interventions which may be necessary when a block cannot be overcome through the use of the other methods listed above.

Personal Analysis/Intensive Psychotherapy and/or Systematic Self-Analysis. The reasons for entering religious life, the fields of psychiatry and psychology, or becoming a pastoral counselor are quite varied. No one reason motivates each person who enters one of these special helping professions. Also, no decision made is a *totally* mature one.

Everyone brings to religious and mental health work primitive motives from childhood. Freud felt that much of people's search for happiness is based on a continuing desire to gratify childhood needs. The person who becomes a pastoral counselor is not exempt from this. Neither is the psychologist or person in ministry. Such immature needs may include the desire to work out personal problems in the process of helping others, a voyeuristic urge to see others in an intimate light, or a need to have the power of one who occupies a position of authority.

Everyone has seen instances of this. There is the psychiatrist who rationalizes being seductive to his patients—possibly to the point of even having sexual relations with them; the minister who uses the pulpit to increase his or her feelings of personal mastery rather than as a means of spreading the word of God; and also the person who enters religious life as a means of running away from his or her feelings of personal or sexual inadequacy at home. Unchecked and unanalyzed, these persons can move forward on a path which is self-destructive and harmful to those they are meant to serve.

Going through a process of personal therapy or systematic self-analysis is a necessary prelude to working as a pastoral counselor. There is no way around it. While working with others in an intense fashion, counselors must have a good grasp on who they are and how they are reacting to their patients. In expecting patients to be courageous and to look at themselves, the counselor must first go through the process personally. The more the counselor understands and has worked through childhood motivations, needs, and conflicts, the greater the chances are of being helpful to patients. The more maturely integrated one is as a person—or, in analytic jargon, the less fractious one's ego is—the less likely it is for that individual to stray into an immature arena of self-gratification at the expense of the patient.

A pastoral counselor then must look carefully inward and attempt to get in touch with unconscious issues. To accomplish this, entering into a contract with an experienced mental health professional for the purpose of a personal analysis or intensive psychotherapy is normally recommended. This is supplemented during and after the personal analysis is terminated with a structured systematic process of self-analysis. (In some cases, people feel that a planned, thorough self-analysis is sufficient of itself without undertaking a personal therapy as well. This is *not* a widely accepted position today.) William Glasser in his book *Reality Therapy* (1965) referred to therapy as "an intensified version of the growth process." Self-analysis is designed to take the knowledge achieved in therapy/analysis a step further out of the consulting room and into the world. Even when therapy is officially terminated, it is carried on by the patient (in this case, the pastoral counseling novice) throughout his or her life.

When a decision is made to go into therapy, the question subsequently arising is: Whom should I get for a therapist? Implied in this question are at least three others: Does the therapist have to be of my own faith? What kind of theoretical orientation should he or she have (i.e., must he or she be an analyst)? Is there some place I can go to find someone so I don't have to just look up a name in the phone book?

These are specific questions that need to be faced by a religious who is looking for a therapist. The answers to the more general ones would require too lengthy a treatment for inclusion here. Also, this information has been sufficiently covered elsewhere. (For a compact discussion, the reader is referred to Chapter 11 in the book *Helping Others*, Wicks, 1982; for a more comprehensive coverage, the reader is referred to the following authors who have recently published books entirely devoted to the topic: Ehrenberg and Ehrenberg, 1977; Kovel, 1976; Mishara and Patterson, 1977; Park and Shapiro, 1976.)

There remain, though, a number of specific questions which relate particularly to the pastoral counselor who is seeking a personal therapist. For instance, there has always been debate about whether a person should seek personal therapy with someone of the same faith. There is no clear answer to this question.

Some would indicate that it might be wise for the pastoral psychotherapy intern to seek a person of the same faith who would be attuned to his or her religious lifestyle. Others would take the opposite position. They would point out that a fresh point of view from someone not steeped in the same religious tradition is preferable.

A possibly more reasonable approach to the issue than either of the previous two extremes is to pick someone who believes in the existence of God and respects the religious way of life. Belief in God would seem to be a baseline since it would be difficult to attain enough empathy with the religious if the therapist did not see God as a relevant, important entity.

With regard to respect, unless there is an appreciation of the religious way of life, bias could interfere. For instance, if there were a lack of respect for a Catholic priest's or sister's vow of celibacy, then the therapist might quickly assume the vow was the problem each time this type of religious came into therapy.

When respect and acceptance are there though, such difficulties can be avoided. A therapist who believes in God may not be someone who focuses strongly on having the Holy Spirit as an affective life-giving element of life. However, this same therapist could still treat pentecostals or charismatic Catholics and respect their type of worship and style of involvement with God.

In line with this respect, there must also be present an ability to question anything about the style of faith the religious holds. Respect for the way a person believes does not preclude this. This point is very important since religion like anything else can be employed defensively.

Therapeutic orientation is also important to ascertain. A pastoral counseling intern need not go into analysis which involves three to five sessions a week for a number of years with a professional whose theoretical base is Freudian or neo-Freudian. Some interns *may* choose this route, but it is not necessary or even the best approach for everyone. On the other hand, the therapist chosen should be someone whose professional orientation includes at least some psychoanalytic theory and practice—in other words, someone who does what we refer to as "intensive psychotherapy."

In reality, most therapists today are labeled as "eclectic." This means that they have integrated a number of schools of thought into their therapy. If the therapist has done this, yet still retains the primary features of psychoanalytically-oriented psychotherapy, then this individual would probably be suitable from a theoretical standpoint. Discussion regarding the therapist's orientation is certainly appropriate in the first session. By the same token, those desirous of doing intensive pastoral psychotherapy themselves someday (which by definition is in part based on depth psychology) are cautioned from having their own personal therapy done by a professional who is far afield from analytically oriented psychotherapy—i.e., Behavorist, Gestaltist, Transactional Analysis therapist, etc.

Help in choosing a particular therapist can be sought from the headquarters of the group to which the religious belongs. For example, many Catholic archdioceses maintain a list of approved therapists for Catholic religious/laity who request mental health assistance. Local theology schools and centers for pastoral counseling and psychotherapy can also provide assistance. Naturally, there is also the less reliable, but frequently helpful, source of other members of one's religious denomination who have had past experiences with therapists residing in the area. Whatever the method used though, this choice is an important one, so it should be made with care.

Supervision. The same principles involved in obtaining a healthy, well-trained, appropriate therapist are applicable in the choice of seeking a counseling supervisor. Supervision is the key to useful consolidation of therapeutic theories and skills. In working with patients, the pastoral counselor begins the delicate process of taking knowledge from lectures, readings, and tapes, and applying this information in actual encounters with other persons.

What may have seemed quite clear in a book can become quite confusing in an *in vivo* situation. Principles are guidelines; they form attitudes, but they do not provide a real understanding of what it is like to be a counselor.

This comes with experience. Supervision provides help in becoming more attuned to one's personal approaches and countertransferences, and is a step toward integrating good theory and practice in a way that ultimately results in positive professional growth and formation.

Expense is often cited as a reason why a supervisor is not obtained after graduation. This is shortsighted since the tuition for a pastoral counseling/psychotherapy program or course is probably much greater than the fees that are paid for supervision. Yet, without supervision the value of having completed a pastoral program would be greatly limited.

Another reason for not obtaining supervision after completing a program is that some supervision is experienced as part of pastoral training. This help, though necessary, is not enough. The completion of formal training is an ideal juncture at which to seek supervision. It is at this point that professional formation and growth are accelerated and consolidated.

In the beginning of supervision there is much focus on countertransference. This information is invaluable. Even for the novice who has undergone a personal therapy, this is the case. After this focus on the countertransference has been given primary attention, a bulk of the time is then given to the technique and style of the counselor. Both of these phases of supervision enable the pastoral counselor/therapist to integrate, solidify, and elucidate a personal—probably eclectic—therapeutic philosophy to the point where it becomes vital and powerful.

Case-by-Case Countertransference Review. Counselors generally take the time to jot down notes on their sessions. This is usually done immediately after the session. The complex aspects of the interaction are fresh then. If time or circumstances do not permit, notes are made at the end of the day after all patients have been seen. Whichever method is chosen, such a time is an ideal opportunity to do a countertransference review as well.

Each session can be reviewed for process and content—the former being the theme and unspoken flow of the session, the latter being the specific issues that were addressed. The process is the music, the content the lyrics; both are important to examine and thus determine how the counselor felt and responded during the session.

Even though immediate monitoring of reactions and feelings is done, a written review of thoughts, feelings, and anxieties felt after the session is also essential. In doing this for each session important revealing patterns develop. This makes it easier to see the consistent, particular technique ("countertransference structure"—Racker, 1968) one is developing and using with different patients.

In conducting a case-by-case review, the following questions are usually presented. What did the person say and how did he or she come across? How did I feel being with the person today? Did my attitude or affect change within, and possibly without (visibly), in my dealings with the patient during certain points in the session? What is my present attitude toward the patient as a result of this past therapeutic encounter with him or her? As these questions are answered the unconscious levels and nuances in the style the patient is using at this point in the therapeutic relationship come to light. By monitoring countertransferences, much can be learned about messages the patient is sending as well as about the therapist's response. As a matter of fact, the process can even aid in arriving at a preliminary diagnosis. This can be seen in the following chart for pastors by Lee (1980, p. 12).

Pastor's Feelings	**Possible Diagnosis of the Person**
Male pastor feels actually aroused	Hysteria
by the female patient	Sociopath or narcissistic
Feeling used or manipulated	Passive-dependent
Feeling guilty	Obsessive-compulsive or passive-
Feeling annoyed, frustrated and	aggressive
angry	Schizophrenia, borderline syndrome
Feeling afraid	or primary affective disorder
Feeling attacked or provoked	Paranoia

So, being in tune with countertransference from the very *first* contact can facilitate counseling and provide invaluable information from which original hypotheses can be developed. As the counseling proceeds, personal feelings should be continually monitored to see if the diagnosis as well as the thrust of the treatment needs to be altered.

Countertransferences represent not only the counselor's own unconscious communication to self, but the patient's unconscious communication to the counselor as well. In the above chart, when the male pastor feels actually aroused by the female patient, he is coming in touch with his own primitive sexual needs (i.e., the need to be loved and recognized, the need for status—to be attractive to others). However, he is also getting the unconscious message from the patient that she wishes to have control, to demonstrate her (sexual) power to win over (conquer) an important person like the pastor. For the patient, the issue is power, not sexual attraction; the hysterical person does not have a mature sexual interest, but is seeking to demonstrate personal mastery over someone else—albeit in an immature aggressive fashion.

This process is all on the unconscious level. Thus, if the pastor responded to the sexual overtones, or even was physically warm in gesture, problems might result. The patient whose behavior is unconsciously motivated might interpret the pastor's putting his arm around her as a gesture that he is seriously. and intimately interested in her. The result of this might be that she would withdraw and accuse the pastor of improper advances, or proceed to think that he wants to become involved with her further. In either case, the pastor is in for difficulty because he did not monitor his countertransference sufficiently to see both his own unresolved needs and the immature style his parishioner was displaying.

Consultation with a Colleague. One of the easiest and most rewarding ways of dealing with the countertransference is to consult with one's colleagues. They are often able to shed new light on a case because of their distance from it. Presenting case material to a colleague helps to get additional data on the flow of the therapy and shows where the pastoral counselor's involvement in it is problematic. In presenting a case for review, the following minimal elements are necessary: case history; transcript of one or two recent sessions; review of personal feelings and questions about the patient with illustrations of what the therapist believes is producing them. In the event one colleague isn't of help, seeking the input of another senior colleague or supervisor is usually in order.

To seek such assistance takes a degree of courage and humility. Yet, in doing this the counselor is merely modeling the courage patients are being asked to have—i.e., to be open to the views and insights of others so it is possible to understand one's own personality and its ramifications more clearly. This point cannot be emphasized enough.

Reanalysis. In some cases, all of the preventive methods and interventions do not seem to help. In such an instance, possibly entry or reentry into a personal psychotherapy is indicated. Sexual involvement with a patient or extreme feelings of depression or anger which cannot be worked through by other methods would indicate that there is a conflict which needs to be examined and dealt with in a direct manner.

When problems arise which are resistant to any kind of normal intervention some counselors unfortunately do not have the courage to ask for help from a colleague or to enter into a personal therapy; instead they build up a new so-called "therapeutic philosophy" based on their defenses. So, rather than trying to see why it is that they are acting-out their impulses to make love or be angry at certain patients, they develop a type of "treatment" (love therapy? confrontation treatment?) which incorporates their sexual and aggressive infantile impulses and actions.

This is sad and unfortunately occurs more often than one would like to think possible.

Link of Countertransference with Burnout. A good deal of attention has been given to dealing with countertransference so it does not reach the proportion where it interferes with the counselor's work with the *patient/ client.* However, there are extreme problems which can result for the counselor as well if countertransference is not noticed in time and curbed. This is clearly presented by Chessic (1974, pp. 166, 167) in his discussion of Wile's (1972) comments on the dire results possible with prolonged unanalyzed countertransference.

> The therapist must systematically struggle within himself to understand and master the forces of countertransference structure, which always interfere with his correct understanding and interpretations to the patient.
>   ...In every psychotherapy the therapist "learns" from his patients. He expands his boundaries of human understanding, increases his maturity, and achieves further ego integration. Conversely, unanalyzed negative countertransference experiences over a prolonged period of time can produce what Wile (1972) calls "therapeutic discouragement," an irrational pessimism regarding his therapeutic work and his personal life. This leads to premature termination of therapy cases, and even to the abandonment of the profession itself, the susceptibility to new fads and short-cut active techniques, or an irrational overoptimism and overconfidence in one's powers of healing. Perhaps worst of all, "Deprived of his sense of purpose and value in what he is doing, the therapist may turn to his patient for compensatory reassurance and affirmation."

In the above quote, we see how countertransference and burnout are connected. If one is constantly trying to gratify childhood needs by letting primitive conflicts and inadequacies rule unchecked and unnoticed, the helper will either end up burnt out and want to leave the field, or will act out in a potentially harmful, exploitive way to the patient. This point is helpful to keep in mind in looking at burnout in terms of the person involved in ministry and pastoral care, for it helps to tie together both the topics of countertransference and burnout, thus providing a common ground from which to work when examining both issues.

Burnout

Some people see the concept of burnout as being unnecessary since the same material (i.e., symptoms and signs) are covered when talking about problems that are already defined in the literature. So, when referring to the signs of burnout and the interventions needed to prevent or lessen its symptoms, some say that it is confusing the issue unnecessarily because we are really talking about symptoms and signs similar to those encountered by therapists when they are experiencing stress, depression and undetected countertransference. Be this as it may, the term is still seen as being helpful here. If for nothing else, it makes it legitimate for counselors to experience such negative feelings. Moreover, it provides an integrated way to look at the emotional stress and depression that human services workers and other invested people commonly experience to some degree in their work.

Gill (1980, p. 21) in an article on burnout in the ministry wryly notes that "helping people can be extremely hazardous to your physical and mental health." When Gill (1980, pp. 24, 25) goes on to indicate which religious are likely to experience burnout, it sounds as if he is certainly talking about (among others) the pastoral counselor:

Judging from the research done in recent years, along with clinical experience, it appears that those who fall into the following categories are generally the most vulnerable: (1) those who work exclusively with distressed persons; (2) those who work intensively with demanding people who feel entitled to assistance in solving their personal and social problems; (3) those who are charged with the responsibility for too many individuals; (4) those who feel strongly motivated to work with people but who are prevented from doing so by too many administrative paper work tasks; (5) those who have an inordinate need to save people from their undesirable situations but find the task impossible; (6) those who are very perfectionist and thereby invite failure; (7) those who feel guilty about their own human needs (which, if met, would enable them to serve others with stamina, endurance and emotional equanimity); (8) those who are too idealistic in their aims; (9) those whose personality is such that they need to champion underdogs; (10) those who cannot tolerate variety, novelty, or diversion in their work life; and (11) those who lack criteria for measuring the success of their undertakings but who experience an intense need to know that they are doing a good job.

In reviewing his list, seeing the role again that countertransference plays in burnout is easy. With a distortion of one's actual role, potential impact, and actual abilities, a pastoral counselor can set himself up for burnout. Likewise when one is not aware of underlying needs and conflicts, being thrust in the direction of overcommitment and resultant physical and mental exhaustion is easy.

In one of the first book-length treatments of burnout among people in the human services, Edelwich and Brodsky (1980, p. 14) define the term as a "progressive loss of idealism, energy, and purpose experienced by people in the helping professions." They and authors like Freudenberger (1980), Malasch (1980), Gill (1980) and others follow this definition or one similar to it and indicate various causes, warning signs, and levels of development of burnout.

Causes, Levels, Signs, and Interventions. Most authors have developed their own unique list of burnout causes. There is much overlap though, and all of them seem to point to the problem as being a *lack* which produces frustration. It can be a deficiency of such things as: education, opportunity, free time, ability, chance to ventilate, institutional power, variety, meaningful tasks, criteria to measure impact, coping mechanisms, staff harmony, professional and personal recognition, insight into one's motivations, balance in one's schedule, and emotional distance from the client population.

Since the factors on the above list are present to some degree in every human services setting, the potential for burnout is always present. When it reaches the point where it becomes destructive, such statements (by pastoral psychotherapists and counselors) can be heard as: "I wish she wouldn't show up to see me today. I'm fed up with her constant demands. So, she's divorced and having problems with her six children; what does she expect me to do anyway?" "If I see one more person who says he is lonely I'm going to scream. Why don't they just go out and shake the bushes and meet someone?" "Another group of cases today. The same old problems with new faces. I could care less." "What's the sense in my helping them? Nothing ever comes of it. I work hard and the rest of the people involved mess it up." "This is ridiculous. I'm way over my head. I don't know what I'm doing, and there's nowhere to turn for some guidance. What a fake I am. How come I don't have anyone to turn to for help?" Frustration, depression, apathy, helplessness, being overwhelmed, impatience— they all appear to some degree at each level of burnout.

Figure 1

Level 1—Daily Burnout:
A Sampling of Key Signs and Symptoms

Mentally fatigued at the end of a day

Feeling unappreciated, frustrated, bored, tense, or angry as a result of a contact(s) with patients, colleagues, supervisors, superiors, assistants, or other potentially significant people

Experiencing physical symptoms (i.e., headache, backache, upset stomach, etc.)

Pace of day's activities and/or requirements of present tasks seem greater than personal or professional resources available

Tasks required on job are repetitious, beyond the ability of the therapist, or require intensity on a continuous basis

There are any number of ways to break down the levels in order to understand the progression of burnout. Gill (1980, pp. 22, 23) does it in the following way: "The first level is characterized by signs (capable of being observed) and symptoms (subjectively experienced) that are relatively mild, short in duration, and occur only occasionally....The second level is reached when signs and symptoms have become more stable, last longer, and are tougher to get rid of....The third is experienced when signs and symptoms have become chronic and a physical and psychological illness has developed."

The above commonsense breakdown is very much in line with the medical model and there is some overlap between levels. While they could be applied to any physical or psychological constellation of symptoms and signs, they provide a reasonable way of delineating a breakdown of the burnout syndrome. The third level is self-explanatory. And in line with what is known about serious prolonged countertransference from earlier in this chapter, the signs, symptoms, and treatment are obvious.

If a counselor is experiencing a life crisis and undergoing notable ongoing psychosomatic problems, then it means that preventive measures and self-administered treatments have failed. Psychological and medical assistance is necessary. This may mean entering or re-entering psychotherapy and obtaining, as advised by the therapist, medical help if necessary. Once this third level has been reached, the burnout is severe and remediation of the problem will likely take a good deal of time and effort.

Figure 2

Level 1—Daily Burnout:
Steps for Dealing with "Daily Burnout"

---

1. Correcting one's cognitive errors so there is a greater recognition when we are exaggerating or personalizing situations in an inappropriate, negative way ("The patient canceled his appointment; I guess he didn't want to see me because I'm not doing a very good job and he didn't like me.")

2. Having a variety of activities in one's daily schedule

3. Getting sufficient rest

4. Faithfully incorporating meditation time into our daily schedule

5. Interacting on a regular basis with supportive friends

6. Being assertive

7. Getting proper nourishment and exercise

8. Being aware of the general principles set forth in the professional and self-help literature on stress management (Schafer, 1978; Selye, 1976; Speilberger and Sarason, 1975, 1977; Sarason and Speilberger, 1975, 1976)

And so, to avoid reaching level three becomes imperative. To accomplish this, one should be attuned to burnout as it is experienced in Level 1 (see Figure 1) and in its more extreme forms in Level 2. Level 1 can be aptly termed "Daily Burnout." Everyone experiences a little bit of burnout each day. In most instances dealing with it is possible by taking some or all of the following steps (see Figure 2).

In Level 2 (see Figure 3), where the burnout problem has become more severe and intractable to brief interventions, a more profound effort is necessary. Central to such actions is a willingness to reorient priorities and take risks with one's style of dealing with the world, which for some reason is not working optimally.

To accomplish this, frequently one's colleagues, spiritual director, and psychological mentor need to become involved. Their support and insight for dealing with the distress being felt is needed. The uncomfortable steps taken to unlock oneself from social problems and the temptation to deal with them in a single unproductive way (repetition compulsion) requires all of the guidance and support one can obtain. In many cases, this also requires

Figure 3

**Level 2—Minor Stress Becomes Distress:
Some Major Signs and Symptoms**

Idealism and enthusiasm about being a pastoral counselor waning; disillusionment about counseling and being a counselor surfacing on a regular basis

Experiencing a general loss of interest in the mental health field for a period of a month or longer

Pervading feeling of boredom, stagnation, apathy, and frustration

Being ruled by schedule; seeing more and more patients; being no longer attuned to them; viewing them impersonally and without thought

Losing criteria with which to judge the effectiveness of work coupled with lack of belief in appropriateness of one's approach

Inability to get refreshed by the other elements in one's life

A loss of interest in professional resources (i.e., books, conferences, innovations, etc.) in the fields of psychology and theology

Intermittent lengthy (week or more) periods of irritation, depression, and stress which do not seem to lift even with some effort to correct the apparent causes

a break from work for a vacation or retreat in order to distance oneself from the work for a time so that revitalization and reorientation can occur.

Everyone experiences Level 1 burnout; most pastoral counselors experience Level 2, and some of us, unfortunately, experience Level 3. This reality indicates why counselors should do all in their power to prevent self-ignorance from replacing self-awareness. Looking at and utilizing personal strengths, readings, experiences, mentors, and interpersonal support groups is essential. Also, riding the inevitable small waves of countertransference and burnout so that they don't turn into an emotional tidal wave is an effort that needs daily repetition.

The literature on burnout, stress and countertransference also implies something else important, namely, that everyone can learn and benefit even from serious problems in living *if there is a willingness to turn to others for help*. It is this last lesson that sorrowfully some mental health and religious professionals don't learn. And it is at this juncture that they either give up and despair, or bring on great denial which leads to the exploitation of others.

Bibliography

Chessick, R. *Technique and Practice of Intensive Psychotherapy.* New York: Aronson, 1974.

Edelwich, J. and Brodsky, A. *Burnout: Stages of Disillusionment in the Helping Professions.* New York: Human Sciences Press, 1980.

Ehrenberg, O. and Ehrenberg, E.M. *The Psychotherapy Maze.* New York: Holt, Rinehard, and Winston, 1977.

Fenichel, O. *The Psychoanalytic Theory of Neurosis.* New York: Norton. 1945.

Freud, S. and Pfister, O. *Psychoanalytic and Faith: The Letters of Sigmund Freud and Oskar Pfister.* H. Meng and E. L. Freud, editors. New York: Basic Books, 1963.

Freudenberger, H. *Burnout.* New York: Anchor Book/Doubleday, 1980.

Fromm-Reichmann, F. *Principles of Intensive Psychotherapy.* Chicago: University of Chicago Press, 1950.

Gill, J. "Burnout: A Growing Threat in the Ministry." *Human Development,* 1 (2), Summer 1980, 21–27.

Glasser, W. *Reality Therapy.* New York: Harper & Row. 1965.

Kovel, J. *A Complete Guide to Therapy.* New York: Pantheon Books, 1976.

Langs, R. *The Technique of Psychoanalytic Psychotherapy.* Volume II. New York: Aronson, 1974.

Lee, R. R. *Clergy and Clients: The Practice of Pastoral Psychotherapy.* New York: Seabury, 1980.

Maslach, C. "Burned-Out," *Human Behavior,* September 1976.

Menninger, K. *Theory of Psychoanalytic Technique.* New York: Basic Books, 1958.

Mishara, B. L. and Patterson, R. D. *Consumer's Guide to Mental Health.* New York: Times Books, 1977.

Natale, S. *Pastoral Counseling: Reflections and Concerns.* New York: Paulist Press, 1977.

Oates, W. E. *Pastoral Counseling.* Philadelphia: Westminster, 1974.

Park, C. C. and Shapiro, L. N. *You Are Not Alone.* Boston: Little-Brown. 1976.

Pattison, E. "Transference and Countertransference in Pastoral Care." *The Journal of Pastoral Care,* 19, Winter 1965, 193–202.

Racker, H. *Transference and Countertransference,* New York: International Universities Press, 1968.

Ruesh, J. *Therapeutic Communication.* New York: Norton, 1961.

Sarason, I. and Speilberger, C. (eds.). *Stress and Anxiety Vols. II and III.* New York: Wiley, 1975, 1976.

Schafer, W. *Stress, Distress, and Growth.* Davis, California: Responsible Action, 1978.

Selye, H. *The Stress of Life* (revised edition). New York: McGraw-Hill, 1976.

Speilberger, C. and Sarason, I. (eds.). *Stress and Anxiety Vols. I and IV.* 1975, 1977.

Tarachow, S. *An Introduction to Psychotherapy.* New York: International Universities Press, 1963.

Tauber, E. S. "Exploring the Therapeutic Use of Countertransference Data." *Psychiatry,* 17: 331–336, 1954.

Wicks, R. *Christian Introspection: Self-Ministry Through Self-Understanding.* New York: Crossroad Book, 1983.

Wicks, R. *Helping Others: Ways of Listening, Sharing and Counseling.* New York: Gardner Press, 1982.

Wile, D. "Negative Countertransference and Therapist Discouragement." *International Journal of Psychoanalytic Psychotherapy,* 1 (2), Summer 1980, 21–27.

Pamela Cooper-White

16. Sexual Exploitation and Other Boundary Violations in Pastoral Ministries

The inclusion of this chapter in the *Clinical Handbook of Pastoral Counseling vol. 3* signals an important and healthy shift in awareness among religious institutions about clergy professional sexual ethics and the problem of sexual misconduct. A great leap in awareness has occurred over the course of the past decade, in part prompted by religious institutions' growing commitment to address other forms of domestic and sexual abuse. Clergy violations of sexual boundaries with members of their congregations, once almost universally cloaked in secrecy, denial, or patterns of blaming the victim, are now much more visible, as religious institutions have begun to make serious efforts toward policymaking, preventative education, screening of candidates for ministry, intervention in reported cases of misconduct, and healing for individuals, families, and congregations in the aftermath of abuse. The codes of ethics of the American Association of Pastoral Counselors (AAPC) and the Association for Clinical Pastoral Education (ACPE) both formally prohibit sexual behavior with clients, patients, and students or supervisees (AAPC, 1994; ACPE, 1999). AAPC further prohibits sexual behavior with research subjects and employees other than spouses or domestic partners. Nevertheless, continued attention to the issue of sexual boundary violations by clergy is necessary, in order to build on the pioneering work done in the past decade and to more fully institutionalize a commitment to making all pastoral ministries and all places of worship harbors of safety for all people.

The focus of this chapter is on clergy sexual misconduct with adult congregants. However, in cases of child sexual abuse in a religious setting, many of the same principles and dynamics may also apply. Child victims of clergy sexual abuse must be treated, as with all cases of child abuse, in accordance with state reporting laws and in cooperation with local law enforcement and child protective agencies. Therapists working with child victims and their family members must also immediately notify appropriate religious authorities to prevent potential harm to other children. Although sexual abuse by clergy or religious leaders is technically extrafamilial abuse, the dynamics resemble incest, especially because clergy and congregational leaders are often treated like trusted relatives by adult family members, and congregations are often referred to as "families of faith." Clergy sexual abuse of children therefore carries all the devastations of incest, including family members' reactions of guilt, rage, or disbelief. It can destroy a child's inner sense of safety and protection, and gravely damage the child's sense of relationship with God. Pastoral counselors doing treatment with child victims and their families should receive specialized training and supervision in child sexual abuse intervention, and should familiarize themselves thoroughly with state laws and local child protective and law enforcement agencies. Clergy who abuse children must be reported to local law enforcement, and clinical treatment must be carried out by therapists specialized in treatment of sex offenders, in cooperation with law enforcement or probation.

The high prevalence of clergy sexual misconduct with adult congregants is increasingly being verified by research (summarized in Fortune, 1997). Surveys of female ministers, rabbis, church workers, and women congregants have shown rates of sexual harassment experienced in the religious context ranging from 21percent to 77 percent. Surveys of ministers in a variety of denominations show self-reported percentages of sexual contact ranging from 5.8 percent to 38.6 percent. In other studies, 70 percent of clergy report knowledge of other ministers who have had sexual contact with congregation members. Forty-two percent of pastoral counselors surveyed in a new study reported that a colleague had told them of committing sexual misconduct. Eighty-seven percent of these pastoral counselors reported treating at least one client who told them of experiencing sexual boundary violations by clergy, and many had treated five or more clients with similar reports (Cooper-White, 1999). Although sexual boundaries can be violated by both male and female clergy, in both heterosexual and same-sex relationships, experts continue to estimate that the vast preponderance of sexual misconduct (90–95 percent) is between male clergy and female congregants. As with all child sexual abuse, sexual abuse of children in religious settings is also committed largely by male heterosexual clergy or congregational leaders.

Pastoral counselors may be called upon to assist in situations of sexual misconduct in several ways: (1) counseling victims of clergy sexual misconduct; (2) counseling clergy who have crossed sexual boundaries with congregation members; (3) couples' and/or family counseling with the families of victims or offenders to deal with the secondary traumatization of family members and the disruptions of family relationships in the aftermath of the misconduct; and (4) consulting to congregations in need of healing during and after the disclosure of sexual boundary violations, and to interim clergy and "after-pastors" who are ministering to congregations in the aftermath of misconduct. This chapter is intended to provide a grounding in basic definitional, ethical and theological, and psychological understandings of the dynamics of clergy sexual misconduct with congregation members, and to offer some basic guidelines for counseling in these several situations. Of course, no one pastoral counselor can or should serve all the many persons affected in any given case of misconduct. A collaborative team approach is recommended, in which pastoral counselors, consultants, and judicatory staff may work together as appropriate, respecting the roles, boundaries, and primary accountabilities of each. In every aspect of this work, the safety of past, present, and future potential victims, the cessation of harmful behaviors, and the re-establishment of safety and justice must be the first priorities. Counselors who plan to specialize in this area, or who find themselves called upon to do this work because of a specific request for help or a referral, can avail themselves of the growing body of literature available on this subject (see chapter references), but they should also seek specialized training and clinical supervision before declaring this as a specific area of competency.

Clergy sexual misconduct has been analyzed from two different but complementary perspectives: (1) ethical and theological analyses, aimed primarily at prevention, appropriate intervention, and justice making; and (2) psychological or psychodynamic analyses, which provide a deeper understanding of why sexual misconduct occurs, how it typically is enacted, and what prevention and intervention measures are needed to address the deeper impact of misconduct on individuals, families, and congregations, and to promote safety in our houses of worship. Both approaches are helpful to pastoral counselors in understanding the complexities of individual cases.

First, some definitions are needed to clarify the various types of clergy sexual misconduct. It should be noted that in actual situations of sexual misconduct, many of these categories overlap or co-exist.

Definitions

Sexual harassment refers to inappropriate sexual language or behavior within the context of an employment, teaching, mentor, or colleague relationship between the persons involved. Sexual harassment, as legally defined by Title VII (Section 703) of the 1964 federal Civil Rights Act, is a form of sex discrimination that is an unlawful employment practice. As defined by the Equal Employment Opportunity Commission (EEOC), sexual harassment includes unwelcome sexual advances, requests for sexual favors, and other verbal or physical conduct of a sexual nature when 1) submission to such conduct is made either explicitly or implicitly a term or condition of an individual's employment, 2) submission to or rejection of such conduct by an individual is used as the basis for employment decisions affecting such individual; or 3) such conduct has the purpose or effect of unreasonably interfering with an individual's work performance or creating an intimidating, hostile, or offensive working environment.

Case law has further applied these EEOC definitions to educational settings under Title IX of the Education Amendments of 1972.

The first two criteria in the law constitute what is understood as *quid pro quo harassment* (from Latin, meaning "this for that"), in which the employee or student is expected to submit to sexualized behavior in exchange for fair supervision, that is, continuation of employment, promotion, fair evaluation, grades, or recommendations. The second criterion, which is sometimes more difficult for victims to prove, is called *hostile environment* or *condition of work harassment,* in which a sexualized atmosphere is created that a victim finds difficult to tolerate. Hostile environment harassment is the more common form of harassment because it is more subtle. But it is equally damaging, since it often has the effect of driving a victim away from an economic, educational, or vocational opportunity, and also frequently results in stress-related health problems. If a victim does manage to tolerate the hostile atmosphere, in the interests of keeping her job or educational situation, this often is taken (erroneously) as proof of her consent. *Gender harassment* is also a form of hostile environment harassment, in which the atmosphere is not necessarily sexualized, but the victim's gender itself is a target of hate speech, often accompanied by discriminatory practices. Racial and gender harassment are frequently combined to target women of color. Sexual and gender harassment are also frequently targeted at gay men and lesbians.

Sexual abuse technically refers to sexual contact with a minor or with an adult person who is legally incompetent to consent. Any physical contact with a person under the age of eighteen constitutes felony abuse, regardless of consent or even invitation by the minor. Even apparently consensual sexual activity with a minor constitutes statutory rape in all fifty states in the United States. Medical professionals, social workers, and counselors are mandated to report child abuse to the proper child protective agencies in all fifty states. Most states also mandate reporting of sexual abuse of adults who are deemed legally incompetent to care for themselves, and all states have adult protective services agencies.

The term *sexual abuse* is also frequently used more generally to refer to any sexual language or behavior that exploits the vulnerability of another person, including vulnerability due to a power differential in roles, for one's own sexual gratification. In fourteen of the fifteen states that have criminalized sexual contact between a psychotherapist and a client, clergy who do counseling for emotional or mental health problems are specifically included under the category of "psychotherapist." Two states, Minnesota and Texas, further specify that sexual contact by clergy with anyone for whom they have provided pastoral or spiritual counsel is also a felony.

Sexual exploitation is a betrayal of trust in a pastoral relationship by the development or the attempted development of a sexual or romantic relationship. Sexual exploitation occurs when any ordained priest, minister, pastor, rabbi, professional pastoral counselor, chaplain, or lay staff member in a defined ministry role (for example, Stephen minister, lay Eucharistic minister, minister of music, youth minister), participates in sexual behavior with any person served in that worker's ministry. Because of the unequal power inherent in all pastoral relationships, this holds true even when the person served initiates or apparently consents to the sexual behavior. Exploitative behavior can range from sexualized verbal comments, overt and covert seductive speech, gestures, and requests for sexual favors, to erotic kissing or touching, to sexual intercourse. In sexual exploitation, both the person who is the recipient of the sexual behavior and the office of ministry itself are being exploited for the sexual gratification of the religious leader who engages in the sexualized behavior.

Sexual misconduct is a violation of professional sexual ethics by clergy, counselors, chaplains, and other helping and teaching professionals, and may encompass any or all of the above categories of behavior.

Ethical and Theological Analysis

Until recently, clergy sexual misconduct was generally understood under the rubric of personal morality of the clergyperson. Sexual behavior with a member of the congregation was, and still frequently is, regarded as an "affair," identifying the wrong done by clergy as adultery, or in the case of single clergy, violating religious norms prohibiting sexual activity outside the marital bond. This view is severely limited, however, in that it fails to recognize the professional ethical and theological dimensions of sexualized language and behavior by clergy with members of their congregations. Recent ethical analyses have recognized that there is not only a personal moral dimension to sexual misconduct, but also a professional duty, or fiduciary responsibility, to care for congregants.

As the Rev. Marie Fortune (1989) has so clearly outlined in her pioneering book *Is Nothing Sacred?*, the primary issue is that in any professional helping relationship, there is an imbalance of power that eliminates the possibility of authentic consent on the part of a congregant. In Fortune's words, "Consent to sexual activity, in order to be authentic, must take place in a context of mutuality, choice, full knowledge, and equal power, and in the absence of coercion or fear. When there is an imbalance of power in a relationship, these necessary factors will not be present." (Fortune, 1989, p. 38) Sexual relating with persons in one's professional care is wrong for four interlocking ethical reasons: violation of professional role, misuse of authority and power, taking advantage of vulnerability, and absence of meaningful consent (Fortune, 1997). The authority of the pastoral office, however much the offending clergyperson may wish to downplay it, precludes a peer relationship in which the term "consenting adults" could be meaningful.

The clergy role carries a great deal of power in and of itself, especially for male ministers, infused with popular ideals about being a "man of God." Clergy may have multiple levels of spiritual and institutional authority in relation to congregants, not only in the general sense, as a visible leader or "CEO" of the congregation and many of its committees and subgroupings, but also with varying degrees of formal institutional authority as an employer, administrator, teacher, supervisor, mentor, and spiritual guide. Clergy frequently also act (with or without formal clinical training) as pastoral or spiritual counselors to congregants and their family members, sometimes briefly, but sometimes over long periods of time, with all the transference inherent in all counseling relationships. Home visitation and pastoral care in hospitals and nursing homes gives clergy and chaplains intimate access to congregation members in their most private settings and at their most vulnerable times.

Because of the unequal power and authority inherent in the pastoral relationship, it is always the responsibility of the clergyperson, as professional, to maintain appropriate boundaries. Although the majority of cases of clergy sexual exploitation occur at the clergyperson's initiative, sometimes members of the congregation attempt to initiate a sexual or romantic relationship. Sometimes vulnerable congregants are attracted by the power of the clergy role itself and the healing it seems to offer. In such cases it is unequivocally the clergyperson's responsibility to recognize the underlying need represented by the congregant's overtures, and to say "No" compassionately but clearly. This both protects the safety and dignity of the congregation member and preserves the integrity and the genuine healing potential of the pastoral relationship.

Clergy sexual misconduct causes harm to both primary victims, those who have been directly harassed, abused, or exploited, and many secondary victims—the families of both victim and offender, members of the congregation, the denomination, and even the surrounding community. Because of the universal imbalance of power between clergy and members of their congregations, and the potential for widespread harm, over the past decade denominations have increasingly developed policies that strictly prohibit sexual contact with congregants and also limit the pastoral counseling role of clergy serving in congregations. In some policies, single clergy dating of single adult members of the congregation is permitted, but is strictly circumscribed by admonitions to openness with congregational leaders and denominational authorities, adequate supervision, and provision of alternate pastoral care of these congregation members. While professional opinions vary on this somewhat (Fortune, 1989; Rutter, 1989; Lebacqz and Barton 1991; Rutter, 1991; Peterson, 1992; Cooper-White, 1995), the practice of single clergy dating single congregation members, even with appropriate disclosure to congregational and denominational leadership, presents a high risk for harm, not only to the member, but also in the potential for divisiveness in the whole congregation, and should be avoided.

Finally, from a theological perspective, the exploitation of congregation members violates fundamental biblical tenets of care for the vulnerable. Clergy sexual misconduct is not only a wrong because it stands outside accepted personal moral standards for both clergy and laity, but because it is a violation of justice. Persons join congregations in good faith, expecting their religious institutions to be places of safety and inspiration. Clergy sexual misconduct profoundly violates this trust. Further, because clergy and religious institutions come to represent the divine in many people's imaginations, sexual violations may even have deep repercussions upon congregation members' ability to trust God.

Psychodynamic Analysis

The issue of keeping good boundaries, while first and foremost an ethical duty, is not *only* an ethical and theological matter, but also a profoundly psychological one. Ethical and theological analyses are crucial in educating clergy about the importance of prevention of harm, and in educating religious institutions more generally about the need for policies with clear-cut reporting procedures, fair processing of complaints, and clear-cut consequences for misconduct that prevent harm to future potential victims. However, policies and prohibitions, no matter how clear, have never altogether stopped an offender caught in the grip of a powerful unconscious impulse.

Because being "above the law" is a common psychological defense in the profile of clergy sexual offenders, ethical education and policies may be regarded as applying to everyone else, but not to him. Some understanding of the unconscious dynamics of sexual misconduct is helpful, both in screening candidates for ministry and in recognizing and intervening in cases of abuse.

The unconscious dynamics of clergy sexual misconduct can be understood in two ways: (1) through the transference-countertransference relationship, and (2) through an understanding of the psychological profile of clergy who cross sexual boundaries with those in their care.

As in all helping relationships, there is a transference-countertransference dynamic operating in and between both the clergyperson and the congregant or student or counselee. *Transference* refers to the expectations, fears, and wishes that a congregation member unconsciously projects or *transfers* onto the clergyperson from early childhood experiences with caregivers and other powerful figures during his or her formative years. *Countertransference* refers to the parallel childhood-based projections transferred by the clergyperson onto the congregant or counselee, as well as a wide range of feelings, thoughts, and fantasies that may be evoked by the transference of the counselee. Transference and countertransference are universal phenomena in helping relationships, whether or not the helping professional is aware of the dynamic.

The less trained or aware the professional is regarding the dynamic of transference and countertransference, the more likely he is to fail to recognize the pulls and impulses arising from the dynamic, and to behave reactively rather than therapeutically. In particular, most psychotherapists are trained to recognize the specific phenomenon of *erotic transference,* involving an intense feeling of love and desire on the part of a counselee. They know not to react sexually but to use this phenomenon as information to guide them in appropriate care for the client. However, many clergy who have had little or no formal clinical background may not recognize the transferential dynamic for what it is, and find themselves feeling flattered and enthralled in a countertransference reaction of grandiosity and sexual arousal.

The element of grandiosity aroused in the countertransference points to the other important aspect of psychodynamics in clergy sexual misconduct, namely, the inner psychological structure of clergy who cross sexual boundaries. Various typologies of offenders have been proposed, including a twofold typology of "wanderer" versus "predator" (Fortune, 1989), and a sixfold typology ranging from uninformed or naïve, healthy or mildly neurotic, severely neurotic and/or socially isolated, impulsive character disorders, to sociopathic or narcissistic character disorder (Schoener and Gonsiorek, 1989; see also Gabbard, 1994; Irons and Roberts, 1995). These typologies can be useful when studied by trained mental health professionals for the purposes of diagnosis, prognosis, and, when deemed possible, appropriate methods and length of time for rehabilitation. One pitfall of these typologies, however, is the misuse of such typologies by judicatory executives and by the offender himself. Because of a widespread culture of optimism within religious communities, offenders may be rushed through inappropriate, brief pseudo-rehabilitation and reinstatement, because judicatory staff, clergy colleagues, and others involved in the situation may have a strong wish to see the offender incorrectly as a "wanderer" or a "neurotic." Experts at rehabilitation of clergy offenders estimate that a very large proportion of all offenders, and generally all repeat offenders, are on the end of the spectrum of more serious woundedness and therefore have a poor prognosis for rehabilitation (Schoener and Gonsiorek, 1989; Gabbard, 1995).

Another way of understanding boundary violations from the inner dynamics of the offenders is related to narcissistic wounding. Because all clergy sexual misconduct involves the exploitation of another person for the gratification of the clergyperson's own needs, a unifying thread of narcissistic wounding can be identified running through the entire range of clergy offenders. Narcissism, because it has its origin in the earliest years of life, is very difficult to heal. It impairs a minister's professional judgment in a way that puts him particularly at risk for crossing boundaries, because it damages his capacity for empathy and causes him to seek gratification of his own needs first, regardless of the cost to others. Kornfeld's (1998) description of the cleric or lay leader with an "unseen-unseeing self" is apt: "Although he does not know it, he is emotionally abusing those whom he unconsciously leads on. Often he engages a woman in intense, intimate conversation. He looks at her deeply, *as if* he truly sees her. He does not see her; he is looking at her *as he wishes to be seen*." (p. 294) Even a "wanderer" or "neurotic" clergyperson may show evidence of narcissistic entitlement through manipulative behaviors, externalization of blame, and a tendency to use others, especially to meet personal needs in times of stress.

Through the lens of self-psychology, it has been proposed that the sexualization of usually nonsexual activities and relationships can be seen as an effort to enliven a sense of deadness inside, or to soothe a sense of inner fragmentation or emptiness, and is, in fact, a hallmark of narcissistic character structure (Goldberg, 1995). Rutter (1989) has also suggested from a Jungian perspective that a male offender may project longed-for aspects of his own inner life onto the woman who has come for help. She may then be used unconsciously by the offender as an *anima*-figure or muse, artificially creating a sense of wholeness that can really only be achieved through an internal process of integration, not through enactment of projection-laden fantasies.

Narcissism begins with early childhood wounding, or deprivation—sometimes quite subtle—in which the normal grandiosity of the very small child is not mirrored, or is even crushed, leaving a great psychic hole to be filled. Unconscious defenses are erected, concealing the core wound, but empathy is seriously impaired, resulting in behavior that may in turn victimize others. The narcissistically wounded professional tends to conceal his insecurities and cravings for attention under a behavioral style of specialness—a style often condoned or even reinforced by the ministry setting. A primary sign of narcissistic wounding is a tendency toward entitlement. Wants are equated with needs. Because manipulation and the projection of a star image are common to narcissistically wounded people, empathy and conscience are often convincingly feigned. But at the core of the person's soul is overwhelming despair, emptiness, and fear. For this reason, there is often difficulty establishing appropriate intimate relationships and peer friendships, often resulting in a "Lone Ranger" style of ministry (Pellauer, 1987). Other people are used compulsively and heedlessly in an attempt to keep the demons of worthlessness at bay. This is why it is also advisable when sexual boundary crossings are uncovered to look for other violations of fiduciary responsibility as well, such as financial misconduct.

Boundary violations that may stop short of sexual involvement but may lead to what some researchers have called the "slippery slope phenomenon" (Gabbard, 1995) include giving of personal gifts, establishing an inappropriately intimate friendship and relying on the congregation member or counselee to set limits, or privately attending concerts or movies together. By showing the congregant or counselee his "private side" by swearing or engaging in activities that others would probably regard as unusual for a clergyperson, or even illicit, such as smoking marijuana together, or engaging her in other behaviors that would normally be considered private, a clergy person creates an aura of specialness around the relationship. Undue special treatment of a congregant or counselee, attempts to isolate her from family and friends, isolating oneself from one's family, friends, and colleagues, seeking repeated reassurance from consultants can also be signs of gradual sexualization of the relationship (Pope et al., 1993). Imposing secrecy on the congregant or counselee about the relationship or any aspect of it is a serious warning sign of the development of an inappropriate relationship. All these behaviors serve to enhance the professional's sense of importance, and the resulting excitement or risk is used unconsciously to inflate an underlying sense of flatness and malaise caused by the original narcissistic wound.

It is perhaps important also to note that there is no single profile for victims of clergy sexual abuse. While offenders often seem to have an uncanny ability to ferret out vulnerabilities and exploit them, no member of a congregation is immune to exploitation because of the transferential dynamic and the power imbalance in the pastoral relationship. Everyone brings certain vulnerabilities and lifelong desires for growth, inspiration, and wholeness to their church or temple, and legitimately so, because the quest for wholeness is at least one central dimension of all religious life. It is precisely the exploitation of these vulnerabilities and desires for wholeness that constitutes such a profound betrayal of trust and causes such psychological and spiritual harm to victims.

Counseling Adult Victims

By the time an adult victim seeks counseling, whether the abuse occurred recently or long ago, she has probably already gone through a significant process of struggle and discernment. She is likely to be aware of a variety of painful and confusing feelings around her attempt to end an exploitative relationship or in its aftermath. She may have read something about clergy sexual misconduct that struck a responsive cord. She may have been suffering in isolation for a very long time, not even knowing how to name her suffering as abuse, or having any idea that there might be somewhere she could turn for healing and justice. She may also be struggling with feelings of guilt for disclosing the nature of the relationship to anyone, even a therapist, because perpetrators often swear victims to secrecy, sometimes with the implication of a holy vow.

Post-traumatic symptoms are common, including nightmares, intrusive thoughts and memories, disturbances in relating with others, and self-destructive behaviors. Depressive symptoms are also common, sometimes to the level of a major depressive episode, including depressed mood, excessive guilt and feelings of worthlessness, sleep disturbances, and changes in appetite.

Most victims initially blame themselves, and threads of this self-doubt may persist for a very long time. In the aftermath of sexual exploitation by a clergyperson, victims often feel confused, hurt, angry, or shaken up, or may be wondering why it seems unusually difficult to heal from the ending of the relationship. However, they may have little understanding that they have been wronged in an institutional, ethical sense. As in other forms of sexual and physical abuse, there is a dynamic of victim/perpetrator splitting, in which the perpetrator generally presents himself as the victim, and the victim as the "true" perpetrator. Within the relationship, victims are often told explicitly or implicitly, "You make me do this; I can't help myself even if I know better." This kind of thinking serves to relieve the perpetrator from feeling responsible, and causes the victim to feel at fault from the very first moment the clergyperson began to fantasize about her. Prevailing myths about the seductiveness of

female congregants and the supposed naïveté and innocence of clergy reinforce this dynamic (Morey, 1988). Some Christian professional journals for
clergy continue to emphasize the pastor's struggle to resist temptation, and
continue to portray clergy as innocent sitting ducks for the seductive wiles of
female parishioners (for example, McBurney, 1998).

Because of these dynamics, there are seven principles that govern the
therapeutic process with victims of clergy sexual misconduct:

1. *Convey your belief in the client's experience.* Because clients are so
   prone to doubting themselves, and because prevailing social and
   institutional views still tend to place blame upon victims, this is
   healing in and of itself. It may be necessary to reinforce many times
   over that both therapist and client can trust her inner process to
   know what is true and how to proceed.
2. *Convey to the client that the abuse was not her fault.* Some educational work is often appropriate, explaining that religious institutions do not condone such behavior by clergy, and that it is always
   the responsibility of the clergyperson to maintain appropriate sexual boundaries. It may also be helpful to refer clients to appropriate
   literature about sexual boundary violations and to current professional ethics standards for clergy, and to provide some direct analysis of the abuse of power inherent in sexually exploitative
   relationships. Such educative efforts may help to validate the
   client's trust in her own perceptions of her experience, and to
   reduce self-blame and shame.
3. To the extent that it is appropriate to your role, *offer some form of
   institutional acknowledgment and apology.* As a religious professional, you may at least in the broadest sense represent institutional
   religion in the client's eyes. It is appropriate to say, "As a
   minister/rabbi/priest myself, I am deeply saddened by what you are
   telling me. The events you describe should never happen to anyone, and I am very sorry for what you have experienced, and the
   pain you are in now."
4. *Respect client self-determination concerning any decision to report
   or take action.* As in all good counseling, the principle "Follow the
   client's lead" becomes even more important when working with
   adult victims of clergy sexual misconduct. Counselors frequently
   may feel outrage on the client's behalf, and feel an impulse to push
   the client toward reporting or taking some other form of action.
   Counselors may even wish to disclose the abuse or take action
   directly with judicatory bodies. Concern about potential future victims and a desire to bring the offending clergy to justice may fuel

these impulses. It is important to remember that, as a responsible adult, the client can only feel empowered by allowing her to reach decisions about action in her own time and her own way. Clients also may need to be helped to recognize that reporting may not necessarily produce all desired results. Clients should report or take legal action only when they are able to do so out of an inner sense of rightness, and not out of an unrealistic expectation that all their needs will be met in the process. Some degree of frustration or disappointment is probably inevitable even when an institution responds well, and many institutions are still not able to make a thoroughly educated or just response. Further, acting or pressing the client to act before she is ready may jeopardize her safety.

5. *The victim's safety is always the first priority.* Any decision to report or act belongs to the victim. Reporting may carry serious risks of re-traumatization, both because the relevant institutional body may not be prepared to make a safe and just response, and because the perpetrator may retaliate. Offending clergy often have a wide sphere of influence in which they can inflict harm to the reporting victim's personal reputation, professional status, and goals. Clergy fearing report or institutional discipline sometimes even threaten physical harm. Therefore, client self-determination must be respected.

6. *State your commitment to confidentiality.* While keeping confidentiality is ethically mandated in all counseling, it is especially crucial to state this clearly and directly to the client in cases of sexual abuse, because the client's trust has already been ruptured by the abuser, and may be particularly vulnerable to re-injury. This commitment may need to be restated at various times, as the client remembers and re-experiences fears and doubts in the area of trust. The usual exceptions to confidentiality, as in cases of abuse of a minor, or where the client has threatened harm to herself or another, must be carefully explained, and whenever possible, handled as collaboratively with the client as possible in order to minimize her further sense of disempowerment and rupture of trust.

7. Finally, *be active in promoting justice.* While it may not be possible to intervene directly in a particular case, due to consideration for the client's own self-determination and safety, it is possible to advocate for wider changes that will advance safety and justice in your own institutional settings and communities. Therapeutic work to empower individual clients is a trust that is strengthened at its foundations by one's own commitment to systemic change.

Counseling Clergy Who Cross Boundaries

Given the psychological profile of clergy offenders offered previously, and in particular the prevalence of narcissistic wounding, the question of rehabilitation and reinstatement becomes a matter of more subtlety and discernment than simply designating a specific period of time for therapy and re-education. The kind of therapeutic process necessary to address such deep-seated characterological patterns at minimum takes years, not months. Even then, evidence of true "amendment of life" for a clergyperson who has crossed sexual boundaries with a person or persons in his care would, at the very least, have to include questions such as, Does the clergyperson genuinely and spontaneously take full responsibility for his past behaviors, without excuse or qualification, or does he still at least partially frame his own experience of the misconduct as one of having been victimized himself (whether by the victim, by the congregation, by his family, or by the judicatory body or "the system")? Is he able to talk about the past, focusing genuinely and spontaneously on the pain that was caused to others, or is this still an area he seems to avoid, minimize, or neglect to bring up until someone else raises it? Does his request for reinstatement to the clergy roster seem motivated by a genuine desire to serve others, or does it still seem driven by his own interests and desire for status?

It is unfortunately very easy for counselors working with offenders to be pulled into an empathic dynamic that joins with the offender's own minimization or denial, or to be distracted by the presentation of other issues. Once uncovered, clergy sexual misconduct is often misattributed, even by mental health professionals, to alcohol abuse, mismanagement of personal stress, or "sex addiction." Treatments designed around these framings of the problem will not bring about genuine rehabilitation, because they fail to address both the ethical and theological issues of abuse of power and the underlying psychological dynamic of narcissistic entitlement.

Counselors working with offenders need to maintain an unequivocal stance that all sexual or romantic relating with congregation members or others in their care is wrong, period. Empathic joining may be possible around a shared desire for rehabilitation, but the goal of therapy is *not* reinstatement per se, but to help the offending clergyperson to take responsibility for his actions. This may or may not lead to reinstatement. Treatment will require a long period of exploration of the deep origins of the clergyperson's sense of entitlement and use of others in attempts to shore up a fragile sense of self. The counselor's empathy should be mobilized away from collusion with the offending clergy's sense of entitlement, and toward uncovering the offending clergy's patterns of disavowal of destructive sexualized behaviors and impulses.

Because of the dangers of being manipulated and co-opted, pastoral counselors interested in working with offenders should avail themselves of specialized education and clinically supervised training hours. Some resources for training are listed at the end of this chapter.

Counseling Family Members

Family members of both victims and offending clergy are often the secondary victims who are forgotten in institutional processes of discipline and healing. There is still little written on this particular aspect of clergy sexual misconduct.

Family members of victims may go through a range of feelings upon learning of the sexual abuse. Shock, betrayal, anger toward the victim, anger toward the offending clergyperson, and anger toward the congregation and the religious institution are common. Family members often blame the victim, asking questions like, "Why didn't you just say No?" and "Why couldn't you see through him?" Feelings of shame, embarrassment, and humiliation can affect family members as well as victims, and these are often displaced onto the victim herself.

Family members often feel tremendously out of control in the aftermath of disclosure of abuse, and may attempt to regain control through conscious or unconscious efforts to control the victim. They may begin to "carry" feelings for the victim herself, such as anger or hurt, making it difficult for the victim to identify her own feelings, and they may co-opt her own process for healing by attempting to direct her responses. They may also displace this need for control onto the religious institution and its representatives. Family members may press religious institutions for a speedy response, and become enraged on behalf of the victim when justice is slow, partial, or not forthcoming.

Family members need support in coming to terms with their own grief and anger, and differentiating these from the reactions of the victim. The usual goal of conjoint therapy of enhancing individual members' capacity for self-differentiation while remaining connected becomes paramount in work with families of survivors of sexual abuse. Family members often need help in withdrawing their own projections about what happened, and processing their feelings and responses as their own. Like the victim herself, family members almost always suffer a sense of betrayal of their own trust, and if they are also members or clients of the congregation or agency in which the abuse occurred, a sense of loss of their own religious community or support system.

Family members of victims can also be helped in strengthening communication skills, in particular learning to listen more empathetically to the victim regarding her feelings, and what kinds of support she does and does not need.

Family members of offenders are also secondary victims of the sexual misconduct. The marital betrayal of the spouse may be doubly harmful, because it carries not only the pain of infidelity to the marriage, but also the pain of infidelity to the office of ministry, about which the spouse may care deeply and may be deeply invested. The spouse of the offending clergy may wish to deny that the abuse occurred, and therefore unconsciously collude with the clergyperson's own patterns of minimization and self-justification. She may feel rage toward the "other woman," and a wish to blame the victim for having seduced the spouse. Spouses of offending clergy not infrequently also report dynamics of power, control, and/or abuse within their own marital relationship. The disclosure of abuse of a member of the congregation may cause the spouse to recognize more fully the abusive dynamics of the marriage.

Often, the family of the clergyperson not only lose their religious community, but a special status or role within it, and experience feelings of shame, humiliation, and loss of privacy when the truth is disclosed. Victim blaming by congregations is sometimes secondarily directed at other prominent women in the congregation, and wives of offending clergy are sometimes blamed for being inadequate spouses, unsupportive of their clergy husbands, or insufficiently involved in the life of the congregation.

Families of offending clergy also suffer direct economic consequences when offending clergy are disciplined. The clergyperson's salary may be terminated, and in cases of church-provided parsonages, housing may be abruptly terminated as well. Legg and Legg (1995) state that some congregations express anger over "sexual sin" through money, causing the offender's family to suffer financial punishment even though they themselves committed no wrongdoing.

Children of both victims and offenders may act out unhealed dynamics in the family after the disclosure of the abuse. Children of both families may blame the victim, lose respect for the clergyperson, and by extension for the office of ministry, and become mistrustful of all institutional religion. Children from both families may be scapegoated, especially if the abuse is given significant media coverage. "Good child/bad child" splits may begin to occur in both family systems, in which many interactions between children, or among children and adults, may begin to take on a perpetrator/victim dynamic.

Spouses and family members of both victims and offenders frequently feel disregarded by institutional processes of adjudication that focus heavily on the victim and the offending clergy but offer little in the way of emotional or material support to families. Counselors can help family members to identify and assert their own needs for support from their religious communities.

Whether the marriage of either the offender or of the victim can be kept intact or dissolved, both families can benefit greatly from therapeutic help. Effective counseling can help families of both victims and offenders to avoid the escalation of destructive projective processes and patterns of denial, and to engage fully in the emotional process of grieving, healing, and ultimately acceptance of new realities and integration of the truth of what occurred.

Consulting to Congregations

There has been increasing recognition among clergy and judicatory executives that congregations are also traumatized by clergy sexual misconduct. It is now generally understood that when congregations are not offered an intentional, well-planned healing process, they continue to carry wounds that can affect future generations of future clergy and lay members, and are likely to pose significant if unspoken obstacles to effective ministry. Congregations are groups or systems that, just like individuals, have unconscious as well as conscious dynamics. Traumatic events in the life of a congregation may be "forgotten," initially because of systemic taboos against telling the truth about what happened. Later, even if every person who was a member at the time the trauma occurred has moved away or died, the post-traumatic dynamics persist. Old patterns of relating, of behavior, speech, and silence, are taken up by new members without a conscious understanding of their origins. Like families with multigenerational patterns of incest, congregational dynamics can also be governed by a sexual abuse secret that is hidden from conscious awareness but can be recognized by the symptoms it produces.

Congregations with unhealed histories of sexual misconduct, whether recent or long past, tend to exhibit certain characteristics (Knudsen, 1995). They exhibit patterns, not unlike the dynamics of a family in which incest has occurred, that serve unconsciously to protect the congregation's "family" secret. These patterns may include unclear lines of communication, taboos and defensiveness about aspects of the congregation's history, tendencies toward scapegoating and rage, hypervigilance, and lack of trust. There may be symbolic expressions of the secret, such as undue preoccupation with the appearance of the church building, with physical boundaries such as altar rails and doors, or with denominational controversies over sexuality statements or policies. It is even fairly common for lay leaders unwittingly to act out the unconscious group dynamic of an unhealed congregation by hiring new clergy who also violate boundaries.

Experts have identified a number of indicators of congregational symptoms in the aftermath of clergy sexual misconduct (Knudsen, 1993):

1. Anger that is displaced toward other authority figures such as congregation staff members, judicatory executives, interims and "after-pastors," and even toward lay leadership;
2. Reactivity in the form of making unwise or hasty decisions;
3. A pattern of divisiveness within the congregation;
4. A sense of depression, malaise, and apathy among members toward routine tasks and programs;
5. Excessive preoccupation with caring for the offending clergyperson (sometimes even after he has left the congregation) without similar apparent regard for other injured parties;
6. A loss of members and/or income that does not resolve in the usual "recovery period" of 6–12 months;
7. A climate of gossip and conjecture resulting from understandable attempts to find out "what happened";
8. Conscious or unconscious embarrassment, leading to isolation from the surrounding community and from other congregations;
9. "Sexualization" of the congregation, in which undue attention is given to matters of human sexuality;
10. "Symbolic fights" (Hopkins, 1993), congregational conflicts that symbolize the pain (for example, conflicts about the priority of children's ministries, about job or role descriptions, about the external appearance of the congregation's building, about the newsletter and other means of communication, about "boundaries" such as keys to the building, office hours, outreach);
11. Nostalgia for the "good old days" or idealization of previous clergy; suspicion or resistance to new ideas, programs, or forms of ministry;
12. Despair about the future of the congregation, resulting in fear of making commitments or taking risks.

In order to heal from sexual misconduct, congregations need intentional, well-trained, and empathic intervention. First and foremost, congregations need information and education. Appropriate disclosure may be made by professionals who have authority in the religious institution with which the congregation is affiliated (judicatory executives), or consultants who are authorized officially to represent the institution by virtue of their particular training and expertise in working with congregations in the aftermath of sexual misconduct. Appropriate disclosure serves two purposes: (1) to reduce the congregation's anxiety about what happened and what has been kept from them; and (2) to model permission for open discussion and truth-telling within the congregation itself. As with all trauma, truth-telling and open processing of feelings are at the heart of any congregational healing process. Information and education should at minimum include:

1. *Appropriate, ample disclosure of facts.* Congregations need fair and honest answers to the question "What happened?" Exceptions to full disclosure, such as withholding the identity of reporting victims to preserve their safety or withholding of any information for specific, concrete legal reasons, should be explained. Secrecy is at the heart of the betrayal of the congregation's trust. The interruption of patterns of secrecy begins from the first disclosure to model a new way of congregational life based on honesty and sharing. Congregations that are "left in the dark" are more likely to engage in gossip, secrecy, victim-blaming, and covering up of the truth.

2. Access to the most recent *policies and procedures* pertaining to the case. They should be "walked through" the steps that will occur in their denomination's adjudication procedure, and be told what to expect at various stages in the process.

3. *Education about appropriate ministerial boundaries, the misuse of power inherent in clergy sexual misconduct, and a theological framework for sexual ethics.* Members should be helped to understand their institution's rules and disciplinary codes concerning clergy professional conduct, and the ethical and theological rationales behind them. Educational efforts should give attention to issues of ministerial trust and responsibility for boundaries, power differentials inherent in the role of ministry, and theological understandings of abuse.

4. *Education about the stages in the congregational healing process,* which are not unlike the stages of grief experienced by a person in bereavement. The variety of commonly experienced feelings, reactions, and behavioral responses can be explained and normalized. A "Trauma De-Briefing Model," as developed by the Rev. Chilton Knudsen (1991), is recommended for initial disclosure and early healing process. Her "Dimensions of Congregational Healing" wheel is helpful in explaining the range of reactions that may occur normally in a congregation in the aftermath of clergy misconduct. Reactions may include shock, denial, bargaining, anger (scapegoating), depression/sadness, anger (righteous rage), and (eventually), acceptance and integration.

A collaborative team approach is recommended, in which mental health or addictions professionals, denominational personnel, area clergy, attorneys, and (as appropriate) law enforcement professionals may all potentially be of help to a congregation in the aftermath of sexual abuse. Lay leaders who have experienced misconduct in another congregation and have sufficiently moved through their own grief process can also be useful resources. Such a "response team" should be balanced to include both women and men, clergy and laity. The team should also include persons of varying ages and sociocultural perspectives, reflecting the nature and diversity of the congregation's own membership. A quiet room and a person designated simply to be a caring listener should be provided at any public meeting or event related to the misconduct. Local counseling resources should be posted so that members who wish to do so may seek further individual consultation and healing. Congregations can be helped in recognizing the need for a plan to respond to media in an appropriate and timely manner.

Finally, a consultant can help the congregation to realize that the healing process will take time. It is the disclosure of the information that initiates the crisis for the congregation, although the crisis was actually caused by the clergy misconduct. Disclosure opens a window for potential healing, but this window may shut again if ongoing support and education are not offered. Healing cannot be accomplished in a single congregational meeting. Follow-up meetings, both large and in small groups, should be planned at regular intervals. As with all grief processes, two years is a reasonable minimum length of time to expect that healing will occur, if the process is being regularly attended throughout that time. Some members may protest, "It's time to move on!" or even urge premature forgiveness of the offending clergy. These protests must be understood at least in part as carrying the group's wish to deny and to distance from the emotional pain of the process (Friberg, 1995). In the long run, Knudsen has written, "No congregation that I know of has ever complained that 'too much was offered to us' for their healing process. Err on the side of offering more rather than less opportunity to discuss, process and accept/integrate the experience" (Knudsen, 1993).

After the initial crisis period, pastoral counselors who are well educated in these congregational dynamics may continue in an ongoing capacity to serve as consultants to interim clergy and "after-pastors." As consultants, pastoral counselors may help these clergy to stay differentiated from the wounded congregational system into which they have been immersed. Consultants can help them recognize post-traumatic "symptoms" as they occur in the congregational system. By integrating this knowledge, "after-pastors" may maintain a constructive, ongoing, "nonanxious" pastoral presence (Friedman, 1985) that helps move the congregation through healing to renewal of ministry and mission.

Pastoral counselors may also be a helpful resource to judicatory executives who need consultation in dealing directly with situations of sexual misconduct (H. Hopkins, 1995). Education in both the ethical and theological ramifications and the psychological dynamics of clergy sexual misconduct, as well as guidance in appropriate methods of prevention and intervention can be invaluable to religious leaders. It is important to remember that judicatory executives are also secondary victims of clergy sexual misconduct. They may experience a range of feelings including shock, anxiety, dread, disbelief, a wish to minimize, a pull to collude with the offender, or a desire to act impulsively from outrage or grief upon the discovery of clergy sexual misconduct in one of their congregations. Consultants can support judicatory executives in maintaining an educated, conscious, nonanxious leadership presence, implementing (or creating) policies and procedures that enact at an institutional level both healing and justice.

Conclusion

Pastoral counselors can make an important contribution to the prevention and healing of clergy sexual misconduct. This contribution can be made in a variety of ways—leading educational workshops for clergy and laity on the clergy sexual ethics and the prevention of sexual misconduct; counseling victims, offenders, and secondary victims; consulting with congregations, judicatory executives, and "after-pastors"; and engaging in active work for justice in our own denominations and institutions. Finally, pastoral counselors must attend to our own ethical and theological mandates, maintaining the highest standards of sexual professional ethics in our own practices, and refraining from colluding or "turning a blind eye" toward colleagues who cross sexual boundaries with clients, patients, congregation members, or others whom we serve. We must continue to strengthen our own policies and procedures, so that our profession is a harbor of safety and justice for all who come to us for help.

References

American Association of Pastoral Counselors (1994). *Code of Ethics.* 9504A Lee Highway, Fairfax, VA 22031-2303. Web site: www.aapc.org

Association for Clinical Pastoral Education (1999). *Standards.* 1549 Clairmont Road, Ste. 103, Decatur, GA 30033-4611. Web site: www.acpe.edu

Benyei, C. R. *Understanding Clergy Misconduct in Religious Systems: Scapegoating, Family Secrets, and the Abuse of Power.* Haworth Press, 1998.

Biele, N. et al. *It's Never OK: A Handbook for Victims and Victim Advocates on Sexual Exploitation by Counselors and Therapists.* Minneapolis: Task Force on Sexual Exploitation by Counselors and Therapists, Minnesota Department of Corrections, 1994.

Cooper-White, P. "Soul-Stealing: Power Relations in Pastoral Sexual Abuse." *Christian Century,* February 20, 1991, 196–99.

———. *The Cry of Tamar: Violence against Women and the Church's Response.* Minneapolis: Fortress Press, 1995.

———. *Therapists' Conceptualization and Use of Countertransference.* Unpublished survey of pastoral counselors and clinical social workers (1999), work in progress.

Erickson-Pearson, J. *Safe Connections: What Parishioners Can Do to Understand and Prevent Clergy Sexual Abuse.* Chicago: Evangelical Lutheran Church in America, 1996.

Fortune, M. *Is Nothing Sacred? When Sex Invades the Pastor-Parishioner Relationship.* San Francisco: Harper & Row, 1989.

———. *Clergy Misconduct: Sexual Abuse in the Ministerial Relationship Workshop Manual,* rev. ed. Seattle, WA: Center for the Prevention of Sexual and Domestic Violence, 1997.

Friedman, E. H. *Generation to Generation: Family Process in Church and Synagogue.* New York: Guilford Press, 1985.

Friberg, N. "Wounded Congregations." In Hopkins and Laaser (1995), 55–74.

Gabbard, G. O. *Sexual Exploitation in Professional Relationships.* Washington, DC: American Psychiatric Press, 1989.

———. "Psychodynamics of Sexual Boundary Violations." *Psychiatric Annals* 21(1991), 651–55.

———. "Psychotherapists Who Transgress Sexual Boundaries with Patients." *Bulletin of the Menninger Clinic* 58/1 (1994), 124–35.

———. *Boundaries and Boundary Violations in Psychoanalysis.* New York: Basic Books, 1995.

Goldberg, A.. *The Problem of Perversion: The View from Self Psychology.* New Haven: Yale University Press, 1995.

Grenz, S. J. and Bell, R. D. *Betrayal of Trust: Sexual Misconduct in the Pastorate.* Intervarsity Press, 1995.

Hopkins, H. "The Effects of Clergy Sexual Misconduct on the Wider Church." In Hopkins and Laaser (1995), 116–39.

Hopkins, N. M. "Symbolic Church Fights: The Hidden Agenda When Clerical Trust Has Been Betrayed." *Congregations: The Alban Journal* (May/June 1993), 15–18.

———. *The Congregational Response to Clergy Betrayals of Trust.* Liturgical Press, 1998.

——— and Laaser, M., eds. *Restoring the Soul of a Church: Healing Congregations Wounded by Clergy Sexual Misconduct.* Collegeville, MN: Alban Institute, in association with the Interfaith Sexual Trauma Institute, 1995.

Hulme, W. E. "Sexual Boundary Violations of Clergy." In Gabbard, G. O., ed., *Sexual Exploitation in Professional Relationships* (1989).

Irons, R. and Roberts, K. "The Unhealed Wounders." In Hopkins and Laaser (1995), 33–51.

Knudsen, C. "Trauma Debriefing: A Congregational Model." *MCS Conciliation Quarterly* (Spring 1991), 12–13.

———. "Pastoral Care for Congregations in the Aftermath of Sexual Misconduct." Unpublished paper, Episcopal Diocese of Chicago, 1993.

———. *"Understanding Congregational Dynamics."* In Hopkins and Laaser (1995), 75–101.

Kornfeld, M. *Cultivating Wholeness: A Guide to Care and Counseling in Faith Communities.* New York: Continuum, 1998.

Lebacqz, K. and Barton, R. *Sex in the Parish.* Louisville, KY: Westminster/John Knox Press, 1991.

Legg, A. and Legg, D. "The Offender's Family." In Hopkins and Laaser (1995), 140–54.

McBurney, L. "Seduced." *Leadership* (Fall 1998), 101–6.

Meloy, J. R. "Narcissistic Psychopathology and the Clergy." *Pastoral Psychology* 35/1(1996), 50–55.

Morey, A. J. "Blaming the Woman for the Abusive Male Pastor." *Christian Century,* October 5, 1988, 866–69.

Pellauer, M. "Sex, Power and the Family of God." *Christianity and Crisis,* February 16, 1987, 47–50.

Peterson, M. R. *At Personal Risk: Boundary Violations in Professional-Client Relationships.* New York: Norton, 1992.

Poling, N. W. *Victim to Survivor: Women Recovering from Clergy Sexual Abuse."* United Church Press, 1999.

Pope, K. S., Sonne, J. L. and Holroyd, J. *Sexual Feelings in Psychotherapy: Explorations for Therapists and Therapists-in-Training.* Washington, DC: American Psychological Association, 1993.

Rutter, P. *Sex in the Forbidden Zone: When Men in Power Abuse Women's Trust.* Los Angeles: Jeremy Tarcher, 1989.

Rutter, P. "The Boundary-Maker in Relationships of Closeness and Trust." In *Closeness in Personal and Professional relationships.* Edited by H. Wilmer, pp. 62–75. Shambhala Publications, 1991.

Schoener, G. and Gonsiorek, J. "Assessment and Development of Rehabilitation Plans for the Therapist." In Schoener et al. (1989), 401–20.
————. Milgrom, J., Gonsiorek, J., Luepker, E., and Conroe, R. *Psychotherapists' Sexual Involvement with Clients: Intervention and Prevention.* Minneapolis: Walk-In Counseling Center, 1989.
Weiser, C. *Healers: Harmed and Harmful.* Minneapolis: Fortress Press, 1994.

Resources

The Center for the Prevention of Sexual and Domestic Violence, 936 N. 34th St. Ste. 200, Seattle, WA 98103. Tel. (206) 634-1903. Web site: www.cpsdv.org Training videos from the Center include: "Not in My Church" (Christian), "Not in My Congregation" (Jewish), "Once You Cross the Line," "Hear Their Cries: Religious Responses to Child Abuse," and "Bless Our Children: Preventing Sexual Abuse."

Interfaith Sexual Trauma Institute (ISTI), St. John's Abbey and University, Collegeville, MN 56321-2000. Tel. (320) 363-3994. Web site: www.osb.org/isti/

Walk-In Counseling Center, 2421 Chicago Ave., South, Minneapolis, MN 55404. Tel. (612) 870-0565. Web site: www.walkin.org

David A. Steere

17. Supervising Pastoral Counseling

Supervision is the principal method of teaching pastoral counseling. Our grasp of counseling theories tends to fade with each step we take away from a formal classroom, unless these ideas take on reality in concrete instances where they apply. Both the conceptual tools and the specific techniques needed to work effectively with others can be mastered only through ordered reflection upon the counseling process itself. And that is what supervision is designed to accomplish—the acquisition of knowledge within the specific context of its use.

The term *supervision* broadly designates the process of overseeing someone else's work. If you agree to supervise me, you assume some responsibility for helping me perform a job, whether it be upholstering a chair, teaching a class, or doing pastoral counseling. Usually, you will have some expertise in the task at hand and some authority in the structure of what is going on. You will assign, regulate, and evaluate my activities with some say-so about my qualifications and advancement.

When it comes to the work of the pastor, supervision is nothing new. It may be as old as Jesus sending out the seventy-two to spread the good news and then talking with them about what happened when they returned. And just as the pastoral task of giving counsel has changed from one age to another, the style of supervising its practice also changed with the beliefs that governed the times (Clebsch and Jaekle, 1964). The church adopted a Thomistic psychology based upon Aristotelian thought in the twelfth and thirteenth centuries. Pastoral counselors embraced the "faculty psychology" of sense, imagination, passions, and reason that followed the Enlightenment. Theological education seized the notion of apprenticeship from the guild system of the Middle Ages and made supervised practice under a tried cleric of higher rank standard in the preparation for priesthood. Pastoral training not only drew upon the existing psychologies of the day to understand its task. It made use of the best supervisory practices of every age to accomplish it.

It comes as no surprise, then, that contemporary theories that govern the supervision of pastoral counseling are the product of a dialogue with professionals in the fields of psychiatry, social work, clinical psychology, education, and marriage and family therapy. This chapter will (1) identify four major traditions in the current practice of supervision in pastoral counseling with some of their varying emphases, (2) advance a model for supervision sufficiently comprehensive to contain and integrate these differing approaches, and (3) discuss three basic dimensions of the supervisory task common to them all.

Four Supervisory Traditions

The word *supervision* can have both broad and narrow meanings. It can mean the oversight of an entire educational process in the clinical setting: designing, administrating, and implementing a training program. It can also designate one particular part of this teaching/learning process—systematic reflection with trainees on the actual process of their clinical practice. Supervision in this latter sense became the core teaching method in the clinical setting and began to develop a theory all its own. Four separate theoretical traditions converge to make up contemporary theories of supervision in pastoral counseling, each with its own distinct approach to the task: Clinical Pastoral Education, the psychodynamic tradition, the humanistic tradition, and the systemic tradition.

Clinical Pastoral Education

Current supervisory practices in pastoral counseling are the clear product of interprofessional cooperation in the clinical setting. The term *clinical* literally means "at the bedside" (Schuster, Sandt, and Thaler, 1972, p. 1). It derives from the Greek word *kline* for the couch in the Temple of Aesculapius where the Greeks went to find a cure for their ills. A clinician is one who gathers data "at the bedside." Clinical medicine is concerned with the actual observation and treatment of disease among patients rather than its study through experimental research in the laboratory. The term was adopted by clinical pastoral educators in the 1920s the way Richard Cabot used it in a famous lecture entitled "A Plea for a Clinical Year in the Course of Theological Study" urging that the clergy be trained to practice theology in the same way physicians learn to practice medicine in the clinical setting (1926, p. 7). Anton Boisen, who conducted what was probably the first program of clinical pastoral education as we know it today, put it another way: the theological student should learn how to read "living human documents" as well as the traditional documents of the church's faith (1951).

The CPE tradition learned and incorporated much from other supervisory traditions in the clinical setting. But it managed to preserve this central focus upon a clinical method of theological inquiry. For Cabot and Dicks, this meant the study of verbatim records of the pastoral conversation in which religious beliefs became the substance of what is done or acted out in the actual process of pastoral care with the patient (1936). What they envisioned was a *clinical theology* setting forth specific ways the pastor's body of theological belief takes shape in concrete methods such as "creative listening." Boisen's emphasis on the study of *living human documents* involved the observation of how the actual beliefs people hold function to direct the course of their lives, for illness or for health, for sin or for salvation.

It remained for Seward Hiltner to draw together these initial commitments to ordered reflection on the pastoral conversation into a formal discipline of *pastoral theology* (1958). Pastoral theology was defined as a branch of theological knowledge and inquiry that brings the pastoral perspective to bear on concrete helping operations drawing conclusions of a theological order from systematic reflections upon them. We begin with theological hypotheses about what will actually be of help to human beings, then reflect on the caring process step-by-step, and emerge with conclusions of a theological order about the theories that govern it. This made the actual task of supervisory reflection a valid and legitimate source of theological knowledge. As Hiltner put it, "The truth about how the truth operates is part of the truth itself" (1958, p. 220).

Supervision in the CPE tradition developed an intense personal relationship between supervisor and student. Its hallmark is the presentation of verbatim records of the pastoral conversation constructed by recall. The case study of religious histories of patients is also important along with a form of group supervision (interpersonal relations group) which deals with the trainee's personal reactions to the entire experience. There has been much debate whether the focus of supervision lies in the acquisition of pastoral skills or in the personal growth of the trainee or both (Steere, 1989). But from the 1920s on, supervision in the CPE tradition saw itself as a theological discipline and not simply as a practice shared with other helping professions. Genuine knowledge about theology itself is acquired, reformulated, and tested again in the crucible of human experience.

The Psychodynamic Tradition

The American Association of Pastoral Counselors (AAPC) was formed in 1963 in order to recognize and credential a rapidly expanding number of pastoral counselors. Most of its founders came out of the CPE movement, and one-quarter of CPE remains a requirement for membership to date. An important difference, however, was present in the situation that spawned it. Standards for the reliable training of pastoral counselors were sought among existing secular disciplines in psychotherapy. Supervision from professional figures in the fields of psychiatry, psychology, or social work was required. This made sense as pastoral counselors sought to raise their expertise to levels comparable to those of their colleagues. In the process, both the psychodynamic and the humanistic traditions of long-standing influence were formally integrated into supervision in pastoral counseling.

The psychodynamic tradition has its roots in psychoanalytic theory where the task of dealing with our unconscious motivations or forces (dynamics) outside our awareness is central to all human change. Sigmund Freud considered anyone making use of the twin phenomena of *resistance* and *transference* to be doing psychoanalysis (1938, pp. 9, 39). *Resistance* is the term for that mental mechanism by which we shut out of our conscious awareness traumatic or seemingly unacceptable aspects of our personal experience. We push from our memory the painful roots of the problems we address. We make constructive changes in our life when someone assists us in circumventing our resistance to bring these repressed experiences to consciousness, thereby gaining insight into how they determine our present striving. For Freud any technique that helps one achieve this is a psychoanalytic one.

The term *transference* was given to the phenomenon of reexperiencing childhood emotions toward significant others with someone else in the present. In its narrowest definition, transference is restricted to instances in the psychoanalytic relationship where the patient projects onto the analyst infantile feelings of libido (love, sexual attraction) and aggression (hate, primitive rage) originally experienced toward a parenting figure. Broader definitions are more common today in which the phenomenon of transference is expanded to include the whole range of relationships in which we may project "the face" of someone significant from our past onto the person we interact with currently with similar affect and behavior.

Both these elements of resistance and transference are prominent in psychodynamic theories of supervision. Therapists in training can be expected to resist awareness of how earlier experiences are determining their present striving, just as their patients do. Their own countertransference toward persons with whom they work can distort their perceptions and inhibit their effectiveness. Learning to do psychotherapy required a corresponding self-encounter in depth on the part of therapists-in-training to manage the whole process.

Accordingly, some form of personal analysis or "didactic analysis" has always been a part of psychoanalytic training. The issue is whether it belongs within the context of supervision. Early in the movement, some argued that the same analyst should analyze and supervise the trainee because you could only supervise people properly if you knew them well enough through conducting their own personal analysis. Others insisted upon separating the two completely. Supervision should be a didactic experience focusing sole attention on how to treat patients and not address issues of personal therapy.

The problem is that psychotherapists-in-training never seem to get all their personal issues settled in therapy and then go to supervision with no further need for insight into their own unconscious motivations and transference. Most psychodynamic supervisors separated the two, but not so completely. Rudolph Ekstein and Robert Wallerstein's *The Teaching and Learning of Psychotherapy* became the classic text in the psychodynamic tradition by mid-century (1958). The authors rejected a patient-centered approach in which the therapist brings technical problems with the patient to the supervisor and is given advice. They also rejected a therapist-centered approach which focused on the therapist's blind spots and countertransference reactions to patients. Instead, they proposed a *process-centered* emphasis on the interaction between patient, therapist, and supervisor with a clear focus on what is happening in this whole system of relationships.

This involved psychodynamic supervision in a number of things that paralleled the psychotherapeutic relationship it addressed. There were points where the therapist's own personal difficulties got in the way of treatment. Ekstein and Wallerstein called these "learning problems" because they continually stood in the way of the student's acquisition of psychotherapeutic skills. Moreover, a similar set of difficulties also appeared in the relationship between the supervisor and the therapist-in-training. In spite of whatever good intentions occupied their conscious minds, students were found to resist learning from supervision. These characteristic resistances to supervision, termed "problems about learning," originated in each trainee's own "unique transference" toward the supervisor.

To make the situation even more complex, psychodynamic theories of supervision soon began to observe a *parallel process* at work between these two sets of problems that were always cluttering up the psychotherapeutic situation and the supervisory relationship at the same time (Doehrman, 1976). Psychotherapists-in-training may give the patient in therapy what they desire from their supervisor, or they may read into the patient elements of their own anxiety in the supervisory relationship. What students see and present from a therapeutic relationship frequently parallels comparable problems they themselves experience in supervision. It is as if the supervisory conversation addresses a constant metaphor in which the patient's problem in psychotherapy may be used to express the therapist's problem in supervision and vice versa. More often than not, resolution of the problem in supervision is accompanied by a similar breakthrough or gain in the therapeutic relationship.

The hallmark of supervision in the psychodynamic tradition is continuous case presentation of the same patient, week by week, following progress across this parallel process we have been considering. Systematic reflection is not confined to the therapeutic relationship the trainee presents, and regularly expands to address the trainee's resistance to the learning process of supervision itself. Since most important data that supervisees bring are personal data concerning their own attitudes, approaches, and feelings toward patients, verbal description, process notes, and personal reflection are the primary means of presenting material. Audio and video recording, while helpful, find their principal use in stimulating immediate recall of one's internal attitudes and intentions at the point of intervention. Ekstein and Wallerstein favored the separation of supervision from administrative oversight of the patients' treatment. They wanted the supervisor free to encourage maximum learning at the supervisee's own initiative and readiness and not be tempted to "treat the patient" through the supervisory process.

The Humanistic Tradition

The humanistic tradition in supervisory theory finds its roots in the work of Carl Rogers and his approach known as "client-centered therapy" (1951). Rogers became the first non-medical practitioner to effectively challenge the reign of psychoanalytic helping theory. His approach was soon labeled *non-directive counseling* because of the permissiveness that characterized it in which the counselor listened, clarified what was being said without interpretation, and attempted to help people arrive at their own solutions to their problems. Rogers himself preferred the term *client-centered therapy* to indicate that the significant activities in therapy were those of the client, not the therapist. In essense:
If the counselor:

1. places a high value on the worth and capacity of the individual,
2. operates on the hypothesis that the individual is capable of self-understanding and self-direction,
3. creates an atmosphere of genuine acceptance and warmth,
4. develops a sensitive ability to perceive experience as it is seen by his client,
5. communicates to the client something of his understanding of the inner world of the client;

then the client:

1. finds it safe to explore fearful and threatening aspects of experience,
2. comes to a deeper understanding and acceptance of all aspects of himself,
3. is able to reorganize himself in the direction of his ideal,
4. finds it more satisfying to be his reorganized self,
5. discovers that he no longer needs the counselor.

(Rogers and Becker, 1950, pp. 33–34)

Rogers's approach had immediate appeal to pastoral counselors, both theologically and practically. Theologically, it expressed in human paradigm the force of God's forgiveness as personal acceptance. Practically, it freed training and supervision from the cumbersome necessity of psychoanalytic methodology. By mid-century, the reigning theory of pastoral counseling expressed a marked affinity to this tradition. Seward Hiltner's "eductive counseling," Paul Johnson's "responsive counseling," and Carroll Wise's "non-coercive counseling" (although he steadfastly refused any label for it) were all constructed along lines similar to Carl Rogers's client-centered therapy (Hiltner, 1949, Johnson, 1953, Wise 1951). The normative helping act was that of "evoking" or "calling forth" resources that were internal to the person receiving help. The same tradition is preserved by Barry K. Estadt, John R. Compton, and Melvin C. Blanchette in their definitive work on the supervision of pastoral counseling: *The Art of Clinical Supervision: A Pastoral Counseling Perspective* (1987). Here, the *core process of supervision* is defined around Robert Carkhuff's helping skills of attending, exploring, and personalizing which embody the primary client-centered orientation of the humanistic tradition (1987).

Supervisory theory in the humanistic tradition soon established itself around modeling the experience it sought to teach. Client-centered therapy turned upon what came to be known as the "therapeutic conditions" of *empathy, understanding, respect,* and *genuineness.* Wherever these conditions prevailed, positive change was facilitated. Not only were they curative factors in psychotherapy; they were found to stimulate creative efforts to develop therapeutic skills in supervision. They were equally applicable to patterns of interaction in groups, so client-centered therapists were increasingly trained as group therapists and supervised in the group setting.

Central to the humanistic tradition in supervision is its faithfulness to the scientist/practitioner model in psychology which undertook extensive research in the implementation and effectiveness of client-centered therapy. Careful one-on-one supervision buttressed by extensive research in techniques that bring effective therapeutic outcomes governed training programs

(Rogers and Dymond, 1954). Wide use was made of electrically recorded data in supervision. Rogers believed that only careful study of the actual interview, preferably with a sound recording and a transcript available, made it possible to determine what purposes were actually being accomplished by the therapist. At the core of supervisory reflection was the task of determining how each response to the client can congruently convey the therapist's fundamental orientation toward that individual's worth as a person. Effective supervision modeled the empathetic understanding, respect, and genuineness which the supervisee was being taught to implement with the client.

The Systemic Tradition

Since mid-century a fourth tradition in supervision has emerged among marriage and family therapists which can be characterized by its emphasis upon systems theory. Proponents cut across traditional lines separating the professions uniting to treat the family system rather than the individual. Regarding a linear, cause-and-effect approach to understanding emotional problems to be too narrow, the systemic tradition began working with concepts of circular causality within the family unit where psychopathology both originated and was sustained. The symptomatic person or the identified patient was found to provide an important role either in maintaining stability or in bringing about change in that system—or both. Treatment came to be conceived in terms of measures that intervened in or altered constructively the way the family system operates as a whole, eliminating whatever within its relationships produced symptomatic behavior. Along with the practice of family therapy came new ways of doing supervision indigenous to its experience of working with relational systems.

One principal innovation was the practice of live supervision that grew up among marriage and family therapists. In general, the term *live supervision* describes any process in which the supervisor guides the therapist during the actual course of treatment itself. The most common way is to observe from behind a one-way glass. Contact with the therapist is maintained throughout the session in any number of ways. Some supervisors knock on the door or interrupt with a buzzer asking therapists to step out for consultation. Others call in on the telephone for a conversation in the midst of treatment. Still others have experimented with putting a "bug" in the ear of the therapist, permitting a running commentary and step-by-step instructions during the whole process. Some supervisors on occasion walk into the room and join the therapist for brief periods of time to undertake specific interventions. Two volumes afford the best introduction to supervision from the systems perspective: *Handbook of Family Therapy Training in Supervision*, edited by Howard A. Liddle, Douglas C. Breunlin, and Richard C. Schwartz, and *Family Therapy Supervision: Recent Developments in Practice*, edited by Rosemary Whiffen and John Byng-Hall (Liddle, 1988, Whiffen, 1982).

Live supervision has many advantages. Trainees may provide a higher quality treatment if their supervisors can guide therapy at strategic points. It eliminates fruitless periods in reflective supervision of sitting through long segments of previously recorded material after therapy has gone awry and the session "lost" in an unproductive direction. Potentially irrelevant and damaging sequences of interaction may be interrupted, building the therapist's confidence through success early in training. Some systemic supervisors are critical of its emphasis upon technique to the neglect of teaching trainees a comprehensive theory of life that organizes their behavior as therapists. Others insist that while live supervision may prove effective in the short run, it can stifle the trainee's long-term growth and autonomy. But some balanced and measured use of it is a growing part of most training programs.

There are wide variations in the use of live supervision throughout the systemic tradition. Structural/strategic supervisors who see issues of power and hierarchy as paramount give authoritative directives to the therapist concerning interventions and the next steps in treatment. Groups behind a one-way mirror may observe and discuss what is going on, but the supervisor directs the entire process, assuming responsibility for its outcome. Supervisors from the Milan School have the group observing behind the window take an active part in the treatment, writing prescriptions, designing rituals and paradoxical directives which are delivered to the family as messages from the "team" behind the glass. Other supervisors with stronger humanistic leanings, who make a larger place for personal choice among, members of the family system, may place the team in the treatment room with the family. Instead of issuing authoritative prescriptions and strategies from behind a one-way mirror, team members openly discuss different ways of looking at the family process in a "reflective dialogue," making supervision an open procedure conducted in the presence of the family and part of the actual course of treatment. The family's responses to the discussion by the supervisor and team members then constitute the next step in therapy.

Systems theorists soon encountered a phenomenon in supervision they called *isomorphism* which proved analogous to what the psychodynamic tradition called *parallel process*. Isomorphism is the tendency for patterns to repeat themselves at all levels of the family therapy system. A particular pattern in the parent/child relationship begins to reappear in the relationship between therapist and parent. Suddenly the same therapist/ parent pattern reappears in the supervisory relationship itself. The father in the family is over-solicitous and placating, reluctant to assert his ideas and take initiative toward his son. The therapist ignores this behavior and fails to recognize and confront it for fear of driving him further into the background. The supervisor is reluctant to intervene, with a vague sense that the therapist lacks the confidence to make a potent demand that the father behave differently. One and the same problem plays itself out at each level of the system of family therapy that confronts it.

Resolution of the isomorphic issue will cascade down the treatment hierarchy from supervisor to therapist to family member. The same parallel process is operative. As the supervisor is successful in assisting the therapist to overcome blocks to self-assertion, the therapist begins to succeed in helping the father engage in appropriate assertive measures with his son who in turn stops apathetically flunking out of school.

To an already existing complexity of supervisory theory and methodology the systemic tradition contributed its practice of live supervision in which both supervisor and supporting group or team can take part in the treatment process itself. Supervision remains a reflective process, but the interval of time between reflection and return for implementation of supervisory decisions is reduced to the immediate present. Supervision has traveled full circle from Ekstein and Wallerstein's separation of it from administrative responsibilities for treating the patient. Now everybody involved may take an active and responsible role in what goes on in the treatment room.

A Reflective Model

Our next step is to advance a model for supervising pastoral counselors that is broad enough to encompass this diversity of contemporary approaches, yet focused enough to provide clarity and integrity to the task. It is constructed from a general model that has been in use at Louisville Presbyterian Seminary for a number of years (Steere, 1969). It has proven sufficiently comprehensive to encompass supervision at both beginning and advanced levels together with its varied forms and formats, whether one is addressing counseling relationships with individuals, groups, couples, or families.

Definition

Supervision in pastoral counseling is a teaching/learning process conducted through an extended relationship in which supervisor and supervisees agree to engage in systematic reflection upon the trainees' concrete practice of pastoral counseling in order to focus all available resources on the supervisees' personal growth in their professional role. The terms of this definition bear some explanation.

1. Supervision takes place in an *extended relationship* that develops across time. It is not a one-shot affair as consultation sometimes is. We benefit through regular engagement in it. There is an accumulative effect, as we learn to use it, which increases over time and experience.

2. Supervision is founded upon a *mutual agreement* between supervisor and supervisee. This involves a clear contract, verbal and usually written, outlining responsibilities and culminating in evaluation.

3. Supervision involves *systematic reflection* upon *concrete practice*. The actual events of the counseling relationship are presented as precisely as possible. There are many ways to do this. They range from simple recall and verbal reconstruction to the use of verbatim records, process notes, case studies, audio and video tape recordings, and various forms of live supervision. Whatever the method, the essence of supervision is disciplined reflection upon the raw data of concrete practice.

4. The supervisory conversation *focuses all available resources* upon understanding what transpired in the data addressed. For pastoral counselors, these resources include the best conceptual understandings available to supervisor and student from the range of theological knowledge they share, on the one hand, and the knowledge of such human sciences as psychology, sociology, and anthropology, on the other. Whatever helping theories are adopted from contemporary professional disciplines must be constantly placed in mutually critical correlations with the pastoral counselor's own theological assumptions. The notion of shared *availability* between supervisor and student is crucial in such efforts. Both parties must possess conceptual tools with sufficient mastery of their meaning and relevance to make them useable in concrete applications to practice.

5. It follows that supervision cannot impart all the information necessary for understanding the resources it employs. It must rely on the larger context of theological education for this. As conceptual resources are increased in the supervisee through seasoned learning and use, so will the depth of that person's experience in supervision.

6. The aim of supervision is *personal growth in one's professional role.* These words are carefully chosen. As in all good education personal growth is an important goal. No one can engage in such close personal reflection upon efforts to counsel others without wrestling with personal changes that are required to increase effectiveness. These often involve basic patterns in attitude or behavior. Whatever the case, supervision concentrates on making

these changes in one's professional role as a pastoral counselor. This distinguishes it from pastoral counseling or psychotherapy.

Three Clinical Poles

Any effort to engage in constructive reflection upon the raw data of counseling will immediately involve participants in what we term the *three clinical poles*. The focus is clearly upon the concrete process of interaction between counselor and counselee, exchange by exchange, transaction by transaction. This is the first pole for clinical reflection. What went on, step by step, in the counseling relationship? What helped accomplish its purposes? What hindered or got in the way? This will inevitably involve a shift of reflective attention between the second and third clinical poles: the pole involving the counselor and what is going on within his or her internal process and the pole involving the counselee or counselees and what is going on inside their internal systems.

The situation is depicted in Figure 1. The focus of supervisory conversation is clearly on the counseling relationship itself (I—Process Pole). This is represented by the larger circle in the center which encompasses everything that transpires within a particular counseling process between the parties involved. Whatever lies within its boundaries is germane to and admissible within supervisory reflection. This, however, necessitates commensurate amounts of attention to the other two clinical poles.

To understand fully what is going on we must know something about what happens inside the counselor (II—Internal/Counselor[s] Pole). What history, attitudes, intentions, beliefs, and behaviors are brought to the counseling relationship? How do they influence participation in this specific transaction? What previous personal issues come into play? Effective supervision will address any factor in the counselor's own life experience that this particular helping process draws within the circumference of attention. This is represented by the shaded elliptical portion of the circle standing for the pastoral counselor overlapping the area of the larger circle designating the process of pastoral counseling. It represents that part of the counselor's personal life that impinges upon this particular pastoral event. The situation becomes even more complex when we add a second counselor (co-therapy) or a team behind the window (live supervision). What goes on within these relationships is an equally important part of the second clinical pole. But here our model draws a boundary to the domain of supervisory conversation. We address only those issues in the internal life process of counselors to which the counseling event at hand gives rise. Other matters from their personal lives in general are the domain of counseling or psychotherapy proper.

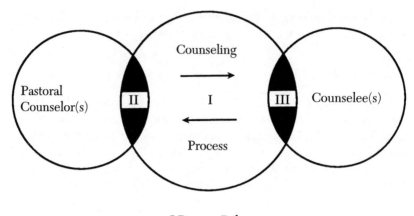

I Process Pole

II Internal/   III Internal/
      Counselor(s)   Counselee(s)
      Pole   Pole

Respirces:

Conceptual: Theological/Psychological
                          Sociological/Anthropological

Methodological: Techniques/Principles/Skills

Figure 1

By the same token, it is equally necessary to concentrate attention upon the person or person receiving counseling (III—Internal/Counselee[s] Pole). We need to know enough about their history, attitudes, beliefs, intentions, and behaviors in order to understand their response to the specific transaction at hand. The deeper the grasp of these factors, the more effective the supervisory conversation in framing strategies, interventions, and interpretations of the process. This becomes even more complex when supervision addresses the internal system of a group, a couple, or a family. Reflective attention to these issues is represented by the elliptical area of the circle designating counselee(s) overlapping the larger circle representing the counseling process itself. It represents what supervision must determine about these persons in order to develop theoretical and methodological skills to provide them with effective pastoral counseling. Research in general about the character of these persons' lives, the structure of relationships that sustain them, or the nature of their beliefs, attitudes, values, and the like belongs beyond the boundaries of supervision and within the domain of some other discipline of study, be it theological, psychological, sociological, anthropological, or whatever. Again, supervision cannot generate within itself the resources upon which it draws.

Among the supervisory traditions we have been considering, we can observe different measures of attention to one or another of these three clinical poles. Anton Boisen's emphasis upon the study of *living human documents* as a source of knowledge about how beliefs function for persons in crisis focused upon Pole III—Internal/Counselee[s]. Cabot and Dicks, through concentrating clinical study on verbatim records of what transpired in the counseling relationship, stressed Pole I—Process. Supervision in the psychodynamic tradition shifted a great deal of attention over to the second clinical pole—Internal/Counselee(s)—as supervisors focused upon the therapists' resistance to learning and countertransference to patients. Yet each approach demands that supervision pay attention to all three. The humanistic tradition, for example, may concentrate supervision on the actual process (I) of counseling through the use of audio and video records of what transpired. But the counselor's congruence in reflecting an inner attitude (II) of belief in each individual's personal worth and capacity to pursue self-chosen solutions to life problems is measured in each counselor-response. And so is the counselor's *empathy* in terms of its accuracy in responding to what is intended in each communication by the counselee (III). Psychodynamic supervisors address their supervisees' unconscious motivations and distortions through countertransference (I) in order to enable them to make accurate interpretations (II) of their patients' internal dynamics (III).

Among supervisors in the systemic tradition there is the same breadth. Structural/strategic supervisors may direct their main attention in live supervision to frame specific interventions in the family system at crucial points (I). Others from the systemic school (systemic, proper) may have the supervisory team engage in a "reflective dialogue" in the family's presence, inventing various accounts of what currently governs its relationships (III) and positively connoting the strategies of individual members. Supervisors who emphasize transgenerational influences may send supervisees back to their families of origin with particular tasks to differentiate themselves from the grips of its emotional process (II), so they may learn how to help clients engage in similar therapeutic missions of their own (III).

Whatever the theoretical tradition of the supervisor, Figure 1 attempts to depict the circular character of supervision as a teaching/ learning process as it addresses its conceptual and methodological resources. Any conceptual understandings of the counseling process that come into play are subjected to their concrete function in understanding the actual process of counseling at hand. Theoretical knowledge finds immediate expression and expansion within the use of each professional skill it dictates, and vice versa, each continually reshaping the other as a certain integrity grows deep within.

Three Dimensions of Supervision

We turn now to identify three dimensions of the supervisory task common to all the approaches we have been considering. Whatever their varying degrees of attention to the three clinical poles, all of them share: (1) a dimension of *administrative oversight* which has to do with maintaining the welfare or treatment of counselees or clients together with whatever institutional structure supports the services that are rendered; (2) a *therapeutic dimension* of personal growth which focuses attention on whatever insight, behavioral change, or other personal conditions must be met by the supervisee in order to increase personal effectiveness; and (3) a dimension of the *working alliance in* the supervisory relationships themselves between supervisee, peers, and supervisor which requires periodic attention to make the whole process work.

Each of these three dimensions provides an essential element to the supervisory conversation. Yet each can become a hook upon which the supervisory process gets caught and subverted. Any one of the three, if permitted to dominate the others to the point of their exclusion, can render the process ineffectual. Yet each is so vital in its time that its neglect disestablishes supervision, giving rise to the clinical axiom: when supervision is stuck in one dimension, switch to another and see where that leads.

Administrative Oversight

In all supervision, there is an inevitable tension between the desire to train the student and a sense of responsibility to oversee the care of clients or patients. What distinguishes supervision from ordinary administrative oversight in general is its central commitment to teach a way of thinking and acting in accord with conceptualizations from a professional role. Its disciplined reflection will always go beyond merely devising more effective strategies and methods. The supervisor is an educator out to create a climate of intensely personal learning in which patterns of thinking and responding are developed that may last a lifetime.

So this first dimension of the supervisory conversation begins with a focus on the task of delivering effective pastoral counseling to the client. But it may take many turns along the way. Allowances may be made for students to learn at their own pace, to make their own mistakes and benefit from them. New concepts may require tentative periods of incubation; new skills may result in awkward periods of uncertain efforts to try on new methods for size to see how they fit. Most good supervisors will make a conscious choice at times to permit supervisees to struggle with their partially-formed understandings that are less than state of the art. In supervision it is always more important that trainees learn to do things for themselves rather than that these things be done as quickly and effectively as possible—for example, by the supervisor stepping in and doing it for them which is a common pitfall in live supervision.

Clinical supervisors from any tradition constantly balance their attention between concerns for personal learning and concerns for the welfare of the patient. There are times when concerns for a counselee's well-being will override personal learning. For example, severely depressed persons who are at risk of suicide require well-established procedures that refrain from excessive nurture, obtain clear contracts against harming themselves, and make appropriate referral which no responsible supervisor would leave to a process of trial and error. There are limits in the minds of most supervisors having to do with protecting counselees from excessive control and domination by a trainee who talks too much or protecting particular individuals who are vulnerable from excessive confrontation or harmful criticism. As liability increases along with litigation against malpractice in the field of mental health, no supervisory program in pastoral counseling will ignore this dimension of administrative oversight in order to protect the services it renders at the institutional level.

Within some traditions where instructions, directives, and demonstrations by the supervisor are a normal part of supervision, there is minimal conflict between administrative and supervisory concerns. Structural/strategic supervisors doing live supervision of family therapy assume full responsibility for the course for treatment and intervene from behind the one-way glass with clear directives to supervisees about what they should do ("Give them my voice"). Their assumption is that competence is learned by being empowered to act effectively rather than left to founder in search of one's own resources.

In other situations, however, a subtle tension between administrative and supervisory concerns follows each step of the way. Take live supervision of a co-leader in group counseling, for example. Will supervisees learn more if the supervisor interrupts and guides at crucial points when the group is at a loss or if the supervisor permits supervisees to struggle for a while to find their own way? How effective is learning when the supervisor takes over at a particular point and demonstrates an alternative when the supervisee is stuck? And how long should the supervisor refrain from doing so in order to give supervisees a chance to discover things for themselves without abdicating shared responsibility in the overall course of the group's life?

It is clear that excessive concern in this dimension of administrative oversight can disestablish learning, particularly if permitted to eclipse the other two dimensions of supervision. But one wonders if any form of supervision can ever be free from some tension between the desire to let supervisees learn by trial and error and the desire to ensure the highest quality of practice the supervisory system can muster, moment by moment. Supervision is always conducted within the context of a larger system of administrative relationships constantly triangling others into its procedures. We have cited examples where our supervisor may represent the welfare of a particular patient or serve as interpreter of institutional policies. At other times the open nature of the supervisory relationship calls for the freedom to question and challenge existing regulations, theories, and practices. Sensitive supervisors will not permit the administrative dimension of their role to dominate it to the exclusion of such concerns.

The Therapeutic Dimension

In the intensely personal task of pastoral counseling, strong measures of self-confrontation are unavoidable. We use ourselves as an instrument to bring about change. In supervision we are faced continually with some personal impasse that gets in our way when we set out to be of help to others. Things happen that demand that we change, too. The therapeutic dimension of supervision focuses attention upon whatever insight, behavioral change, or other personal conditions need to be met by the supervisee in order to function effectively in the role of pastoral counselor.

There are a number of ways to look at this therapeutic dimension. One is to recognize a certain inner integrity that all good counselors have. It makes us reluctant to expect others whom we counsel to deal with anything we must avoid or have not yet mastered in our own lives. We cannot help a counselee unearth a hidden rage that has been denied for years if we fear or deny a similar anger in our own experience. We cannot counsel a couple deeply divided over parenting their children without encountering the difficulties marking the relationships in our own marriage and family. In supervision we are always bumping into our own unfinished business. In this sense, each new troublesome client bears a gift of self-confrontation that brings us up short before our next issue of personal growth, regardless of how experienced we think we are.

Consequently, each supervisory tradition allowed for this therapeutic dimension in particular ways. Supervisors in the psychodynamic tradition sought to provide the same intensely personal relationship that the therapist provides in psychotherapy, permitting trainees to identify and work through personal issues that inhibited both their learning and their effectiveness with clients. In many schools of group therapy, a treatment experience as a member of a therapy group became a standard part of supervisory training to lead one. Supervisors in the humanistic tradition founded the supervisory experience upon providing supervisees the same therapeutic conditions of empathetic understanding, respect, and genuineness their trainees were taught to extend to clients. From the beginning the CPE tradition included a group experience for supervisees as a formal part of supervisory efforts to address personal issues evoked by training.

For supervision within the tradition of systems theory, the issue has not been so clear-cut. Transgenerational schools had no difficulty including specific tasks of differentiation from the therapist-in-training's family of origin within supervision. But systems theorists who always address the marital and family unit as a whole had no place for dealing with personal behavior apart from its context. They confronted specific relational issues among trainees within the isomorphic character of their appearance through the system of supervised therapy which we described earlier. The therapist's problem with the family becomes the supervisor's problem with the therapist in supervision, permitting necessary changes in relational behavior to be dealt with in the context of the supervisory relationship itself.

It is no accident that all of our supervisory traditions set out to model in the supervisory relationship the essence of what they regard to be curative or therapeutic in the psychotherapy they supervise. This is more than practicing what you preach or demonstrating what you teach. It is a necessary step in the training of effective counselors. It is one thing to go off in private and to get our act together in personal psychotherapy. It is another to keep that act together through continual entry into and involvement in the many personal and interpersonal systems of others we seek to help. The latter constitutes the therapeutic dimension of supervision.

The therapeutic dimension of our model maintains a clear boundary between these two domains of psychotherapy and supervision. Any personal issue that supervision addresses must originate within the supervisee's professional relationships. The supervisory conversation need not impose an unnatural restriction on discussing its specifics. Supervisees are free to generalize to the presence of similar conflicts throughout their lives, fitting their present experience into the larger mosaic of their own personal history. But our model limits the attention given to working for personal change in those professional relationships to whatever is occurring here and now. It does not extend attention to one's personal past or present family life or other non-professional relationships. Within these boundaries anything therapeutic that can be accomplished within supervision is a responsible use of time and energy. Supervisors may model good counseling procedures in identifying and exploring the problem. Specific strategies to work through its grips in the present sphere of clinical relationships with administrators, peers, supervisors, and patients are well within the bounds of supervisory conversation.

The therapeutic dimension of supervision can also become a hook that subverts its process. Occasionally a trainee's personal problems become so great that they dominate the supervisory hour. The focus of reflection upon concrete clinical practice is surrendered and supervision is converted into personal therapy. We have identified this as a supervisory game called "Sick" in training workshops for supervisors. In its common form, both supervisor and supervisee subtly agree at a covert level that the supervisee is so "troubled," "mixed up," "stressed," or "confused" that each supervisory hour is converted into counseling regarding these problems. Responsible presentation and assessment of clinical materials is avoided. The student is "Sick" and cannot be expected to perform competently. The supervisor gets to demonstrate the role of "Wonderful Counselor." In its more subtle forms, clinical learning is undermined by referring everything to one's current personal issue, excusing oneself from substantial, critical reflection upon the work at hand. This is a temptation for more seasoned players who would rather be "Sick" than "Stupid." Resolutions are found through referring the trainee's personal issues to a proper setting for psychotherapy outside supervision where they can receive adequate time and attention. Supervision then may reestablish its focus in the first dimension of administrative oversight.

The Working Alliance

The third dimension of supervisory reflection is the working alliance in the supervisory relationship itself. The term is borrowed from the psychodynamic tradition to describe a quality of collaboration in supervision similar to the one in psychotherapy between analyst and patient (Bordin, 1982). At the heart of this collaboration for change is a bonding aspect of working together in cooperative endeavor. It is like the rhythmic "Heave Ho!" through which a team of persons moves a heavy object. It demands that the parties succeed in building up, repairing, and maintaining this working relationship.

Supervisors can count on experiencing some substantial resistance from each person entering supervision with them. Psychodynamic supervisors offer a vivid description of characteristic forms of resistance encountered among psychotherapists-in-training (Ekstein and Wallerstein, 1958, pp. 142–156). Some students approach learning through vigorous denying, warding off the impact of supervision by reducing it to the familiar or refusing to acknowledge that any help can accrue. Others learn only through submission, the too easy manner of adopting the supervisor's offerings, leading to an imitative assumption of external trappings of content without truly effective learning. Still others react with a *"mea culpa"* attitude which constitutes a response with embarrassment and readied acknowledgement magnifying one's own feelings to the point of caricature and learning only by being beaten. Still others evade supervision by awarding the supervisor the task of achieving results, refusing to accept a role of responsible participation. Others have problems finding a problem to discuss or escape through over-involvement by maintaining so many conflicting interests that training is obtained "on the run."

There are any number of ways in the literature on supervision to conceptualize the particular forms this resistance may take. Supervisors from several traditions have elected to use Eric Berne's metaphor of psychological games to identify a number of "supervisory games" that can be observed between supervisors and supervisees (Kadushin, 1968; Steere, 1969; McCarty, 1978). Such games involve supervisor and student in an unconscious collusion to avoid the demanding task of supervision through a repetitive series of transactions (moves), governed by an ulterior and complementary alliance of which they are unaware, progressing to a predictable outcome (payoff) that frustrates the professed aims of both parties (Berne, 1964). A typical example is "Look What You Made Me Do" in which the supervisee shifts increasing responsibility to the supervisor ("You're the Super") who eventually designs some strategy for the supervisee's counseling. The supervisee meticulously executes the task, unsuccessfully returning with clinical data to the effect of "Look What You Made Me Do," disestablishing the professional and personal well-being of both parties.

Others conceptualize resistance in terms of "irrational beliefs" and "self-defeating philosophies" with which supervisees needlessly upset themselves. The three most common ones are: (1) "I *must* do well in supervision and be approved by my supervisor"; (2) "My supervisor *has* to be competent and treat me fairly"; (3) "The supervision program *must* be well arranged and effective, and *I can't stand it if it isn't*" (Wessler and Ellis, 1982).

Whatever one's perspective, some reflection upon the character of the supervisory relationship itself proves necessary to establish and maintain its working alliance. Whatever self-defeating patterns of feeling, thinking, and acting its parties carry into everyday life will eventually emerge to disrupt collaboration and mutual trust. If permitted to go unattended, the quality of this working alliance deteriorates, yielding unvoiced frustration with one another and increasingly ineffective supervisory hours.

Whenever the supervisory conversation addresses this dimension of its working alliance, it also enters the fertile field of exploring what we have described as *parallel process* and the *isomorphic character* of the entire system surrounding the therapeutic relationship. We have noted this recurrent tendency of the therapist's issues in the treatment relationship to reappear in the supervisory relationship and vice versa. For example, an otherwise cooperative and forthright trainee presented in a somewhat defiant and obscure way his work with a client who himself was rebelliously nondescript about his own life experience in the counseling hour. Before either party was aware of it, the supervisor was probing for information that was missing and not forthcoming from the supervisee who became more defensive and guarded, replicating the frustrating experience in the counseling relationship upon which the two reflected.

Psychodynamic explanations of this parallel process view the counselor as identifying with the counselee and unconsciously presenting this emotional material to the supervisor in the way it was encountered. Such efforts can persist for lengthy periods of supervision when the counselee's issue is sufficiently similar to something in the counselor's own personal life that persists and begs for resolution. First dimension efforts at clinical reflection are increasingly frustrated and ineffective as both the treatment and its supervision become bogged down in this impasse of parallel process. Third dimension resolutions through reflection upon the supervisory relationship not only serve to restore effective collaboration but present the counselor-in-training with a corrective experience that is normally accompanied by a similar breakthrough with the counselee in counseling.

The experience of *isomorphism* reported by systemic supervisors, however, suggests that we are dealing with an even broader phenomenon. This same parallel process appears to manifest itself throughout the entire system of relationships surrounding marriage and family therapy. For example, during a session of live supervision, therapy with a family behind the glass suddenly became confusing and chaotic as both parents criticized each other. Anxiety rose and communication became tangential. The hapless co-therapists emerged from the room for consultation with the "team" behind the glass with mounting anxiety, feeling both confused and critical of each other. Conversation among team members was equally chaotic, and efforts by the supervisor to focus feedback were met with tangential responses. The supervisor became critical of the team and anxious about restoring some order and potency to the therapy. It was as though the whole system of relationships surrounding the family therapy had been unwittingly inducted into one and the same problem-determined system.

I have come to regard such isomorphism as not only common but inevitable among sensitive and caring human systems. There are a number of metaphors by which to comprehend its effect and contemplate appropriate awareness, detachment, and intervention. The *hypnotic* metaphor is one. Through involvement and joining efforts we are inducted into the family system at some level of its emotional fusion, thereby beginning to feel the way its members feel, think the way its members think, and respond the way its members do to the problems at hand. Constructive intervention demands that we somehow break this trance.

Another is the metaphor of the *game* as it is used by Berne and Palazzoli (Berne, 1964; Palazzoli, Cirillo, Selvini, and Sorrentino, 1989). The game metaphor preserves the notion of a number of players beneath their level of ordinary awareness being drawn into an elaborate system of interaction which progresses to a repetitive and well-defined outcome. It effectively integrates the notion of general rules governing the players' interactions (systemics—holistic thinking) and moves made by individual subjects (strategic thinking) embodying ideas of conflict and deception. Whenever we address a human problem with any depth and reflect upon it in supervision, we all become players from our own specific vantage point: therapists, supervisors, referring parties, administrators, families, supporting figures, etc. To become involved is to enter the game at some point as a player with a position and a role. To change the outcome involves supervision in the necessary task of reflection in this third dimension with sufficient detachment and differentiation from present rules and personal strategies to function as part of the solution rather than part of the problem.

I am reminded of the old German fairy tale in which a boy steals the magic goose and becomes stuck to it. Subsequently, anyone who touches the boy or the goose or anyone touching the boy or the goose also becomes stuck. Any effort to extricate or free participants involves the next person becoming stuck, and what we encounter in such a problem-determined system as a game are numbers of people wandering across the countryside all stuck together. Supervision begins and ends with the search for effective means by which supervisor and supervisee can unstick themselves, so that they can help other people in the system to unstick themselves.

Bibliography

Berne, E. *Games People Play.* New York: Acove Press, 1964.
———. *Principles of Group Treatment.* New York: Oxford University Press, 1966.
Boisen, A. T. "The Challenge to Our Seminaries," *Journal of Pastoral Care,* Spring 1951, pp. 8–12.
Bordin, E. S. "A Working Alliance-based Model of Supervision," *The Counseling Psychologist* 11 (1):35–42 (1982).
Cabot, R. C. *Adventures on the Borderline of Ethics.* New York: Harper & Brothers, 1926.
Cabot, R. C. and Dicks, R. L. *The Art of Ministering to the Sick.* New York: Macmillan Co., 1936.
Carkhuff, R. *The Art of Helping VI.* Amherst: Human Resources Development Press, 1987.
Carter, E. A., "Supervisory Discussion in the Presence of the Family," in R. Whiffin and J. Byng-Hall, eds, *Family Therapy Supervision.* London: Gruss and Stratton, 1982, pp. 69–90.
Clebsch, W. A. and Jaekle, C. R. *Pastoral Care in Historic Perspective.* Englewood Cliffs, N.J.: Prentice-Hall, Inc., 1964.
Doehrman, M. J. G., "Parallel Process in Supervision and Psychotherapy," *Bulletin of the Menninger Clinic,* March 1976, pp. 9–104.
Ekstein, R. and Wallerstein, R. S. *The Teaching and Learning of Psychotherapy.* New York: Basic Books, 1958.
Estadt, B. K., Compton, J. R., and Blanchette, M. C., eds., *The Art of Clinical Supervision: A Pastoral Counseling Perspective.* Mahwah: Paulist Press, 1987.
Freud, S. "The History of the Psychanalytic Movement," in *The Basic Writings of Sigmund Freud,* trans. and ed. A. A. Biell. New York: Random House, 1938.
Hiltner, S. *Preface to Pastoral Theology.* Nashville: Abingdon Press, 1958.
Hoffman, L. W. *Old Scapes, New Maps: A Training Program for Psychotherapy Supervisors.* Cambridge: Milusik Press, 1990.
Kadushin, A. "Games People Play in Supervision," *Social Work,* July 1968, pp. 23–32.
Laing, R. D. *Politics of the Family.* New York: Vintage Books, 1972.
Liddle, H. A., Breunlin, D. C., and Schwartz, R. C., eds., *Handbook of Family Therapy Training and Supervision.* New York: London: Guilford Press, 1988.
McCarty, D. *The Supervision of Ministry Students.* Atlanta: Southwest Baptist Home Mission Board, Southern Baptist Convention, 1978.
Mead, D. E., ed. *Effective Supervision.* New York: Brunner/Mazel, 1990.

Palazzoli, M. S., Cirillo, S., Selvini, M. and Sorrentino, A. M. *Family Games*. New York and London: W. W. Norton & Co., 1989.

Practical Applications in Supervision. A Manual Written by the California Association for Marriage and Family Therapists Educational Foundation, 1990.

Ritterman, M. *Using Hypnosis in Family Therapy*. San Francisco: Jossey-Bass, 1983.

Rogers, C. R. *The Clinical Treatment of the Problem Child*. Boston: Houghton Mifflin Co., 1939.

————. *Client-Centered Therapy: Its Current Practice, Implications, and Theory*. New York: Houghton Mifflin Co., 1951.

———— and Becker, R. J. "A Basic Orientation for Counseling," *Pastoral Psychology*, February 1950, pp. 26–34.

———— and Dymond, R. F., eds. *Psychotherapy in Personal Change*. Chicago: University of Chicago Press, 1954.

Schuster, J. J., Sandt, J. J., and Thaler, O. F. *Clinical Supervision of the Psychiatric Resident*. New York: Brunner/Mazel, 1972.

Simon, R. "Behind the One Way Mirror: An Interview with Jay Haley," *Family Therapy Networker*, Sept.–Oct. 1982, pp. 18–25, 28, 29, 58, 59.

————. "Deeper, Deeper, Deeper…The Family's Hypnotic Pull," *Family Therapy Networker* 9 (March–April 1985), pp. 20–28, 69–71.

Steere, D. A., "An Experiment in Supervisory Training," *Journal of Pastoral Care*, December 1969, pp. 202–217.

Steere, D. A., *The Supervision of Pastoral Care*. Louisville/Westminster: John Knox Press, 1989.

Wessler, R. and Ellis, A. "Supervision in Counseling: Rational Emotive Therapy," *The Counseling Psychologist* 11 (1):443–449, 1982.

Whiffin, R. and Byng-Hall, J. Jr. eds. *Family Therapy Supervision: Recent Developments in Practice*. London: Grune and Stralton, 1982.

Whittaker, C. A. "Hypnosis and Family Depth Therapy," in *Eriksonian Approaches to Hypnosis and Psychotherapy*, Jeffrey K. Zeig, ed. New York: Brunner/Mazel, 1982.

Joanne Marie G. Greer

18. Research in Pastoral Counseling: A Responsibility and an Opportunity

Introduction

According to Strunk (1985), *modern* pastoral counseling is tied both to theology and to a group of human sciences which were nonexistent during much of the history of pastoral counseling. This highlights a specific research dilemma in pastoral counseling: to what extent is the pastoral counseling researcher to be guided by belief, and to what extent by state-of-the-art science? The answer to this question is neither obvious nor simple, but is an important first step in delineating the nature of pastoral counseling research. In this chapter I will attempt to identify some reasonable responses to this global definitional question, and will also survey the armamentarium of social science research techniques to identify those techniques most congenial to the pastoral counseling research effort. Finally, I will address the training of future researchers in pastoral counseling.

Section 1. Can Pastoral Counseling Be Simultaneously "Pastoral" and "Scientific"?

Pastoral counselors represent a recent-day rapprochement between (psychological) science and religion. It is useful to consider an earlier rapprochement between these two fields: the shaman-healer evolved into the physician-healer. It is noteworthy that clinical psychology and psychiatry, as the heirs of the religious shaman, still retain some qualities of the religious side of humankind. Even the secular mental health worker is to some vestigial extent influenced by the religious heritage of mental health work. For example, it is difficult to persevere in the work of psychotherapy without something very like the religious virtue of hope. But the greater weight of influence for the secular mental health worker comes from the secular scientific world. What is the appropriate balance between religion and secular science for the pastoral counselor, and, more specifically, for the pastoral counseling *researcher?*

The worldview of the pastoral counselor is somewhat different, and may be *very* different from that of the secular health professional. A number of decades have been dedicated to studying the interface of faith and psychological science for the practitioner pastoral counselor. While these clarifications and reflections can partially inform pastoral counseling research, other important issues remain to be addressed. These questions are specific to the triple interface of the *pastoral* role, the *counselor* role, and the *researcher* role.

The most simplistic approach to structured research is found in the straightforward application of laboratory scientific method: the formulating and testing of hypotheses and the rejection of (or failure to accept) unsupported beliefs. This research process appears to be, in its narrowest form, antithetical to the life of faith, which consists *precisely* in the acceptance of unsupported beliefs. Where, then, can there be a rapprochement between the scientific method in behavioral science research and the faith basis in pastoral counseling? This is the most difficult question which this chapter will attempt to address.

There are several types of pastorally-oriented research to consider in attempting to define "pastoral counseling research":

1. Studies of believers as sociological groups. An example might be "A comparative study of child-rearing practices of believers and non-believers." This type of study is not pastoral counseling research, but rather belongs to the sociology of religion, an academic field. While certainly these studies are often interesting to religious persons (what group does not enjoy reading about itself?), they are of only peripheral use in the professional work of the pastoral counselor. These studies may expand a counselor's knowledge of the individual subculture within which a client lives, but these studies do not add to the knowledge of how best to perform pastoral counseling, or how to assess the *intrapsychic* outcomes of pastoral counseling.

Precisely because sociological studies are *sociological* rather than religious, they are easier to execute with technical precision. Sociology-of-religion researchers do not have to struggle with the interface of faith and their academic discipline, and deal only in a limited way with intrapsychic life. Rather, they simply follow good general research practices to observe the presumed effects of faith or church membership and activities in their area of interest: social behavior.

2. Research aimed at proving, through psychological or behavioral observations and measurements, the positive effects of various beliefs and belief systems on the mental health status and social behavior of believers.

These studies are similar in abstract structure to well-known studies of relationships between belief systems and *physical* health: e.g., the studies showing positive health impact of the dietary practices of the Seventh Day Adventists.

Such studies belong to a type of research I would like to designate by the term "motivated research." A flippant formulation of the hypotheses of such studies might be "Jesus cures" (either instead of or in addition to "Jesus saves"). Clearly, motivated research reaches out toward the non-believing community with a variation of what an Anglican pastor of my acquaintance calls "rice Christianity," i.e., the practice of missionaries in feeding non-believers in order to later convert them. Motivated research strives to *prove* that believers are better off (better fed) in the here-and-now than the non-believers are, with the evident intent of promoting esteem for and interest in religion. Therefore, motivated research has a type of open or covert apologetics function. One might almost call it marketing research on behalf of God as the good psychological product. Critiquing the theology behind such research hypotheses is beyond the scope of my paper. But it is important to understand that purposeful studies of this ilk are generally disrespected in the secular academic community because such studies violate long-standing principles of scientific research. A key ideal of secular scientific research is a neutrality toward the outcome of a study; properly designed and executed research does not seek so much to prove a pre-conceived position as to explore what might be so. In my opinion, motivated research has no reasonable audience. To the educated non-believer this research is likely to be an object of ridicule, while for the believer this research could easily be understood as offering a false set of reasons for the continued practice of faith, hope, and love, and could therefore actually be deleterious to faith development. Both of these outcomes seem highly undesirable.

For all these reasons, I feel that motivated research should not be practiced in the pastoral counseling community any more than it should be practiced in medical or scientific studies.

3. Theoretical psychological studies which seek to *identify psychological factors* that facilitate or hamper the life of faith or the identification of and fulfillment of one's place in creation in the here-and-now. Concomitantly, one must also include research seeking to identify efficient pastoral-therapeutic strategies to *remove intrapsychic obstacles* to the life of faith or to the identification of and fulfillment of one's place in creation. This latter research would correspond to what is known in secular psychology as "research on technique."

These types of research seem most appropriate to designate as "pastoral counseling research" because such studies represent an appropriate melding of the psychological and the faith knowledge bases found in pastoral counseling. An example of the first category might be "a study of the environmental and developmental factors *which may facilitate* the life of faith within a marriage commitment." An example of the second category might be "a study of optimal psychological distance and intimacy within the pastoral counseling dyad for *facilitating* progress of the client." The phrasing of hypotheses in terms of *facilitating* rather than *causing* a spiritual/psychological outcome seems an important distinction which should be found throughout pastoral counseling research. The pastoral counselor presumably believes in the primacy of God as the ultimate source of human spiritual, social, and psychological growth. At the same time, the pastoral counselor as mental health worker is also involved in a human apostolate, in furthering the work of God, and thus may reasonably turn to research in order to identify better ways to carry out his or her human collaboration in the work of God.

Section II. Some General Ideas About Method in Research: What Is "Methodology"?

Methodology in any research field consists of a few broadly defined activities: (1) development of statements of models to explain data of interest to the particular discipline; (2) development of formal definitions and measures of the constructs in the model(s); (3) development of formal tests of the explanatory power of any model, as compared with competing models; (4) extension of knowledge by application of inductive and deductive reasoning to make extrapolations from validated models. Specifics of this process are necessarily influenced by the particular discipline's accumulated body of knowledge. However, the general structure of necessity conforms to certain basic rules of logic, no matter what the discipline.

What is a "model"? Our intuitive idea is sound when we think of a "model airplane" or a "model community mental health center." A model unites into a formal relationship all the parts which we find necessary to some idea such as "airplane" or "mental health center." The model airplane is a better example because it has an element of *simplification* which is ordinarily found in a research model. A research model is a statement of the essential relationship(s) among a set of concepts and/or objects of interest. The non-essential is stripped off, to better examine the underlying skeleton.

As the reader may immediately suspect, a regular area of contention among researchers in any particular field is whether or not this or that attribute is essential. Such disputes are negotiable, based on further research. Here is a pleasing example, from educational research. For many years educational researchers maintained that class size was an important variable in any school-based learning model. A researcher who suspected that class size was irrelevant did a naturalistic study of class sizes in public schools. He gathered achievement data on the children in various class sizes found in public school, ranging from fifteen to forty children per class. He found no difference in their achievement, after statistically adjusting for differences in IQ, social status, etc. A dissenting researcher replicated the study, looking at class sizes between five and fifteen. He found that class size *in that range* was a significant factor in learning. These two researchers were able to resolve their dispute, based on one's partial replication of the other's research.

This is a particularly nice example because it conveys the spirit of testing models with data—a process which is cumulative and to a great extent collaborative. It is unlikely that any one researcher will have all the relevant insights on a specific problem. Therefore, a necessary aspect of methodology is the *standardization* of descriptive and inferential processes to make communication with other researchers possible. Such standardization also makes possible parsimonious and elegant variations, replications, tests, challenges, and extensions to another researcher's work.

An essential aspect of the standardization of method is the *abstracting* of both the model and hypotheses into some form of notation. Math-haters in any field usually have to be persuaded that this translation is necessary. A Danny Kaye joke gets this point over very effectively:

Two Persons at a Cocktail Party
Speaker 1: How did you like the Himalayas?
Speaker 2: Loved him; Hated her.

The point is, words don't mean the same to different people. Before you and I can either argue or agree, we must unambiguously communicate. We must struggle with the process of setting down our hypotheses in a mutually understood, standard form. Research methodology gives us the tool for this. During this century, logicians, mathematicians, statisticians, philosophers, operations research analysts, linguists, psychologists, engineers, and others have evolved a set formal vocabulary with which to explicate and debate models. Pastoral counseling has absolutely no choice but to master this language. Further, it is certainly possible for pastoral counselors to do so. This is clearly so because the needed material is being taught at the master's level in almost all post-bachelor's curricula in social sciences, behavioral sciences, and education.

On the other hand, research courses need not be *heavily* mathematical, and indeed should not be, at all levels of instruction except the most advanced. Mathematical foundations are necessary for the average user only to the extent that they help a person understand what to do. As Roberts notes,

> The essence of statistics is only incidentally mathematical: It embraces the systematic formulation of decision and inferential problems, including the recognition that there is a problem; the formulation of tentative statistical models to guide data analysis, which requires understanding of the assumptions or specifications required for proper application of the models; and the diagnostic checking and fitting of these tentative models. In the process of teaching these things we need to stress real problems, not finger exercises for arithmetic....Further, the tools of statistics given highest emphasis should be those of highest potential in the student's field of application (Roberts, 1978).

Non-mathematicians often think that mathematics as a discipline is both inflexible and exact. John Von Neumann noted that these are in fact misconceptions, and mathematicians actually disagree about what constitutes adequate proof, and which parts of the discipline are proven beyond doubt. He felt that a more important contribution of mathematics to our thinking is that it has demonstrated an enormous flexibility in the *formation of concepts,* a degree of flexibility to which it is very difficult to arrive in a non-mathematical mode (J. Von Neumann, 1963).

One aspect of testing models where mathematics is both unavoidable and extremely helpful is the process of devising measures. A measure can be as simple as a tally of occurrences of a certain type of material in a client's sessions. Other measures are simply categories: male/female, child/adult, etc. Some measures are relatively continuous like IQ, income, and age. The process of manipulating and combining measures without violating logic is a tricky business, because the measures are only imperfect representations of the idea being measured.

Elementary measurement theory is easily mastered by beginning research design students, and most also find it very interesting. This is another area where it is most efficient to learn a little for oneself, even when consultants are available. After all, no consultant will have a truly personal insight into one's own data and one's own planned comparisons and contrasts.

A pastoral counselor researcher-to-be must learn to state an unambiguous research hypothesis, identify relevant data with which to test it, evaluate alternative measures, select a technically adequate measure, take proper account of competing explanations of change, and decide whether the results of the study support or disprove the hypothesis.

Section III. Does Correct Methodology *Really* Matter?

Methodology is sometimes scorned as mere "number-crunching." One cannot deny that research methods are but the handmaiden of the research itself. Nevertheless, proper research design always elucidates the truth, while slapdash designs may hopelessly obscure it. Several humorous books have built upon this fact, including *How to Lie with Statistics* (Huff, 1954) and *Science Is a Sacred Cow* (Standen, 1950). Good methodology makes a disciplined researcher.

If the content of one's discipline is of emotional importance, it becomes difficult to remain aware of the line between facts and beliefs (Martin, 1983). Methodology converts beliefs, hunches, clinical judgment, and accumulated experience into testable hypotheses which can then be *objectively* validated. Method is the researcher's protection against self-deception. The author of *Science Is a Sacred Cow* twits the biased researcher with an apocryphal tale of the research subject who gets drunk on whiskey and soda water on Monday, brandy and soda water on Tuesday, gin and soda water on Wednesday, etc. What caused his drunkenness? Obviously the common factor, soda water. What is the methodology lesson in this tale? Competing explanations for the same data must be given a fair chance to emerge (Standen, 1950, at p. 25).

A more subtle example of a poor research design is the following. A mental health researcher looked at the correlation between certain brain scan data and characteristics of the "Multiple Personality" diagnosis. To do this the researcher repetitively reused a small sample of twelve subjects to compute fifteen correlation coefficients, one by one. It requires a fairly good knowledge of statistical research methodology to recognize that these computations are fatally flawed and therefore the results are uninterpretable. The results are meaningless because a relative balance must be preserved between the number of computations to be extracted from the data and the number of research subjects, known as degrees of freedom. Ignoring requisite degrees of freedom for one's desired computations will give-results. which are indeterminate, i.e., uninterpretable.

Even if there were an adequate number of subjects, this particular study also has a second design flaw. It reuses the same subjects fifteen times for fifteen simple computations, rather than using a more complex overall significance test. As a result, the probability levels for the fifteen statistical tests will be incorrect and misleading. This second example was deliberately selected to have less obvious flaws, in order to bring home the impossibility of relying on untutored logic to develop a viable research design. Issues such as degrees of freedom and repeated reuse of the same subjects are sometimes complex, and are best taken care of by including a statistician on the planning team for a research project. However, for many small studies this is not practical. Consequently, any researcher must master the general concepts and a few rules of thumb about sample selection.

A basic course in research design can be thought of as a map to the mine field which lies in the researcher's way as he or she struggles to concretize and test hypotheses. Teachers of these courses sometimes joke about the sincerity model, i.e., the attitude that "I have a worthy hypothesis and I am sincere in seeking the truth, therefore I need not worry about all these technicalities" (Patton, 1978). The pursuit of probable truth is a harsh business. It *does* matter whether or not the data are sufficient to support the hypotheses. If not, the researcher's situation is similar to that of the person who believes he can walk safely out of a tenth-story window. Disaster strikes just as surely whether he believes he is safe or not.

A philosophical side benefit of formal research designs is their unrelenting reminder that a model is just a model, and not a reality. The reification of constructs such as ego, superego, id, or self is an ongoing problem in mental health theorizing. Such failures of logic can be avoided by recalling the fact that the data and not the model is the ultimate reality. Theorists from a wide variety of fields find themselves struggling against the wish to reify constructs. Noted psychometric researcher Lee Cronbach once commented, "The true IQ is a hero-figure as well known to us as the Lone Ranger; we try to tell about it and suddenly realize that not even Wechsler himself knows what the "true Full Scale IQ" might mean" (Cronbach et al., 1972).

Testing of treatment models for efficacy and specificity can only be accomplished by formal confrontation of model with data. In the process one grasps firmly that models and constructs are not *things* but *ideas*. In the end, the model must bow to the data. As one enthusiastic statistician's T-shirt proclaimed, "Data Is Everything!" Respect for the data is the most important principle of research. If the data don't fit the model, it is the model that is suspect, because the model is only an idea, while the data are a part of reality.

It is also extremely important to insist upon precise variable definitions. Here we will find the solution to such seeming dilemmas as research studies which purport to prove that untrained counselors are as effective as highly trained ones, or that short-term behavioral modification is as effective as long-term insight oriented counseling. The treatment situations are most probably *not* equivalent in their outcomes. They may seem so simply because the data gathered are too simplistic for an accurate test of the hypotheses. When the correct contrasts are identified, and the appropriate data has been gathered, it will be possible to demonstrate the differences we hypothesize to exist. For example, studies which purport to prove that short-term behavior modification is equal to long-term insight-oriented therapy use a less complex model of human functioning. Few pastoral counselors would be satisfied with a treatment regimen which merely got a client to go to work every day and stop making trouble at home. Yet these are two common criteria for short-term mental health treatment success.

Section IV. Hypothesis Testing: "Did Anything Really Happen?"

A very major concern of methodology is separating random fluctuation, often called "error" or "noise," from *meaningful* ups and downs in the data. The central classical data-analytic technique, Analysis of Variance (ANOVA), separates the fluctuations in the data into (1) variations within groups and (2) variations between groups. This permits the researcher to consider whether the differences *between* two groups (either treatment-1 versus treatment-2, or treatment versus control) are considerably greater than the differences among the clients *within* each of the groups. If the subjects are assigned to their groups randomly, then the variation *within* any group represents expectable human variability, as opposed to variability due to treatment. In contrast, the variability *between* two groups will represent the true differences duo to treatment. The ratio of these two types of variability is "tested for significance." If the ratio is favorable, the treatment is promising.

If the data do not show a difference, however, the formal method merely withholds judgment. For this reason, careful researchers speak of "failing to reject the hypothesis of no differences" rather than "accepting the hypothesis of no differences." This is an important point for pastoral counselors to grasp, because it is quite possible that finding ways to study pastoral counseling with formal scientific method may take time. The learning process may involve some failures, and it is important to understand that these should in no way be taken to prove that pastoral counseling is without a unique impact.

To make clearer the advantages of formal comparisons across randomized groups, let's consider the most commonly used defective research design, the "one group pre-test/post-test study." The usual form of such comparative studies is a pre-treatment and a post-treatment measure. As Rogosa and Willett (1985) note, however, designs with only two observations are usually inadequate for the assessment of systematic individual differences in growth. This is because the subtle movements forward and backward during the period of change are lost when measures are taken at only the beginning and the end of the treatment period. Further, this design offers no means to measure and to separate out the common human variability from the variability due to the treatment effect. This design was often seen a generation ago in mental health treatment research. Introduction of a second group, a control group, has led to the surprising finding that some people get well with no treatment at all! Consequently, any claims for treatment efficacy must be superior to the effect of simply leaving the client alone. To demonstrate this incremental efficacy, one needs a control group.

Other kinds of variability besides unwanted random variability must also be controlled. For example, an intake process before counseling may have a biasing effect on the measure of counseling effectiveness. The "Solomon four-group design" controls for this problem:

Time

Group-1	Intake	Treatment	Post-test
Group-2	Intake	No Treatment	Post-test
Group-3	No Intake	Treatment	Post-test
Group-4	No Intake	No Treatment	Post-test

Here the effects of the post-test can be measured on Group-4, and the effects of the pretest can be measured by Group-2 minus Group-4. The effect of the treatment will be measured by the scores of Group-1 minus Group-2, while the effect of the treatment plus the post-testing process can be seen in Group-3. This kind of sophisticated control is important in treatment research, because evaluation and interviewing are known to have some short-term therapeutic effect. It is necessary to control for this short-term artifact in order to measure the effect specifically due to the treatment under formal consideration.

In another example, consider the evaluation of different styles of supervision and/or specific supervisors for effectiveness. In such a study the order of exposure to supervisors and also the learning stage of the trainee must be controlled. These are two sources of variability which are extraneous to the matter of real interest, i.e., the comparison of supervisory techniques. This particular design problem has surfaced over and over in educational research, where the personal style of a teacher may interact with a teaching method. Further, a personal attribute of the learner may also interact with a teaching method. When the interfering variable is an easily identifiable one, such as gender, its effect can be anticipated and controlled by manipulations of the data during the planning and data analysis. If the effect is unique, such as one supervisor's personality, it can be controlled by spreading it evenly across the whole study, e.g., by rotating each trainee through the entire supervisor roster. A further problem which will then arise is whether it makes a difference whether a trainee gets Supervisor A before or after Supervisor B. An elegant research design which takes care of all these problems is the so-called Latin Square. In the supervision research example, supervisors would

be arrayed across columns, and trainees down the rows of the research proto-
col. The sequence of pairing for supervisor/trainee pairs would then be randomized by a third code at the row and column intersections:

Supervisor 1	Supervisor 2	Supervisor 3	Supervisor 4	
a	b	c	d	Trainee 1, 5, 9, etc.
b	c	d	a	Trainee 2, 6, 10, etc.
c	d	a	b	Trainee 3, 7, 11, etc.
d	a	b	c	Trainee 4, 8, 12, etc.

The order of supervisors for the first group of trainees would be 1, 2, 3,
4 because their cells are coded a, b, c, d. For the second group of trainees,
the order of supervisors would be 2, 3, 4, 1 because their cells are coded b, c,
d, a. And so on. All of the following can be studied via this design:

—comparisons of technical approaches a, b, c, and d
—comparisons of supervisors 1, 2, 3, and 4
—comparisons of *order* of presentation of approaches
—comparisons of *order* of presentation of supervisors.

Furthermore, the comparisons of supervisors are controlled (balanced) for
method and for trainee maturity, while the comparisons of methods are controlled (balanced) for individual characteristics of supervisor and trainee
maturity. To study the impact of the order of presentation of the four supervisory styles, you would sum trainee ratings across the four rows, while to
compare the supervisory styles themselves, you would sum ratings down the
four columns. Unfortunately, this design does not give a direct measure of
random fluctuation, but this might not be a concern in a study in which the
participants had been so carefully screened.

The Latin Square must be square, but the dimensions are optional. It
could be 5 x 5, 6 x 6, etc.—all depending on the number of treatments,
approaches, or styles one wanted to compare. This is an excellent example of
the usefulness of a planned design even for a research undertaking which
will not yield any numerical data at all! The data gathered in such a study
could well be purely impressionistic ratings, based on expert judgment. The
rotational pattern would nevertheless serve to control extraneous factors in
the study, whether they are due to attributes of the supervisor or trainee, or
to the order of presentation of each supervisor to trainees.

Much of the technical work in designing a particular research study is
the identificat ion and control of *unwanted* causes of fluctuation, so that the

fluctuation due to the effect to be studied can be teased out and exposed if it is present. Statisticians focus a great deal, of their research on developing research designs which minimize unwanted fluctuation and maximize meaningful information, while holding down costs and numbers of subjects needed. Optimizing the research design is a process of minimizing the variation in the data which is due to unwanted fluctuation, while maximizing the variation in the data which is due to the variables of research interest. In situations where the data are expensive to gather, a further concept of efficiency of design comes into play: the relative payoff in control of unwanted fluctuation for the cost of the various design possibilities is computed. In this way the researcher can choose the design which gives the most experimental control for the project funds available. Design efficiency will be an area of great importance in designing pastoral counseling studies, because the natural form of the data is costly, involving both long periods of time and highly trained observers.

Section V. Using "Standard" Methodology: How To Begin?

Any researchers in need of formal methodological skills can take one of two approaches. They can either study the topic area or seek a consultant. Consultation may prove difficult for pastoral counseling researchers, since some consultants have neither the interest nor the patience to understand the multiple facets of pastoral counseling data. Conversely, the pastoral counselor will almost certainly find it a strain to understand and defer to the consultant's technical concerns. This difficulty occurs in other esoteric fields as well; ultimately many content areas develop their own methodologists to solve this problem. Many graduate school programs attempt to place the potential researcher in a middle ground; they give enough training in methodology so that the candidate can design simple studies and can also function as an intelligent shopper for data-analytic services. This approach appears desirable for the potential pastoral counseling researcher. Conceptualizing a workable research project and getting the best service from consultants is laborious or even impossible without minimally "speaking the language."

Section VI. Not All Useful Theories Can Be Proved

It is important that pastoral counselors begin to systematize their theories and chip away at validating them. Such a validation process will yield not only confirmation of the familiar, but discovery of the unknown. In the process, pastoral counselors can take comfort in the fact that no reasonable person expects any discipline to function solely on a basis of fully proven theory. All disciplines also rely for everyday operation on insight, hunch, approximation, and expert opinion.

The pastoral counselor modifies use of scientific research studies in yet a further way, beyond insight and hunch. He or she relies also upon faith and divine guidance. It is important for the growth of pastoral counseling as an academic discipline and a professional field to realize that there is no inherent conflict between careful research about pastoral counseling work and the life of faith as a pastoral counselor. Simply because the insights about pastoral work gleaned from research will be seen "in a glass darkly" does not mean that this limited vision will not be useful in the here-and-now.

Not only pastoral counseling data, but any form of mental health data has a high level of complexity and ambiguity. Further, the learning of the therapist's or counselor's role and tasks consumes great time and energy. Pastoral counselors, often lacking even basic methodology skills, are perhaps insufficiently aware of how simple, and sometimes how flawed, the methodology approaches are in some published treatment research (Salsburg, 1985). With relatively little further investment in training time, pastoral counselors could become recognized participants in the general mental health research community.

Is it important for pastoral counseling to come in this way under the dominance of formal research methodology? Yes, it is, for several reasons. The isolation of pastoral counselors from the mental health research community would suggest to critics a shrinking back from the tests to which other treatment researchers submit their procedures. Undoubtedly, critics would be underestimating the work involved in formal tests of such complex hypotheses, but their point would be nonetheless valid. Pastoral counselors must learn and use the methodology of statistical evaluation, rather than proclaiming it irrelevant to their special theories and hypotheses. At the same time, a part of their identity as pastoral counselors will be to remain aware that the explanations of human change which they find within their research about their counseling methods are only part of the whole story. In summary, good pastoral counseling research will embody a continual reflection on, and alternation between, the poles of faith and action in carrying out God's work in the psychological world.

Bibliography

Cronbach, Lee J., Goldine C. Gleser et al. *The Dependability of Behavioral Measurements: Theory of Generalizability for Scores and Profiles.* New York: John Wiley and Sons, 1972, p. 387.
Huff, Darrell. *How to Lie with Statistics.* New York: Norton, 1954.

Martin, James A. "Science and Democracy in the Age of Technology: Separating Fact from Value," *American Statistician*, 37, No. 4, Part 2, 1983, pp. 367–373.

Patton, Michael Quinn. *Utilization Focused Evaluation*. Beverly Hills: Sage Publications, 1978, p. 13.

Roberts, Harry V. "Statisticians Can Matter," *American Statistician*, 32, No. 2, 1978, pp. 45–51 at 50.

Rogosa, David R. and John B. Willett. "Understanding Correlates of Change by Modeling Individual Differences in Growth," *Psychometrika*, 50, No. 2, June 1985, pp. 203–228.

Salsburg, David S. "The Religion of Statistics as Practiced in Medical Journals," *American Statistician*, 39, No. 3, 1985, pp. 220–223.

Standen, Anthony. *Science Is a Sacred Cow*. New York: E. P. Dutton and Company, 1950.

Strunk, Orlo, "A Prolegomenon to a History of Pastoral Counseling," in Wicks et al., *Clinical Handbook of Pastoral Counseling*. Mahwah: Paulist Press, 1985.

Von Neumann, John. "The Role of Mathematics in Science and Society," in *Collected Works*, Volume VI. New York: Macmillan Co., 1963.

About the Editors

ROBERT J. WICKS is Professor in the Graduate Program in Pastoral Counseling at Loyola College in Maryland. His two areas of expertise are the prevention of secondary stress and the integration of psychology and spirituality. He is editor of the *Handbook of Spirituality for Ministers*, Vols. I and II; his latest authored works include a book on mentoring *(Sharing Wisdom)* from Crossroad, *Living a Gentle, Passionate Life* (Paulist Press), and a co-authored work with Joseph Ciarrocchi entitled *Psychotherapy with Priests, Protestant Clergy and Catholic Religious* (Psychosocial Press/JUP).

RICHARD DEAN PARSONS is Professor in Counseling and Educational Psychology at West Chester University in Pennsylvania. Dr. Parsons has published extensively in the areas of mental health prevention and intervention. In addition to his three seminal texts in mental health consultation, Dr. Parsons' most recent works include *The Ethics of Professional Practice* (Allyn and Bacon), *The Skilled Helper* (Allyn and Bacon), and *Action Research* (Wadsworth).

DONALD CAPPS is William Harte Felmeth Professor of Pastoral Theology at Princeton Theological Seminary. He was president of the Society for the Scientific Study of Religion in 1990–1992 and holds an honorary Th.D. degree from the University of Uppsala. His most recent books include *Men, Religion, and Melancholia* (1997); *Living Stories: Pastoral Counseling in Congregational Context* (1998); *Social Phobia: Alleviating Anxiety in an Age of Self-Promotion* (1999); and *Jesus: A Psychological Biography* (2000).

Notes on the Contributors*

SHEILA BARRY holds a Ph.D. in Pastoral Counseling from Loyola College in Maryland, where she is now Adjunct Professor in the Pastoral Counseling Department. She is a fellow in AAPC and an advanced Imago relationship clinician. She is married with five children and practices with Cornerstone Pastoral Counseling on the eastern shore of Maryland.

RICHARD BYRNE, O.C.S.O., is a monk of the New Melleray Abbey, Dubuque, Iowa. Currently he is director of the Institute of Formative Spirituality at Duquesne University, Pittsburgh, Pennsylvania. His teaching and research focus upon the following areas: the new discipline of formative spirituality and its relation to Christian mystical tradition, the contribution of formation science to pastoral counseling and spiritual direction, and contemporary personality theories in relation to transcendence development. He has conducted numerous workshops nationally and internationally on these topics.

PAMELA COOPER-WHITE is an Associate Professor of Pastoral Theology at the Lutheran Theological Seminary at Philadelphia. She is an Episcopal priest and a certified Fellow in the American Association of Pastoral Counselors.

DAVID W. FOY currently holds professorships in psychology at the Neuropsychiatric Institute, UCLA Medical School, and the Graduate School of Psychology, Fuller Theological Seminary. He also serves as Director of PTSD Research and Training at West Los Angeles VA

---

*Contributors' biographical sketches appear as they originally did in the early editions.

Medical Center, Brentwood Division. His primary interests involve study and treatment of survivors of traumas.

WILLIAM C. GAVENTA, JR., is an American Baptist clergyman and CPE Supervisor who has worked in a variety of roles with people with disabilities, their families, service providers, advocates, and religious communities. He serves as Volunteer Executive Secretary of the Religious Division of the AAMR.

JOANNE MARIE G. GREER, Director of Research for the Pastoral Counseling Department at Loyola College in Maryland, has dual specialties of research methodology and psychoanalytic psychology. She received a B.S. in mathematics from St. Mary's Dominican College, New Orleans, and a Ph.D. in Research Design and Statistics from the University of Maryland, where she concentrated on psychological measurement. She also holds a post-doctoral diploma in psychoanalysis from the Washington Psychoanalytic Institute. Formerly with the U.S. Department of Health and Human Services, she is the author of numerous journal articles and government monographs on various technical subjects in health services research.

HAROLD G. KOENIG, M.D., is Associate Professor of Psychiatry and Associate Professor of Medicine at Duke University Medical Center in Durham, North Carolina. He is founder and director of Duke's Center for the Study of Religion, Spirituality, and Health and author of *The Healing Power of Faith* (Simon & Schuster, 1999).

CONSTANCE M. MUCHA, DPC, RNCS-P, is a nurse psychotherapist, who began working as a grief therapist in 1989. She received her doctorate in Pastoral Counseling from Loyola College in Maryland. She has published articles on grief and loss. Her most recent article was *Counseling the Dying*.

CHRISTIE COZAD NEUGER is an Assistant Professor of Pastoral Theology at Princeton Theological Seminary. An ordained United Methodist minister, she worked as a parish pastor, a hospital chaplain, and a pastoral counselor before coming to Princeton Seminary. She received a B.A. from the University of Minnesota, M.Div. from United Theological Seminary of the Twin Cities, and the Ph.D. in Personality and Theology from the School of Theology at Claremont. She lives in Princeton with her husband, Win, and her two teen-aged children.

REBECA M. RADILLO, D.Min., is the Pastoral Care Studies Program Director at Blanton-Peale Institute, Pastor of the Waterloo United Methodist Church, Adjunct Professor of Pastoral Care, Supervised Ministry and D.Min. Program at Drew University. She received her M.Div. from Emory University; did her Pastoral Psychotherapy Residency at Blanton Peale. She is originally from Cuba and now maintains a private practice in New Jersey. She is also an AAPC Fellow.

REV. STEPHEN J. ROSETTI is a Catholic priest of the Diocese of Syracuse, New York. He is currently the President and Chief Executive Officer of Saint Luke Institute in Silver Spring, Maryland, a residential treatment and education program for clergy and religious of all faiths. He was a member of the National Conference of Catholic Bishops' Think Tank on Child Sexual Abuse and is a founding member of the board of Directors of Saint John's University Interfaith Sexual Trauma Institute. He is the editor of *Slayer of the Soul: Child Sexual Abuse and the Catholic Church,* which won a Silver Gryphon award and the author of the newly released *A Tragic Grace: The Catholic Church and Child Sexual Abuse.*

STEVE SANGKWON SHIM is Adjunct Professor in the Graduate School of Christian Studies at Soonsil University in Seoul, Korea. He is an AAPC Diplomate, Certified Counseling Psychologist, and is Executive Director of the Korea Christian Institute of Counseling and Psychotherapy in Seoul.

WALTER J. SMITH, S.J., Dean and Clinical Professor of Psychology and Pastoral Care at Weston School of Theology, Cambridge, Massachusetts, has worked for almost two decades with individuals facing life-threatening illnesses. His book *Dying in the Human Life Cycle: Psychological, Biomedical and Social Perspectives* (Holt, Rinehart and Winston, 1985) summarizes many of the issues he has treated in his clinical practice. His book on AIDS pastoral care, *AIDS: Living and Dying with Hope* (Paulist Press, 1988), was named "Best Pastoral Book in 1989" by the Catholic Press Association.

DAVID A. STEERE is Professor of Pastoral Care and Counseling at Louisville Presbyterian Theological Seminary. He is a Certified Supervisor with the Association of Clinical Pastoral Education, a Diplomate with the American Association of Pastoral Counselors, an Approved

Supervisor for the American Association of Marriage and Family Therapy, and a Clinical Teaching Member of the International Transactional Analysis Association. He is the author of *Bodily Expressions in Psychotherapy* and the editor of *The Supervisor of Pastoral Care.*

GAIL LYNN UNTERBERGER is Assistant Professor of Pastoral Care and Counseling at Wesley Theological Seminary in Washington, D.C. A United Methodist minister, she received the Ph.D. in Personality and Theology form the School of Theology at Claremont, California. She is finishing a book on feminist pastoral counseling.

EDWARD P. WIMBERLY is an Associate Professor in the Graduate School of Theology at Oral Roberts University. He received his Ph.D. in Pastoral Psychology and Counseling from Boston University. An ordained United Methodist minister, Dr. Wimberly has pastored several churches and led many seminars and workshops on Pastoral Care throughout the Eastern United States.

Name Index

Subject Index

Abuse. *See* Family abuse and violence

Acculturation, 110–11

Addiction, 212–13; *see also* Sexual addiction

Affirmation, 190, 192, 193, 194, 201–2, 203–4

Afro-American women, 22, 66–67

Afro-Americans, 61, 63–69; case study, 73–75; counseling, 70–73; countertransference, 69; family systems, 65–67; growth model, 70–73; HIV infections, 297; transference, 69

Aged, 38–59; Alzheimer's disease, 52–54; anxiety and fear, 51–52; chronic physical illness, 42–45; counselor, 48–49; depression, 46, 47–51; disability and dependency, 38, 46; family caregivers, 54–56; loss of meaning and purpose, 56, 57; memory loss, 40; normal aging, 40–42; problems of aging, 39–40; religion, 43–45, 49; suicide, 50–51

AIDS, persons with. *See* HIV, persons with

Alzheimer's disease, 38, 52–54; caregivers, 54–56

American Association for Marriage and Family Therapists, 8

American Association of Pastoral Counselors, 8, 153, 155, 342, 368–69

American Association on Mental Retardation, 123

American Psychiatric Association, 152, 183, 212, 275; AIDS Education Project, 289

American Psychological Association, 20, 152

Analogical Imagination, The (Tracy), 197–98

Anxiety: in aged, 51–52; in caregivers, 56; in HIV-infected persons, 306; religion and, 52; *see also* Stress

Application, 192, 194–95, 202–3

Appraisal, 192–93, 194, 197–98, 199, 201, 203

Apprehension, 192, 194, 196–97, 198, 201, 203

Art of Clinical Supervision, The (Estadt, Compton, and Blanchette), 372

Asian Americans, 63, 77–100; Chinese Americans, 80–82; clinical methods and approaches, 92–97; clinical procedures, 93; common cultural values, 87–92; ethnic-oriented issues, 91–92; Japanese Americans, 82–83; Korean Americans, 83–85; referrals, 96–97; religion, 81–82, 83, 85; resources for supportive networks and referrals, 96; termination of counseling, 93

Association for Clinical Pastoral Education, 342